MODERN MOVEMENTS IN EUROPEAN PHILOSOPHY

Richard Kearney

Manchester University Press
Manchester and New York

Distributed exclusively in the USA and Canada by St. Martin's Press

Published by Manchester University Press
Oxford Road, Manchester M13 9PL, UK
and Room 400, 175 Fifth Avenue,
New York, NY 10010, USA

Distributed exclusively in the USA and Canada
by St. Martin's Press, Inc.,
175 Fifth Avenue, New York, NY 10010, USA
Reprinted 1987, 1989, 1991, 1993

British Library Cataloguing in Publication Data

Kearney, Richard
  Modern movements in European philosophy.
  1. Philosophy, Modern—20th century
  2. Philosophy, European
  I. Title
  190'.9'04   B804

Library of Congress cataloging in Publication Data

Kearney, Richard
  Modern movements in European philosophy.
  Bibliography: p.
  Includes index.
  1. Philosophy, Modern—20th century.   2. Philosophy,
  European—History—20th century. I. Title.
  B804.K37   1986   142   86–2824

ISBN 0–7190–1747–5 *paperback*

Typeset in Linotron Ehrhardt by
Northern Phototypesetting Co Ltd, Bolton
Printed and bound in Great Britain by
Biddles Ltd, Guildford and King's Lynn

CONTENTS

ACKNOWLEDGEMENTS

I wish to thank the following colleagues and friends who read parts of the manuscript, at various stages of its evolution, and offered helpful suggestions: Kevin Barry, Kathleen Fitzpatrick, Cormac Gallagher, Patrick Hederman, Mike Kelly, Gerard McNamara, Dermot Moran, Redmond O'Hanlon, Fran O'Rourke, Jennifer Todd, Brian Torode, Ronan Sheehan and Ross Skelton. My special gratitude is due to my wife, Anne, and my daughter, Simone, for their endless patience and loving support.

AUTHOR'S NOTE

The titles of works cited in the main text are, with few exceptions, given in English. On the first occasion of their citation they are followed by the date of the original publication (German, French, Italian etc.), unless otherwise stated. The publication information and date for the English translations of these works are, where available, given in the select bibliographies of 'primary texts' at the end of the book. The bibliographies of 'secondary texts' are equally selective and also serve as acknowledgements by the author of secondary sources consulted or quoted.

In the interests of the advanced reader, the appendix format has been used on occasion at the end of chapters for a more extended presentation of certain specialised arguments. These appendices may be passed over by the general reader.

INTRODUCTION

European philosophy in this century has responded in various ways to a world increasingly dominated by technocracy, the positive sciences and the threat of totalitarian control over human intelligence. The question of meaning could no longer be taken for granted. New models of understanding were required.

Phenomenology and existentialism attempt to relocate the origins of meaning in our concrete lived experience prior to the impersonal 'objectivism' of a narrow scientific attitude. Structuralism emphasises the hidden or 'unconscious' structures of language which underpin our current established discourses – social, cultural, economic etc. While Critical Theory develops the insights of Hegel and Marx into a radical interrogation of the ideologies at work in advanced industrial society.

In contrast to certain reductionist trends in Anglo-American thinking, modern European philosophies have consistently stressed that so called 'neutral' analysis of logic and fact cannot be divorced from critical questioning. The reason *why* we quest for knowledge remains a matter of fierce controversy and committed debate. Philosophy, it is claimed, is not to be pursued in a vacuum. It is situated in its time and responds to its distinctive innovations and upheavals.

The principal intention of this publication is to offer a systematic if selective overview of three major movements of European (by which I understand Continental) philosophy – phenomenology, structuralism and critical theory. It presents some key ideas of six central thinkers from each of these movements, demonstrating how they develop from or contest one another. By presenting the three movements together in a single work, it is hoped to provide the reader with a more comprehensive grasp of the rich and varied nature of modern Continental thinking.

All three movements testify to a sense of imposing crisis. There is a common feeling that the classical systems of ideas – which had a place for everything and had everything in its place – no longer suffice. The sacrosanct notion of one philosophical mind of Europe has lost credibility; and the attendant collapse of a globally accepted system of social, political and religious values has seriously undermined the ideal of a Western rational tradition destined to historical progress and unity. In a century which has witnessed Enlightenment Europe founder before the devastating impact of totalitarian and fascist movements, and two world wars, modern European philosophies have responded, each in a distinctive way, by advancing new models of understanding.

The philosophical movements discussed in this book also display concerted opposition to the modern spread of positivism, an essentially anti-philosophical philosophy based on the empirical methods of the natural sciences. The upshot of positivism has been to reduce the life of ideas to a cult of verifiable certainty; and this reductionist fixation upon 'objective facts' is accompanied by a total ignorance of those ulterior factors – human, historical and structural – which determine in the final analysis the *meaning* of such facts. In short, phenomenology, critical theory and structuralism are each in their own way fundamentally anti-positivist in perspective. While positivism sees truth exclusively in terms of a one-dimensional surface observation, these modern methods open up *other* dimensions of meaning concealed behind the empirical manifestation of things: the intentional activities of consciousness (phenomenology); the historical strategies of domination and liberation (critical theory); the unconscious codes of language (structuralism).

Lastly, the three movements share a common conviction that philosophy needs new methods of inquiry more accurately attuned to the particular circumstances of Western culture in this century. All three illustrate how such innovations in methodology mark a transition from the traditional philosophy of *substance* (which assumed that the truth of a being exists in itself prior to its relationship to other beings) to the modern philosophy of *relation* (which argues, contrariwise, that the truth of a being is only constituted in and through its relationship to beings, or to systems of meaning, other than itself).

Each of the three movements is characterised by a specific choice of method corresponding to a specific category of relation. The phenomenological method privileges the *intentional relation* of consciousness to the meanings of the world. The method of critical theory highlights the *social relation* of the human subject to the historical conditions of production or alienation. While the structuralist method underscores the *structural relation* of individual speech to the code systems of language which ultimately determine it. We offer here a precursory outline of these three movements.

PHENOMENOLOGY

Phenomenology was committed to a new form of 'concrete thinking'. The phenomenological method was developed by Edmund Husserl at the turn of the century; it claimed to redeem philosophy from academic abstractions by enabling us to return to the origin of ideas in our concrete lived experience of the 'things themselves'. Thus Jean-Paul Sartre, for example, writes of his enthusiasm when he discovered in the early thirties how the German phenomenologists had made it possible to "philosophize about everything. They could spend the night in describing phenomenologically the essence of a gas street lamp". He provides the following account of just how revolutionary he felt this philosophy to be:

> I was carried away: nothing appeared to me more important than the promotion of street lamps to the dignity of a philosophical object. I had the obscure recollection of a thought that perhaps I have never had: truth drags through the streets, in the factories and, apart from ancient Greece, philosophers are eunuchs who never open their doors to it. One year later, I read Husserl in Berlin; everything was changed forever ('Merleau-Ponty I').

Martin Heidegger expressed a similar sense of intellectual discovery when he proclaimed in *Being and Time* that the phenomenological method permitted modern man to retrieve the fundamental question of the meaning of Being by relating it to the concrete concerns, moods and projects of our lived existence. Phenomenology, he argued, at last provided the philosophical means for understanding Being in terms of man's everyday being-in-the-world. Merleau-Ponty vividly echoed this enthusiasm in his preface to the *Phenomenlogy of Perception* with the claim that phenomenology enables us to "bring back all the living relationships of experience, as the fisherman's net draws up from the depth of the ocean quivering fish and seaweed". Merleau-Ponty insisted that phenomenology is not some speculative system with ready-made solutions but a unique style of thinking which must be experienced by each questioning person for himself. "It is less a question of counting up quotations", he writes, "than of determining and expressing in concrete form this *phenomenology for ourselves* which has given a number of present-day readers the impression, on reading Husserl and Heidegger, not so much of encountering a new philosophy as of recognizing what they had been waiting for."

Because of this openness of appeal, the phenomenological method lent itself to multiple interpretations. While Heidegger applied the method to the question of Being, Sartre to the question of human freedom and Merleau-Ponty to the question of our bodily relationship to the world, subsequent disciples of phenomenology further extended its range of application. Paul Ricoeur, for example, saw it as the basis for a new interpretation of signs and symbols operating in such diverse areas of cultural experience as myth, religion, literature and the unconscious. And Jacques Derrida explored and exposed the limits of phenomenology, maintaining that all traditional Western notions of truth as centralising identity must be 'deconstructed' to reveal an endless play of multiple meanings.

CRITICAL THEORY

Critical theory provided a radical stimulus to a new generation of European philosophers by combining the dialectical methods of Hegel and Marx. This gave rise to a distinctive brand of socially committed analysis often described as Hegelian or humanist Marxism. Lukács and the Frankfurt School theorists were the most influential pioneers of this new intellectual departure. They also believed that philosophy must retrieve its true vocation as 'concrete thinking'. But the ultimate meaning of our world, they held, could not be divorced from its historical and political context. This position entailed not just a repudiation of the abstract speculative systems of traditional metaphysics but also of orthodox scientific Marxism which reduced the liberating flexibility of historical dialectics to a crude mechanistic materialism. The revolutionary insights of Hegel and Marx needed to be preserved in constant dialogue. To understand the historical genesis of meaning in terms of a narrow economic determinism, governed by casually necessitated laws, is to misunderstand it, to dehumanise it. Thus we find Georg Lukács declaring in *History and Class Consciousness* that if history is indeed shaped by the forces of labour and production this is because such forces embody the power of human consciousness to overcome the constraints of capitalist exploitation – in which human relations are 'reified' or frozen – in order to project new potentialities of social existence. Antonio Gramsci makes a similar point in his *Prison Notebooks* when he argues that without a theoretical critique of the political and cultural structures which dominate human existence in our modern industrial society, the concrete liberation of men and women will be forever postponed.

This 'humanist' reading of Marxism received additional support from the German publication of Marx's *1844 Economic and Philosophical Manuscripts* in 1932. In the same year, Herbert Marcuse, one of the founding figures of the Frankfurt Institute for Social Research, published an important essay entitled 'The foundations of historical materialism'. Marcuse hailed the Manuscripts as providing indisputable evidence of the philosophical humanism of Marx's critique, redefining it as a theory of revolutionary praxis which develops rather than dismisses the dialectical methods of Hegel. This emphasis was, of course, anathema to the more orthodox 'scientific' Marxists who strenuously denied any link with the humanist philosophy of Hegel and the German idealists. Marcuse and his Frankfurt colleagues, Adorno and Horkheimer, insisted that Marx's central concept of labour be rescued from the straitjacket of economic determinism and restored to its properly human status as a power of historical transformation which resists the 'objectivications' of material and ideological domination. The revolutionary overcoming of the conditions of alienation presupposes that labour is both a form of concrete practice *and* understanding. For without the freedom of critical consciousness man remains a slave to the blind mechanisms of economic exploitation. 'The abolition of alienation', writes Marcuse, 'can be based only on the penetration of reification i.e. on the *practical insight* into the activity of objectivication in its historical-social situation.' In his subsequent works Marcuse proceeded to challenge the various ideological constraints – social, economic and cultural – placed upon human subjects in advanced technological society. And, not surprisingly, he and his colleagues looked increasingly to art and literature for sustaining evidence of the creative resources of man.

Walter Benjamin, Ernst Bloch and Jürgen Habermas each developed the dialectical method of humanist Marxism in its dual capacity as a critique of ideology and a project of emancipation. What all these thinkers held in common, despite their differences of emphasis, was a basic debt to Marx's original recognition that it was only by combining our practical and reflective activities – that is, the material and intellectual aspects of our existence – that we may effectively combat the prevailing forces of domination.

STRUCTURALISM

If critical theory was concerned primarily with the *social* origins of meaning, and phenomenology with the *existential*, structuralism may be said to have privileged the *linguistic*. But the term linguistic is deployed by Saussure and the structuralists in a substantially different sense to that current in analytic philosophy. Rather than analysing the ordinary 'common sense' use of words, as is the wont of much Anglo-American linguistic philosophy, structuralism penetrates beneath surface meanings to the concealed structural laws which predetermine such meanings. Everyday language usage is thus treated as a system of 'coded' utterances which usually mean something other than what they *appear* to mean. Structuralism thus disputes the claim of analytic philosophy that our everyday language is entirely in order as it is. It also resists the analytic view – regrettably some would argue – that 'what can be said can be said clearly'. For a structuralist, language is never transparent. Meaning is always masked, hidden, oblique. Furthermore, structuralism understands the functioning of signs in a much broader sense than that of traditional or analytic linguistics. Saussure and his followers spoke of a science of signs (semiology) which extends far beyond the established norms of language to embrace a wide variety of signifying systems. Roland Barthes offers a useful account of the implications of Saussure's discovery of the structural method in the following passage from *Elements of Semiology*:

> In his *Course in General Linguistics*, first published in 1916, Saussure postulated the existence of a general science of signs, or semiology, of which linguistics would form only one part. Semiology therefore aims to take in any system of signs, whatever their substance and limits; images, gestures, musical sounds, objects, and the complex associations of all these, which form the content of ritual, convention or public entertainment: these constitute, if not *language*, at least systems of signification. There is no doubt that the development of mass communications confers particular relevance today upon the vast field of signifying media, just when the success of disciplines such as linguistics, information theory, formal logic and structural anthropology provide semantic analysis with new instruments. There is at present a kind of demand for semiology, stemming not from the fads of a few scholars, but from the very history of the modern world.

Barthes' own most original contribution to structuralism was perhaps his incisive decoding of the signs of the mass media and popular culture. Others applied the structural method of analysis to different modes of signification: Lacan to the dreams and symptoms of the unconscious; Lévi-Strauss to the rites and symbols of anthropology; Foucault to the strategic discourses of power and knowledge; and Althusser (though he disliked the label 'structuralist') to a critical discrimination between ideology and science. What all these thinkers shared was a determination to decode the surface meanings of our familiar and all too often unsuspecting discourses in order to uncover the 'deep structures' of language which covertly condition such meanings. And this structuralist procedure entailed the controversial dismantling of Western concepts of the autonomy and centrality of the human subject. Structuralism thus presented itself as a rival to humanism and existentialism. It operated according to the motto that it is not man who speaks language but language who speaks man.

The tripartite classification of the eighteen thinkers discussed in this work has necessarily involved some degree of simplification. The kind of 'ideal typology' employed presupposes the abstraction, isolation and compression of certain significant philosophical trends under three broad headings. Quite evidently, such an approach has made it impossible to do justice to the complex and often overlapping intellectual biographies of the various thinkers or to convey adequately the multi-dimensional relations existing between the three movements. Sartre and Merleau-Ponty, for example, successfully combined the methods of phenomenological and Marxist critique, particularly in their postwar work (e.g. Sartre's *Critique of Dialectical Reason* and Merleau-Ponty's *Adventures of the Dialectic*). In a more comprehensive survey these philosophers could have been considered in terms of their contribution to *both* phenomenology and critical theory. It might similarly be noted that the Marxist theorists, Lukács and Marcuse, were influenced by phenomenology in their formative thinking in the 1920s. And an even more complex problem of classification arises with Althusser. Though commonly associated with the structural methods of analysis, Althusser's work almost certainly owes more to Marx than to Saussure or Lacan. But his unambiguous opposition to humanist Marxism which he saw as contaminating the science of Marx with the 'ideological' philosophising of Hegel, precluded our treating him under the heading of critical theory. So, *faute de mieux*, we have included Althusser in the structuralist movement. Finally, there is the case of Ricoeur's wide-ranging hermeneutics which relates the phenomenological model of inter-pretation, borrowed from Heidegger and Gadamer, to both the Marxist critique of ideology and the structuralist critique of the subjective cogito. And here, once again, we have been obliged to focus on one aspect of the thinker's work (albeit the most central) at the expense of others.

A further problem arising from our limitation of each of the three movements to six representative figures is the inevitable exclusion of other thinkers one might reasonably expect to see discussed in an exhaustive treatment of these movements: Gadamer and Levinas in the case of phenomenology, for instance, or Adorno and Horkheimer in the case of critical theory. To diminish somewhat the extent of such omissions, I have tried wherever possible to make comparative reference to the 'excluded' thinkers in my discussion of those 'included' (e.g. to Gadamer in the chapter on Ricoeur and to Adorno and Horkheimer in the chapter on Habermas).

The method of our survey is essentially one of commentary and conden-sation rather than of critique. What is offered is a 'sympathetic' reading of each of the eighteen thinkers, an internal exegesis which does not presume to challenge, dispute or refute. I have expressly tried to avoid making weighted preferences for certain movements or thinkers over others. Not out of a scruple that philosophies should be presented in terms of some putative 'neutral objectivity' free from critical judgement, but so that the reader may be allowed as much scope as possible to make such judgements for him/herself. In other works – particularly *Dialogues with Contemporary Continental Thinkers* and *Poétique du Possible* – I have had occasion to engage several of the philosophers dealt with in this survey in critical debate. My brief in the present work is of a more self-effacing and perhaps serviceable nature: to draw up a map of modern European thought and to place within it a representative sample of individual thinkers.

Contemporary Continental philosophies have proved at times to be highly technical and even obscure. In writing this book I have become increasingly aware of the difficulty of explaining such philosophies in a language accessible to a non-specialised readership. While several of the chapters will no doubt be intelligible to the general reader interested in a basic introduction, there are other chapters (and, of course, the appendices) which are more suitable for advanced students of philosophy. Such considerations notwithstanding, it is hoped that the overall result of this publication will be to facilitate access to some of the key debates of modern thinking.

In recent years, these modern movements have been somewhat overtaken by the 'post-modernist' trend in Continental philosophy known as *deconstruction*. Thus we find Jacques Derrida and his disciples deconstructing the phenomenological theories of Husserl and Heidegger as ultimate instances of the traditional 'metaphysics of presence'. The 'deconstructive turn' transgresses the conventional boundaries between philosophy and literature; it rejects such a division, arguing that both discourses are ultimately bound to an endless play of language whose 'signifiers' cannot be retraced to some transcendental 'signified' (i.e. some putative 'origin' of meaning located in a consciousness or Being existing beyond language).

One also finds structuralism being 'deconstructed' by some of its former exponents, in particular Roland Barthes and Michel Foucault. The late Barthes – e.g. of the 1977 'Inauguration Lecture' at the Collège de France – repudiates the orthodox structuralist claim to identify 'deep' structural meanings behind the surface play of discourse. He replaces the scientific model of Saussurian linguistics with a literary model which celebrates 'the splendour of the permanent revolution of language'. The essence of language, Barthes now claims, is to be found not in some covert political message – as Marxist theory and the early Barthes himself held – but in an open-ended 'displacement' of signifiers which can never be brought to a close by being assigned a 'fixed' reference. Literature thus becomes the privileged locus of Barthes' post-structuralist philosophy in so far as it makes knowledge 'festive'. "It stages language", says Barthes, "instead of simply using it . . . Through writing, knowledge ceaselessly reflects on knowledge, in terms of a discourse which is no longer epistemological, but *dramatic*". By breaking with the scientific habit of using words as instrumental means towards ends, the literary text transforms words into 'explosions, vibrations, devices, flavours'. Knowledge is thus reconverted into desire, acknowledging itself as a playful signification to be hedonistically savoured. Barthes's deconstructive manoeuvres aspire to that utopian condition where the subject may know, without remorse or repression, the bliss of speaking 'according to his perversions, not according to the Law'. For post-structuralism, the two main aims of reading texts are: 1) to subvert the authoritarian claim to definitive knowledge and; 2) to give voice to the prohibited desire for *jouissance* (the very essence of language as surplus of signifier over signified). This deconstructive strategy, concludes Barthes, represents a moment "at once decadent and prophetic, a moment of gentle apocalypse, a historical moment of the greatest possible pleasure" ('Inauguration Lecture'). Michel Foucault echoes this preference for the anarchic pleasures of deconstructive play in several of his later writings. A typical example is his recommendation in *Language, Counter-Memory and Practice* (1977) that we "renounce the *will-to-knowledge* and its sacrifice of life", embracing instead "a certain practice of stupidity".

Where these various deconstructive tendencies are leading is not yet clear. What *is* clear is that the basic motivation of phenomenology, structuralism and critical theory to disclose 'deep' or 'hidden' meanings behind the surface play of language is being strategically eroded. It is equally certain, of course, that this rejection of a hierarchical order of meanings does not imply a return to positivism – for positivism is devoted to a strict classification of facts utterly opposed to the deconstructive paradigms of play and ambivalence. At this point in time, it is still impossible to tell whether the 'deconstructive turn' represents an ephemeral fad of Parisian dilletantism, the much rumoured 'end of philosophy', the last intellectual death-rattle of post-industrial capitalism or, like the new physics, the discovery of revolutionary models of understanding.

PHENOMENOLOGY

Edmund Husserl

Phenomenology has proved one of the most influential philosophies of our time. It originated in Germany at the turn of the century. Edmund Husserl, its founder, published his seminal *Logical Investigations* in 1900. And Martin Heidegger, his most celebrated disciple, published his epoch-making phenomenological analysis of human existence, *Being and Time*, in 1927. But it was arguably thanks to the French phenomenologists – Sartre, Merleau-Ponty and Ricoeur – that the movement gained wider and more popular currency after the '30s. French phenomenology succeeded in translating the innovatory insights of Husserl and Heidegger into more accessible and engaging idioms. It applied the phenomenological method to a wide gamut of human concerns – psychology, literature, politics, religion, sociology etc. The translation of phenomenology from German into French was, therefore, not simply a matter of clarifying the notoriously difficult terminology of Husserl's and Heidegger's philosophy but also of extending its range of relevance.

One of the most enduring features of Husserlian phenomenology was an open-ended method of enquiry which invited a rich variety of inter-pretations. Thus we have the *existentialist* interpretation of Heidegger, Sartre and Merleau-Ponty; the *hermeneutic* interpretation of Gadamer and Ricoeur; and the *deconstructionist* interpretation of Derrida. Each of these tendencies shall be examined in the following chapters. This opening essay will outline some of the main characteristics of Husserl's own formulation of phenomenology. It will concentrate mainly on the insights of the later Husserl whose conviction that all objective or scientific truth is ultimately grounded in a human *life-world* (*Lebenswelt*) of experience, proved a central inspiration for subsequent developments in phenomenology.

I

Edmund Husserl was a German philosopher of Jewish origin whose prolific output, counting over twenty major publications, was the result of forty years of teaching and research in the universities of Göttingen and Freiburg, where he exerted a lasting influence on a new generation of European thinkers in the early decades of this century. Beginning with a philosophical study of mathematics – his first book *The Philosophy of Arithmetic* was published in 1891 – Husserl gradually became convinced that the 'objective' truths of mathematics and logic, as of all the sciences, required to be grounded anew in the living acts of human consciousness. Even the nature of such abstract entities as numbers could only be explained by the way they come into our knowledge.

This grounding of truths in experience called in turn for a new method capable of describing the various ways in which human consciousness originally constitutes meaning through pre-reflective acts of perception, imagination and language. Husserl referred to this method, which he outlined in *The Logical Investigations* (1900), as 'phenomenological' since it aimed to return to the origins of knowledge by examining how the world first *appears* (Greek, *phaino*) to human consciousness. The meanings of the world, he argued, can only be properly recovered as *phainomena* of consciousness.

By leading us 'back to the things themselves' (*zu den Sachen selbst*) as they first become manifest to us, prior to the 'objectifying' constructions of our conceptual judgments, phenomenology aims to demonstrate how the world is an *experience which we live* before it becomes an *object which we know* in some impersonal or detached fashion. The most decisive manoeuvre of phenomenology was therefore to relocate that primary point of contact between man and world, that original relation which precedes the conventional separation of our experience into the opposite poles of subject and object. The *phenomenon* upon which Husserl strives to redirect our philosophical attention is precisely this experiential interface or midpoint where subject is primordially related to object and object is primordially related to subject. In this manner, the traditional category of 'substance' is replaced by the category of 'relation'. Relation, insists Husserl, is not something which occurs between two distinct substances – e.g. man and world – as if they formerly existed independently of each other. Man and world are first and foremost in relation; it is only subsequently, at the reflective level of logic, that we divide them into separate entities.

For Husserl, phenomenology is more than an academic matter. Upon it depends the future development of the Western sciences which Husserl believed were in crisis in our modern age due to the fact that they had lost their sense of rootedness in man's life-experience. And this crisis of European science and reason was itself reflected, he charged, in the contemporary crisis of Western civilisation as a whole. Man had forfeited his essential identity because he had become an impersonal object among objects, divorced from the inner or 'transcendental' life of experience. Reason was, accordingly, under threat to the extent that it had been separated from spirit. The result was either an arid intellectualism (neo-Kantianism) or an historicist irrationalism (Diltley). To combat such extremes of scientism and relativism, Husserl resolved to restore reason to its true spiritual vocation as the transcendental production of meaning in and through the human life-world.

Nowhere is Husserl's project of the retrieval of reason more poignantly and urgently expressed than in his 'great last work', as it came to be called, *The Crisis of European Sciences and Transcendental Phenomenology*. This decisive work was written between 1934 and 1938, mostly in Vienna and Prague, as Husserl, then over seventy, was denied any public platform in Nazi Germany on account of his Jewish origin. Only two parts of the *Crisis* were completed and published before Husserl's death in 1938. Faced with the realisation that the "general faith in the idea and the practical ideal of Europe, that of a harmonious unity of the life of nations with its source in the rational, has been undermined" – a realisation made brutally evident by the rise of anti-rational fascist movements in the thirties – Husserl affirmed that Western man was being confronted with "the imminent danger of the extinction of philosophy in this sense, and with it necessarily the extinction of a Europe founded on the spirit of truth" (*Crisis*). But these turbulent events of his final years made Husserl more convinced than ever of (i) the urgency to "reflect upon the origins of our critical scientific and philosophical situation" (*Crisis*), and (ii) the necessity to do so by means of a phenomenology of human meaning.

Husserl proposed phenomenology as a radical beginning. It was to be radical in the sense that it would offer modern consciousness a means of returning to the root (*radix*) of philosophical questioning. Phenomenology proclaimed the need to begin philosophy all over again, to wipe the slate clean, as it were, so that we might relearn to *see* the world anew, as it really is in our original *lived* experience. In short, Husserl claimed to provide a theoretical representation of the ways in which reality appears to us in our *pre*-theoretical experience. Rather than prejudging the manner in which we know the world, phenomenology wished to eliminate all prejudice, to suspend all our easy answers to fundamental questions, all our taken-for-granted attitudes. It would disclose the world in all its concrete richness. As Sartre, one of Husserl's most brilliant disciples, remarked when he first read phenomenology:

> I was filled with the hope that . . . one would return I know not what absolute to perceptible objects, that the truth of the green was precisely this green leaf, that the glare of the sun was the truth of light. I wanted man to be the measure of everything because I was only interested in him and I had built I know not what

ethic on the joy of seeing and touching what *is* . . . Our generation no longer had anything to do with the culture which created us, a hackneyed positivism which was tired of itself. . . . This discipline (of phenomenology) brought us everything". (Memorial essay on *Merleau-Ponty (1)*, 1961)

From the outset, Husserl argued that phenomenology's main purpose is to remind us that the primordial *meaning of the objective world* is its mode of engaging human consciousness. And by the same token, it reminds us that the *meaning of our subjective consciousness* is the mode in which it opens up towards the world. The positivist attitude of much modern science, by contrast, reduces the world to an isolated object and consciousness to a disembodied subject. Human subjectivity is thus alienated from its creative activities or operations (*Leistungen*) in the life-world. It ceases to participate in its own creation of meaning and becomes instead a mere thing among things.

Husserl endeavoured to recover philosophy's true vocation as phenomenology by showing how the two poles of objectivity and subjectivity – which positive science tended to segregate in terms of a polar opposition – are in fact inseparable, each being co-determined by the other in a primordial relation. The world is disclosed accordingly as a world that is always *for* consciousness (i.e. its meaning being constituted only in and through consciousness). And likewise consciousness is disclosed as a consciousness *of* something other than itself – consciousness of the world. Indeed it was Franz Brentano, the nineteenth-century philosopher of scholastic formation who first taught Husserl that the human mind is an *intentional* activity which always moves beyond itself towards reality. (Husserl worked with Brentano in Vienna between 1884 and 1886 and was particularly impressed by his work, *Psychology from the Empirical Standpoint*). Phenomenology rests upon the radical conviction that meaning is neither in the mind alone, nor in the world alone, but in the intentional relationship between the two. We exist in the world before we are reflectively *aware* of either our own separate existence or the world's separate existence. This means that consciousness can no longer be considered as a box which contains perceptions or images of objects *within* itself. The object is not, as Hume and the empiricists maintained, a representation or faded impression inside my head. To say that consciousness is 'intentional' is to recognise that when I perceive or imagine an object my consciousness is already out there reaching toward the object itself. As Husserl's disciples, the existentialist phenomenologists put it, man is primordially a *being-in-the-world*.

II

The phenomenological attitude – particularly as advanced by the later Husserl – claimed to overcome the traditional extremes of idealism and realism. It rejected the efforts of philosophical idealism to overcome the subject-object dualism by confining meaning to a solitary consciousness cut off from the world (e.g. in the manner of the Cartesian Cogito or Kantian noumenal Ego). But phenomenology was equally unequivocal in its resistance to the opposing philosophies of realism and materialism which sought to resolve the subject-object dualism by subordinating consciousness to the pre-established realities of the external world. Both of these extremes denied the intentional rapport *between* consciousness and world which Husserl believed alone provides us with the 'immediate evidences' of our lived experience. Only such immediate evidences could serve as the presuppositionless basis of a genuine philosophical science.

Husserl passionately believed that phenomenology could provide the scientific ideal of knowledge with a rigorous foundation. He was deeply suspicious of attempts to apply the model of the natural or positive sciences to the understanding of human consciousness. This limited model is what Husserl calls 'naturalism' or the 'natural attitude'. While naturalism acknowledges the need for a scientific philosophy, it in fact precludes the genuine possibility of such a philosophy in that it only credits as real that which is physically given (*positum*). Naturalism is narrowly positivistic for it either denies the life of consciousness altogether or else 'naturalises' it as a 'fact' of physical reality. The phenomena of consciousness are thereby deprived of their essential status as living intentional experiences (*Erlebnisse*) and are considered to be of the same nature as the objective facts of such empirical sciences as physics or chemistry.

In his rejection of naturalism, Husserl would appear to share Dilthey's determination to establish a distinction between the criteria of the natural sciences (*Naturwissenschaften*) and those of the properly human sciences (*Geisteswissenschaften*) of which philosophy would be the ultimate foundation. (In most other respects, however, Husserl rejected Dilthey's 'historicist' model of the human understanding which he believed was open to the charge of relativism.) Since philosophy deals with the spiritual or 'transcendental' phenomena of human experience which transcend the mechanistic causality of facts, it is impossible for the positive sciences to provide a foundation for philosophy (as the psychophysical models of nineteenth-century naturalist psychology – what Husserl called *psychologism* – had attempted). On the contrary, it is philosophy, in the form of a phenomenological science, which alone can provide its own absolute foundation and, by extension, the foundation of the positive sciences. Modern science is in crisis, Husserl argued, precisely because it has forgotten its own roots in the lived experiences of our *human* life-world. Even the ideal of objectivity which positive science invokes to identify and classify its 'facts', is itself a product of this phenomenological experience. Husserl is not therefore denying a legitimate role to natural science; he is simply arguing that its very legitimacy presupposes a phenomenological investigation of the intentional origins of knowledge. The natural attitude cannot claim to found the phenomenological attitude for the simple reason that the former ultimately precedes the latter.

Moreover, since naturalistic psychology insists on treating consciousness as a physical thing among things, rather than a spiritual relationship between things, it remains bound to the contingency of empirical existence; and so it cannot lay claim to a necessary, absolute, presuppositionless foundation. Such a foundation for knowledge can only be secured, Husserl believed, by a rigorous method which returns to the intuitive evidence of the immediate experience of consciousness. Put in another way, one can only know the 'things themselves' by interrogating the life of that interior transcendental consciousness which intends these things. Whereas the physical 'facts' of nature are governed by causal laws of empirical observation, the 'phenomena' of consciousness operate according to non-causal laws of intentional relation which preexist the objectified world of nature. In the following passages from a lecture delivered in 1935, entitled *Philosophy and the Crisis of European Man*, Husserl outlines his famous critique of naturalism:

> There are all sorts of problems that stem from naiveté, according to which objectivistic science holds what it calls the objective world to be the totality of what is, without paying any attention to the fact that no objective science can do justice to the subjective life that achieves science. . . . Psychology with its claims to scientific exactitude wants to be the universal fundamental science of the spirit. Still, our hope for real rationality, that is for real insight, is disappointed here as elsewhwere. The psychologists simply fail to see that they too study neither themselves nor the scientists who are doing the investigating nor their own vital environing world. They do not see from the very beginning that they necessarily presuppose themselves as a group of men belonging to their own environing world and historical period. By the same token, they do not see that in pursuing their aims they are seeking a truth in itself, universally valid for everyone. By objectivism psychology simply cannot make a study of the soul in its properly essential sense, which is to say, the consciousness that acts and is acted upon. Though by determining the bodily function involved in an experience of evaluating or willing, it may objectify the experience and handle it inductively, can it do the same for purposes, values, norms? Can it study reason as some sort of (empirical) 'disposition'? Completely ignored is the fact that objectivism, as the genuine work of the investigator intent upon finding true norms, presupposes

just such norms. . . . There can, however, never be any improvement so long as an objectivism based on naturalism is not seen in all its naiveté, until men recognize thoroughly the absurdity of the interpretation of the world, according to which nature and spirit are to be looked upon as realities in the same sense. . . . The spirit and in fact only the spirit is a being in itself and for itself; it is autonomous and is capable of being handled in a genuinely rational, genuinely and thoroughly scientific way only in this autonomy. In regard to nature and scientific truth concerning it, however, the natural sciences give merely the appearance of having brought nature to a point where for itself it is rationally known. For true nature in its proper scientific sense is a product of the spirit that investigates nature, and thus the science of nature presupposes the science of spirit. (*ibid.*)

In short, Husserl criticises the 'natural attitude' of the positive sciences for taking the 'objective' status of reality for granted and for neglecting to put its own 'subjective' presuppositions into question. The natural attitude fails accordingly to analyse what Husserl refers to as the 'ultimate foundation' (*letzte Begründung*) of our knowledge in a pre-reflective experience which eludes all fixed, positivistic categories. And by this failure, naturalistic psychology commits the error of reducing the intentional acts of consciousness, wherein meaning is first constituted, to quantifiable data of a purely empirical kind. Husserl thus accuses the positive sciences of forgetting that what they consider to be neutral facts are really no more than abstractions divorced from their original genesis in our life-world.

Phenomenology works to recover the forgotten origins of scientific knowledge by declaring that 'meaning' is not something objectively existing but a relationship of consciousness which must be retraced to a pre-objective intuition of the 'things themselves' in their 'flesh and blood presence'. To this end, Husserl formulated a phenomenological method capable of redirecting philosophical attention to the primordial ways we perceive the world prior to the reifying prejudices of the natural attitude. He thus invites us to rediscover the hidden intentionalities of consciousness so that we may examine their essential structures in a new, presuppositionless manner. (For a critique of Husserl's claim that phenomenology can provide such a presuppositionless knowledge see the first section of our chapter on Ricoeur).

III

Husserl's formulation of the method is complex and indeed manifold. In each of his major works, he presents it from a new angle, adding, subtracting, revising and expanding. In some works his approach is distinctly Cartesian, in others it is more Kantian or Hegelian. But regardless of his specific point of departure, Husserl considers the goal of his method to be a transcendental experience of consciousness capable of producing universally valid knowledge. What follows is a summary outline of five principal phases of the method.

Firstly, Husserl proposes a bracketing (*epoche*) or suspension of the empirical and metaphysical presuppositions of the 'natural attitude'. Foremost among such bracketted presuppositions is the question of beings existing independently of our consciousness. Husserl thus intends to concentrate our awareness on the ways in which meanings appear to us *qua* phenomena, regardless of whether they exist as empirical entities outside of our consciousness. Within this heightened phenomenological perspective, consequently, the evidence of fiction (e.g. of non-empirical or 'possible' experience) is considered just as reliable as that of fact. Both are equally valid experiences of consciousness. The mind is thus freed from its servile attachment to literal 'reality' which we normally take for granted, and comes to know its own intentionality more intimately and more accurately.

Secondly, there is the phenomenological *reduction* which enables us to return (*reducere*) to the generating axis of our intentional experiences before they are overlaid by objectifying constructs. By means of such a reduction Husserl believed we could regain access to a presuppositionless world of transcendental immediacy where being becomes identical with its manifestation to consciousness. In other words, *being* becomes 'reduced' – in the non-reductive sense of being retrieved and opened up – to the *meaning of being*.

Thirdly, there occurs what Husserl terms *free variation*. Having undergone the *epoche* and the *reduction*, meaning is no longer confined to empirical actualities but unfolds in a free play of pure possibilities. So that in the unfettered horizon of our imagination, we can now liberally vary or modify any given thing – a table, tree, person etc. – until an invariant structure is revealed, common to all the possible appearances of the thing to our consciousness. This invariant structure is what Husserl terms the essence or *eidos* of the thing intended.

The fourth stage of the method entails an *intuition* of the essence as it emerges passively from the overlap of the multiple acts of our freely varying intentionality. This essential intuition involves an active repossession of the passive play of possibilities, reuniting them in a single immediate grasp. In this manner, phenomenology contrives to repeat the pre-reflective acts of our intentional experience in a reflective fashion. By means of a transcendental intuition, consciousness becomes reflexive, critically coinciding and taking hold of itself in an absolute way. One might say, therefore, that while the *content* of our empirical experience and our phenomenological experience is the same (i.e. there can be a strict parallelism between a factual and a possible table) the *attitude* towards this content is in both cases radically different. A phenomenological intuition of essences is the result of a methodical conversion or change of mind. It can only occur when we no longer attend simply to taken-for-granted objects but reorient our attention to the manner in which these objects are intended by our consciousness. The table intuited is still a table; but it is now intended and grasped in a more fundamental manner – that is, in all its hitherto hidden dimensions. Moreover, it is only by means of such intuition that the world ceases to be a self-evident given and becomes instead a gift of meaning, an explicit reappropriation of all its implicit meanings.

Fifthly, the method culminates with a *description* of the essential structures of both intended thing (*noema*) and intending consciousness (*noesis*), as these essences emerge from the free variation of imagination into the grasp of a united intuition. The descriptive stage is that which records the preceding phases of the method and makes them available to others as a theoretical document of the entire phenomenological analysis. Although Husserl repeatedly denied that phenomonelogy represented a *system* of philosophy, he certainly saw it as an ongoing movement – a kind of open-access archive with each phenomenologist contributing new registrations of our intentional experience. The descriptive phase of the method, is, in short, that which renders essential intuitions permanent and thus eligible for communication to others in the universal pursuit of knowledge.

Let us try to put some flesh on this rather abstract outline by taking an example of how the method works. In his *Cartesian Meditations* (1929), Husserl offers the following description of the intuition of a table:

Starting from this table-perception as an example, we vary the perceptual object, table, with a completely free optionalness, yet in such a manner that we keep perception fixed as perception of something. Perhaps we begin by fictively changing the shape or the color of the object quite arbitrarily, keeping identical only its perceptual appearing. In other words, abstaining from acceptance of its being, we change the fact of this perception into a pure possibility, one among other quite 'optional' pure possibilities – but possibilities that are possible perceptions. We, so to speak, shift the actual perception into the realm of non-actualities, the realm of the as-if, which supplies us with 'pure' possibilities, pure of everything that restricts us to this fact or to any fact whatever. As regards the latter point, we keep the aforesaid possibilities . . . as a completely free 'imaginableness' of fantasy (*ibid.*)

By thus effecting a methodological shift from a perceptual mode of intentionality to an imaginative one, Husserl believes he can liberate consciousness from the contingency of particulars into an 'eidetic' intuition of a universal essence (*Greek, eidos*). In our imagination, in other words, we can amplify any given perception of a table, here and now, so that our consciousness includes all kinds of *possible* perceptions of this particular table or other tables (e.g. round or square; three-legged or four-legged; seen from the side, the top or from underneath; recalled from memory, dreamt about or anticipated as future possibility of perception – and so on). To the extent that we are dealing with the 'free variation' of objects, we treat every *fact* – that is, every actual perception of a table here and now – as merely exemplifying one of a whole range of *possibilities*. Husserl thus gives priority to the 'essential' character of an object (as a totality of perceived or imagined possibilities) vis-à-vis its 'empirical' character (as an isolated, literal actuality).

Husserl's analysis focuses not just on the *objects* of consciousness – e.g. a table – but also and more fundamentally on the *acts* of consciousness – perception, imagination, signification etc. – which intend the object. Indeed, Husserl shows that, strictly speaking, there is no such thing as an isolated fact. The meaning of an object for the phenomenologist, is the sum of the ways in which it is intended by consciousness. We perceive the world in a series of profiles (*Abschattungen*) by means of which the object is presented ever more fully from a variety of different angles and in a variety of different aspects. The table is perceived in its colour, width, length, extension, solidity, from the left, from the right, from the four sides and so on. In order to grasp the total essence of a table, therefore – that is, the table in all its multiple dimensions of tableness – it is far more effective to move beyond this particular aspect of the empirical table here and now, into the 'symbolic' intentionality (of imagination or signification) where more comprehensive modes of intending a table may be experienced. Symbolic consciousness allows for spatio-temporal freedom. With regard to time, it permits us to perceive the table not just as it is now (present), but as it has been (past) or might be (future). Similarly, symbolic consciousness enables us to describe a table in a rich plurality of spatial perspectives. It is by means of such imaginative and signifying intentions, which vary any present perception in an open horizon of alternative perceptions, that the invariant essence of the table may eventually emerge.

For phenomenology, the science of facts becomes, as it were, an art of fictions. Thus, in *Ideas* (1913), Husserl could affirm the phenomenologist's interest in the "rich use of fiction for perfect clarity and the free transformation of data", adding that "we can draw extraordinary profit from what art and particularly poetry have to offer us in this regard". Without the freedom of imaginary variation, exploration and description, we would never be in a position to transcend the limits of particular empirical facts so as to intuit universal essences. In short, the truth of the real is most fully attained through the symbolic. As Husserl rather mischievously remarks in *Ideas*: "If anyone loves a paradox, he can really say, and say with strict truth if he will allow for the ambiguity, that the *element which makes up the life of phenomenology as of all essential science is 'fiction'*, that fiction is the source whence the knowledge of 'eternal truths' draws its sustenance". (For a more detailed analysis of Husserl's treatment of the three primary modes of intentionality – perception, imagination and signification – see Appendix).

IV

To sum up, phenomenology's overall task is, for Husserl, to secure an 'ultimate grounding' of meaning in a 'questioning back' (*Rückfrage*) to the origins of our intuitive experience. The ultimate grounding is a self-grounding in that it presupposes nothing and so is absolutely original and scientific in a genuine sense, for it obviates all those speculative abstractions which naively mistake themselves for ultimate reality.

Phenomenology is therefore a science of science; it criticises the pseudo-scientific pretentions of naturalism for ignoring the fundamentally intentional nature of the 'experience' it purports to invoke as a principle of empirical verification. As Paul Ricoeur, one of Husserl's most distinguished disciples, put it: "Phenomenology is not situated elsewhere, in another world, but rather is concerned with natural experience itself, in so far as the latter is *unaware* of its meaning" ('Phenomenology and Hermeneutics' in *Hermeneutics and the Human Sciences*, 1981). In short, the suspension of the natural attitude which sets the phenomenological analysis in motion, is not a departure from our worldly experience into some Platonic heaven of immutable essences. On the contrary, it solicits a greater fidelity to our natural and temporal experience so that we may come to grasp its concealed depths, to re-cognise, as it were, the *giving* acts of intentional consciousness behind the *givens* of the natural attitude. To put it in another way, we could say that phenomenology seeks to uncover the *positing* acts of human subjectivity which originally produce the *positum* of any so-called objective fact.

In several of his works, particularly *Ideas* and *The Cartesian Meditations*, Husserl seems to have believed that such a self-grounding of knowledge could only be achieved in the pure immanence of a transcendental subjectivity, unadulterated by the contingencies of empirical experience. Indeed some of Husserl's disciples would regard his 'transcendental reduction' to the absolute interiority of a spiritual consciousness existing in and for itself, as a relapse into another form of idealism – and this in spite of all Husserl's efforts to surpass previous idealist philosophies, Platonic, Cartesian, Kantian, Hegelian etc. There are indications in his late writings, however, and particularly in *The Crisis of the European Sciences*, that Husserl himself was becoming aware of the dangers of a transcendental solipsism and sought to overcome them by showing how all subjective consciousness is in fact grafted upon an *intersubjective* community which opens up the transcendental ego to a life-world of existential communication. The following passage from *The Crisis* is a good case in point:

> In our continually streaming perception of the world we are not isolated but rather stand within it in contact with other men. . . . In *living with one another* each can participate in the life of the other. Thus, in general, the world does not exist for isolated individuals but for the community of men; and this is due to the communalization of the straightforwardly perceptual. . . . It is only by making oneself understood that we have the possibility of *recognizing* that the things which one sees are the *same* as those which the other sees. (*Ibid.*)

This passage would seem to suggest that we arrive at an intuition of universal meanings not from within the solitary resources of transcendental subjectivity (as the early more 'Cartesian' Husserl tended to argue) but by means of a communal validation wherein each subject reciprocally corrects or confirms the other's phenomenological description of his experience. Essences are therefore disclosed by the later Husserl as being neither eternal ideas nor *a priori* constructs of an autonomous ego. They are the result of an historical harmony of communication between human subjects. This is why phenomenology remains an endlessly open and collective enterprise, a proposal rather than a self-contained system, a task rather than a solution.

Husserl's discovery in *The Crisis* of the primacy of historical intersubjectivity over a timeless self-grounding subjectivity, already anticipates the necessity of re-opening the brackets which had suspended the ontological question of being. In this manner, Husserl's own phenomenological essentialism ultimately indicates the possibility of a phenomenological existentialism – a possibility which Husserl's disciples would realise. But this discovery also prompted Husserl to reinterpret the entire history of philosophy and science as an ongoing series of attempts, beginning with the Greeks and reiterated by all the great classical, medieval and modern thinkers, to realise in however partial a form the ultimate aim of phenomenology – an all-encompassing and rigorous science of knowledge. Phenomenology is thus revealed as a teleological project, anticipated by all former great philosophers and finally made known to itself and set on a firm footing by Husserl himself, but still susceptible to further self-fulfilment by those subsequent thinkers who take up and extend the phenomenological quest for a genuinely human reason. Indeed, Husserl interpreted this quest as an ethical responsibility of Western European civilisation. Husserl's dramatic conclusion to *Philosophy and the Crisis of European Man*, written and delivered in 1935 while in exile from Nazi Germany, represents a passionate plea for the revival of philosophical reason in the face of that irrational barbarism which threatened to destroy the very spirit of European culture:

> The crisis of European existence, which manifests itself in countless symptoms of a corrupted life ... becomes manifestly understandable against the background of the philosophically discoverable teleology of European history ... To get to the concept of what is contra-essential in the present crisis, the concept Europe would have to be developed as the historical teleology of infinite goals of reason; it would have to be shown how the European world was born from ideas of reason, i.e., from the spirit of philosophy. The crisis could then become clear as the seeming collapse of rationalism ... The collapse of a rational culture does not lie in the essence of rationalism itself but only in its exteriorization, its absorption in naturalism and objectivism. The crisis of European existence can end in only one of two ways: in the ruin of a Europe alienated from its rational sense of life, fallen into a barbarian hatred of spirit; or in the rebirth of Europe from the spirit of philosophy, through a heroism of reason that will definitively overcome naturalism. Europe's greatest danger is weariness. Let us as 'good Europeans' do battle with this danger of dangers with the sort of courage that does not shirk even the endless battle. If we do, then from the annihilating conflagration of disbelief, from the fiery torrent of despair regarding the West's mission to humanity, from the ashes of the great weariness, the phoenix of a new inner life of the spirit will arise as the underpinning of a great and distant human future, for the spirit alone is immortal. (*Ibid.*)

Husserl clearly believed that philosophers are not some rarefied and ineffectual elite but 'functionaries for mankind', as he remarked in his introduction to *The Crisis*. What the philosopher thinks affects the human community at large, for "the genuine spiritual struggles of European humanity as such take the form of struggles between the philosophies" (*The Crisis*). Phenomenology cannot afford to remain the privileged concern of a handful of academics. The stakes are simply too high. Upon the future development of phenomenology, Husserl remained convinced, depends the entire destiny of Western culture.

APPENDIX: THREE MODES OF INTENTIONALITY

Husserl recognises three major modes of intentionality: perception, imagination and signification. In the sixth of his *Logical Investigations* (1900), Husserl describes in detail how these three modes of intentional consciousness interrelate. Perception intends its object as an immediate reality. Here the act of consciousness which intends or aims at an object fulfils itself by presenting this object to itself as a literal presence. For example, if I intend a tree in perception, this particular tree is given to my consciousness here and now.

To imagine a tree, by contrast, is to present a tree to my consciousness as a quasi-presence, as an *unreal* presence. Consciousness is fulfilled therefore in a symbolical rather than literal fashion. In imagination, I intend the tree in its absence but *as if* it were present. Something is indeed given to consciousness. But it is not a real tree, in any empirical sense; it is a picture or representation of a tree. Indeed, the tree as imagined may never have existed in empirical reality. For example, the chestnut tree as symbol of mystical unity described by Yeats in his poem *Among School Children*, has surely never existed, any more than his idealised fisherman – 'A man who does not exist / A man who is but a dream'. But that does not prevent Yeats or his readers from enjoying an imaginary experience of such ideal entities. But imagination is by no means confined to the world of art and dream. Everytime we remember the past or anticipate the future we are already engaged in making experience imaginatively present in its absence (the past as *no longer present* and the future as *not yet present* in the full perceptual sense). Moreover, Husserl will use his method of reflective analysis to show that even our perceptions are always given in terms of temporal horizons which extend into our past and future experiences – experiences which are rendered co-present to our actual perception by acts of imaginary 'retention' and 'protention'. To perceive this actual tree here and now in any meaningful or essential way already presupposes such imaginary acts. For without the imaginative ability to *recall* our past experiences of trees or to *anticipate* this empirical shape before me in the intended fulfillment of all its essential features, it would be impossible to recognise this shape as a tree in the first place.

Lastly, there is the intentional mode of signification. This designates consciousness as an empty intention (what the French phenomenologists call *une visée à vide*) before it is fulfilled by either a perception or image. The most common example of this is the way in which consciousness uses the signs of language to conceptualise meaning in an abstract way. I can use the word *mankind*, for instance, without actually perceiving or imagining this or that particular human being. Signification refers therefore to imageless or non-perceptual thinking which intends things as pure absences without any fulfilment of our intention in terms of a literal or imaginary presence. Mathematics and logic provide the most explicit instances of such conceptual language. $1 + 1 = 2$, regardless of whether it is apples, unicorns or chickens. And the same goes for such logical signs as S, P, Q and so on. It is precisely this ability of our signifying consciousness to intend meaning in an empty way that makes conceptual thought or abstraction possible. But it is also that power which keeps our perceptual and imaginative consciousness open to *new* meanings, absent meanings which have not yet found their fulfilment in any kind of presence, real or unreal. In short, signification keeps consciousness open to the infinitely extending horizon of the future.

While Husserl insists that perception, imagination and signification represent distinct *sui generis* modes of intentionality, he also insists that they constantly overlap and support one another. Without imagination and signification, perception would be limited to the literal presence of empirical facts (materialism). Without imagination and perception, signification would be lost in its own empty abstractions, devoid of any anchorage in the lived experience of the world as a 'flesh and blood' presence (conceptualism). And without perception and signification, imagination would become fascinated by its own self-engendering fantasies, cut off from both the reality of the present and the undiscovered novelty of the future (solipsism).

To illustrate concretely how these three modes of intentionality converge and cooperate to furnish consciousness with a comprehensive intuition of an object, let us briefly examine Husserl's own example in *Ideas* of the way we might intend the meaning of Dürer's engraving of *The Knight, Death and the Devil*. Suppose we begin by reading the title of the engraving. Here we have pure signification which intends a meaning in the form of three allegorical abstractions – the Knight as emblem of human courage and faith; the Devil as emblem of evil temptation and despair; Death as the neutral emblem of decision which will yield victory to the Knight or the Devil. We remain at this conceptual level until we *perceive* the engraving before us. But what do we begin by perceiving? Not the Knight, Devil or Death, but merely 'the engraved print as a *thing*', that is, as an undetermined mass of black lines on vellum paper. The perception only becomes *meaningful* as an aesthetic experience when it combines with the signifying intention of the title to yield an imaginative intuition of the three figures which the black lines serve to illustrate. As Husserl explains: "In the aesthetic observation, we do not consider the small colourless shapes as the objects of our attention, but *what is portrayed in the picture* . . . the Knight of flesh and blood, and so on". The Knight, Devil and Death portrayed remain *absent* from the engraving until such time as they are represented – in the form of a fictional quasi-presence – by our imagination.

All three modes of intentionality are necessary for the full intuition of the meaning of the portrait. Without the signifying title, we would not know what to expect to find in the perceptual data of black strokes on paper. Without the perceptual data there would, of course, be nothing given at all, but only an empty abstraction or idea. And without imagination to enliven the empirical data before our eyes and thus fulfil the empty signification of the title, there would be no aesthetic recognition of the unreal or fictional personages depicted in and through the engraving; there would, in other words, be no *representation* of the imaginary scenario which the perceptual presence of these particular lines on vellum illustrates.

Martin Heidegger

Martin Heidegger was born in Messkirch in southern Germany in 1889. He was a prolific thinker whose collected works comprise some fifty-seven volumes. Heidegger has exerted an enormous influence on contemporary thinking, extending beyond the realm of philosophy proper to embrace such diverse fields as psychology, theology, linguistics and modern theories of the text – most notably the hermeneutic theory of Gadamer and Ricoeur and the deconstructive theory of Derrida.

Heidegger's philosophy has proved both contentious and controversial. He has been denounced by some as a mystificatory wizard of wordplay and hailed by others as the most original thinker of the century (Hannah Arendt described him as the 'secret king of thought' and George Steiner as the 'great master of astonishment'). Either way, however, Heidegger is acknowledged by ally and adversary alike as a pivotal figure in the history of philosophy, one who takes his place alongside Plato, Artistotle, Descartes, Kant and Hegel. Following Husserl's lead, Heidegger recalled modern philosophy to the basics, alerting it to the danger of an era which has lost the power to question deeply, and pointing to the possibility of a new beginning. "We are too late for the gods and too early for Being": this was to become the abiding motto of Heidegger's philosophy.

Having spent several semesters in a Catholic seminary studying theology, the young Heidegger soon discovered his philosophical vocation on reading Brentano's thesis on Aristotle's inquiry into the multiple meanings of Being. Heidegger worked and taught for most of his life at Freiburg University, where he joined Husserl as an assistant and apprentice in 1916. Fascinated from the outset by his mentor's phenomenological project, Heidegger gave numerous courses on Husserl's *Logical Investigations*, edited and introduced his lectures on the *Phenomenology of Internal Time Consciousness*, collaborated with him on the crucial article on *Phenomenology* for the *Encyclopaedia Britannica*, and finally succeeded him to the chair of philosophy in Freiburg in 1928. It was, however, with the publication of his first major work, *Being and Time*, in 1927 that Heidegger definitively reworked Husserl's original method and pointed phenomenology in a new direction. Though *Being and Time* was dedicated to Husserl and acknowledged a profound debt to the master, it represented a radical reformulation of the phenomenological project. In a short study entitled 'My Way to Phenomenology' (1963), Heidegger reflects as follows on his formative relationship to Husserl:

My academic studies began in the winter of 1909–10 in theology at the University of Freiburg. But the chief work for the study in theology still left enough time for philosophy which belonged to the curriculum anyhow. Thus both volumes of Husserl's *Logical Investigations* lay on my desk in the theological seminary ever since my first semester there . . . I had learned from many references in philosphical periodicals that Husserl's thought was determined by Franz Brentano. Ever since 1907 Brentano's dissertation 'On the Manifold Meaning of Being according to Aristotle' had been the first help and guide of my first awkward attempts to penetrate into philosophy. The following question concerned me in a quite vague manner: If being is predicted in manifold meanings, then what is its leading fundamental meaning? What does Being mean? . . . From Husserl's *Logical Investigations*, I expected a decisive aid in the question stimulated by Brentano's dissertation . . . Husserl's teaching took place in the form of a step-by-step training in phenomenological 'seeing' which at the same time demanded that one relinquish the untested use of philosophical knowledge . . . Husserl watched me in a generous fashion, but at bottom in disagreement, as I worked (after 1919) on the *Logical Investigations* every week in special seminars with advanced students . . . There I learned one thing – at first rather led by surprise than guided by founded insight: what occurs for the phenomenology of the acts of consciousness as the self-manifestation of phenomena is sought more originally by Aristotle and in all Greek thinking and existence as *aletheia*, as the unconcealedness of what-is-present, its being revealed, its showing itself. That which phenomenological investigation rediscoverd as the supporting attitude of thought proves to be the fundamental trait of Greek thinking, if not indeed of philosophy as such. The more decisively this insight became clear to me, the more pressing the question became: Whence and how is it determined what must be experienced as the 'things themselves' in accordance with the principle of phenomenology? Is it consciousness and its objectivity (as Husserl maintained) or is it the Being of beings in its unconcealedness and concealment? ('My Way to Phenomenology' in *On Time and Being*)

Heidegger gave phenomenology an 'existentialist' orientation which gained it international acclaim and attracted such talented and original young minds as Sartre, Merleau-Ponty, Hannah Arendt, Marcuse and many others. In the thirties, Heidegger's thinking underwent its famous 'turn' (*Kehre*) from a phenomenology of human existence, based on a concrete description of man's moods and projects as a *being-in-the-world*, to a phenomenology of language which stressed the priority of the word of Being over the human subject. This second phase of Heidegger's philosophy has been identified by some commentators with his works on Hölderlin and Nietzsche composed during the Nazi dictatorship of Germany in the thirties and forties. Heidegger ultimately regarded the rise of fascism and totalitarianism in our century as symptomatic of the historical conjunction of European nihilism and 'planetary technology', a fateful event whose dehumanising consequences called for an urgent rethinking of man's relationship to Being. Heidegger argued that this relationship had been forgotten in Western metaphysics whose historical development signalled a movement away from a thinking centred on Being (which characterised early Greek thinking from the pre-Socratics to Aristotle) towards a thinking more and more concerned with exclusively 'anthropocentric' notions of calculable certainty, technical mastery and wilful productivity. The emphasis on the meditative and revelatory aspect of poetic language in Heidegger's later writing, powerfully illustrated in such works as *On the Way to Language* and *Poetry, Language, Thought* (both published in English in 1971), indicates the necessity for a radically innovative approach to philosophy transcending the established limits of traditional metaphysics and logic. Apart from some rare visits to France after the war (prompted by his desire to meet the French poet, René Char) and to Greece in 1962, Heidegger spent most of his mature life in seclusion in Germany, where he died in his native Swabian village of Messkirch in 1976.

The following presentation of Heidegger's philosophy is divided into two main parts, dealing respectively with his early and late thinking.

I

Heidegger revised Husserl's phenomenological method so that it might properly respond to the question of Being. He re-opened the brackets and let existence back in. But existence was now to be understood neither as mere subjectivity nor mere objectivity, but as a fundamental openness to the Being of beings.

Husserlian phenomenology had operated largely at the level of epistemology, that is, of an inquiry into the origin of knowledge (Greek, *episteme*) as it is constituted by our intentional experience. This had required, Husserl believed, a suspension of the ontological question of Being (Greek, *on*) in order to focus on the workings of consciousness. Heidegger goes a step further than his master; he shifts the emphasis from the *meaning of consciousness* to the *meaning of Being*. He accepts nonetheless the overriding conviction of phenomenology that an analysis of the essential structures of meaning necessitates a movement beyond the subject–object dualism in order to lead us back to our originary experience of the world, that is, to 'the things themselves'. But where Husserl identified this originary experience as a consciousness-of-the-world, Heidegger interprets it as a being-in-the-world. In this wise, phenomenology graduates from the epistemological question – What does it mean to *know*? – to the ontological question –

What does it mean to *be*?

Heidegger proposes to recover the original question of Being which *founded* Greek metaphysics, and by extension, Western culture as a whole. The search for such a 'fundamental ontology' is no easy task, however, for the entire history of metaphysics from Plato to Kant has developed, Heidegger argues, in forgetfulness of its own original questioning. And so man's primordial experience of Being in terms of his temporal being-in-the-world, has been concealed in the elaborate speculative edifices of consecutive metaphysical systems.

As a result, the question of Being has become for us today the emptiest and vaguest of all questions. Metaphysics has increasingly replaced our temporally and existentially lived experience of Being (*Sein*) with objectified abstractions of timeless beings (*Seiendes*): Principal among these are *On*, the most generalised abstraction of being, and *Theon*, the most elevated abstraction of being. Metaphysics has thus become what Heidegger calls an *onto-theology* which ignores the originally phenomenological character of our existence as being-in-the-world (*In-der-Welt-Sein*). Ontotheology tends towards a polarised dualism of subject and object, expressing itself either as idealism (being as a worldless subject) or realism (being as a subjectless world). And in the process metaphysics becomes oblivious to our primordial being-in-the-world and degenerates into a series of scholastic systems providing us with abstract answers divorced from the originating concrete questions. The original 'ontological difference' between *Sein* and *Seiende* is forgotten.

Heidegger champions phenomenology as a means of recovering and restating the fundamental question of Being: 'Why is there something rather than nothing?' This question goes beyond the certainties of dogmatic speculation or science; it is not concerned with determining *what* things are so that they may be classified, objectified or controlled. It inquiries instead into the ultimate *why* of being, restoring a sense of wonder that things should *be* at all rather than *not be*. While recognising that this ontological question has become irrelevant for our contemporary culture and no longer commands our attention, Heidegger proclaims the possibility, indeed the necessity, of reviving this question by 'deconstructing' (*Ueberwinden*) Western metaphysics and thereby 'retrieving' (*wiederholen*) the original existential experience of Being, whence metaphysical questioning first arose.

In *Being and Time* Heidegger employs phenomenology to redirect our attention away from traditional metaphysics to the 'fundamental ontology' which originally founds it. As the title suggests, the ontological question will be reactivated by a concrete description of man's being-there (*Da-sein*) in the temporal world. *Being and Time* opens with the question: 'What does it mean to be?' And it proceeds on the assumption that since man is the only being capable of asking this question, our inquiry into *Being* as such must first engage in a phenomenological analysis of *human being* as it concretely exists in the everyday world. I shall summarise the central features of Heidegger's celebrated description of *Dasein* under ten main headings.

(1) Existence

Man's essence lies in his existence. This is because, from a phenomenological standpoint, there is no essential self or given *cogito* before there are intentional acts (of our concrete lived existence) which constitute the 'self' as a meaning-project. Only humans can ask the question of Being, because we are the only beings who can stand back from (*ex-sistere*) the objective condition of things (*qua Seiendes*) and so put ourselves into question. Properly speaking, only human beings can ex-sist in this critically self-conscious or reflective manner. Man is, accordingly, the only being whose existence, as Heidegger puts it, "is an issue for him". Precisely as existence, man never truly understands himself simply as a fixed object amongst objects, a self-identical entity; he is a being who is perpetually reaching beyond himself towards the world, towards horizons of meaning beyond his present given condition. Human existence is, in brief, an activity of endless transcendence. *Existenz* is *Transzendenz*.

(2) Temporality

The essence of human being is *temporality* (*Zeitlichkeit*), Heidegger argues, for we can only understand ourselves in the present by referring to the temporal horizons of our existence, that is, by recollecting our past and projecting our future. Man is temporality precisely because what he is, here and now, always presupposes what he has been and what he will be. Heidegger describes *Dasein*, in consequence, as a mode of being which is always projecting itself beyond itself towards its *possibilities*. Human existence cannot simply be conceived as a determined fact or given actuality, in the manner of a stone or a tree. It must be understood as a project of possibility (*Entwurf der Möglichkeit*.) 'Because we exist in time, we are what we are *not* – in the sense of being what we are 'no longer' (our past) or 'not yet' (our future). As one poet observed: "We look before and after and pine for what is not". Here Heidegger's analysis owes a profound debt to Husserl's *Phenomenology of Internal Time-Consciousness* (1905–1910) which he edited and which was published in 1928.

(3) Facticity

It is true, of course, that *Dasein* always finds itself in a given situation. As such, our self-understanding is always limited by certain environmental cultural, social, psychological or economic conditions – what Heidegger calls our *facticity*. In other words, our existence is always conditioned by a certain given state of mind (*Befindlichkeit*) which is governed by actual historical circumstances. But this historical situatedness never definitively predetermines *Dasein* to be this or that particular thing. *Dasein* understands even its own facticity in terms of possibility; for it reinterprets its given circumstances, past or present, in terms of the open horizon of its future. In this way, Heidegger observes, we make the world *meaningful* for us, we make it our own.

(4) Freedom

Dasein is freedom to the extent that its existence as temporal transcendence towards the possible, is irreducible to the sum of its conditioning circumstances in the present. I am indeed, as Heidegger puts it, a being-in-the-world-*alongside-entities*. I am not some free-floating disembodied *cogito*, but inherit a world that is not of my own making, a world into which I have been *thrown*. Nonetheless, while I am bound by this finite condition of *thrownness* (*Geworfenheit*), I remain free to choose how I will reappropriate the meanings of this world for myself in order to project (*entwerfen*) them into an open horizon of futural possibilities. In other words, *Dasein* is free to redetermine the predetermined, to reinterpret actuality in the light of possibility. "Dasein is in every case what it *can* be", writes Heidegger, "and in the way in which it is its possibility" (*Being and Time*).

(5) Resoluteness

Dasein is free according to the resoluteness of its decision. Thus, for example, Raskolnikov in Dostoyevsky's *Crime and Punishment* is able to transform the past meaning of his existence – his criminal relationship to the world – by resolving to be different in future, that is by converting his former contempt for others into a loving relationship with Sonia. This does not alter the *fact* of his crime committed in the past; but the *meaning* of this act is radically altered as his understanding of it undergoes a profound change. In short, Raskolnikov's change of heart and mind demonstrates how even our past acts can be reinterpreted in different *possible* ways in the light of our future projects. My understanding of myself in the future does not have to be the same as my understanding of myself in the past. While I may be born into a certain family, religion, nationality, language, political system etc., nothing prevents me from deciding to respond to these conditioning circumstances in a new or different way. As Joyce's hero, Stephen Dedalus, exclaims in *A Portrait of the Artist as a Young Man*: "I will not serve that in which I no longer believe, whether it call itself my home, my fatherland or my church ... you talk to me of nationality, language or religion. I shall try to fly by these nets". As a temporal being who reinterprets his past or present in the light of his future, as one who perpetually projects his meaning into an horizon of possibilities, man's understanding of the world always involves a decision of self-understanding.

(6) Understanding

The term 'understanding' is not confined by Heidegger to analytic or reflective consciousness. It refers primarily to those pre-reflective 'moods' (*Stimmungen*) of our lived experience – e.g. anguish, guilt, fear, concern, wonder and so on – which Heidegger identifies not simply as psychological emotions but as ontological acts of *pre-understanding (Vor-Verständnis)*. For instance, Heidegger argues that our common experience of anguish, which frequently goes by the name of 'depression', is irreducible to the sum of ostensible causes which might be adduced at the level of an empirical psychology. We are not simply depressed because we failed exams, had influenza or crashed a car. These are no more than occasions which disrupt our normal patterns of behaviour, leaving us exposed to a fundamental void or nothingness at the heart of our existence. At its deepest level, Heidegger argues that anguish is an ontological 'mood' which expresses being-in-the-world as an experience of non-being. Unlike fear, for instance, anguish lacks any identifiable object; it occurs precisely where 'nothing' is the matter.

Heidegger sees his phenomenological analysis as a way of bringing the moods of our lived pre-understanding to the level of a reflective self-awareness. For Heidegger we exist before we are objectively aware that we exist. Our existence is pre-understanding – in the sense of a pre-reflective interpretation of the world as a project of possibilities for our existence – *before* we come to reflectively understand it as such. In short, *Dasein's* understanding is existential before it is philosophical; it is lived before it is conceptualized. Moreover, human existence constitutes what Heidegger terms 'a hermeneutic circle' to the extent that it implicitly interprets (*Greek, hermeneuein*) Being in terms of its everyday moods and projects before it raises this interpretation to the level of an explicit philosophical questioning. We already know – however vaguely – what we are looking for when we ask the question of Being. If we did not, the question would be meaningless and we would be unable to recognise what we find.

(7) Being-towards-death

Man is a being-towards-death in so far as his existence, as a perpetual projection toward his future, ultimately culminates in death. Since we are beings who exist in time, death represents the *end* – in both the sense of conclusion and goal – of all our possibilities. Death, as Heidegger remarks, is our final and sovereign possibility – the impossibility of any further possibilities. Our experience of Being is thus radically finite because limited by non-being, that is, by the possibility of our non-existence which cannot be gainsaid. All our existence is haunted at every moment by an awareness, which we usually conceal from ourselves, of our own ultimate nothingness – our being-towards-death. This awareness of death is experienced as anguish (*Angst*), which for Heidegger is the most fundamental of all our existential moods.

(8) Death

Death is experienced as anguish to the extent that it reveals itself as a nothingness *within* us, as the very basis of our existence. This experience of nothingness dispels our view of our existence as a self-enclosed subjectivity. We come to realise that nothingness lies concealed as the very groundless ground of our being-in-the-world. This realisation does not involve an objective observation of death (and if it did we would not experience anguish). In fact, it renders such an observation impossible. We cannot have a detached or impersonal 'representation' of nothingness; for it is the realisation of the self itself and of all objective entities as ultimately groundless. The self thus discovers that it *is* nothingness. And so it breaks through the field of normal consciousness which separates existence into purely subjective thought (e.g. the Cartesian *cogito*) on the one hand, and purely objective beings (the *seiendes* of the natural sciences) on the other. By thus unsettling the clearly defined boundaries of our natural consciousness, anguish discloses nothingness as residing at the root of all that exists. In anguish, the being of the self and of all things is 'nullified' – though obviously not 'annihilated' – and becomes a question mark. We reach down to an ontological mode of existence which goes deeper than psychology or the concepts of the positive sciences. We are brought to the threshold of Being itself (*Sein*) as that which is *not* a being (*Seiende*).

(9) Care

But anguish is not an end in itself. As an experience of our ultimate non-being, it also serves as an openness to Being. The anguish of *Dasein* can thus become a clearing (*Lichtung*) for a more fundamental manifestation of *Sein* itself, as something totally *other* than what is commonly known in our everyday existence. Since anguish reveals us to ourselves as an ultimate nothingness, it dispossesses us of the illusion of being a timelessly self-contained entity and thus prepares us for the question of Being – 'Why is there something rather than nothing?' This question, Heidegger insists, expresses itself ultimately in an existential attitude of *care*. Anguish may be said accordingly to function as a prelude to a caring for Being; it is that call of conscience (*Gewissen*) which reminds us that the meaning of the world is not simply invented out of our private subjectivity but is given to us by Being itself. Answering the call of conscience and acknowledging the hidden ontological message of anguish as the revelation of our nothingness, we become more care-ful of Being. We no longer take our being-in-the-world for granted; we question its ultimate meaning, we seek its ultimate foundation. This is what Heidegger means when he describes our experience of nothingness as 'the veil of Being'.

(10) Authenticity

Dasein is authentic when it ceases to take the world for granted as some objective entity 'present-at-hand' (*vorhanden*), recognising it instead as an open horizon of possibilities 'ready-to-hand' (*zuhanden*) – possibilities which concern *Dasein's* projects of the future. Being is revealed authentically, therefore, through the temporal horizon of *Dasein* as it is lived towards its final possibility of death and so remains open to the otherness of Being. But *Dasein* can only accede to an authentic awareness of Being as *other* by first acknowledging its own existence as its *own* (*eigentlich*). In order to open myself to Being, I must first assume responsibility for my being-towards-death as my ownmost (*eigenst*) possibility. To choose resolutely to live towards my death, thereby appropriating the experience of my ultimate nothingness, is to live my freedom authentically, without alibi. Inauthenticity, by contrast, is the refusal of my being-towards-death. And it is, consequently, a refusal of the revelation of Being which my experience of nothingness makes possible. I exist inauthentically to the extent that I flee from my awareness of freedom, responsibility and death, seeking refuge in the security of the anonymous 'They' (*Das Man*) which tells me what to think and what to be. The 'They' defines me as a fixed actuality rather than a free possibility. It wards off anguish by concealing the experience of death. It lulls me into a passive attitude of mindless distraction and conformity. To experience anguish, however, is to return to the authentic awareness that I am a displaced person, forever out of joint with the 'They' and indeed with myself. It is to recognise that nobody can die for me, not even the 'They'. I can never read my own obituary – only that of others. And this simple point illustrates how my death can never be made into an 'object' external to me, a mere fact to be impersonally observed in the manner of the 'they'. I experience death in my deepest interiority, as the very texture of my existence, as that ultimate possibility which haunts me at every moment however much I seek to flee from it. My being-towards-death is therefore inalienably *my own*. By thus retrieving the authentic self from the inauthentic crowd, *Dasein* confronts its ontological condition of homelessness (*Unheimlichkeit*). It begins to care for Being. Heidegger concludes that the authentic attitude leads naturally to reflection, recalling that our existence is at issue for us. And in so doing, it reawakens the dormant question of Being.

II

In his later writings, Heidegger supplemented his existential analysis of *Being and Time* in two principal ways. First, with a philosophy of 'overcoming' (*Überwindung*); and second, with a philosophy of language. Both of these philosophical 'paths', he believed, would lead to a deeper understanding of the question of Being (*Sein*).

The first of these paths, already announced in the introduction to *Being and Time*, consisted of a series of deconstructive readings of the great thinkers of the Western metaphysical tradition – Plato, Aristotle, Augustine, Kant, Schelling, Hegel and Nietzsche. These readings aimed to take a 'step back' (*ein Schritt zurück*) from the ontotheological framework of metaphysics – which reduced Being to objectified entities – in order to disclose the underlying and hitherto 'unthought' presuppositions of all metaphysical inquiries. For Heidegger, this 'unthought' origin of metaphysics is none other than the phenomenological horizon of the temporal experience of *Dasein* wherein Being first manifests itself to man. Thus, for example, when Plato or subsequent metaphysical thinkers speak of ultimate Being in terms of a permanent presence – *nunc stans, parousia, aei on, ipsum esse subsistens* and so on – they are already obliquely referring to Being in its temporal character of the *present* (rendered timeless to the extent that it is abstracted from the past or the future). As Heidegger observes in his deconstructive re-reading of Kant in *Kant and the Problem of Metaphysics* (1929):

> What is the significance of the fact that ancient metaphysics defined the *ontos on* – the Being which is Being to the highest degree – as *aei on* (timeless Being)? The Being of beings is obviously understood here as permanence and subsistence. What projection lies at the basis of this comprehension of Being? A projection relative to time, for even eternity, taken as the *nunc stans*, for example, is as a 'permanent' *now* conceivable only through time. What is the significance of the fact that Being in the proper sense of the term is understood as *ousia, parousia*, i.e., basically as 'presence', the immediate and always present possession, as 'having'? This projection reveals that 'Being' is synonymous with *permanence in presence*. In this way, therefore, that is, in the spontaneous comprehension of Being, temporal determinations are accumulated. Is not the immediate comprehension of Being developed entirely from a primoridal but self-evident *projection of Being relative to time?* Is it not then true that from the first this struggle for Being takes place within the horizon of time? (*Ibid.*)

By subjecting the metaphysical thinkers of the Western tradition to such a phenomenological deconstruction, Heidegger hoped to demonstrate how the history of philosophy represents the history of Being as it discloses itself in and through its own concealment. He insists accordingly that phenomenology does not seek to abolish metaphysics, only to rethink its hidden temporal foundations in a more rigorously faithful way. In short, to 'deconstruct' Plato, for example, is to try to think his thought through in a more fundamental way than Plato himself had done. The question of presumptuous hindsight notwithstanding, Heidegger's deconstructive project is intended not as a repudiation of metaphysics, after the fashion of empiricism or materialism, but as a reinterpretation of its suppressed dimensions. As such, indeed, it may even be construed as a *heightened* fidelity to the essential questioning of metaphysics. Deconstruction, in other words, enables metaphysics to retrieve its own origins by recovering from its forgetfulness of the temporality of Being. This abiding allegiance to the history of metaphysics is made clear in the following passage from the first volume of Heidegger's *Nietzsche* (1961):

> The more clearly and simply a decisive inquiry traces the history of metaphysics back to its few essential stages, the more that history's power to reach forward, seize and commit grows. This is especially the case where it is a matter of deconstructing (*überwinden*) such history. Whoever believes that philosophical thought can dispense with its history by means of a simple proclamation will, without his knowing it, be dispensed with by history . . . He will think he is being original when he is merely rehashing what has been transmitted and mixing

together traditional interpretations into something ostensibly new. The greater a revolution is to be, the more profoundly must it plunge into its history. (*ibid.*)

The second major way in which Heidegger's later work endeavours to develop the existential analysis of *Being and Time* is by means of a philosophical reappraisal of language, and particularly poetic language. It might be said that Heidegger's preoccupation with language serves as a connecting thread between his early and late philosophy. Already emerging as a central mode of Being's disclosure in *Being and Time*, it was to become the most constant theme of his subsequent writings. (For an outline of the early Heidegger's systematic approach to language see our *Appendix* to this chapter). The remainder of this section is devoted to a summary presentation of the later Heidegger's analysis of language as a means of disclosing Being.

In the modern era dominated by an increasingly technologised and rationalised use of language, the caring for the word which Heidegger commends to both the thinker and the poet, requires us to reach back into the silent abyss in search of a language capable of speaking Being in all its otherness. The task of creating such a poetic utterance in our 'destitute times' is both hazardous and difficult. "One of the essential theatres of speechlessness", Heidegger observes, "is dread in the sense of the terror into which the abyss of nothing plunges us. Nothing, conceived as the pure *other* than the things that are, is the veil of Being" (*What is Metaphysics?*).

Language, for Heidegger, is not an entity which exists (*Seiend*) but the very giving of Being (*Es gibt Sein*) whereby everything exists. It is not a present object but presencing. It is not something true but the very coming to be of truth – the horizon of meaning wherein all things appear to us *qua phenomena*. Consequently, if phenomenology is precisely the 'science of the appearing as appearing' (*phainesthai*), language is its ultimate horizon: the act of bringing things to light as appearances (*phainomena*) which does not itself appear as such. It presences in absence. Unlike beings (*Seiendes*) which *are*, language as Being (*Sein*) *is not*, for it is that whereby beings exist without itself being something that exists. Logos, in short, is the *nothing* which lets *things* be, the voice of silence.

In his later work – and particularly those essays collected under the titles *Poetry, Language, Thought, On the Way to Language* and *Discourse on Thinking* (1959) – Heidegger argues that language functions poetically as a 'house of Being' where genuine thinking is fostered. With frequent allusion to the writings of such German authors as Rilke, Hölderlin and Trackl, Heidegger states that the vocation of the poet is to listen and respond to the 'silent tolling' of language (*das Geläute der Stille*) (*PLT*). Only by attending to the concealed origins of language can we learn again to speak words originally. Poetry, Heidegger suggests, is the 'conscience' (*Gewissen*) of the Word of Being which upsets our natural consciousness and invites us to experience the *strangeness* of things.

But poetry is far more than an act of individual conscience. It involves a communal recollection. Heidegger cites Hölderlin's feastday hymn 'Remembrance' as a celebration which "gathers a people together" in the common pursuit of their origin-ality. Authentic poetry can remind a community that they have been exiled from their tradition which must be sought after anew. But if this seeking is to be a genuine 'homecoming' it must avoid the danger of a reactionary regression to some antique memory of self-possession. On the contrary, it must expose the community to an experience of uncanny dispossession (*Unheimlichkeit*) in order that it may open itself to a genuine future. If Hölderlin speaks therefore of poetry allowing us to come home, he means it, according to Heidegger, not in the sense of some triumphalistic return to a fixed past (*Heimkunft*), but rather in the sense of a futural arriving which can never finally arrive (*Heimkommen*) – an arriving which, in Heidegger's phrase, preserves itself as a perpetual advent (*Ankunft*). Homecoming, in short, is not a mystificatory nostalgia but a responsible expectancy. "Just as every work", writes Heidegger, "is itself responsible for the awakening and formation of the generation that will set free the world hidden in that work, the growth of the work in turn must *hear ahead* to the tradition it is responsible for" (*Commentaries on Hölderlin's Poetry*, 1951).

Heidegger affirms accordingly that the communal vocation of poetry entails an historical project whereby we may recover what is no longer present as what is still to come (utopia). And so Heidegger concludes that Hölderlin's poetry of 'homecoming' acts as a summons to others to become hearers of the word that is coming, to become a deliberating and patient community which will eventually turn from its abuse of language as mere idle talk or technical manipulation and return to the essence of language as a caring for the mystery of origins. The poet cannot inaugurate this homecoming by himself; he needs *others* to listen to his language of care and to take the burden of that care upon themselves. "Once spoken, the word slips away from the guardianship of the caring poet . . . so the poet must turn to the others, in order that the remembrance can help the poetic word be understood, with the result that the homecoming self-appropriately transpires for each in his destined way" (*Ibid.*)

In *On the Way to Language*, Heidegger claims that poetry becomes a 'piety of thinking' (*Frömmigkeit des Denkens*) whenever the poet enters the 'play of language' thereby suspending the common approach to speech as a utilitarian vehicle of information. As such, poetry sponsors a non-objectifying disposition to the very 'saying' of language. In answer to the question, 'what is speech?', the poet replies in the manner of the mystic Silesius, that 'saying is that which says' (*Die Sprache spricht*). Refusing to reduce language to an objectifiable concept – by standing *above* it or speaking *about* it – the poetic thinker experiences and thinks language from *within*. We do not 'represent' language to ourselves; language presents itself to us and speaks through us.

But when Heidegger speaks of poetry as a 'sacred' or 'mysterious' language, he insists that this does not entail an elitist cult of transcendental otherworlds. "Authentic poetry", he writes," is never merely a higher plane of ordinary language. On the contrary, ordinary speech is a forgotten and worn-out, overworked poem, out of which the call is scarcely audible anymore" (*On the Way to Language*). In this sense, poetry is a fidelity to the concealed richness of our everyday speech and experience. By using language in a strange way, the poet estranges us from our familiar use of words in order to restore a sense of newness to their earthly origins. Far from endorsing some occultist escape into a Platonic heaven of timeless essences, the poetic 'strangeness' of words elicits a concrete existential quest to dwell poetically in the innermost Being of things:

> The word (strange) we are using – the German '*fremd*' . . . really means – forward to somewhere else, underway toward –, onward to the encounter with what is kept in store for it. The strange goes forth, ahead. But it does not roam aimlessly, without any kind of determination. The strange element goes in its search toward the site where it may stay in its wandering. Almost unknown to itself, the 'strange' is already following the call that calls it on the way into its own. The poet calls the soul 'something strange on the earth'. The earth is that very place which the soul's wandering could not reach so far. The soul only *seeks* the earth; it does not flee from it. This fulfils the soul's being: in her wandering to seek the earth so that she may poetically build and dwell upon it, and thus may be able to save the earth *as* earth (*On the Way to Language*).

For Heidegger, the notion of poetry as a 'piety of thinking' approximates to the pre-Socratic model of language as *logos*. By *logos* the pre-Socratics understood not some logical correlation between objects, but a hidden ontological attunement (*harmonia*) of the Word of human thinking (*logos* as *psyche*) and the Word of Being (*logos* as *eon*). Heraclitus could affirm accordingly that *logos* remained irreducible to a purely anthropocentric framework: "If you have heard not me but the *logos*, then it is wise to say – all is one". Post-Socratic metaphysics, by contrast, reduced the *logos* to logic and made of thinking a matter of correct judgement – a matter of adjudicating Being reductively in terms of the categories of technical thinking. Heidegger tries to restore to language that poetic status it once enjoyed as a measure of balance between the opposite poles of Being and thinking. He invokes Parmenides' famous maxim that if one listens to the word of truth, "it is the same thing to think and to be". Thus Heidegger counsels us to reverse the traditional substitution of logic for *logos* – a substitution which resulted in: i) the reduction of the *presencing* of Being (as *a-letheia* or dis-closure) to the juridical *representation* of entities according to a predetermined set of idealist categories (e.g. the transcendental Ideas of Platonism or the innate ideas of Cartesianism); and (ii) the reduction of language as an harmonious attunement of opposites to the logical principle of non-contradiction which excludes and polarises opposites (If *A* is *A* it cannot be *B*). Heidegger explains this decisive capitulation of the *logos* to logic as follows:

> In the service of thought we are trying precisely to penetrate the dark from which the essence of thinking is determined, namely *aletheia* and *physis*, Being as unconcealment, the very thing that has been lost by 'logic' . . . When did the development of logic begin? It began when Greek philosophy was drawing to an end and becoming an affair of schools, of organization and technique. It began when *eon*, the Being of things, was represented as *Idea* and as such became the 'object of knowledge (*epistéme*). Logic arose in the curriculum of the Platonic-Aristotelian schools. Logic is an invention of schoolteachers, not of philosophers. When philosophers took it up it was always under more fundamental impulsions, not for the sake of logic itself . . . logic was able to arise as an exposition of the formal structure and rules of thought only after the division between Being and thinking had been effected . . . Consequently logic itself and its history can never throw adequate light on the essence and origin of this separation between Being and thinking. (*Introduction to Metaphysics*, 1953).

Heidegger concludes that the reign of an exclusively instrumental logic has reached global and sometimes dangerous proportions in the modern technological era:

> In place of the old world-content of things that was formerly perceived and used to grant freely of itself, the object-character of technological dominion spreads itself over the earth ever more quickly, ruthlessly and completely. Not only does it establish all things as producible in the process of production; it also delivers the products of production by means of the market. In self-assertive production, the humanness of man and the thingness of things dissolve into the calculated market value of a market which not only spans the whole earth as a world market, but also, as the will to will, trades in the nature of Being and thus subjects all beings to the trade of a calculation that dominates most tenaciously . . . (*ibid.*)

Only by means of poetic thinking, claims Heidegger, attentive to the original *harmonia* of Being and thought, can adequate light be thrown on the priority of the *logos vis-à-vis* logic. Poetry may thus enable philosophy to reclaim its own origins in that thinking which corresponds to the saying of the *logos*. Heidegger makes this point clearly in the following passage from *What is Philosophy?* (1955):

> The unfolding correspondence . . . is attuned to the voice of the Being of beings. This correspondence is a Saying in the service of *language*. What this means is difficult for us to understand today, for our current conception of language has undergone strange changes. As a consequence, language appears as an instrument of expression. Accordingly it is considered more correct to say that language is in the service of thinking rather than that thinking, as co-respondence, is in the service of language. Above all, the current conception of language is as far removed as possible from the Greek experience of language. To the Greeks the nature of language is revealed as the logos. (*ibid.*)

Poetic thinking, which lies at the root of genuine philosophising, is a mode of speaking in accord (*homo-legein*) with Being – a speaking (*Sprechen*) in co-respondence (*Ent-Sprechen*) with language itself (*Sprache*). The poetic logic does not, therefore, re-present Being *in* words so much as bring Being to presence *as* words. Heidegger cites here Stefan George's couplet: "Where word breaks off no thing can be". Poetry "tells of the origin of the word", Heidegger suggests, by reminding us of the primary "mutual belonging of saying and Being". But this reminder requires us to foresake our habitual approach to language as no more than a means of predicating things and accept that language is the very genesis of things themselves. Things do not exist as independent empirical facts. They only come into being in so far as they are summoned by language which bestows their meaning upon them. As Heidegger remarks: "According to poetic experience and to the oldest tradition of thought, the word *gives*: Being'" (*On the Way to Language*). We must, in other words, relinquish our natural inclination to be so taken up with our own immediate interests that we no longer pay attention to the silent, originating call of language. For it is only when we consent to abandon our will-to-power over language that language can itself speak and thus become a disclosure of Being.

By deconstructing the purely utilitarian or technical functioning of language in favour of a more poetic saying, Heidegger proposes to retrieve the forgotten Word of Being. And upon such a retrieval, he claims, depends the very future not only of Western philosophy but of Western civilisation as a whole.

CONCLUSION

If philosophy is to revive the motivating question of its history – *Why is there something rather than nothing?* – it must transcend the established certainties of both common sense and science which reduce beings to commonplace dispensable entities; and it must do so in order to rediscover the extraordinariness of each being as a place for the unconcealing of Being. "To philosophize", as Heidegger reminds us in *Introduction to Metaphysics*, "is an extraordinary inquiry into the extraordinary."

In our own age Being has become the most vague and empty of abstractions due to modern man's obsession with technical prediction, economic profit and political control. So enthralled have we become with the immediate production and consumption of beings that we have forgotten Being itself. Denying this tendency of contemporary industrial society, West or East, to treat man and the world as mere 'commodities', Heidegger urges that we ask the question of Being once again by putting our own being (*qua Dasein*) into question.

Such questioning calls for a new mode of thinking. Whereas technological thinking – like the metaphysical thinking which preceded it – is initiated by the autonomous human subject (as cogito, transcendental ego or productive will), and seeks to make everything in the world an 'object' for the subject, the kind of meditative or poetic thinking sponsored by the late Heidegger sees itself as a response to Being which calls. Genuine philosophical thinking is summoned by Being rather than man; it is a matter of Being 'presencing' to man rather than of man 'representing' Being to itself and thereby reducing all things to objects present-at-hand (*vorhanden*) in the trade of calculation.

For Heidegger the most essential form of thinking (*Denken*) is thanking (*Danken*), that is, an openness to and guardianship of the truth of Being. Western metaphysics, as the history of the forgetfulness of this truth, culminates in the current reign of technocratic positivism where thinking degenerates into a system of efficiency, self-assertion, domination and security (from investment security to national security). In contrast to such technocratic thinking, the *Denken* which Heidegger counsels is a non-objectifying, non-systematic, non-calculative receptivity which enters the play of Being by giving thanks. But in order to be thankful for thought we must first become aware that we have forgotten thought. "Most thought-provoking about this thought-provoking time", writes Heidegger, "is that we are still not thinking." It is in this sense that Heidegger devoted his entire philosophical career to the provocation of thought.

APPENDIX:
HEIDEGGER'S WAY TO LANGUAGE

Heidegger's philosophy of language was motivated from the outset by an ontological concern. He wished to show how language bespoke Being by expressing our being-in-the-world. To this end, Heidegger identified four main modes of language (*Sprache*): (i) *Assertion (Aussage)*, (ii) *Discourse (Rede)*, (iii) *Idle Talk (Gerede)*, and (iv) *Saying (Sagen)*.

(i) Language as assertion (logical propositions)

Traditional philosophies, Heidegger maintains, tended to reduce language to formal or abstract expression. Language was more often than not considered in terms of grammar and logic – in its scientific capacity of assertion.

Assertion generally served the threefold purpose of *designating* (this thing here); *predicating* (this thing here is white); and *communicating* (the exchange of such designated or predicated information – "letting someone see with us what we have pointed out by way of giving it a definite character"). Language thus became a matter of propositional logic concerned with the representation and classification of the world. Words were used impersonally to define or map reality as a collection of objects 'present-at-hand' (*vorhanden*). And in the process language was tailored to the requirements of a one-dimensional objectivisation. Henceforth it was only recognised in terms of its 'objectively valid character' – in the sense of words being deployed as a mere propositional calculus valid for regulating and standardising the relationship between word and thing.

In assertion, therefore, words are frequently treated as little more than lifeless entities for the abstraction and computation of reality: "Words are proximally present-at-hand, that is to say, we come across them just as we come across things." (*Being & Time*). This slide towards the reification of words reached its most restrictive extreme in the modern reign of logical positivism. Heidegger proclaims the necessity of "reestablishing the science of language on foundations which are ontologically more primordial", in order to emancipate meaning from the hegemony of logic which, in the scientific approach to language, is "still accepted as the standard today and is oriented towards discourse as *assertion*" (*Being & Time*).

(ii) Language as interpretive discourse (existential hermeneutics)

The purely formal functioning of logical assertion presupposes a more existential mode of language – what Heidegger calls interpretative or hermeneutic discourse. Here language is seen to have its roots in man's everyday existence in the world as a primordial interpretation (*hermeneuein*) of Being: it enables us to interpret a thing *as* something which is intimately related to our project of being-in-the-world. For example, discourse does not simply *assert* that a rock is there (designation) or that it possesses a series of objective characteristics such as weight, colour, width etc. (predication); it also and more fundamentally interprets the rock *as* something which is useful or meaningful for my existence – the rock is interpreted in its existential everydayness as something to be employed by me as a weapon, barrier, sculpting stone, building block or whatever.

If logical assertion treats things as objects present-at-hand (*vorhanden*), hermeneutic discourse recognises them as instruments ready-to-hand (*zuhanden*) for our existential concerns. Each thing is now disclosed as the bearer of a specific *message* (hence the derivation of the term 'hermeneutic' from Hermes, the Greek messenger of the gods). Everything serves as a 'sign' which addresses our concrete projects – of survival, pleasure, comfort, creativity, beauty and so on. We thus interpret the things of the world *existentially*, that is, no longer as logical entities but as lived *possibilities* to which we commit our existence. In short, hermeneutic discourse reveals beings in terms of their possible serviceability *for me*. And it does this by releasing them from the abstract quarantine of a timeless present into the temporal horizons of my concrete historical concerns – retrieving the meaningfulness of these entities from my *past* experience or projecting such meaningfulness into my *future* possible experiences.

Heidegger argues that the 'communicative' function of language as assertion – i.e. as a logical exchange of coded information from one empirical subject to another – is merely a derivation from the more primary mode of communication as an existential sharing of a world with others. Communication is more deeply understood, accordingly, as the interpretation of a common life-world which involves us *responding* to the other's project of meaning – and vice versa. The things of our *Dasein* are thus disclosed as symbols of our relationship to other *Daseins*. The world we inhabit through language is already replete with the cultural, historical and socio-economic meanings which we inherit from the whole intersubjective community of mankind which has preceded us. In this fashion, hermeneutic discourse defines our individual being-there (*Dasein*) as a communal being-with-others (*Mitsein*), i.e. as history and tradition.

Heidegger makes an important distinction here between *authentic* and *inauthentic* forms of existential discourse (*Rede*). The authentic form he calls 'Saying' (*Sagen*). This he identifies with our ability to remain responsible for our speech by remaining *silent* so as to *listen* and thus genuinely *respond* to the voice of Being. The inauthentic form he calls 'Idle Talk' (*Gerede*), which he goes on to define as an opinionated chatter totally unmindful of, because unresponsive to, the claim of other *Daseins*. "Keeping silent authentically", writes Heidegger, "is possible only in genuine discoursing. To be able to keep silent, *Dasein* must have something to say – that is, must have at its disposal an authentic and rich disclosedness of itself, in that case one's reserve makes something manifest and does away with idle talk . . . As a mode of discoursing, reserve articulates the intelligibility of *Dasein* in so primordial a way that it gives rise to a potentiality for hearing which is genuine, and to a being-with-one-another which is transparent" (*Being & Time*). I will now briefly outline these respective modalities of *Idle talk* and *Saying*.

(iii) Language as idle talk (public opinion)

Language as discourse-with-the-other (*Rede-mit-ein-ander*) can easily degenerate into idle talk (*Gerede*). This occurs whenever the speaker ceases to respond individually to the address of the other and is content to merely correspond to the anonymous chatter of 'public opinion'. Here the existential responsibility of each 'I' – qua *Dasein* – capitulates to the unthinking sway of the 'They' (*Das Man*). Accordingly, my speech ceases to be authentically *my own* (the German term for authentic, *eigentlich*, literally means 'own'): it is deformed into a mere commodity in the exchanges of fashionable gossip.

In Idle Talk words become strategies for escaping from ourselves; we cease to communicate decisively on the basis of our own lived experience. The challenging strangeness of the world is thus covered over with a film of convenient familiarity. Our existence is no longer lived *by us*; it is lived *for us* by the impersonalised 'They' who make decisions on our behalf. And so we fill up the hollow gaps within us by chattering away according to the rules of fashionable averages. Idle Talk or 'they-speak' interprets our being-with-the-other inauthentically to the extent that the world is considered to be what it is, not because *I* say so (in genuine response to the other) but because *One* says so.

Heidegger defines this alienated condition of language as an ontological 'groundlessness' (*Bodenlosigkeit*) wherein it becomes impossible to distinguish between a genuine utterance of our being and mere verbalising. Furthermore, the speakers whose discourse has been averaged out by the They, will "not want any such distinction, and do not need it, because of course, they understand *everything*". Idle Talk underwrites our *entrée* to the public world by cosmetically masking the unique differences of each individual's experience in order to present a veneer of unchallenging and uncritical indifference. Heidegger writes: "Idle Talk is the possibility of understanding everything without previously making the thing *one's own*. If I were to make something *my own*, Idle Talk would founder; and it already guards against such a danger. Idle Talk is something which anyone can rake up; it . . . releases one from the task of genuinely understanding and develops an undifferentiated kind of intelligibility" (*Being & Time*). Such indifference, which permits something to be said groundlessly by passing it along in mindless repetition, ultimately reduces the act of disclosing (*erschliessen*) truth to an act of closing off (*verschliessen*) truth. Otherwise put, Idle Talk operates as a form of *closure* which suspends any authentic interpretation of our being. Pretending to know everything, it in fact serves to discourage "any new enquiry and any disputation". The talk of the They thus ensures the "dominance of the public way . . . prescribes one's state-of-mind and determines what and how *one* sees" (*Being & Time*). Anonymous clichés and catchwords protect us from self-interpretation, from the need to use language *thoughtfully*; and by skimming over the surface of things, one contrives to suppress the fundamental question of our *rootedness in Being*.

Heidegger concludes accordingly that "this uprooting becomes our most everyday and most stubborn reality". The two most common ways in which this uprooted talk is conveyed are Curiosity (*Neugier*) and Duplicity or Double-Speak (*Zweideutigkeit*). Curiosity epitomises an inauthentic being-with-others in so far as it seeks to possess and consume everything without having to commit itself to anything. Idle Talk becomes curious talk to the extent that it knows a little about all and a lot about nothing. It is cocktail party conversationalism which prides itself on being *au courant* with anything worth talking about. And so, instead of 'tarrying' with the other, Curiosity is only interested in others in so far as they are deemed to be 'interesting', that is, in so far as they provide occasions of distraction or amusement: "It seeks novelty only in order to leap from it anew to another novelty . . . It seeks restlessness and the excitement of continual novelty and changing encounters" (*Being & Time*). Unlike the being-with-others of authentic language, curious talk has nothing to do with marvelling at the world (what the Greeks termed *Thaumazein* affirming it to be the root experience of all philosophical questioning). To be sure, curiosity does concern itself with a certain kind of knowing, but just in order to *have known* and *be known*. As Heidegger sums up:

> Both this *not tarrying* in the environment with which one concerns oneself, and this *distraction* by new possibilities, are constitutive items for curiosity; and upon these is founded (another) essential characteristic of this phenomenon, which we call the character of *never dwelling anywhere* . . . Idle Talk controls even the ways in which one may be curious. It says what one 'must' have read and seen. In being everywhere and nowhere, curiosity is delivered over to Idle Talk (*Being & Time*).

(IV) Language as Saying (Poetry)

For Heidegger poetic language is the most authentic mode of our being-with-others. Here language obviates the uprootedness of both Idle Talk (where the other is reduced to the socialite game of Who's Who) and of logical assertion (where the transcendence of the other is dispensed with altogether for the sake of scientific clarity). Poetry allows language to recover its primordial hermeneutic function of interpreting the world as the revelatory *text* of our existential projects. The world is thereby revealed as an open horizon of possibilities, each one of which speaks to us as a symbol or cypher of Being.

But if poetry recognises the rootedness of language in our authentic being-in-the-world, it also confronts us with the realisation that our being is itself ultimately rooted in death – the possibility of our non-being. Poetic language thus reaches down into the abyss which subtends all my interpretations of the world as a series of service possibilities (*zuhanden*). In poetry the meaning of Being surpasses *my* interpretation of *my* world; it is 'deworlded' in the sense of being released from the pragmatic contexts of mere economic or political or informational exchange. In this manner, the other is allowed to stand before me as strange and unique, irreducible to my functional projects. And by the same token, I too am 'deworlded' by the other, emancipated from my customary pragmatic approach to people and things.

Taking a more specific example, we could say that in poetry a rose is no longer considered in terms of a mere horticultural object of scientific observation (*vorhanden*); nor in terms of a mere flower to be watered, plucked or admired as part of my immediate environment (*zuhanden*); nor indeed in terms of a mere emblem of national identity (e.g. the Rose of England), sexual purity (e.g. Blake's 'Rose thou art sick') or regenerative resurrection (e.g. the Christian mysticism of the crucified and risen Rose). In poetic utterance, the rose exceeds all of our hermeneutic projects and is allowed *to be itself*: it reveals itself to be 'without why'; as the German mystic Silesius put it – a rose is a rose is a rose (*Der Satz vom grund*, 1957).

Heidegger affirms that man is ultimately grounded in poetic language in so far as it "reveals beings by enabling man to experience Being" (*On the Way to Language*, 1971). This experience of Being frequently occurs when poetic language dispenses with words as logical or utilitarian instruments related to particular practical concerns and empowers them to confront us with an experience of death. Poetry is a privileged means for revealing us to ourselves as being-towards-death (*Sein-zum-Tode*), for reminding us that our existence is finite, that it eventually comes to an end. Being itself speaks poetically to us through our awareness of our own mortality, disclosing itself as something which *is not*, that is as *nothingness* (as a no-thing-for-me). In poetry Being is made manifest in all its otherness; it exposes the limits of our individual projects. This is what Keats called 'negative capability' – the poetical ability to "experience mystery, uncertainty or doubt without that irritable reaching after fact and reason".

By putting into check the tendency of ordinary speech to take things for granted, poetic speech opens us to habitually closed-off dimensions of Being. It is when the objects and instruments of our world are transfigured by the poetic power of words that we see them as themselves, very often for the first time. Poetry enables us, as Heidegger observes, to take a 'step back' from things (*ein Schritt zurück*) whereby we may experience the world in a new way. Consequently if the thinker is to rethink and resay Being in an original manner, he is well advised to attend to how the poet reworks the language of Being:

> Obedient to the voice of Being, thought seeks the word through which the truth of Being may be expressed. Only when the language of historical man is born of the word does it ring true . . . The thought of Being guards the word and fulfils its function in such guardianship, namely care for the use of language. Out of long-guarded speechlessness and the careful clarification of the field thus cleared, comes the utterance of the thinker. Of like origin is the naming of the poet . . . since poetry and thinking are most purely alike in their care of the word (*What is Metaphysics?*).

Jean-Paul Sartre

Sartre was born in Paris in 1905. His father was a Catholic, his mother a Protestant; Sartre, who made a virtue of his atheism, was neither. When he was only two, his father died at war and Sartre often commented on his fatherless existence as a formative experience which taught him that each human being transcends the conditioning circumstances of his past and creates himself, as it were, out of nothing. For Sartre, the ultimate condition of twentieth-century man is one of abandonment, anguish and total freedom.

Sartre commenced his intellectual career as a teacher of philosophy at Le Havre in 1931. In 1933 he went to Germany to study phenomenology at first hand and this apprenticeship with the masters of phenomenology was to deeply influence his entire subsequent philosophical development. After his return from Germany, Sartre wrote a major work on the phenomenology of imagination in the thirties as well as his bestselling first novel *Nausea* in 1938, a work which, like many of his subsequent novels and plays, expressed in vivid literary terms the pivotal insights of his philosophical writings. Sartre went on to publish several other phenomenological studies on such themes as emotion and literature, but it was with the publication of his monumental *Being and Nothingness* in 1943 that Sartre succeeded in establishing himself as a highly original thinker in his own right, being hailed by many as the greatest modern philosopher of freedom. It was also at this time that Sartre founded the celebrated French journal *Les temps modernes* and participated with Simone de Beauvoir, Merleau-Ponty, Camus, Aron and others in some of the most arresting intellectual debates of our century.

The influence of Sartre's writing, both philosophical and literary, was immense. And his reputation was by no means confined to his native France. By the fifties, the name of Sartre had become synonymous with existentialism throughout the world; and existentialism had established itself, in large part thanks to Sartre's controversial stance and polemical style, as the most representative philosophy of twentieth-century man. In his later career, after the publication of *Being and Nothingness* and the highly popular *Existentialism and Humanism* (1946), Sartre's thinking tended to move beyond the limits of phenomenological existentialism to embrace a more political philosophy of humanist Marxism, deeply inspired by Lukács as is evident in *The Critique of Dialectical Reason* (1960). In his final years, after all the activism of the rebellious sixties, Sartre returned to more 'aesthetic' questions, publishing his massive three-volume study of Flaubert in 1971. Sartre died in Paris in 1980.

Since our brief in the present study is to deal explicitly with Sartre's contribution to the phenomenological movement, we have been obliged to forego discussion of his later Marxist and aesthetic writings, confining our attention instead to the formative period of his thought in the thirties and forties.

I

Sartre's philosophy of existence became, in his own words, the intellectual 'scandal of the century'. If Heidegger had adapted phenomenology to the question of Being, Sartre readapted it to the question of freedom. He agreed with Heidegger that Husserl's method should be developed in an existentialist direction. But he differed from Heidegger in declaring existentialism to be the basis of a radical *humanism*. For Sartre, man not Being occupies the centre of the existential stage. Meaning is not a gift of Being, it is an invention of the human individual. As the phenomenological analysis of Husserl indicated, man can no longer be considered as some timeless essence or substance but only as an intentional activity which is constantly surpassing itself and reconstituting itself throughout its existence. Sartre affirms accordingly that truth, far from being grounded in some ontological source other than human existence, is the sum of each individual's freely chosen actions. Nothing more, nothing less. 'Man is what he makes of himself.' This, insists Sartre, is the first principle of existentialism.

The most popular formulation of Sartre's phenomenology of freedom is to be found in *Existentialism and Humanism*. Written and published in 1946, this work is a passionate plea for existentialism as the most adequate philosophical response to the crisis, both social and cultural, which prevailed in Europe in the wake of the war. Sartre rose to the challenge with great gusto, directly addressing a population disillusioned with traditional systems of meaning. He declared that whatever meaning was to survive the collapse of European civilisation would have to be created *ex nihilo*, as it were, from the sole resources of each subjective consciousness. Only the individual could find within himself or herself the means of beginning all over again with the freedom and responsibility of an absolute choice. Traditional norms and conventions could no longer serve as an objective court of appeal. To this end, Sartre combined the Kierkegaardian maxim that 'the crowd is untruth: truth is subjectivity' with the phenomenological message that we must return to our 'lived experience' (*le vécu*) in order to rediscover an intentional and creative relationship with the world. Sartre advanced his humanistic brand of phenomenological existentialism in the belief that it provided the best possibility of a radically new beginning. *Existentialism and Humanism* offers a blueprint for authentic existence. Unlike Heidegger, however, Sartre invokes 'authenticity' as a guide to a 'fundamental anthropology' rather than a 'fundamental ontology'. His overriding concern is with *human being* rather than *Being in general*. To exist authentically, for Sartre, means to recognise that man's 'existence precedes his essence'.

Traditional philosophies from Plato to Kant had taught that our essence preceded our existence, that we were predetermined to be what we are by some innate or *a priori* principle such as God (*qua* First Cause of all things), Nature or Reason. According to this model, we possess a given human 'character' or 'essence' which it is the business of our temporal existence in this world to faithfully realise. We are like actors on a stage reciting a script which has been written for us beforehand. Sartre calls this traditional attitude 'sincerity' or 'seriousness' in contrast to authenticity. He ascribes it to those who believe that existence is a matter of living out a preestablished role in society, of occupying an appointed place in the universe. Like Lucien Fleurier, in Sartre's story, *The Childhood of a Leader* (1939), the sincere person is one who contrives to avoid the anguish and responsibility of freely choosing how to exist by presuming that this existential choice has been made for him, by some natural or divine destiny. Sincerity is the plain man's version, so to speak, of the traditional divine right of kings. Sartre describes Lucien's final succession to his father's privileged position as factory owner in Férolles in the following satirical passage:

> Generations of workers (would) scrupulously obey the commands of Lucien; they would never exhaust his right to command; rights were beyond existence, like mathematical objects and religious dogma . . . He had believed that he existed by chance for a long time, but it was due to a lack of sufficient thought. His place in the sun was marked in Férolles long before his birth. They were *waiting* for him long before his father's marriage; if he had come into the world it was to occupy that place . . . a graceful, uncertain adolescent had entered this café one hour earlier; now a man left, a leader among Frenchmen. (*ibid.*)

For the sincere person, therefore, existence is a way of remaining faithful to his pre-ordained essence, of being true to his given self.

The authentic person, on the other hand, begins by acknowledging that there is no given self to be true to; that our existence precedes our essence;

and that we invent ourselves as we go along. This means we make our own identity in and through our free decisions and actions. Accordingly our 'essence' is nothing other than that which we choose to be. We are what we are – good, bad or indifferent – not because we were born like that, or created so by God, or determined so by our environmental conditioning, genetic heritage, family upbringing or social and religious training, but because *we made ourselves* like that.

Sartre does not, of course, wish to deny that we choose within limits. He is the first to acknowledge that our existence is always *situated* in a concrete historical context. I do not choose to be born, nor do I choose my physical or biological condition, nor what economic class or political state or national culture I am born into. But I *do* choose how to exist within the limitations of these circumstances. As Sartre explains in *Being and Nothingness*, I cannot be an invalid, for example, "without having chosen the way in which I regard my infirmity as humiliating, intolerable, to be hidden, to be exhibited as a source of pride or as a justification of failure". In short, man is what he makes of himself in spite of the conditioning influences of his factual circumstances. We are free because we *define* what we are and how we are by a series of free choices which culminate only in death.

The root meanings of the opposing terms 'sincerity' and 'authenticity' are instructive. The former derives from the Latin, *sine-cera* meaning literally 'without wax', that is, without veneer or make-up. To be 'sincerely' true to oneself, therefore, is to refuse to wear masks, to reject the temptation to pretend that we could be other than what we are. This attitude is exemplified in Polonius' counsel to his son Laertes in *Hamlet*: 'This above all, *to thine own self be true*, / And it must follow, as the night the day, / Thou canst not then be false to any man". The sincere person is one who refuses to play games or experiment with his identity; he accepts his self as part of the naturally ordained order of things. In short, sincerity presupposes a belief in some kind of natural law.

The term, 'authenticity', by contrast, derives from the Greek roots, *auto-hentes*, meaning to make or create onself. To be authentic is to embrace our existence as an open-ended field of multiple possibilities of self-identity from which we choose. Authenticity demands consequently that we negate or transcend our 'objective' essence in order to invent new roles to play, new personae to identify with, new masks to express our numerous projects of existence. Only by opening ourselves to an experimental horizon of possible identities can we then choose freely in any given circumstance. "What is alarming in the doctrine I am proposing", writes Sartre in *Existentialism and Humanism*," is that it confronts man with a possibility of choice." There is little doubt that Sartre's description of authenticity is influenced by the existentialist theories of Søren Kierke-gaard, and particularly by his 'aesthetic' portrayals of the romantic heroes, Faustus, Don Juan and Prometheus, all three of whom transgressed the natural and divine order in order to assert their individual liberty.

The existentialist demand for free choice issues in a correlative demand for free *action*. If one grants that man is a given essence created by God or predetermined by genetic, environmental and socio-economic factors, then the individual is reduced to a quietism of inaction. There is nothing to be done, because everything is done for us before we arrive on the scene. My life is little more than a replay of a pre-established scenario authorised by anonymous forces which precede my individual actions. In the case of theism, for example, "god makes man according to a procedure and a conception, exactly as the artisan manufactures a paperknife following a definition and a formula" (*Ex. and Hum.*).

The affirmation of a radical humanism requires as a necessary conse-quence a repudiation of theism. There is no such thing as 'human nature' because there is no Divine Mind to preconceive it. Each individual is a 'leap towards existence' who wills and conceives of himself. Only by rejecting theism and all other forms of collectivist dogmatism can each person reappropriate his/her authentic role as author of his/her own world. When we say, therefore, that man's existence precedes his essence, declares Sartre, "we mean that man first of all exists, encounters himself, surges up in the world – and defines himself afterwards". Man *is* what he *does*.

Sartre confirms Dostoyevsky's maxim that 'if God is dead then all is permitted'. Existentialism, he argues, registers the terrifying drama of existence without God, drawing the necessary consequence of His absence right to the end. Emancipated from theism, we exist without excuse or alibi; we can no longer deflect our responsibility for existence onto any authority outside of ourselves. At every moment we are free to invent our identity. Atheism, as a philosophy of radical freedom, thus finds its truest expression in existentialism.

But Sartre is equally dismissive of attempts made by Enlightenment rationalism to replace a theological dogmatism with a secular dogmatism which presumes that certain values are good in themselves *a priori* on the basis of some positivistic notion of universal reason or progress. This is simply to substitute an atheistic determinism for a theistic one. Even the Marxist reading of historical revolution as the ineluctable liberation of the proletariat is, for Sartre, ultimately answerable to the individual freedom of action. For while the Russian revolution took place in 1917, as Sartre observes in *Existentialism and Humanism*, one cannot say that it has inevitably led to the triumph of the proletariat. It might well have led to the opposite. Nothing is assured for good and all. History is an open book, with new chapters waiting to be written. Only our free commitment to action can write them. Existentialism calls for a *phenomenology of action*.

At an ontological level, Being (*on*) can only have meaning, Sartre insists, in terms of the temporal project of our existence. Unlike a tree or a stone, which simply is what it is without any free choice in the matter, human being is a temporal projection "which propels itself towards a future and is aware that it is doing so". Whatever the conditioning limits of our past or present, our future offers itself to us as a blank canvas waiting to be filled in. Here Sartre confirms Heidegger's phenomenological description of our being-in-the-world as temporality – as a perpetual transcendence towards an open horizon of possibilities. Before this temporal projection of ourselves, nothing exists. Central to Sartre's existentialism is a *phenomenology of temporality*.

But in so far as we define ourselves by our projects in time, each of us is entirely responsible for the creation of meaning. Since our existence, as the free projection of the present self towards its future possibilities, is prior to our essence, "man is responsible for what he is. Thus the first effect of existentialism is that it puts every man in possession of himself as he really is and places the entire responsibility for his existence upon his own shoulders." To those who object that man is simply the result of environmental influences, Sartre replies that each one of us is responsible for what he or she has become. We could have been otherwise – under exactly the same circumstances. On the basis of our given conditions (class, nationality, language etc.), we create a unique role for ourselves. Paul Valéry, as Sartre tersely remarks, was indeed a *petit-bourgeois* Parisian, but not every *petit-bourgeois* Parisian became a Valéry! Sartre's existentialism entails accordingly a *phenomenology of individual responsibility*.

Because of this omnipresent responsibility, man is condemned to be free. Even the choice to have no choice is itself a choice. To demonstrate this, Sartre cites the example of a student who sought his counsel during the war. The student was in a dilemma as to whether he should join the resistance movement in Britain in order to fight the Nazis or stay in Paris and look after his ailing mother. Sartre refused to take responsibility for the student's own choice, reminding him "You are free, therefore choose". He pointed out to the student, moreover, that if he were to go and seek the advice of somebody else, a priest for example, he would still have to choose *which* priest. In other words, to seek the advice of a priest is to have selected this or that priest (e.g. a priest sympathetic to the resistance or to the collaboration movement), knowing more or less what he would advise. To choose an advisor is to have already committed oneself by that choice. Sartre's existentialism is a *phenomenology of choice*.

This realisation of the inescapability of choice is accompanied by the experience of anguish. When we choose we are filled with anguish because we become aware that there is no objective criterion of value which could guarantee or vindicate our actions in any absolute fashion. The authentic existence is one which accepts the inevitability of anguish and does not seek to hide from it. Furthermore, our anguish results from the fact that our choice of action is not just a choice of each individual self for itself but for all men. (Here Sartre endorses Kant's dictum that we should act in such a way that our actions are universalisable for all other individuals also.) The inauthentic individual, by contrast, sponsors the illusion that it is the universal (mankind) that legislates for the particular (individual men), rather than the contrary. Dispensing with the traditional idea of a transcendent value system which pre-ordains a set of natural laws, Sartre states uncompromisingly that "anguish is the very condition of action – for action presupposes that there is a plurality of possibilities and in choosing one of these, we realize that it has value only because it is chosen" (*Ex. and Hum.*) Existentialism involves therefore a *phenomenology of anguish*.

Sartre concludes *Existentialism and Humanism* by proposing that we might best understand the drama of human existence in terms of an *aesthetic* analogy. Just as we do not judge Proust's genius on the novels he could or might have written but on the ones he actually wrote, so too each individual's existence must be judged on the basis of those actions to which he has committed himself. This means for Sartre that "in life, man commits himself, draws his own portrait and that there is nothing but that portrait". Sartre develops this crucial analogy as follows:

Moral choice is comparable to the construction of a work of art . . . Does anyone reproach an artist when he paints a picture for not following rules established *a priori*? Does one ever ask what is the picture that he ought to paint? As everyone knows, there is no pre-defined picture for him to make; the artist applies himself to the composition of a picture, and the picture that ought to be made is precisely that which he will have made. As everyone knows, there are no aesthetic values *a priori*, but there are values which will appear in due course in the coherence of the picture, in the relation between the will to create and the finished work. No one can tell what the painting of tomorrow will be like; one cannot judge a painting until it is done. What has that to do with morality? We are in the same creative situation. We never speak of a work of art as irresponsible; when we are discussing a canvas by Picasso, we understand very well that the composition became what it is at the time when he was painting and that his works are part and parcel of his entire life. It is the same upon the plane of morality. There is this in common between art and morality, that in both we have to do with creation and invention (*Ex. and Hum.*)

Sartre admits that this aesthetic analogy of existence is intolerable for many. For it means that people must assume responsibility for being what they are. The coward must accept responsibility for being a coward and the hero for being a hero; and as a consequence both must accept the possibility of ceasing to be what they are and of becoming something else. For this reason, Sartre categorically rejects the accusation that his existentialism is a recipe for pessimism and inaction. It is, he retorts, the very opposite – an appeal to the total freedom, responsibility and commitment of action. And this is the utmost act of optimism, for it places the destiny of man squarely in man's hands. "Those who hide from this total freedom, in the guise of solemnity or with deterministic excuses", concludes Sartre with customary directness, "I shall call cowards. Others who try to show that their existence is necessary, when it is merely an accident of the appearance of the human race on earth, I shall call scum" (*ibid.*)

II

Sartre's philosophy of freedom derives from a series of phenomenological descriptions of the intentional activities of human consciousness which he published in the thirties and forties. Principal among these are *The Psychology of Imagination* (1940), *Sketch for a Theory of Emotions* (1939) and *Being and Nothingness* (1943).

It is highly significant that Sartre's first two major books comprised a phenomenological investigation of the power of human imagining. The first of these, *Imagination* (1936), is a refutation of classical theories of the image which identified it reductively as a 'thing' in consciousness, passively derived from sensation, rather than as an 'act' of consciousness. Sartre champions Husserl as the first to describe imagination as an intentional activity, thereby liberating it from the servile role it had acquired in traditional epistemologies. The second work, *The Psychology of Imagination* (the original title was *L'Imaginaire: Psychologie Phénoménologique de l'Imagination*), signalled a more original contribution. Here Sartre developed Husserl's analyses of intentionality in the *Logical Investigations* into an innovative reassessment of imagining as the most fundamental act of our being-in-the-world.

Sartre begins *The Psychology of Imagination* with a phenomenological analysis of perception and imagination as two distinct modes of human intentionality. Defining both as acts of consciousness, Sartre distinguishes between perception as an act which presents an object in its presence and imagination as an act which presents an object in its absence. I cannot – to take one of Sartre's examples – perceive and imagine Pierre at the same time. If I perceive Pierre in this room here in Paris, it is not possible to simultaneously imagine him in Berlin. And by the same token, in order to imagine Pierre in Berlin – in his absence – I must negate what is perceptually present to me here and now. Sartre defines imagination accordingly as the negation of perception. For to imagine something we must absent ourselves from what is present (in perception) in order to present to ourselves what is absent. The image of something is its *presence in absence*. (For a more detailed analysis see the Appendix on *Sartre and Imagination*).

Sartre concludes his phenomenological description of the intentional operations of imagination by declaring that while man is ontologically limited by his being-in-the-midst-of-the-world (by the 'facticity' of perceptually present realities), he is ontologically free by virtue of his being-beyond-the-world (by the transcending power of imagination which negates the actual world in its projection of new, futural possibilities). "For a consciousness to be able to imagine", writes Sartre, "it must be able to escape from the world . . . in a word, it must be free.' And by the same token, it is precisely "because man is transcendentally free that man can imagine". If it were possible to conceive for a moment of a consciousness which could not imagine, it would have to be conceived as completely engulfed in the actuality of the present moment, and therefore incapable of grasping anything other than this actuality. But this could not be, insists Sartre, "for all existence as soon as it is posited is surpassed by itself" – surpassed that is, towards something which it is *not*. Thus Sartre prefigures his celebrated definition of man in *Being and Nothingness* as a being who is not what he is and is what he is not. As soon as I realise myself as I am now, I am already imagining myself as I am no longer (my past self) and as I am not yet (my future self). My present self is haunted by past and future absences. To imagine is, therefore, a temporal act in which I constitute myself as both nothingness (i.e. no actual given *thing* here and now) and freedom.

In his *Sketch for a Theory of the Emotions* (1939), Sartre extrapolates the implications of his phenomenology of imagination for a phenomenology of man's so-called 'irrational' emotional behaviour. In a series of vivid phenomenological descriptions, Sartre endeavours to demonstrate that our emotions are not, as many classical and behaviourist psychologists believed, reflex reactions to external stimuli, but purposeful intentions of consciousness. Once again we find Sartre employing phenomenology to show that the traditional division of man into a rational soul and an irrational body (which would include such pre-reflective phenomena as imagination and emotion) is untenable. Emotion and imagination, he argues, are not reducible to mechanistic models of explanation. They are not simply the products of empirical causes but express a highly strategic consciousness.

Sartre's analysis of emotion shows it to be teleological rather than causal. He defines it as 'an ordered pattern of means directed towards an end (*telos*).' In other words, emotion is less an automatic bodily response to a physical cause than an act of consciousness whereby I negate the world as it is in order to transform it into a world of unreality. Sartre affirms accordingly that we may 'speak of a world of emotions as we speak of a world of dreams'. Emotion occurs when our normal avenues of behaviour – what Sartre calls our 'hodological maps' (Greek, *hodos*, means path or way) – no longer seem functional or simply prove too difficult to pursue in a conventional manner. Thus confronted with what appear to be 'impossible situations', we depart from the pragmatic patterns of so-called 'rational' behaviour and have recourse instead to 'magical' behaviour. But this magical behaviour is just as intentionally structured as the rational behaviour it replaces. Put in another way, once the real world proves 'non-utilisable' or 'unmanageable', we deploy emotion to transmute this world into an unreal one where the normal laws of behaviour no longer operate. In short, we negate the world in order to better cope with what appears to be an irresolvable problem. Far from being a 'passing disorder of the organism', therefore, emotion is revealed as a highly ordered strategy which apprehends the world in an unreal way. "Emotion is not an accident", writes Sartre, "it is a mode of our conscious existence, one of the ways in which consciousness understands its being-in-the-world . . . by transforming the determinist world in which we live into a magical world" (*Ibid.*)

Emotion is thus construed by Sartre as a pre-reflective act of imaginative consciousness. For, strictly speaking, what it transforms is not the world itself – which remains as unmanageable as before – but the *manner in which we intend the world*. Emotion is magical behaviour to the extent that it pretends to change the world by changing *itself*, that is, the way in which we present the world to ourselves. In other words, by altering our attitude to the world, emotion provides imaginary solutions to real conflicts.

Sartre rehearses many examples to support his thesis. The common emotional attitude of 'sour grapes', for instance, expresses a transformation of our attitude of desire (we reached for the grapes because we desired to eat them) into an attitude of couldn't-care-less rejection (unable to reach the grapes, we act 'as if' they were green and so undesirable). In this way, we contrive to resolve the tension of our frustration by changing our intention towards the object. And so doing, we choose to believe our own illusion, pretending that our subjective change of mind corresponds to an objective property in the object. We attribute 'sourness' not to ourselves but to the intended goal of our original desire. In reality, however, it is of course only our emotional frame of mind that is 'green' not the grapes themselves.

Sartre also examines the emotion of horror. A woman alone in a country house perceives a face staring through the window and screams. She screams – that is, has recourse to the emotional behaviour of terror and fear – precisely because the normal modes of pragmatic behaviour (e.g. inquiring who is there, locking the doors, calling for help, seeking a weapon of self-defence etc.) are too difficult to entertain in such a moment of tension. By screaming, the woman does not of course alter the real fact of a real face at a real window. But by positing the face as too 'horrible' for words or actions, the 'horrified' woman is in fact presuming to negate the world of reality by negating her perceptual consciousness of it. As Sartre explains: "The horrible is not possible in the deterministic world of the utilizable. The horrible can only appear in a world which is such that all the things existing in it are magical by nature, and the only *defences* against them are magical". In a similar if more mundane fashion, when we refer to the sea as 'cruel' or the weather as 'bleak' or the season as 'joyful', we are not speaking about these things themselves but of the ways in which consciousness presents them to itself.

One final example which usefully illustrates Sartre's phenomenological theory of emotions, is that of a young girl who weeps hysterically when confronted with her doctor to whom she has a painful incident to confess. According to the models of mechanistic psychology, the girl cries because she can say nothing or because the doctor is disapproving. But Sartre points out that the girl resorts to emotional grief *before* the doctor has reacted in any way whatsoever. The girl weeps hysterically, concludes Sartre, not *because* the doctor disapproves but *in order* that he will not disapprove; not *because* she can say nothing but *in order* to say nothing. Her emotional behaviour is not causally determined therefore in terms of a stimulus/response mechanism; it is teleologically intended.

By means of such phenomenological descriptions, Sartre shows that far from being a 'lawless disorder', emotion is a specific mode of our pre-reflective intentionality. Like imagination, emotion is an act of 'magical incantation' whose aim it is to render the inescapable escapable and the impossible possible, by transmuting what is into what it is not. To say that one was 'emotionally disturbed' or 'hysterical' when one committed a certain action, is not for Sartre to deny our responsibility for that act. Even emotion is a matter of choice. In this way, Sartre furthers his existentialist argument that human existence is irreducible to the sum of the external causes which condition it, remaining in all cases an intentional activity which freely projects its meanings onto the world.

III

In *Being and Nothingness* (1943), probably his most complex, rigorous and systematic work, Sartre sets out to provide an ontological foundation for his phenomenology of human freedom. Hence the subtitle of the work – *An Essay on Phenomenological Ontology*. Taking up his concluding analysis to *The Psychology of Imagination*, Sartre describes human existence as a dialectic between the ontological poles of 'nothingness' (as an imaginative being-beyond-the-world) and 'being' (as a perceptual being-in-the-midst-of-the world). From the ontological category of 'nothingness' he deduces the existential phenomena of *consciousness for-itself (pour-soi), freedom, transcendence, subjectivity* and *anguish*. Under the ontological category of 'being', by contrast, Sartre lists the opposing phenomena of *consciousness in-itself (en-soi), necessity, facticity, objectivity* and *shame*.

Existence is *for itself* in so far as it operates as a consciousness which negates the given world in order to project itself towards a new horizon of possibilities. Our consciousness becomes *for itself* whenever it posits the factual entities surrounding it as instruments for its own intentional projects: a mountain, for example, is interpreted as *for me*, something to be mined, skied on, climbed over, jumped off and so on. By contrast, our consciousness becomes a thing *in itself* whenever our free subjectivity is reduced to the deterministic condition of an object amongst objects. So that if the *for itself* expresses our subjective freedom, the *in itself* designates the counter-position of objective necessity.

The consciousness that exists *for itself* exists, Sartre maintains, in 'anguish'. The existential experience of anguish accompanies the recognition that the world is my own creative project and that I bear responsibility for its meaning. Sartre describes this phenomenon succinctly in the following passage from *Being and Nothingness*:

> I emerge alone and in anguish confronting the unique and original project which constitutes my being; all the barriers, all the guardrails collapse, nihilated by the consciousness of my freedom. I do not have, nor can I have, recourse to any value against the fact that it is I who sustain values in being. Nothing can ensure me against myself, cut off from the world . . . by this nothingness which I *am*. I have to realize the meaning of the world and of my essence; I make my decision concerning them – without justification and without excuse. (*ibid*)

The experience of being *in itself*, on the other hand, is described by Sartre as 'shame'. Here my consciousness is reduced to an object that is judged and determined by forces outside of myself, typified by the objectifying 'look' of the other (*le regard de l'autre*). Sartre terms this 'look' a 'medusa glance' which 'petrifies' all that it comes in contact with. Shame occurs when my subjective activity of intentional 'looking' is transformed by the other into a passive being-looked-at – an objective condition of being like a stone, a fixed presence, a thing in itself deprived of its temporal projections into past and future. Sartre illustrates this experience of shame with the example of a voyeur spying on somebody undressing through a keyhole. The voyeur is a subject for itself and the naked woman an object in itself. The situation is dramatically altered, however, when a neighbour passes in the corridor and catches the voyeur in the act, thereby freezing him in the role of 'peeping Tom'. Thus judged by the 'look' of the neighbour, the voyeur has become an object in itself. Shame, says Sartre, results from this experience of being reified, of the other fixing my identity as if I were a thing (*res*) among things. Petrified by the medusa glance of the other I become a coward or a hypocrite, a hero or a voyeur etc. in the same manner as an inkwell is an inkwell or a table a table. But only a human existence can experience shame, of course, for it alone can be conscious of being reduced to the condition of a thing *in itself*.

If I existed in a world that was *for me* and only for me, then I would experience anguish but no shame; I would exist as a pure interiority of consciousness. But because I exist in a world with others, I am frequently alienated from my interior freedom by the other's objectifying 'look'; I become reduced to the condition of a bodily exteriority. Shame, Sartre affirms accordingly, is the feeling of "recognizing myself in the degraded, fixed and dependent being which I am for the other (*Ibid*). It is the experience of having 'fallen' into a world of objects.

But the possibility of becoming a thing *in itself* can also provide us with an excuse – albeit an illusory one – for not choosing. This attempt to flee from the responsibility of having to choose an identity for ourselves – by presuming this identity can be determined for us by others – is denounced by Sartre as 'bad faith'. To illustrate this refusal to choose, Sartre offers the dramatic example of a young woman who is invited to a restaurant by an 'admirer' with very definite sexual designs. She is well aware of these designs yet also flattered by the thought that she is an object of desire for the seducer. But she doesn't wish to be only that – the pure *in itself* of a desirable body. She also wants to preserve her free transcendence as a subject *for itself* interested in discussing spiritual and intellectual matters. In other words, the young woman wants to be respected as a spiritual consciousness, yet doesn't want respect to be only respect. She knows she will soon have to make a decision as to whether she will succumb to her companion's amorous advances. But she defers this decision for as long as possible, playing a double role of spiritual subject (above all considerations of the flesh) and of appetising object open to all offers. Then the man places his hand on hers. Now it seems, she will have to choose one way or the other. If she withdraws her hand she will have broken the spell of ambiguity and chosen to be a spiritual subject rather than a bodily object. Alternatively, she can leave her hand under his, thereby acknowledging her willingness to consent to his sexual desires. But Sartre describes how the young woman ingeniously contrives to postpone this choice yet again. She leaves her hand under his while pretending not to have noticed! She does not notice, explains Sartre, "because it happened by chance that she is at this moment all intellect. She draws her companion up to the most lofty regions of sentimental speculation: she speaks of life, of her life, she shows herself in her essential aspect – a personality, a consciousness. And during this time the divorce of the body from the soul is accomplished; the hand rests inert between the warm hands of her companion – a *thing*" (*Ibid*). This refusal to choose is 'bad faith'.

Because we live in a world with others, Sartre affirms that we are condemned to a *conflict of freedoms*. The other threatens my freedom and makes me aware that the world is not my own. He steals the world from me. He takes over my projects and gives them another meaning, his meaning. He rewrites my script. My existence thus ceases to be a soliloquy and becomes a drama of colliding subjectivities. Sartre maintains that intersubjective relations are doomed to failure by virtue of the ontological division between being and nothingness. One of the subjects in a human relationship is obliged, for ontological reasons, to become an object for the other. It is impossible for two freedoms to co-exist harmoniously, for the reason that each freedom can only exist *for itself* by negating an object *in itself* which it is not. There is, of course, no problem when that which is other than my negating consciousness is a thing – such as an inkwell or a tree. But when that which my consciousness negates, in order to preserve its free transcendence as a nothingness for itself, is another human consciousness – that is, an opposing power of free negation – then conflict is inevitable. One of the freedoms will have to be negated and thus reduced to the condition of an object in itself, so that the other can exist as a subject for-itself. In short, for one human subject to remain a *no-thing* the other must become a *thing*. Two nothingnesses cannot coexist simultaneously.

On the basis of this ontological analysis of human relations, Sartre reformulates Hegel's dialectic of master and slave. To the extent that I consider myself to be a solitary freedom, the world is my dominion and I am sovereign master of it. But precisely as my sole project, the world is not founded in any objective necessity outside of my empty choosing will. The meaning of my world is thus revealed to me as no more than the result of my arbitrary choice. And with this awareness my magisterial consciousness becomes, like Macbeth's, 'cabined, cribbed, confined, bound in by saucy doubts and fears'. To overcome this anguished realisation that my project is absurd, because devoid of any 'objective' justification, I feel the need to have it confirmed or justified by another. But as soon as I enter into relation with another subjectivity to secure such confirmation, I expose myself to conflict. One of us will be obliged to abandon his freedom to the other. In other words, one will have to become a master and the other a slave. Faced with this dilemma, Sartre outlines three opinions.

1. In order to be confirmed by another, I must first attract his or her attention. But this requires that I become an object of interest or desire for the other, that I renounce my own desire for the sake of conforming to the other's desire. And in so reducing myself to the seductive condition of a 'desirable object' I become a slave and the other becomes my master. Having escaped the *anguish* of a solitary freedom, I now experience the *shame* of a servile unfreedom. I have traded in my nothingness for the dubious privilege of becoming a thing for the other. This strategy is what Sartre calls 'masochism'.

2. The masochistic option is, of necessity, self-defeating, for what I sought in becoming a desirable object for the other was, paradoxically, the confirmation of my subjectivity precisely as a free being for-itself. Realising this, I may now resolve to recapture my former freedom from the other. But I can only do this by reducing the other to my project, that is, by reversing the masochistic scenario and by making the other into an actor in *my* play. In this way, I become the master and the other the slave. Since, however, the other will most probably resist my efforts to deprive him or her of free subjectivity, I am obliged to resort to coercion, or even violence. This strategy Sartre calls 'sadism'.

But sadism is equally self-defeating. It is true that I am now at last confirmed in my freedom by the other. But this is of little satisfaction, since the other who now confirms me does not do so willingly – but merely as a slave reduced to the condition of a mere object. Quite clearly, if someone declares 'I love you' because I have tortured him/her to do so, I can take no comfort from this love. And so the master is once again isolated in his unfounded freedom. The wheel comes full circle and his original anguish returns to plague him.

3. A third strategy considered by Sartre is 'indifference'. Since masochism (the choice to become an object for the sake of the other as master)

and sadism (the choice to become a master by reducing the other to an object) are both equally conflictual, Sartre analyses how one may be tempted to resort to indifference in order to escape the vicious circle of master and slave. If I could become indifferent to all intersubjective relations by denying any possibility of a rapport with others, would this not offer at least a partial solution? Sartre shows, however, that indifference is no less doomed to failure than the other two options. He points out how in our determination to completely ignore others, we remain perpetually obsessed by them. To try to persuade myself that I am not thinking of any other persons is of course a sure way of thinking about them. To spend my time negating others as a threat to my freedom, is to continue defining myself *vis-à-vis* others. "I wish to rid myself of the existence that is obsessing", writes Sartre, "and not only of the existence of a particular other but of all others" (*ibid*). But this is impossible, for "he who has once been for-others is contaminated in his being for the rest of his days even if the other should be entirely suppressed; he will never cease to apprehend his dimension of being-for-others as a permanent possibility of his being" (*ibid*). Even the hermit is haunted by memories of people he has met in the past or by anticipations of people he may meet in the future. Given the ontological impossibility of relating to others *and* of not relating to them at all, it is not surprising that Sartre concludes that 'hell is other people'.

Sartre analyses two further attempts to overcome the ontological dualism of the *for itself* and the *in-itself* by shifting the emphasis from an interpersonal to an impersonal level. These analyses take the form of a critique of the sociological phenomenon of the scapegoat and of the theological phenomenon of God. Both, Sartre argues, involve a flight from freedom.

The phenomenon of the scapegoat tries to overcome the antagonism of freedoms by creating an inauthentic social consensus over and against a commonly negated object – the persecuted outsider. A society may work to establish a sense of intersubjective solidarity amongst its members by falsely attributing responsibility for all that is considered 'evil' in that society – war, economic scarcity, disease, famine, revolt etc. – to a collectively identified scapegoat. In this way, an ostensible sense of harmonious belonging and social community is created by negating some solitary outcast or minority group (e.g. Jews, negroes, communists, dissidents and so on) which the 'established' society is *not*. The members thus feel at one by virtue of their shared hatred of the outsider; they participate in a common *consciousness for-itself* negating a common *object in-itself*. This project of the scapegoat as a collective flight from individual responsibility is brilliantly described by Sartre in his *Anti-semite and Jew* (1946). The anti-semite is like all persecutors of scapegoats, observes Sartre, in that he is someone afraid of his own consciousness, freedom and responsibility, of everything except the 'outsider':

> He is a coward who does not want to admit his cowardice to himself; a murderer who represses and censures his tendency to murder without being able to hold it back, yet who dares to kill only in effigy or protected by the anonymity of the mob
> . . . The existence of the Jew merely permits the anti-semite to stifle his anxieties at their inception by persuading himself that his place in the world has been marked out in advance, that it awaits him, and that tradition gives him the right to occupy it. Anti-semitism, in short, is fear of the human condition. (*Anti-Semite and Jew*)

By projecting all its anxieties on to an imaginary effigy outside of itself, society becomes a collective consciousness which exists in 'bad faith'. But once again this strategy of self-evasion is self-defeating. For the society which persecutes the scapegoat is secretly aware that this outsider is not really responsible for all its problems and conflicts; it must know that its projection of evil onto the scapegoat is no more than a fiction because it has invented this fiction in the first place. Desperate to flee from its anguish, society practises a double-think whereby it chooses to believe in its own lies. It realises that its project is false even though it pretends to itself that it is true. The scapegoat phenomenon is thus interpreted by Sartre as yet another example of inauthentic imagination.

Finally, in his famous conclusion to *Being and Nothingness*, Sartre demonstrates the ontological impossibility of theism as a solution to the conflict of human existence. God, for Sartre, is the human projection of an ideal synthesis of the for-itself and the in-itself, of nothingness and being. Traditionally defined as an *ens causa sui* – the Supreme Being that is both pure freedom for-itself and its own necessary cause in-itself – God represents the ultimate imaginary project of all human existence. 'Man is the desire to be God.' But this is an absurd project for the simple reason that God is an ontological contradiction in terms. On the phenomenological plane of finite, temporal being – which is the only plane Sartre admits of as being philosophically legitimate – freedom and necessity can only exist in perpetual opposition. The *for-itself* and the *in-itself* are mutually exclusive; they cannot relate to each other except as contradiction. God must be denounced, consequently, as a contradictory project of the human imagination: an ideal which remains forever unrealisable. To believe in God is, according to Sartre, the ultimate form of 'bad faith', for it is to believe in the ultimate lie, our most supreme aesthetic fiction, our most ingenious confidence trick.

Thus exploding the ontological premise of theism, Sartre demands that we lucidly acknowledge the inescapable absurdity of our existence – without justification or illusion. To attribute the solution to life's problems to a non-existent deity, is not only to deny our responsibility for our existence, it is also to deny ourselves for nothing. "The idea of God is contradictory", concludes Sartre, "and we lose ourselves in vain – man is a useless passion." Man is authentic when he accepts his human condition as a useless passion; he is inauthentic when he refuses it.

Sartre's phenomenological analysis of existence issues in an ontology of absolute dualism and conflict. The freedom of the for-itself remains incorrigibly at odds with the necessity of the in-itself. Man is condemned to self-division, to be what he is not and not to be what he is. In several works after *Being and Nothingness*, most particularly *What is Literature?* (1947) and *The Critique of Dialectical Reason* (1960), Sartre made valiant efforts to modify his dualist ontology by incorporating a Marxist analysis of social praxis as an ongoing struggle for the universal goal of liberty for all. But even here, Sartre's existentialist conviction that any legitimate notion of 'universal' value must be authenticated by the free choice of each human subject survives. In the final analysis, Sartre would appear to have remained faithful to the first principle of his existentialism: man is what he makes of himself.

APPENDIX: SARTRE AND IMAGINATION

In *The Psychology of Imagination*, Sartre proceeds to describe imagination as a *quasi-observation*. When I imagine Pierre, I observe him as existing in a quasi-time and quasi-space. The image transgresses the spatio-temporal limits of the perceptual world here and now. So that if I read a fiction like *War and Peace*, for example, I can travel freely through different minds, countries and generations. In the fictional world, I attain a freedom over space which permits me to be in Paris one moment, in Berlin the next and in Moscow the next. Similarly, I acquire a freedom over time which enables me to concentrate the temporal experience of a hundred years (of several generations of fictional characters for instance) into a few hours (the time it takes to actually read Tolstoy's novel). Or conversely, fiction can allow me to enlarge one moment into several hours or days (as happens in some of Borges' stories). Our dreams and reveries provide even more familiar examples of our imaginative freedom to manipulate time and space in the form of a quasi-observation. In a dream, as everyone has experienced, we can observe ourselves as several different people in several different places at several different times. Imagination is the power to be other than we are.

This power of temporal and spatial transcendence, Sartre calls the *spontaneity* of imagination. Taking the example of observing a cube, Sartre points out that whereas we can only 'perceive' a cube by means of a *succession* of perspectival aspects – that is, we are obliged to perceive each of its four sides one after the other – we can 'imagine' all of its sides and aspects simultaneously – that is, in one single, spontaneous act.

But this intentional freedom and spontaneity of imagination is accompanied by what Sartre calls an 'essential poverty'. After all, the image of the cube or of Pierre offers us not a real but only a *quasi*-observation. The free spontaneity of imagination results from a negation of the inexhaustible presence of the object as a perceptual reality. Sartre defines imagination, accordingly, as an 'unrealising' (*néantisant*) power of consciousness which can only present a thing as a *no-thingness* (in the sense of *not* being an empirical thing in reality). The object of perception overflows consciousness constantly; the object perceived is always *more* than our intention of it. But the object of imagination is never more than my consciousness of it; and so I cannot learn from an image more than I already know. To illustrate this 'poverty' of imagination, Sartre remarks that we cannot count the columns of the Parthenon in our imagination – unless, that is, we already know how many columns there are before we begin to count.

The price we pay for freedom over the world is the annihilation of the world. For in imagination we experience the world as an unreal nothingness. To say I have an image of Pierre is equivalent to saying not only that I do not see Pierre but that I see nothing (i.e. nothing real). Sartre writes:

Alive, appealing and strong as an image is, it presents its object as not being. This does not prevent us from reaching to the image as if its object were before us . . . But the false and ambiguous condition we reach thereby only serves to bring out in greater relief what we have just said: that we seek in vain to create in ourselves the belief that the object really exists by means of our conduct towards it. We can pretend for a second, but we cannot destroy our immediate awareness of its nothingness. (*The Psychology of Imagination*)

If I have a mental image of my loved one before me, therefore, I may well experience feelings of affection or even of passion. But what I am being 'moved by' here is in fact not my beloved as a really existing person but my own subjective projection of her. "It is my love for Annie", explains Sartre, "that causes her unreal (imaginary) face to appear to me, and not the unreal face of Annie that excites a glow of love for her" (*Ibid*). In short, by defining imaginative consciousness as an intentional negation of perceptual reality, Sartre is determining not only the *temporality* of human existence – that we are perpetually transcending the present towards the future, projecting beyond the actual towards the possible – but also the essential *solipsism* of human existence. To imagine is to be condemned to the self (*ipse*) alone (*solus*).

Sartre is thus compelled to admit that consciousness purchases the privilege of *creative activity* (in imagination) by forfeiting the solidity of the real world (in perception). "A perceptual consciousness", Sartre writes, "appears to itself as passive. An imaginative consciousness, on the contrary, presents itself to itself as an active consciousness, that is as a *spontaneity* which creates and holds on to the object as an image. This is a sort of indefinable counterpart of the fact that the object occurs as a nothingness. The consciousness appears to itself as being creative, but without positing what it has created as a (real) object" (*Ibid*).

This creative power of imagination may be understood, Sartre suggests, as a kind of aesthetic *magic*. Even though we know that our images are no more than self-projections we continue to react to them magically, *as if* they were real. If I look at the portrait of King Charles VIII in a Florentine gallery, I know this King is long dead and buried; and yet the imaginary lips, nose, eyes and forehead of the portrait act on my feelings in such a way that I 'magically' transform the lines and colours that are perceptually present on the canvas into the unreal image of the King. In this aesthetic experience, I imagine that the dead King is here before me:

> It is he we see, not the picture, and yet we declare him not to be there. We have him only as an image by the mediation of the picture. Here we see that the relationship that consciousness posits in the imaginative attitude between the portrait and the original is nothing short of magical. Charles VIII is at one and the same time absent and present (*ibid*.)

In similar fashion, primitive peoples lived in a magical world of imagination when they practised voodooism (the absent person being manipulated by means of an imaginary effigy), or buried their royalty along with visual simulacra (which were considered to render them immortal by preserving their presence in spite of their absence); or painted bisons on the walls of their caves to make the hunt fruitful. And lest we presume we have completely outgrown such primitive superstitions, Sartre asks us to consider how we still relate, for instance, to photographs or other imaginary representations of people dear to us. How many of us would unflinchingly pierce the eyes of a photographed loved one, even though we know that our loved one is not *really* present in the celluloid representation? The magical power of imagination is not a quaint phenomenon of antiquity; it is an essential structure of human consciousness. Twentieth-century Western man no longer paints bisons or practises black magic, but he does go to the cinema, read novels, look at television and simply dream. Human beings, according to Sartre, will always experience a fundamental need to negate the world as it is in order to imagine it as it might be. We will never cease to translate fact into fiction.

The imaginative power to negate reality is the precondition of our freedom in so far as it can liberate us from the oppressive constraints of the perceptual, given present. But it can also degenerate into its own kind of unfreedom. This occurs most obviously and most tragically in pathological cases of psychosis or schizophrenia. Here human consciousness completely capitulates to its own imaginings and mistakes them for reality. No longer able to face up to the burdens of existence, some people seek refuge in a magical world believing that their imaginary projects are not created by them but by others – e.g. by God, by society or by some determining unconscious 'other' who possesses them. Sartre describes this 'unfreedom' of imagination as a 'chained' consciousness which ceases to recognise that it is responsible for its own imaginary projections. He insists, however, that we are not concerned here with external *determinism* (conditioning consciousness from without) but with an internal *fatalism* (consciousness becoming alienated from itself in the form of a 'counter-spontaneity' which the person takes to be *other* than itself). A fatalistic consciousness is one which has become captive to itself, thus forfeiting its power to replace one imaginary project by another. No longer capable of keeping imagination open to a futural horizon of possibilities, consciousness latches on to one of its *images* as if it were a determining reality. In short, 'fatalism' occurs whenever we loose the freedom of aesthetic play – our awareness of the 'as if' character of our own imaginings – and begin to take our fictions literally.

The aesthetic attitude differs from the pathological attitude in that it remains conscious of the fundamental intentional distinction between the imaginary and the real. If we go to the theatre, for example, and see Hamlet pierce Polonius with his sword, we do not stand up in the auditorium and shout 'Murder!' We do not, in other words, mistake the fictional for the literal. So too, we preserve the aesthetic freedom of imagination by not confusing our imaginary projects with some intractable reality existing independently of our creative choices. It is precisely this freedom of creative self-consciousness which the 'chained' consciousness lacks. And to this extent, it becomes a prisoner of itself. Sartre offers the following lucid description of the way in which a psychaesthenic becomes incarcerated in a vicious circle of its own imaginings:

> It is my fear of the obsession which causes it to be reborn; every effort 'not to think of it' is transformed spontaneously into obsessing thoughts; if it is at times forgotten for a moment, the patient suddenly asks himself: 'But how calm I am!

etc . . . Consciousness is here a victim of itself, clinched in a sort of vicious circle and every effort to get rid of the obsessing idea is precisely the most effective means of bringing it about . . . It is in this sense, and in this sense only, that the obsession 'imposes itself' on consciousness. (*ibid.*)

Sartre concludes accordingly that the pathological imagination is one which is both victim and executioner. As such, the cure can only come when the patient is reminded that he is being obsessed by himself and so is free to transcend this closed circle towards an horizon of alternative possibilities of being. Sartre rejects the Freudian model of the unconscious as some kind of impersonal 'id' that could impose itself on our consciousness against our will. He denounces this interpretation as a modern revamping of the traditional doctrine of demonic possession. Against Freud, Sartre points out that the only reason a patient can hide the true cause of his neurosis (e.g. a particular childhood trauma) from the analyst and even from himself – in a subterfuge of symbols which disguise the original event – is that the patient *already knows*, albeit pre-reflectively, what the true cause is. We can only lie to ourselves and to others if we already know what truth is. Or to put it in another way: we cannot hide something unless we know what it is we are hiding. Sartre takes this simple fact to mean that the psychoanalytic model of the unconscious cannot be invoked as a means of foisting the responsibility for our behaviour onto some 'cause' outside of ourselves (because outside the ken of our consciousness). The fact that human being is consciousness through and through – be it reflective or pre-reflective – means that we are always free to choose, even if this sometimes involves a choice to deceive ourselves that we are not free. By means of this distinction between a liberating imagination of aesthetic play and an incarcerating consciousness of self-obsession, Sartre lays the foundation for his ontological distinction between authentic and inauthentic existence.

Maurice Merleau-Ponty

Maurice Merleau-Ponty was born in France in 1907. He was professor of philosophy for many years at the Collège de France in Paris and has been hailed as one of the foremost academic French thinkers of the postwar period. Like Sartre, a lifelong philosophical companion whom he first met at L'école normale supérieure in Paris in the late twenties, Merleau-Ponty scorned what he saw as the 'petty rationalism' of modern positivism. Meaning, he asserted, ultimately arises from man's primary 'insertion in Being'. The positive sciences have succeeded in manipulating things because, as Merleau-Ponty observed in *Eye and Mind* (1964), they ceased 'living in them'. By contrast, phenomenology – which Merleau-Ponty discovered in the early thirties via Sartre and de Beauvoir – provided the most effective method of combating positivism by enabling us to describe our lived experience as beings-in-the-world. Sartre makes this point with customary poignancy in his famous obituary essay on Merleau-Ponty: "He was fascinated by 'real life', by the sorrows and days of men. What do they do, what does one make of them, what do they desire, and what do they see?" All Merleau-Ponty's work was an attempt to witness the 'genesis of man by the world and of the world by man': a reciprocal relation which the phenomenological analysis of 'intentionality' and of the 'life-world' revealed. "We found", Sartre continues, "in our first experience, the same master, Husserl, made and waiting for us. Neither one of us knew him, although he was still living, but his work – besides 'intentionality' – gave us, without his then explicitly saying it, the other indispensable tool: we discovered that we were 'situated'. Hardly had we received these weapons than we became brothers without knowing it; across conflicts and moods we remained so up to the end" (Merleau-Ponty I, 1961). Despite many bitter disputes, usually over their different interpretations of the role of postwar Marxism in their spirited contributions to *Les temps modernes* (an intellectual journal which they edited together), Merleau-Ponty and Sartre remained allies in their promotion of phenomenology.

For Merleau-Ponty phenomenology made possible the recognition that the body is not an object amongst objects, to be measured in purely scientific or geometric terms, but a mysterious and expressive mode of belonging to the world through our perceptions, gestures, sexuality and speech. It is through our bodies as living centres of intentionality, he consistently argued, that we choose our world and that our world chooses us. This was the cardinal insight which informed Merleau-Ponty's entire philosophical career from the *Phenomenology of Perception* (1945) to his final and unfinished work *The Visible and the Invisible*, published in 1964, three years after his untimely death.

"We shall find in ourselves, and nowhere else, the unity and true meaning of phenomenology. It is less a question of counting up quotations than of determining and expressing in concrete form this *phenomenology for ourselves* which has given a number of present-day readers the impression, on reading Husserl or Heidegger, not so much of encountering a new philosophy as of recognizing what they had been waiting for." It was with this prophetic-sounding appeal to the primacy of lived expectation over academic abstraction that Maurice Merleau-Ponty prefaced his monumental *Phenomenology of Perception*.

Merleau-Ponty shared with Sartre the distinction of developing French phenomenology in an existentialist direction. But while Sartre emphasised the 'negating' power of consciousness as an act of transcendence beyond the material *in-itself* of being, Merleau-Ponty stressed the centrality of 'embodied' consciousness. Imagination, the latter insisted, could not be divorced from perception. Merleau-Ponty thus rejected what he considered to be Sartre's exclusivist equation of freedom with our imaginative consciousness and of facticity with our perceptual consciousness. He argued that phenomenology, by disclosing the intentional nature of *all* our acts of consciousness, calls for a dialectical rather than a dualist model of experience. Against Sartre, who tended to construe human existence as some free-floating subjectivity which becomes *for-itself* by negating the *in-itself* of its bodily presence in the real world, Merleau-Ponty retorted that man is first and foremost a *body-subject* – at once presence *and* absence, incarnation *and* transcendence, being *and* consciousness. "There is no inner man", writes Merleau-Ponty in the *Phenomenology of Perception*," man is *in* the world, and only in the world does he *know* himself.' Consequently, where Sartre was compelled to regard our intersubjective relations with others as a threat to the freedom of each individual consciousness, Merleau-Ponty sees this as the very precondition of authentic consciousness: "Thought is the life of human relationships as it understands and interprets itself" (*Ibid*).

In this manner, Merleau-Ponty worked to correct what he saw as a 'Cartesian' bias in Sartre's existentialism. He rejects the idea of the body as an exterior manipulandum of an interior cogito; and so doing, he hopes to rescue consciousness from Cartesian idealism and restore it to its primordial habitation in the flesh. A phenomenology of the body-subject, affirms Merleau-Ponty, "does away with any kind of idealism in revealing me as being-in-the-world" (*ibid*). But it is equally concerned to avoid the danger of a reductive materialism. The chief virtue of a phenomenology of the body-subject is to steer through the Scylla of scientific empiricism and the Charybdis of metaphysical idealism, overcoming both extreme subjectivism and extreme objectivism with its notion of consciousness as irrevocably 'incarnate' in the world. As such, Merleau-Ponty's phenomenology finds its true vocation in a philosophy of *ambiguity*. Instead of opposing consciousness and world, it reveals their prior overlapping as an indissoluble knot. The 'phenomenon' of our embodied consciousness is precisely that 'in-between' realm – *l'entredeux* – which pre-exists the division into subject and object.

The implications of this philosophy of incarnation are highly significant. It calls for a reinterpretation of the phenomenological method itself, and by implication of our attitudes to such diverse topics as science, art, language and history. In respect of the first of these, it requires that we cease to envisage Husserl's famous 'reduction' as an annihilation of our embodied relationship to the world in order to attain a pure interiority of transcendental consciousness. True, the reduction serves to slacken the intentional cords which attach us to the world; but it does so only in order that these primordial ties may be brought more fully to our notice. Phenomenology is thus interpreted by Merleau-Ponty as a method whereby we become reflectively aware of our pre-reflective incarnation in the world *without ever ceasing to remain incarnate*. The reduction is understood as an effort to bring the world to light as it is *before* any falling back on ourselves has occurred in terms of philosophical or scientific judgement. "It is its ambition", writes Merleau-Ponty, "to make reflection emulate the unreflective life of consciousness. I aim at and perceive a world . . . The world is not what I *think*, but what I *live through*. I am open to the world, I have no doubt that I am in communication with it, but I do not possess it; it is inexhaustible" (*Ibid*). To the extent that Husserl's 'return' to an intuition of essences is thus construed not as an amputation of our bodily life-world but as a means of recovering this world in all its hitherto hidden riches, Merleau-Ponty believes it obviates the anti-corporal prejudices of traditional idealism. "Husserl's essences", he maintains, "are destined to bring back all the living relationships of experience, as the fisherman's net draws up from the depths of the ocean quivering fish and sea-weed . . . The essences still rest upon the ante-predicative life of consciousness" (*Ibid*).

Phenomenology is 'ambiguous', according to Merleau-Ponty, in that it looks in two directions at once – towards the *origin* of consciousness in the lived experience of our embodied being-in-the-world and towards the *end* of consciousness in the theoretical knowledge of predicative judgement (logic, science, reason etc.). The phenomenological attitude, he argues, suspends the 'objectifying' pretentions of the 'natural attitude' without removing us from our primordial belonging to the natural world. The essences which are disclosed by the phenomenological reduction can never therefore be possessed in the manner of apodictic certainty or completion – as the early Husserl had once presumed. They remain open to alteration, augmentation and revision. Phenomenology concerns itself with what Merleau-Ponty terms 'morphological essences' forever bound to their temporal genesis in the open horizon of our life-world. That is why the essential truth of phenomena sought by phenomenology can never be construed as a *fait accompli*. It remains a 'problem to be solved, a hope to be realized' (*ibid.*). The ideal of a pure presuppositionless consciousness, so cherished by the early Husserl, is thus renounced by Merleau-Ponty. It is not the business of the phenomenological reduction, he charges, to lead beyond presuppositions, but rather to lead us back to them so that we reflectively grasp them in all their lived complexity. This revised understanding of the phenomenological method enables Merleau-Ponty to outline a new critique of science, language, history and Being. We shall examine each of these critiques in turn.

I: CRITIQUE OF SCIENCE

"Science manipulates things and gives up living in them", observes Merleau-Ponty in *Eye and Mind*. Phenomenology functions as the 'conscience' of science, reminding it of its first, if forgotten, allegiance to our primordially lived experience from which its so-called 'objective' categories originally derived. Merleau-Ponty states his critique cogently in the following passage from the preface to the *Phenomenology of Perception*:

> I cannot conceive myself as nothing but a bit of the world, a mere object of biological, psychological or sociological investigation. I cannot shut myself up within the realm of science. All my knowledge of the world, even my scientific knowledge, is gained from . . . some experience of the world without which the symbols of science would be meaningless. The whole universe of science is built upon the world as directly experienced, and if we want to subject science itself to rigorous scrutiny and arrive at a precise assessment of its meaning and scope, we must begin by reawakening the basic experience of the world of which science is the second-order expression. Science has not and never will have, by its nature, the same significance *qua* form of being as the world which we perceive, for the

simple reason that it is a rationale or explanation of that world . . . Scientific points of view, according to which my existence is but a moment of the world's, are always both naive and at the same time dishonest, because they take for granted, without explicitly mentioning it, the other point of view, namely that of consciousness, through which from the outset a world forms itself round me and begins to exist for me. To return to things themselves is to return to that world which precedes knowledge, of which knowledge always *speaks*, and in relation to which every scientific schematization is an abstract and derivative sign-language, as is geography in relation to the countryside in which we have learnt beforehand what a forest, a prairie or a river is. (*ibid.*)

It is the business of phenomenology to recall science to the critical realisation that its theoretical constructs are built upon a prior foundation, that is, upon pretheoretical acts of lived experience which Merleau-Ponty designates as our 'operative intentionality'.

Merleau-Ponty's critique of science owes much to the argument of the later Husserl that the crisis of the natural sciences stems from the fact that they have forgotten that their 'naturalistic attitude' of objectivity entails an 'artificial' rupture with man's intentional relation to the world. Phenomenology lays bare this rupture and protests against it. It demonstrates that all scientific and logical 'objects' are no more than abstractions of originally lived 'phenomena'. Instead, therefore, of trying to explain our existential experience in terms of scientific models of objectivism, phenomenology urges us to explain these models in terms of their existential genesis. This genesis is described by Merleau-Ponty as the 'logos of the aesthetic world'. He understands the term 'aesthetic' in the original Greek sense of *aisthesis*, meaning a primary mode of experiential expression which embraces *both* perception *and* imagination. By thus reversing the tendency of both traditional metaphysics and modern science to subordinate the 'aesthetic' (our pre-reflective carnal experience) to the 'analytic' (our reflective conceptual judgement), Merleau-Ponty denies that objective ideas are born *ex nihilo*. He rules out the possibility of cognitive autonomy. Ideas are neither otherworldly (Platonism), innate (Cartesianism), *a priori* (Kantianism), nor indeed mechanical combinations of impressions made upon some *tabula rasa* of the mind (Empiricism). Ideas, for Merleau-Ponty, are intentional projects first constituted in the pre-theoretical operations of the body-subject. By recognising the 'aesthetic' genesis of our ideas, phenomenology has enabled us to reconstitute the original incarnation of mind in body; and in so doing it has restored the body to its intentional status as a meaning-giving subject. Thus exploding the mind/body antithesis, Merleau-Ponty describes how the rediscovery of the primacy of the body-subject permits us to bypass the false alternatives of an objectivism in-itself and a subjectivism for-itself, returning to the original unity of consciousness and world.

The consequences of this discovery for science are radical. It means that scientific reason can no longer think of itself as some kind of privileged sanctum removed from the transformations of the temporal process. This very idea of reason is now exposed as a 'retrospective illusion' whereby science could take its claim to 'objective knowledge' for granted, forgetting that it is no more than the end product of the intentional production of meaning in our live-world. In short, science strives to remain oblivious to the temporalising origins of its own timeless 'objects'. It presumes its truths to be fixed and eternal acquisitions. But these truths are in fact never more than provisional approximations in the ongoing quest for universal meaning. Even science is bound by the temporal limits of past and future. Reason does not exist in a vacuum. It is radically situated in time in so far as it always inherits meanings *already constituted* in the past (this Merleau-Ponty calls the phenomenon of 'sedimentation') and anticipates meanings *still to be constituted* in the future (i.e. the phenomenon of 'projection').

Such a disclosure of the temporality of scientific reason entails a correlative disclosure of its *intersubjectivity*. Precisely because reason is at once passively constituted by the past and actively constitutes its future, it shares a common project with others – that is, with all those generations of minds which precede and excede it as historical tradition. As such, reason is both the assumption of meanings bequeathed to it by an antecedent intersubjective community and the appeal to a future intersubjective community which will assume and develop its own labours. Just as the body-subject experiences itself as an 'ambiguous' perceiving/perceived (like the hand, to cite Merleau-Ponty's favourite example, which can both touch and be touched), so too reason is a bilateral process which both receives its truths from others and recreates these truths for others. Reason, be it metaphysical or scientific, does not exist in itself, in the manner of some self-thinking-thought or autonomous cogito. It is radically intersubjective, a communal text which each scientific mind co-authors with others.

II: CRITIQUE OF LANGUAGE

The fundamental intersubjectivity of the body-subject prompts Merleau-Ponty to confirm Heidegger's equation of truth and language. "When I speak", he notes in *Signs*, "I experience the presence of others in myself and of myself in others." While this phenomenon of intersubjective reciprocity was first described in the *Phenomenology of Perception*, it was in his subsequent works – most notably *Signs* (1960) and *Sense and Non-Sense* (1948) – that Merleau-Ponty fully explored the implications of a dialectical interpretation of language, and by extension, of culture and art.

The later phenomenology of signs and symbols extends rather than excludes the earlier phenomenology of perception. Perception is never, for Merleau-Ponty, simply a neutral intuition of factual data. 'Perception already stylizes', he insists. The perceptual intentionality of the body-subject is itself a mode of *signifying*. To perceive the world is already to make sense of it, to transform it into signs by expressing an intentional project of meaning. Our carnal interrelationship with others is therefore indicative of an intentional 'signification' even if it remains at the level of bodily gestures not yet articulated in words. In an essay in *Signs*, entitled 'Indirect Language and the Voices of Silence', Merleau-Ponty offers the following example of how such a 'body language' operates:

A woman passing by is not first and foremost . . . a coloured mannequin or a spectacle; she is an individual, sentimental, sexual expression. She is a certain manner of being flesh which is given entirely in her walk or even in the simple shock of her heel on the ground – as the tension of the bow is present in each fibre of wood – a very noticeable variation of the norm of walking, looking, touching, and speaking that I possess in my self-awareness because I am incarnate (*ibid*)

The perceptions of the body-subject, Merleau-Ponty pursues, are never simply empirical givens. We do wrong to consider them as objective data to which imaginary and signifying projects are subsequently added like decorative clothing on a naked body. From the outset, each of our perceptions is involved in a symbolising signification which expresses, in however inchoate or tentative a manner, a particular project of being-in-the-world. Not surprisingly, therefore, we find Merleau-Ponty endorsing Heidegger's view that language can be pre-linguistic (in the sense of pre-verbal). Language includes silence as a listening to others or as a style of behavioural gesture. The way in which Humphrey Bogart smokes a cigarette, Mao-Tse-Tung smiles or the Queen of England waves, each bespeaks an existential project – a distinct manner of signifying their intentions to others. These 'styles' – and every human being is marked by a particular style just as he is marked by a particular fingerprint – already function as 'signs'. They constitute a 'mute' language from which all 'spoken' language ultimately derives. Language as gesture precedes language as word.

Merleau-Ponty makes an important distinction here between what he terms 'the primary expression' of our aesthetic experience (in the broad sense of the stylising perceptions of the body-subject) and the 'secondary expression' of conceptual assertion (which reaches its most abstract and exact formulation in logical and scientific language). The 'objective' statements of our reflective judgements are thus shown to presuppose the preobjective expressiveness of our carnal intersubjectivity. In short, thought is a translation of language; and language, as verbal expression, is itself a translation of the 'silent or indirect voices' of our gestures and styles as body-subjects.

Since the most primary mode of expression is located in the stylising projects of our perceptions, which already transmute the apparent chaos of events into patterns of meaning, Merleau-Ponty argues that artistic forms such as painting, music and poetry provide a privileged access to the hidden workings of language. Behind the transparency of secondary expression, art reveals the *indirect* voices of primary expression. These voices are oblique, allusive, lateral. Merleau-Ponty compares them to the functioning of the body: "The words, lines and colours which express me come out of me as gestures" (*Signs*). While painting or the visual arts obviously come closest to the model of language as indirection or silence, Merleau-Ponty maintains that literary works also function in this primary way. In literature, he claims, we can "detect beneath spoken langauge an operative or speaking language whose words live a little known life and unite with and separate from one another as their lateral or indirect signification demands, even though these relations seem *evident* to us once the expression is accomplished" (*Signs*). The language of literary works, though verbal, is for Merleau-Ponty closer to painting than to science. It works by a tacit and implicit accumulation of meaning rather than by abstracting meaning into a pure state of clarity. In *Signs*, Merleau-Ponty offers the following example of how Stendhal deploys the 'indirect' voices of language in his novel *Scarlet and Black*:

Like a painting, a novel expresses tacitly. Its subject, like that of a painting can be recounted. But Julien Sorel's trip to Verrières and his attempt to kill Mme Renal after he has learned that she has betrayed him, are not as important as that silence, that dream-like journey, that unthinking certitude and that eternal resolution which follow the news. Now these things *are nowhere said*. There is no need of a "Julien thought" or a "Julien wished". In order to express them, Stendhal had only to insinuate himself into Julien and make objects, obstacles, means and hazards appear before our eyes with the swiftness of the journey. He had only to decide to narrate in one page instead of five. That brevity, that unusual proportion of things omitted to things said, is not even the result of a *choice*. Consulting his own sensitivity to others, Stendhal suddenly found an imaginary body for Julien which was more agile than his own body. As if in a second life, he made the trip to Verrières according to a cadence of cold passion which itself decided what was visible and what was invisible, what was to be said and what was to remain unspoken. The desire to kill is thus not in the words at all. It is between them, in the hollows of space, time, and signification they mark out, as movement at the cinema is between the immobile images which follow one another. (*Signs*.)

By providing us with a formal presentation of our pre-objective modes of experience, art opens up a 'universal' realm of primary expression. This universal realm is what Merleau-Ponty calls the 'aesthetic logos of the life-world', or alternatively *une pensée sauvage* (a term also used by Lévi-Strauss). It refers to a language common to all body-subjects, prior to the classifications of dictionaries and grammars. This is the language of music, painting or gesture which pre-exists the differentiation of signs into different linguistic systems – English, French, German, Chinese etc. A painting by Picasso or Leonardo Da Vinci is in principle as capable of communicating to a Chinaman as to a Spaniard or an Italian. Indeed it is precisely because verbal systems of language are themselves expressions of this universal mode of primary signification, that translation from one language to another is possible. The distinct language systems of each culture or nation share a common pool of primary meanings. And this, observes Merleau-Ponty, is what allows for communication between them.

At the other end of the spectrum of language, we have the 'second order' universality of scientific models of expression – logic, mathematics, computer alphabets and so on. Here we are also concerned with signs which transcend the limits of the different national linguistic codes – but in the opposite direction. Scientific language constitutes an 'objective' universality in contrast to the 'pre-objective' universality of art. But Merleau-Ponty insists that the former presupposes the latter and is ultimately derived from it. In both cases, however, the universality takes the form of a project rather than an acquisition. The primary language of art, no less than the secondary language of science, is incapable of achieving a 'totalised' universal. Even though the signs of the aesthetic logos precede the explicit division into distinct linguistic systems, they are nonetheless bound to an open-ended signifying process. And as such, they remain forever partial and unfinished, aspirations to universality situated in the temporal experience of concrete body-subjects. Art cannot lay claim to an absolute point of view any more than knowledge can. For universal meaning is a task to be accomplished, an adventure of culture which never comes to an end. "Culture never gives us absolutely transparent significations", declares Merleau-Ponty: "The genesis of meaning is never completed. We can only contemplate truth in a symbolic context which situates our knowledge" (*Signs*).

To sum up, we may say that the central intuition of Merleau-Ponty's phenomenology of language is that meaning first arises in the implicit form of corporeal signs and only subsequently takes on the explicit form of abstract cognition. The logic of science presupposes the logos of the cultural world – what Merleau-Ponty refers to as the 'wild order of carnal signification'. This formulation of priorities reverses the traditional tendency to distrust symbolic expression as a lesser form of thought, a derived order of expression which alienates or adulterates the 'pure and distinct' ideas of the mind. Merleau-Ponty goes to great lengths to demonstrate that the opposite is true, that it is the temporalising expression of the body-subject which renders possible the subsequent conceptual construction of so called 'timeless ideas'. Science, he concludes, must reopen a dialogue with art lest it ignore its own temporalising genesis in the indirect language of primary expression. No system of cognition can "ever wholly free itself from the precariousness of mute forms of expression, reabsorb its own contingency, and waste away to make the things themselves disappear . . . Expression is not one of the curiosities that the mind may propose to examine but is its *existence in act*" (Signs).

Finally, the aesthetic model of primary expression furnishes Merleau-Ponty with an overall blueprint for the *intersubjective* phenomenon of language. Paintings or poems are not just creative expressions for their authors. They also require audiences. The significance of a work of art, consequently, is not something fixed once and for all by the artist to be passively consumed by the audience. Each artwork articulates a particular *style* of expression which opens an horizon of interpretative possibilities for reader or viewer. Put in another way, the meaning of an artistic project is determined as much by the audience's recreation as by the author's original creation.

III: CRITIQUE OF HISTORY

In opening us to a dialectic of intersubjectivity, art re-inserts us into a dialectic of history. It reminds us that meaning is generated in an historical life-world, not some Platonic other-world. Even modern abstract art retains an historical reference to the world. The modernist abandonment of traditional forms of figurative art does not imply a total renunciation of history. The move away from representational realism simply requires us to view reality in terms of our contemporary 'lived experience' of alienation. "How would the painter or poet express anything other than his encounter with the world?", enquires Merleau-Ponty. "What does abstract art speak of, if not of a negation or refusal of the world? Now austerity and the obsession with geometrical surfaces and forms . . . still have the odour of life, even if it is a shameful or despairing life. Thus the painter always says something which demands precisely this particular upheaval, and it is in the name of a *truer* relation between things that their ordinary ties are broken" (Signs). The strangeness and distance of abstract art do not remove us from the world; these qualities, rather like those of the phenomenological method itself, serve to expose the world in new and unfamiliar ways.

Merleau-Ponty strenuously resists all formalist efforts to dehistoricise art by reducing it to an autonomous play of structures. But he equally resents the Romantic cult of the artist as elitist genius singled out by destiny, removed from the world of common mortals and emancipated from all historical reference. The modern concept of the museum itself epitomises the separation of art from history, attempting to transplant aesthetic experience from its rootedness in the intersubjecive life-world:

> One should go to the Museum as the painters go there, in the sober joy of work; and not as we go there, with a somewhat spurious reverence. The Museum gives us a thief's conscience . . . [It] adds a false prestige to the true value of the works by detaching them from the chance circumstances they arose from and making us believe that the artist's hand was guided from the start by fate. Whereas the style of each painter throbbed in his life like his heart beat, and was just what enabled him to recognize every effort which differed from his own, the Museum converts this secret, modest, non-deliberated, involuntary, and, in short, living historicity into official and pompous history. (*Signs*)

But if Merleau-Ponty rejects the total separation of art from history, he is also suspicious of attempts to completely subordinate art to history in some determinist manner. Merleau-Ponty welcomes the willingness of psychoanalysis and Marxism to relate art to its historical conditions of production (personal history in the case of the former and collective history in the case of the latter). However, he is insistent that this historical reference be reinterpreted in the phenomenological sense of a lived experience. Any reductionist reading which construes the art work as a mechanical effect of, rather than a creative response to, the personal and social conditions of experience is ruled out as inadequate. Art remains for Merleau-Ponty a 'miracle of creative expression' precisely because it transmutes naked events into the intentional signs of a 'style':

> The reason why Leonardo is something other than one of the innumerable victims of an unhappy childhood is not that he has one foot in the great beyond, but that he succeeded in making a means of interpreting the world out of everything he lived – it is not that he did not have a body or sight, but that he constituted his corporeal or vital situation in language. When one goes from the order of events to the order of expression, one does not change the world; the same circumstances which were previously submitted to now become a signifying system . . . If we take the painter's point of view in order to be present at that decisive moment when what has been given to him to live as corporeal destiny, personal adventures or historical events, crystallizes into 'the motive' (i.e. the style), we will recognize that his work, which is never an effect, is always a response to these data and that the body, the life, the landscapes, the schools, the mistresses, the creditors, the police and the revolutions which might suffocate

painting are also the bread his work consecrates. To live in painting is still to breathe the air of this world – above all for the man who sees something in the world to paint. And there is a little of him in every man. (*Signs*).

Of course, Merleau-Ponty readily assents to Sartre's view that art is the realm of freedom. He qualifies this assent, however, by affirming that it is less a freedom *from* the historical world than a freedom *for* it. In art, we still breathe the air of this world, but we 'breathe it in a *freer* manner'. The language of art is a formal concentration and deepening of the living expressiveness of body-subjects. Far from negating history, therefore, aesthetic language reinterprets it in an unprecedented way, transforming meaning as it has *already been expressed* into meanings *yet to be expressed*. At this point in his analysis, Merleau-Ponty parts company with Sartre's existentialism and rejoins Heidegger's view of language as a 'hermeneutic circle' wherein we retrieve lost meanings (*Wiederholung*) and project new ones (*Vorhabe*) at one and the same time. History is not a threat to the individual's project of meaning. It is that intersubjective horizon which functions as its condition of possibility. "A philosophy of history", writes Merleau-Ponty," does not take away any of my rights or initiatives. It simply adds to my obligations as a solitary person the obligation to understand situations other than my own and to create a path between my life and that of others, that is, to express myself. Through the action of culture, I take up my dwelling in lives which are not mine. I confront them, I make one known to the other, I make them equally possible in the order of truth, I make myself responsible for all of them, and I create a universal life" (*Signs*).

Merleau-Ponty's reconciliation of creative subjectivity and historical intersubjectivity debunks the 'hypocrite eternity of art'. This is why he insists that the artist is not obliged to resort to some imaginary realm of nothingness in order to create, but can fully assume the historical origins of his project which in turn enable him to address an historical future of shared intersubjectivity. Thus Merleau-Ponty interprets Stendhal's claim that he would be read in a hundred years to mean less a vainglorious boast than a call to others to participate in his own creative initiative: "His freedom invites a world as yet in limbo to become as free as he was by recognizing as acquired what he has had to invent" (*Signs*). In short, the writer's creative expression is a search for universal meanings which each particular reader never ceases to reinterpret and make his own.

This model of cultural intersubjectivity is invoked by Merleau-Ponty as a blueprint for the broad workings of history itself. It requires a repudiation of the traditional view of history as mere plaything of a timeless and transcendent God. History is not created by some Divine First Cause whose 'vertical transcendence' would remain untouched by the dialectic of human meaning. If anything, history is the very precondition of the idea of God as a dialectical project. Unlike Sartre, however, Merleau-Ponty argues that Christianity offers the possibility of reinterpreting God as an historical dialectic rather than a vertical transcendence – though the latter view has prevailed in Western metaphysics and theology:

> It is a little too much to forget that Christianity is, among other things, the recognition of a mystery in the relations of man and God, which stems precisely from the fact that the Christian God wants nothing to do with a vertical relation of subordination. He is not simply a principle of which we are the consequence, a will whose instruments we are, or even a model of which human values are the only reflection. There is a sort of impotence of God without us, and Christ attests that God would not be fully God without becoming fully man. Claudel goes so far as to say that God is not above but beneath us – meaning that we do not find Him as a suprasensible idea, but as another ourself which dwells in and authenticates our darkness. Transcendence no longer hangs over man; he becomes, strangely, its privileged bearer. (*Signs*)

For Merleau-Ponty, the idea of vertical transcendence is a construct of metaphysical idealism, just as, from another angle, is the idea of autonomous subjectivity. Both abolish the reality of history as an intersubjective dialectic. In a collection of political essays entitled *Adventures of the Dialectic* (1955), Merleau-Ponty takes Sartre to task in rather polemical fashion for reducing history to a subtle version of wilful subjectivity. Sartre's ideal of a pure action of individual choice, he maintains, dissolves the opaque complexity of history into an imaginative *fiat* which presumes "to impose itself on things only to suddenly return to the unreal from which it derives" (*ibid*). For Sartre, consequently, revolution could be no more than a form of 'self-imagination', a voluntaristic subjectivity which subsumes the collective horizon of intersubjectivity into itself. History is thus subjectivised in a "vertiginous freedom, the magic power that is ours to act and to make ourselves whatever we want" (*Ibid*). Merleau-Ponty suspects Sartre's later turn to Marxism as little more than a projection of his subjectivist existentialism onto an historical scenario. He denounces his 'ultrabolshevism' (i.e. his view that the decisions of the elite vanguard of the Communist Party must reign supreme), declaring it to be a disguised form of idealism whereby history becomes the invention of the proletariat, the proletariat the invention of the party, and the party itself an invention of Sartre's own individual project. "The proletariat", he observes, "is untouchable because it exists only in the pure action of the party, and this action exists only in Sartre's thought" (*Ibid*). Once history is reduced to the pure choice of an imaginative act and is thus divorced from the intersubjective dialectic, it degenerates into 'narcissism' – the absolute negation of history.

Merleau-Ponty recommends that we reinterpret the Marxist dialectic of history not on the basis of imagination but of language. This would enable us to conjoin the creative intention of imagination with the receptive intention of perception, and to recognise accordingly that history is a dialectical interrelationship of body-subjects at once free and situated, actively projecting meanings for themselves on the basis of meanings inherited by the former projects of others. History must not be collapsed into imagination (pure transcendence) nor imagination into history (pure determinism). The truth lies somewhere between these two extremes – in a dialectical interworld of 'ambiguity':

> A consciousness that is truly engaged in a world and a history on which it has a hold but which goes beyond it is not insular. Already in the thickness of the sensible and historical fabric it feels other presences moving, just as the group of men who dig a tunnel hear the work of another group coming toward them . . . The question is to know whether, as Sartre says, there are only *men* and *things* or whether there is also the interworld, which we call history, symbolism, truth-to-be-made . . . Politics and culture are reunited, not because they are completely congruent or because they both adhere to the event, but because the symbols of each order have echoes, correspondences, and effects of induction in the other . . . Literature and politics are linked with each other and with the event, but in a different way, like two layers of a single symbolic life or history.
> (*ibid*)

Merleau-Ponty's critique of the early Sartre's political philosophy in no way implies that existential phenomenology and Marxism are incompatible. But it does imply that their compatibility presupposes a reinterpretation of both. Sartre's mistake was to try to equate the extreme subjectivism of his early existentialism with the extreme collectivism of 'party' Marxism. Merleau-Ponty rejects both extremes in his reading of history as language, that is, as an intersubjective interworld where political and cultural factors can coalesce. (To be fair to Sartre, however, it must be pointed out that he too rejects both extremes in his later political philosophy – advanced in *The Critique of Dialectical Reason* (1960), a work which incorporates several of the critiques levelled against him by Merleau-Ponty in *Adventures of the Dialectic* five years previously.) By means of his dialectical phenomenology, he can allow that our socio-economic situation deeply influences our existential projects, but as a 'motivation' rather than a 'determination'. "If existence", he notes in *Phenomenology of Perception*, "is the permanent act by which man takes up, for his own purposes, and makes his own a certain *de facto* situation, none of his thoughts will be able to be quite detached from the historical context in which he lives, and particularly his economic situation. Precisely because economics is not a closed world, and because all motivations intermingle at the core of history, the external becomes internal and the internal external.' Anticipating Sartre's famous use of the Paul Valéry example in the *Critique of Dialectical Reason*, Merleau-Ponty goes on to argue that while it would be quite ridiculous to regard Valéry's poetry as a mere determination of economic disturbance, it is not at all unreasonable to seek in the social and economic drama of his times a 'motivation' for his poetic awareness. There is no cultural phenomenon that does not have, among others, a socio-economic significance. So that if a work of art is never reducible to the material base of economics, it never totally surpasses it either. It is no more possible to equate existence exclusively with economics or exclusively with cultural creation than it is to reduce individual life to bodily functions or to knowledge alone. Just as all life, according to Merleau-Ponty, inhabits a sexual atmosphere without our being able to isolate a single content of consciousness which is 'purely sexual' or 'purely asexual', so too our socio-economic background provides each one of us with an omnipresent context which we set about deciphering and reappropriating in our own distinct way. "The act of the artist or philosopher is free", concludes Merleau-Ponty accordingly, "but not motiveless." Their freedom consists in reinterpreting a *de facto* situation by endowing it with a symbolic meaning which goes beyond its given one:

Thus Marx, not content to *be* the son of a lawyer and student of philosophy, *conceives* his own situation as that of a 'lower middle class intellectual' in the new perspective of the class struggle. Thus does Valéry transmute into pure poetry a disquiet and solitude of which others would have made nothing. Thought is the life of human relationships as it understands and interprets itself. In this voluntary act of carrying forward, this passing from objective to subjective, it is impossible to say just where historical forces end and ours begin, and strictly speaking the question is meaningless, since there is history only for a subject who lives through it, and a subject only in so far as it is historically situated. There is no one meaning of history; what we do has several meanings, and this is where an existential conception of history is distinguishable from materialism and from spiritualism. (*Phenomenology of Perception*).

IV: THE CRITIQUE OF BEING

A phenomenology of ambiguity entails not only a dialectical understanding of history but of Being. In his later works, most notably the posthumously published *Eye and Mind* (1964) and *The Visible and the Invisible* (1964), Merleau-Ponty takes issue with the dualist ontologies of metaphysical idealism. He resists in particular the Cartesian and early Sartrian division of Being into an alternativism of pure freedom (for-itself) and pure necessity (in-itself). Ontology, he argues, must be understood in a more 'fundamental' manner as a dialectic between 'sense and non-sense' – a reciprocal interaction between self and world wherein we are unable to say exactly what meaning comes from us and what from things outside of us. This dialectical principle of 'intertwining' leads Merleau-Ponty to speak of an *ontology of the 'flesh'* as the ultimate conclusion of his initial phenomenology of perception. The 'flesh' cannot be understood as a compound of two separate substances – a subjective 'consciousness of' and an objective 'other'. It is a relation of the visible with its own invisible depths which lie latent within it. As such, the flesh is that element of Being which traverses me and constitutes me as a seer who is at one and the same time seen by others. It is described by Merleau-Ponty as an 'anonymous visibility' which precedes the bifurcation into self and other: a universal dimension of Being prior to the division into particular beings. Being must no longer be understood therefore in terms of the traditional models of a linear movement from one distinct entity to another; it must be reinterpreted as a reversible circle of intercorporeal Being: "this circle which I do not form, which forms me, this coiling over of the visible upon the visible, can traverse, animate other bodies as well as my own" (*The Visible and the Invisible*).

In many respects, the later Merleau-Ponty shares Heidegger's project to rediscover an experience of Being which excedes the limits of metaphysical categories. In *The Visible and the Invisible*, he explicitly endorses the Heideggerean preference for pre-Socratic ontology as a model which articulates a primordial belonging together of consciousness and Being in a common 'element'. Instead of always starting from consciousness and then trying to construct a subsequent relation with Being as if it were an 'objective' entity, Merleau-Ponty believes that his ontology of the flesh enables us to comprehend Being as something which *gives to* us (Heidegger's *Es Gibt*) at the same time as it is *given by* us. Reiterating his analysis of the primary language of painting, Merleau-Ponty shows how it offers a form of 'Vision' which belongs properly neither to the body-subject *qua* fact nor to the world *qua* fact, but epitomises a coupling more real than either of them – a reciprocal intertwining of the one in the other. He writes:

> The seer is caught up in what he sees . . . the vision he exercises, he also undergoes from the things, such that, as many painters have said, I feel myself looked at by the things, my activity is passivity . . . so that the seer and the visible reciprocate one another and we no longer know which sees and which is seen. It is this Visibility, this anonymity innate to Myself that we have called flesh, and one

knows there is no name in traditional philosophy to designate it. The flesh is not matter, in the sense of corpuscles of Being which would add up or continue on one another to form beings. Nor is the visible (the things as well as my body) some 'psychic' material that would be – God knows how – brought into being by the things factually existing and acting on my factual body. In general, it is not a fact or a sum of facts 'material' or spiritual' . . . The flesh is not matter, is not mind, is not substance. To designate it, we would need the ancient term 'element', in the sense it was used to speak of water, air, earth, and fire, that is, in the sense of a *general thing* midway between the spatio-temporal individual and the idea, a sort of incarnate principle that brings a style of Being wherever there is a fragment of Being. The flesh is in this sense an 'element' of Being. (*Ibid*).

The break with Sartre's early ontology of for-itself and in-itself could hardly be more explicit. Sartre had no option but to define consciousness as an absolute subjectivity of negation – for he had defined Being in itself as brute matter devoid of any meaning other than that which the individual consciousness chooses to project onto it. The freedom and creativity of human consciousness thus remained for Sartre in incorrigible opposition to Being. It would have been quite impossible for him to speak of Being as an *Es Gibt* – as some universal element which gives meaning. As a consequence, human actions could only be considered either totally free (and hence absurd or useless because divorced from the reality which they negated) or else totally determined (in which case they succumbed to the inertia of brute Being in itself and ceased to be human). Against Sartre, Merleau-Ponty advocates a phenomenology of Being which permits us to appreciate that "man is neither a no-thing nor a thing but a product/producer in whom necessity can turn into concrete freedom" (*Sense and Nonsense*).

Merleau-Ponty's ontology of flesh reveals that meaning is both within and without, both subjective and objective, spiritual and material; it reveals that Being is not some mindless in-itself which threatens our free expression, but an intercorporeal life-world which gives us meanings and summons each body-subject to recreate these meanings for itself. In *Eye and Mind*, his final work, Merleau-Ponty describes this ontology of dialectical interaction in the following evocative manner:

There really is inspiration and expiration of Being, action and passion so slightly discernible that it becomes impossible to distinguish between what sees and what is seen, what paints and what is painted . . . Vision is not a certain mode of thought or presence to self; it is the means given me for being absent from myself, for being present at the fission of Being from the inside – the fission at whose termination only I return to myself . . . Every visual thing is the result of a dehiscence of Being . . . There is no break at all in this circuit; it is impossible to say that nature ends here and that man or expression starts here. It is mute Being which itself comes to show forth its own meaning. (*ibid*.)

We might sum up the adventures of Merleau-Ponty's phenomenological dialectic in terms of this multiple, reversible equation: *I think* (consciousness) – *I perceive* (nature) – *I express* (language) – *I create* (art) – *I relate with others* (history) – *I exist in the flesh of the world* (Being). One of the conspicuous strengths of Merleau-Ponty's phenomenology is its refusal to subordinate any one of these dimensions of experience to any other. Epistemology, cosmology, linguistics, aesthetics, politics and ontology interact reciprocally in a multifaceted philosophy of uncompromising ambiguity. Merleau-Ponty's thinking is characteristically modern in that it is offered to each reader as an unfinished task. Like works of art and literature, which it so frequently invokes in support of its reasoning, this dialectical phenomenology records meaning as it comes to birth in an intersubjective world. As a fragment of an ongoing movement of thought, which knows itself to be so, it resolves to remain irresolute, in the sense of remaining open to the plural interpretations and reinterpretations it summons into existence. "The unfinished nature of phenomenology", as Merleau-Ponty explains in his preface to the *Phenomenology of Perception*, "and the inchoative atmosphere which has surrounded it, are not to be taken as a sign of failure, they were inevitable because phenomenology's task was to reveal the mystery of the world and of reason. If phenomenology was a movement before becoming a doctrine or a philosophical system, this was attributable neither to accident, nor to fraudulent intent. It is as painstaking as the works of Balzac, Proust, Valéry or Cézanne – by reason of the same kind of attentiveness and wonder, the same demand for awareness, the same will to seize the meaning of the world or of history as that meaning comes into being. In this way it merges into the general effort of modern thought" (*ibid.*).

Paul Ricoeur

Paul Ricoeur is another French philosopher who reworked German phenomenology in a new direction. Taking a lead from Heidegger and Gadamer, he moved beyond both 'eidetic' and 'existentialist' phenomenology towards a 'hermeneutic' phenomenology. Where Sartre had tended to privilege the intentional role of negating imagination and Merleau-Ponty that of an embodied perception, Ricoeur emphasised the primacy of a symbolising signification. This emphasis led him to advance a general hermeneutics where phenomenology confronts its own limits – that is, where the intuition of essences ends and the interpretation (Greek, *hermeneia*) of symbols begins.

Ricoeur was born in Valence, France, in 1913. It was as a prisoner in Germany during the second world war that he became intimately acquainted with the works of Heidegger, Husserl and Jaspers. After his release, Ricoeur returned to France where he published major works on Jaspers and Marcel in the late forties, followed by an important commentary and translation of Husserl's *Ideas* in 1950. Ricoeur began his professional academic career as professor of the history of philosophy at the University of Strasbourg (1948–1956). He was subsequently appointed to the chair of metaphysics at the Sorbonne (1956–1966) and at the University of Paris X, Nanterre (1966–80). Ricoeur also served as Director of the *Centre Phénoménoligique et Herméneutique* (CNRS) in Paris, where he worked closely with Levinas and Derrida, tutoring a new generation of French phenomenologists. He still holds the post of professor of philosophy at the University of Chicago.

But Ricoeur's international repute as a philosopher arose not only from his influential role as exegete and teacher of phenomonology, but more importantly from his own highly original contribution to the 'hermeneutic' turn which the phenomenological movement took with Heidegger and Gadamer. Ricoeur has defined hermeneutics as 'the art of deciphering indirect meaning'. His major hermeneutic works from the fifties to the present day have been devoted to the interpretation of the multiple 'mediations' of meaning through symbol, myth, dream, image, text, narrative and ideology.

In some of his early phenomenological studies of the human will, e.g. *Freedom and Nature. The Voluntary and the Involuntary* (1950), Ricoeur analyses certain limit situations where 'freedom' comes face to face with 'necessity'. Here the voluntary intentionality of our consciousness encounters involuntary or opaque experiences – such as birth, death, the unconscious, suffering, evil, or indeed transcendence – which are irreducible to the subjective transparency of intuition (i.e. Husserl's model of phenomenology). By describing how our finite and historically situated existence transgresses our subjective intentions, Ricoeur was able to affirm one of the guiding principles of his hermeneutic project: we do not *begin* with a pure reflective consciousness; this remains a *task* to be accomplished by means of a long 'detour' through those significations of history and culture which reside outside of our immediate consciousness. The human subject thus comes to realise that he can only interpret himself by interpreting the 'signs' of an external world not his own. He is not a self-sufficient cogito but an embodied being who discovers that he is placed in language before he possesses himself in consciousness.

Human being, for Ricoeur, is always, therefore, a *being-interpreted* – an existence that cannot start from itself or simply invent meanings out of itself *ex nihilo*. Instead of proceeding according to the model of the Cartesian *concept* – a pure and distinct idea transparent to itself – hermeneutics is committed to the primacy of the *symbol*, where meaning emerges as indirect, mediated, enigmatic, complex and multiform. "In contrast to philosophies concerned with starting points," Ricoeur explains, "a meditation on symbols starts from the fulness of language and of meaning already there; it begins from within language which has already taken place and in which everything in a certain sense has already been said; it wants to be thought, not presuppositionless, but in and with all its presuppositions. Its first problem is not how to get started, but from the midst of speech to recollect itself" ('The Hermeneutics of Symbols and Philosophical Reflection', 1962, in the Ricoeur *Anthology*, 1978).

Ricoeur does not for all that renounce the ideal of rationality proposed by philosophical reflection. He simply points out that such an ideal must always presuppose the *revealing* power of symbolism. The ideal of rationality remains therefore a project rather than a possession, the end of philosophy rather than its beginning. Ricoeur argues furthermore that the hermeneutic meditation of symbols answers to the particular situation of philosophy in our modern culture. It corresponds to the recogntion that there is no 'first truth', no 'absolute knowledge', no transcendent vantage-point of lucid consciousness where the dispersal into multiple meanings could be definitively overcome in one final synthesis.

Ricoeur's hermeneutics exposes phenomenology to a radical awareness of the limits and obstacles of consciousness. It opens reflection to the world of the unconscious and the supraconscious. And this *hermeneutic detour*, as Ricoeur calls it, through the hidden or suppressed meanings of symbolic significations – preceding and exceeding the immediacy of intuitive consciousness – is less an option than a necessity. Thus we find Ricoeur's hermeneutic trajectory progressing as a series of reflections upon the primary sources of symbolic interpretation: the symbols of religion and myth (*The Symbolism of Evil*, 1960); the dream symbols of the unconscious (*Freud and Philosophy: An Essay on Interpretation*, 1965); the signifying structures of language, ideology, fiction and socio-historical action (*The Conflict of Interpretations*, 1969, *The Rule of Metaphor*, 1975, and *Hermeneutics and the Human Sciences*, 1981, *Time and Narrative*, 1984). All of these works share a common project – the retrieval of thought in symbol and the extension of symbol into thought. The overriding maxim of this general hermeneutics is Ricoeur's celebrated claim that the 'symbol invites thought' (*le symbole donne à penser*):

> This maxim that I find so appealing says two things. The symbol invites: I do not posit the meaning, the symbol gives it; but what it gives is something for thought, something to think about. First the giving, then the positing; the phrase suggests, therefore, both that all has already been said in enigma and yet that it is necessary ever to begin and re-begin everything in the dimension of thought. It is this articulation of thought . . . in the realm of symbols and of thought positing and thinking that I would like to intercept and understand ('The Hermeneutics of Symbols and Philosophical Reflection'.)

I: THE CRITIQUE OF HUSSERLIAN PHENOMENOLOGY

Before proceeding to analyse Ricoeur's development of the hermeneutic programme, we shall take a brief look at his decisive departure from Husserl's original formulation of phenomenology. Ricoeur considers that the extension of phenomenology into hermeneutics requires a critique of Husserl's 'idealist' model of consciousness (as advanced in such texts as *The Cartesian Meditations* or *Ideas*). He rejects Husserl's notion of an ultimate foundation of knowledge to be achieved by an 'absolute suspension of presuppositions'. Ricoeur argues that the call for a presuppositionless starting point in the self-immediacy of consciousness, labours under the illusion that there exists an order of full intuition where the contingency of meaning could be reduced to the pure immanence of a transcendental subjectivity. In what Ricoeur refers to as his 'idealist' phase, Husserl maintained that such a realm of pure immanence could be reached by means of a 'transcendental reduction' which would bracket out the temporal and historical context of our experience – that context which makes all knowledge inexact in so far as it evolves through successive horizons or profiles (*Abschattungen*). By removing consciousness from the contingency of the natural world, Husserl believed that he could attain a transcendental knowledge that would be self-grounding and thus certain of itself. This realm of transcendental immanence was granted an immunity against doubt by Husserl, "because it was not given by profiles and hence involved nothing presumptive, allowing only the coincidence of reflection with what has just been experienced" ('Phenomenology and Hermeneutics', 1975, in *Hermeneutics and the Human Sciences*,). Ricoeur concludes that Husserl, by proceeding in this manner, reduced phenomenology to an idealism wherein knowledge could be considered autonomous and self-positing, and therefore alone responsible for its own meanings.

Against this idealist reading of the early Husserl – and some might add the early Sartre – Ricoeur protests that phenomenology requires a surpassing of itself towards hermeneutics. Instead of issuing a refusal to history (understood in the broad sense of a transsubjective dispersal of meaning in the world), hermeneutics makes good the intention of phenomenology to return to our lived experience, by embracing history as its ultimate challenge. Here Ricoeur endorses the initiatives of Heidegger, Merleau-Ponty and also indeed of the later Husserl. He confirms that the ideal of knowledge as an absolute self-justification encounters its limit in the phenomenological description of man's being-in-the-world. This description lays bare the radical 'finitude' of consciousness, the fact that we exist in a historical horizon of language whose meanings precede our own subjective creations. As Heidegger's phenomenological ontology clearly showed, consciousness is bound by a relation of *belonging* to past sedimentations and future projects of meaning, a 'hermeneutic circle' wherein each subjectivity finds itself already included in an intersubjective world whose significations encompass it and escape it on every side. Consequently, it is not sufficient simply to describe meaning as it *appears*; we are also obliged to interpret it as it *conceals* itself. And this leads us beyond a phenomenological idealism of pure reflection to a phenomenological hermeneutics of interpretation which acknowledges that meaning is never first and foremost *for me*.

"Interpretation" writes Ricoeur, "is interpretation *by* language before it is interpretation *of* language" ('What is a Text?', 1970, in *Hermeneutics and the Human Sciences*). We belong to a language that has been shaped and formed by others before we arrive on the existential scene. And this language can only be recovered for reflection by a long process of decipherment. Hermeneutics reveals how we are always bound to an ontology of prior signification (what Ricoeur calls the 'tradition of recollection'). It attests to the priority of ontological pre-understanding (based, as in Heidegger, on a description of our being-in-a-world-with-others) over the epistemological category of an autonomous subject which posits itself in some absolute present. Thus Ricoeur counters the Husserlian demand for a return to the transcendental immediacy of intuition with the claim that all understanding is of necessity mediated by meanings which are not constituted by the self alone. In 'Existence and Hermeneutics' (1974), he settles his account with the master as follows:

> It remains that the early Husserl only reconstituted a new idealism, close to the neo-kantianism he fought: the reduction of the thesis of the world is actually a reduction of the question of Being to the question of the sense of being; the sense of being, in turn, is reduced to a simple correlate of the subjective modes of intention. (Existence and Hermeneutics' in the Ricoeur *Anthology*).

Ricoeur does acknowledge, however, that the later Husserl came to see the inadequacies of his early idealism, particularly in the *Crisis* where he began to sketch an ontology of the intersubjective life-world. He remarks that if the final writings of Husserl "point to this ontology, it is because his effort to reduce *being* failed and because, consequently, the ultimate result of phenomenology escaped the initial project" (*Ibid.*) It is only in the wake of this escape that one can begin to speak of a phenomenological hermeneutics.

II: PHILOSOPHICAL ENCOUNTERS

Ricoeur's critique of Husserlian idealism and his subsequent reformulation of phenomenology was influenced by a number of philosophical encounters. Firstly, there was the lasting impact of his formative encounter with the 'concrete ontologies' of Gabriel Marcel and Karl Jaspers in the thirties and forties. It was in fact these non-phenomenological existentialists who initially impressed upon Ricoeur the radicality of the confrontation between freedom and finitude. Any philosophy of reflection, Ricoeur became convinced, would have to reckon with Marcel's analysis of 'incarnate existence' and Jaspers' notion of 'limit situations' (death, war, disease, crisis etc.). This seminal conviction resulted in the publication of *Gabriel Marcel and Karl Jaspers* in 1947 and *Karl Jaspers and the Philosophy of Existence* (co-authored with Mikel Dufrenne) in the same year.

During these same postwar years, Ricoeur was working on his major critical commentary and translation of Husserl's *Ideas*. Not surprisingly, the combination of Husserl's reflective phenomenology with the concrete ontology of Marcel and Jaspers, initially prompted Ricoeur in the direction of an 'existential phenomenology' which approximated in several important respects to the work of Heidegger, Sartre and Merleau-Ponty. Thus in *The Voluntary and the Involuntary, Fallible Man* and *The Symbolism of Evil*, we find Ricoeur exposing Husserl's phenomenology of reflective consciousness to the challenge of an existential appraisal of man's limiting experiences of necessity, facticity and alienation. This exposé took the form of an existential phenomenology of such related themes as 'guilt', 'finitude', 'fallibility' and 'fault'. Consciousness could no longer be described as a sovereign choosing will transparent to itself. The transcendental cogito was exploded in the collision with the 'involuntary' limits of human existence. But this collision, as we noted, already necessitated a transition from a pure phenomenology of consciousness to a hermeneutics of symbols. Ricoeur sees this transition not as a betrayal of phenomenology but rather as a fidelity to its original discovery that the intentional meaning of consciousness resides *outside of itself*. The analysis undertaken in *The Symbolism of Evil* was to be of crucial importance here. Ricoeur writes:

> The servile condition of the evil will seemed to elude an essential analysis of phenomena. So the only practicable route was that of a detour via the symbols wherein the avowal of the fault was inscribed during the great cultures of which ours is the heir: the primary symbols of stain, guilt and sin; the secondary symbols or myths of tragic blindness, of the fall of the soul, of wandering or decline; the tertiary symbols and rationalisations of the servile will or of original sin. *The Symbolism of Evil* thus marked the turning of Husserlian phenomenology, already extended to the problematic of fallibility, towards a hermeneutics of symbols. By 'symbols' I understood . . . all expressions of double meaning, wherein a primary meaning refers beyond itself to a second meaning which is never given directly ('Introductory Response by Paul Ricoeur' in *Hermeneutics and the Human Sciences*).

Ricoeur's intellectual itinerary of 'hermeneutic detour' was also deeply affected by his open debate with two of the major modern rivals to the phenomenological movement – psychoanalysis and structuralism. The former's emphasis on the hidden structures of the unconscious and the latter's on the hidden structures of language, added further dimensions to the dramatic struggle between the voluntary and the involuntary. The possibility of reconciling these opposing claims became a projected goal rather than a starting point, a limiting dialectical idea (in the Kantian sense) rather than an essential intuition (in the Husserlian sense). This meant for Ricoeur that phenomenological hermeneutics would have to renounce the idealist concept of a universal canon of exegesis whereby the alienations and diversifications of consciousness could be united in a totalising subjective synthesis. It would have to accept that there are "only disparate and opposed theories concerning the rules of interpretation" (*Freud and Philosophy*). By disclosing the ways in which the unconscious structures of dream symbols subvert the sovereignty of our immediate consciousness, psychoanalysis compelled phenomenology to advance towards an open-ended hermeneutics "internally at variance with itself" (*ibid.*). Ricoeur assesses the impact of Freudian psychoanalysis on his hermeneutic project as follows:

> In my earlier works, the great detour via signs had not called into question the primacy of the subject. I found in Freud not only the counter-pole to hermeneutics conceived as recollection of symbols, but also an incisive critique of the whole reflective tradition to which I continued to link myself through Kant and Husserl ... The notion of a semantics of desire ... introduced me to the theme of *The Conflict of Interpretations* ('A Response by Paul Ricoeur').

The hermeneutic field was enlarged in yet another sense by the encounter with structuralist linguistics. This confrontation enabled Ricoeur to amplify the model of hermeneutic ontology inherited from Heidegger, by incorporating a model of language as an unconscious system of deep structures common to both the 'intentional' symbols of a phenomenology of existence and the 'disguised' symbols of psychoanalysis.

> It appeared that the linguistic dimension of all symbolism had not been made the object of a distinct and systematic treatment in my earlier works, in spite of the fact that the detour via symbols had, since *The Symbolism of Evil*, taken the form of a detour of reflection on the self via an investigation of the mediating *signs* of this reflection. It is upon this terrain of the investigation of language that I encountered a new challenge, that of French structuralism, which eliminated any reference to a speaking subject from its analysis of signifying systems. I thus discovered a convergence between the structuralist critique originating from linguistics and the psychoanalytic critique originating from Freud, a convergence in what I called collectively the *semiological challenge* ('A Response by Paul Ricoeur.')

This semiological challenge was to motivate the final phase of Ricoeur's philosophical project. It set in train a methodological overhaul which resulted in a new definition of hermeneutics based on the model of the *text*. Where his earlier hermeneutics had been limited to symbols as expressions of double or split intention, the new hermeneutics extended this model of interpretation to embrace all phenomena of a textual order. And these phenomena would include, for Ricoeur (as for such structuralist thinkers as Barthes and Lévi-Strauss), reference to a 'social imaginary' in the broadest cultural sense. In this way, hermeneutics inaugurated a new dialogue with the human and social sciences.

In short, Ricoeur responded to the semiological challenge by privileging the concept of the text as the guiding thread of his investigations into the creation and recovery of meaning. He aimed to show how the text is the exemplary level at which the 'structural explanation' of the scientific approach and the 'hermeneutic understanding' of the phenomenological approach confront one another:

> It was then necessary, however, to expand the hermeneutical project . . . to the dimensions of the problem posed by the passage from the structure immanent in every text to its extra-linguistic aim (*visée*) – the aim or reference which I sometimes designate by other related terms: the matter of the text, the world of the text, the being brought to language by the text ('A Response by Paul Ricoeur'. For an extended discussion of this complex theme see our Appendix, 'The Hermeneutic Model of the Text').

III: TOWARDS A GENERAL HERMENEUTICS

Ricoeur's mature exposition of the hermeneutic model of the text, required not only a revision of the original project of phenomenology but of the hermeneutic tradition itself.

Hermeneutics first arose within the framework of biblical exegesis. Its traditionally motivating question was: how are we to understand the divine intention of Holy Scripture given its successive reinscriptions throughout the historical generations of Jews and Christians? Within the more specific tradition of Christian theology, hermeneutic models were proposed to deal with the fact that texts could have several different layers of signification – e.g. historical or spiritual – which a logic of univocal meanings could not adequately account for. St Augustine's *De Doctrina Christiana* was a good case in point. The guiding impulse of such hermeneutic exercises was to overcome the distance of the different historico-cultural reinterpretations in order to restore the original meaning of the texts of Revelation, making the divine inspiration of the past contemporaneous with the exegetical reading of the present.

Ricoeur (following Schleiermacher, Dilthey and Heidegger) argues that hermeneutics is not limited to the specialist science of biblical exegesis. He insists that the phenomenon of 'polysemy' – that is, of multiple meaning – is a fundamental feature of all language, not just theological language. Hermeneutics can thus be raised to the level of a universal philosophy which acknowledges that when we use language we are already interpreting the world, not *literally* as if it possessed a single transparent meaning, but *figuratively* in terms of allegory, symbol, metaphor, myth and analogy. In this manner, philosophical hermeneutics relates the technical problem of textual exegesis to the general problem of language as a whole.

The first steps towards such a general philosophy of hermeneutics were taken in the late nineteenth century by Friedrich Schleiermacher and Wilhelm Dilthey. In *The Origin of Hermeneutics* (1900), Dilthey raised the problem of how the historical and human sciences (*Geisteswissenschaften*) could acquire a method of interpretation different to the positivism of the natural sciences (*Naturwissenschaften*). How, he asked, could a specifically human science be founded in the face of the methodological hegemony of empirical objectivity. Dilthey advanced a 'psychological' model designed to explain how one finite understanding could transpose itself beyond the 'objective' limits of empirical facts so as to emphatically coincide with another human understanding, removed from it in time and space. But Ricoeur criticises the hermeneutics of Schleiermacher and Dilthey for remaining within the limits of a romantic epistemology which saw all forms of 'objective knowledge' as a negation of self-understanding. The ideal of a lived interiority of consciousness, secured by becoming one with the original experience of another historical consciousness, remained the touchstone of romantic hermeneutics. As such, it succumbed to 'psychologism' and 'historicism', treating cultural artefacts as 'alienated' expressions which can only be salvaged by an 'empathic reliving' (*Nacherleben*) of the original spirituality of their authors. Dilthey's *Lebensphilosophie* tended to construe hermeneutics accordingly as a form of *psychological transposition*, whereby I transcend the horizons of my present historical situation in order to relive the privileged life-experience of the author's original subjectivity. In this way, it worked to render the self 'contemporaneous' with another creative understanding, prior to the latter's alienation in the objectified expressions of cultural documents, artefacts or institutions.

Thus romantic hermeneutics, no less than idealist phenomenology, tended to view the historical 'distanciation' of meaning as a threat to reflective subjectivity. Ricoeur, by contrast, sponsors a phenomenological hermeneutics which will give priority to the historical symbolisations of understanding over the pure interiority of consciousness. "History", he writes, "precedes me and my reflection; I belong to history before I belong to myself. Dilthey could not understand that, because his revolution remained epistemological and his reflective criterion prevailed over his historical awareness ... Dilthey still begins from self-consciousness; for him subjectivity remains the ultimate point of reference. The reign of *Erlebnis* (lived experience) is the reign of the primordiality which I am. In this sense, the fundamental is the *Innesein*, the interior, the awareness of self" ('Hermeneutics and the Critique of Ideology', 1973, in *Hermeneutics and the Human Sciences*).

In response to the shortcomings of romantic hermeneutics, Ricoeur chooses to raise interpretation from the level of epistemology to that of ontology. Together with Heidegger and Gadamer, Ricoeur considers interpretation not on the basis of a psychological self-consciousness, but against the historical horizon of a finite being-in-the-world. But while Heidegger takes the 'short route' to Being, where interpretation culminates, Ricoeur and Gadamer opt for the 'long route' which examines the various inevitable detours which interpretation undergoes through language, myth, ideology, the unconscious and so on – *before* it arrives at the ultimate limit of Being. Man's final project is indeed a being-towards-death whose fundamental encounter with 'nothingness' provokes the question of Being. But between birth and death, human understanding is compelled to traverse a range of hermeneutic fields, where meaning is dispersed, hidden, withheld or deferred. Ricoeur's hermeneutic project resolves to occupy this conflictual terrain of inquiry, a terrain which he locates *between* Dilthey's epistemology of interpretation and Heidegger's ontology of understanding. In 'Hermeneutics and the Critique of Ideology', Ricoeur explains his medial position thus:

> The long route which I propose also aspires to carry reflection to the level of ontology, but it will do so *by degrees*, following successive investigations . . . My problem will be this: what happens to an epistemology of interpretation, born of a reflection on exegesis, on the method of history, on psychoanalysis, on the phenomenology of religion etc., when it is touched, animated, as we might say inspired by an ontology of understanding? (*ibid.*)

Ricoeur embraces the challenge of rival interpretations which he believes is the hallmark of our contemporary understanding. Heidegger circumvented this challenge, by confining his attentions to a fundamental ontology of Being in general (*Sein Uberhaupt*), thereby relegating the conflict of interpretations to 'regional ontologies' concerned with this or that particular kind of being (e.g. the natural and social sciences, religion, psychoanalysis, linguistics and so on). Ricoeur chooses otherwise. He enters the fray and works his arduous passage towards a fundamental ontology by first debating with the various contesting models of interpretation. The phenomenon of multiple meaning – in its alienated or creative forms – becomes for him the primary hermeneutic focus. The notion of a universal field of Being – where the plurality of meanings would find an ultimate grounding – is preserved as a final possibility, but one which cannot be realised in the immediate present.

IV: THE CONFLICT OF INTERPRETATIONS

The conflict of interpretations is for Ricoeur a logical consequence of the symbolic nature of language. Because signs can have more than one meaning, they often say more than they appear to say at first sight. The ostensible meaning of a word frequently conceals another meaning which surpasses it. It is this typically equivocal or multivocal character of symbolic language which calls for the the deciphering activity of the interpreter. Ricoeur defines as symbolic "any structure of signification in which a direct, primary, literal meaning designates, in addition, another meaning which is indirect, secondary and figurative and which can be apprehended only through the first" ('Existence and Hermeneutics'). The decipherment of expressions with double or multiple meanings thus prescribes the hermeneutic field. Interpretation, as the dialectical counterpart of the symbol, is described accordingly as "the work of thought which consists in deciphering the hidden meaning in the apparent meaning, in unfolding the levels of meaning implied in the literal meaning" (*ibid.*).

The 'hidden' meaning of symbolic expressions can be interpreted in a variety of different ways. Nietzsche, for example, interprets it as articulating the strength or weakness of a Will to Power; Freud as a transposition of the repressed desires of the unconscious libido; the theologian as a cypher of divine transcendence; the poet as a projection of the creative imagination; the Marxist as an ideological disguise of class domination – and so on. The common feature of all these hermeneutic models is a certain architecture of multiple meaning whose function is to 'show while concealing'. However much their conclusions may contradict each other, Ricoeur demonstrates how each is concerned with the symbolic transfer of meaning from one plane to another through the linguistic agencies of metaphor, allegory, simile, metonomy etc.

It is the business of philosophical hermeneutics, Ricoeur urges, to provide a 'criteriology' which would situate and demarcate the theoretical limits of each hermeneutic field. The critical task of such a hermeneutics is to arbitrate between the absolutist claims of the respective interpretations, demonstrating how each one operates within a specific set of theoretical presuppositions. In other words, every particular hermeneutic translates a *surplus* of meaning, produced by the multiple determination of symbolic expressions, according to its own 'key' frame of reference. Ricoeur cites the following example of how rival interpretations arise:

> The phenomenology of religion deciphers the religious object in rites, in myth, and in faith, but it does so on the basis of a problematic of the sacred which defines its theoretical structure. Psychoanalysis, by contrast, sees only that dimension of the symbol . . . which derives from repressed desires. Conse-

quently, it considers only the network of meanings constituted in the unconscious, beginning with the initial repression and elaborated by subsequent
secondary repressions. (*The Conflict of Interpretations*).

But Ricoeur maintains that psychoanalysis cannot in itself be reproached
for its exclusivity, any more than the phenomenology of religion. The
methodological limits of these respective readings are their .ery *raison
d'être*. Since psychoanalytic theory confines the rules of its decoding of
dream-texts to a semantics of libidinal desire, it stands to reason that it can
only discover there what it seeks. It is entirely logical that it will interpret
religious symbols and rites as instances of 'obsessional neurosis'; just as a
specifically religious hermeneutics will interpret obsessional neurosis as a
disguised longing for the sacred.

The task of hermeneutics is not, insists Ricoeur, to try to resolve such
conflicts of interpretation; it is to clearly establish the particular
frameworks of pre-understanding – what Wittgenstein would call 'lan-
guage-games' – within which our various interpretations arise, predispos-
ing us to this or that reading of the signs. To dissolve this contest prematurely by appeal to some metalanguage of univocal meaning or some
absolute consciousness *à la* Hegel, is to succumb to the temptation of a
reductive idealism.

But Ricoeur equally resists the temptation to reduce hermeneutics to a
purely linguistic analysis of meaning. This would be to treat significations
as totalities closed in on themselves. Ricoeur takes his distance here from
what he terms the 'ideology of an absolute text' which came into vogue with
structuralism. He does not wish to deny that as soon as discourse is
inscribed in a text, the author's intention ceases to coincide with the
meaning of this text. He readily concedes the structuralist claim that the
text's career escapes the situated horizon lived by its author: "What the text
says now matters more than what the author meant to say, and every
exegesis unfolds its procedures within the circumference of a meaning that
has broken its moorings to the psychology of its author" ('The Model of the
Text'). But to acknowledge that the text suspends the *direct* reference to a
situation commonly experienced by the interlocutors of a spoken discourse,
is not the same as saying that the text has no reference at all. Language,
even as inscribed in an autonomous text, cannot fail to be *about* something.
Nearly all texts speak in some manner or other about a world. It is, of
course, true that the text suspends the situational reference to the author's
original experience, and is thus free to enter into relation with other texts.
This, Ricoeur notes, is what allows for the creation of the world of
literature. Here we speak of symbolic worlds – e.g. the Greek world or the

Byzantine world – that are *represented* in texts rather than *presented* or shown in a spoken situation. But in such instances, reference is not entirely obliterated; it is simply deferred. To suggest that we suppress the referential function altogether, is, Ricoeur charges, to abandon meaning to 'an absurd game of errant signifiers'.

Instead of adopting the structuralist ideology of the absolute text, therefore, Ricoeur's hermeneutic proposes to retain the link with a phenomenological ontology. This allows him to show how the text (e.g. a Greek tragedy) can indeed free itself from its initial direct reference to both an author (e.g. Sophocles) and to the circumstantial reality (e.g. Sophocles's Greece) of a historical situation and still retain the notion of reference – albeit a radically revised and as it were trans-historical reference to the symbolic projection of possible worlds. Ricoeur makes a fundamental distinction here between a situational reference to an actual world (*Umwelt*) and a non-situational reference to a symbolic world (*Welt*).

> In the same manner that the text frees its meaning from the tutelage of the mental intention, it frees its reference from the limits of ostensive reference. For us, the world is the ensemble of references opened up by the texts. Thus we speak about the 'world' of Greece, not to designate any more what were the situations for those who lived them, but to designate the non-situational references which outlive the effacement of the first and which henceforth are offered as possible modes of being, as symbolic dimensions of our being-in-the-world. For me, this is the referent of all literature; no longer the *Umwelt* of the ostensive references of dialogue, but the *Welt* projected by the non-ostensive references of every text that we have read, understood and loved. To understand a text is at the same time to light up our own situation, or, if you will, to interpolate among the predicates of our situation all the significations which make a *Welt* of our *Unwelt*. It is this enlarging of the *Umwelt* into the *Welt* which permits us to speak of the references *opened up* by the text – it would be better to say that the references *open up* the world. Here again the spirituality of discourse manifests itself through writing, which frees us from the visibility and limitation of situations by opening up a world for us, that is, new dimensions of our being-in-the-world ('The Model of the Text').

In this manner, Ricoeur's hermeneutic model renounces the structuralist hypostasis of language – the cult of the text as an end in itself. It remains faithful to the discovery of phenomenological ontology that the basic intention of the sign is to say something *about* something; which, in the case of symbolic language, means to designate *possible modes of existence* which surpass the limits of any given, present situation. "Language itself, as a signifying milieu", Ricoeur states, "must be referred to existence" (*ibid*).

But Ricoeur points out that if language refers to a world, it also addresses an audience. It always says something about something *to someone*. At the same time as it instigates a new mode of reference, symbolic expression also instigates a new mode of communication. The meaning of a textual symbol is not therefore confined to its original creator but addresses an actual or potential audience that it itself makes possible. In short, it is an open-ended communication whose addressee is just whoever knows how to read or interpret it. In referring to possible worlds, the symbol remains open to an infinite horizon of possible interpretations. Indeed, it is precisely because there is no one true reading of a symbol or text, that we find ourselves condemned to a conflict of interpretations.

Ricoeur assesses this condemnation in positive terms. Because my ontological self-understanding as a being-in-the-world can only be 'recovered by a detour of the decipherment of the documents of life' – that is by means of a hermeneutic critique of the various 'signs' of existence – it always remains a *desire to be*, a project of interpretation that can never be completed in any total or absolute sense. Finding ourselves thus exposed to an inevitable plurality of interpretations, we learn that a philosophy of consciousness which holds to the hegemonic claims of the cogito is a philosophy of *false* consciousness. To reduce the *desire to be* to the immediacy of self-consciousness, removing it from the mediating detour of interpretation, is to hypostasise it. The *desire to be* can never relinquish its role as a *being-interpreted*. Fully cognisant of the propensities of consciousness to contrive premature solutions, Ricoeur conjoins 1) the project of phenomenological hermeneutics and 2) the critique of 'false consciousness' advanced by the three 'masters of suspicion' – Marx, Freud and Nietzsche.

These three hermeneutic models of suspicion – Marxian, Freudian and Nietzschean – are welcomed by Ricoeur as reminders that there exist levels of signification removed from the immediate grasp of consciousness. Freud, for example, dismantled the prejudices of the *ego cogitans*, by disclosing how 'unconscious' meanings can be organised and structured in a site beneath the jurisdiction of our sovereign consciousness. Similarly, Nietzsche showed how our so-called timeless concepts of value and reason are in fact 'genealogically' determined by the hidden strategies of the Will to Power. Finally, Marx's critique of ideology discloses how the meanings of human existence are often conditioned by socio-historic forces of domination which surpass the ken of the self-possessed subject. Ricoeur holds that these masters of suspicion teach us that we can only hope to recover our ontological *desire to be* by first understanding ourselves as we exist *outside of ourselves*. All three recognise that meaning, far from being transparent to itself, is in fact an enigmatic process which conceals at the same time as it reveals. Thus Ricoeur can write that if "we are to succeed in understanding together the theory of ideologies in Marx, the genealogies of ethics in Nietzsche, and the theory of ideas and illusions in Freud, we will see the configuration of a problem – hereafter posed before the modern mind – the problem of *false-consciousness*" ('The Critique of Religion', 1973, in the Ricoeur *Anthology*).

Ricoeur believes that the 'hermeneutics of suspicion' makes possible a new critique of culture. Admittedly, it remains a negative hermeneutics of 'demystification'. But precisely as such, it deals with falsehood and illusion not just in the subjective context of epistemological error, but as a dimension of our social discourse as a whole. Thus Marx conceived of false-consciousness as a reflection of the class struggle; Nietzsche as the resentful vengeance of the weak against the strong; and Freud as a history of human desire repressed by cultural prohibition. All three were motivated by a common scruple of *hermeneutic doubt* which, observes Ricoeur, compelled them to demythologise the established cultural codes in order to decipher concealed strategies of domination, desire or will. And to the extent that it recognises the duplicitous workings of meaning and strives to unmask the ploys of consciousness, this moment of doubt marks an essential contribution to the general project of hermeneutics:

> The problem of false-consciousness could only appear by way of a critique of culture where consciousness appears in itself as a doubtful consciousness. But ... this doubt can only work through a totally new technique which is a new method of deciphering appearances. This deciphering will enable us to grasp what we have to say about demystification. What distinguishes false-consciousness from error or falsehood, and what motivates a particular kind of critique, of denunciation, is the possibility of signifying another thing than what one believes was signified, that is, the possibility of the masked consciousness. Consciousness is not transparent to itself ... but a relation of conceal/reveal which calls for a specific reading, a *hermeneutics*. The task of hermeneutics has always been to read a text and to distinguish the true sense from the apparent sense, to search for the sense under the sense ... There is then, a proper manner of uncovering what was covered, of unveiling what was veiled, of removing the mask ("The Critique of Religion').

Ricoeur contends, consequently, that hermeneutics cannot afford to dispense with this strategy of unmasking. It is only by smashing the idols of false consciousness, he remarks, that we can begin to allow the genuine symbols of our culture to speak. We cannot affirm the positive ontological content of our significations – that is, the projection of authentic possibilities of being – without demythologising their false content. Nor can religion presume to obviate this hermeneutic discrimination. The atheistic critique championed by the 'masters of suspicion' is an essential ingredient of the mature faith of modern man. We must incorporate the critique of religion as a mask of 'fear, domination or hate'. As Ricoeur concludes: "A Marxist critique of ideology, a Nietzschean critique of resentment and a Freudian critique of infantile distress, are hereafter the views through which any kind of mediation of faith must pass" ('The Critique of Religion').

V: A HERMENEUTICS OF AFFIRMATION

Only when we have become critically aware of the discontinuities and estrangements of our cultural expressions, insists Ricoeur, can we genuinely embark on a hermeneutics of *affirmation*. But we now appreciate that a universal ontology of understanding is a project rather than a *fait accompli*. The proper ontology for hermeneutics is therefore an *implied* ontology. It is only in and through a conflict of rival hermeneutics that we perceive something of the Being to be interpreted. For the philosophical subject cannot begin to ask the question of the fundamental meaning of Being until it has been dispossessed of the illusion that it already possesses this meaning. And so to complement psychoanalysis, which reveals an *archaeology of the subject* where meaning emerges *before* or *behind* our subjective consciousness, Ricoeur endorses a 'philosophy of spirit' which reveals a *teleology of the subject* where the origin of meaning is also displaced, but this time *in front of consciousness*. In this manner, Ricoeur contrives to rehabilitate and conflate the respective models of Freud and Hegel within the hermeneutic project.

The archaeological and teleological arcs of hermeneutic inquiry both effect a decentering of the traditional concept of the subject – the former as a return to the archaic meanings of the unconscious which precede it; the latter as an anticipation of new meanings which stretch out before it. Ricoeur argues that these two hermeneutic directions constitute man as a movement of interpretation beyond himself as a given, self-centering subject. They demonstrate how the human subject always understands his present significations in terms of 'other' signs implicit in the past and future horizons of what Ricoeur broadly calls *culture*. "Philosophy remains hermeneutics", asserts Ricoeur, "that is, a reading of the hidden meaning inside the text of the apparent meaning. It is the task of hermeneutics to show that existence arrives at expression, at meaning, and at reflection only through the continual exegesis of all the significations that come to light in the world of culture. Existence becomes a self only by appropriating this meaning which first resides 'outside', in works, institutions and cultural monuments in which the life of the spirit is objectified" (*The Conflict of Interpretations*).

Finally, Ricoeur affirms that man's ontological *desire to be* – expressed in

the archaeological recovery of lost meanings and in the teleological anticipation of proposed meanings – finds its ultimate articulation in an *eschatology of the sacred*. This third hermeneutic direction represents, for Ricoeur,
the most complete displacement of the Cartesian subject. The symbols of
the sacred designate both the alpha of archaeology and the omega of
teleology. They represent the irrecoverable origin *before* the beginning
(*arche*) and the unrealisable goal *after* the end (*telos*). "This alpha and this
omega", observes Ricoeur, "the subject would be unable to command.
The sacred calls upon man and in this call manifests itself as that which
commands his existence because it posits this existence absolutely, as effort
and desire to be" (*The Conflict of Interpretations*). In short, the sacred
demands that consciousness divest itself of the illusion of self-sufficiency
and acknowledge its ultimate dependence on a meaning that exists beyond
the self.

Precisely as something that cannot be possessed, repossessed or pre-
possessed, the eschatology of the sacred remains the paramount example of
the *risk* of interpretation. Contrary to the teaching of much traditional
metaphysics, it does not sanction a triumphalist ontology which would
break from the circle of interpretation. On the contrary, it at best solicits
what Ricoeur refers to as a 'militant and truncated ontology' which con-
signs us ever more intensely to the internal warfare of conflicting interpretations. It requires an absolute renunciation of the self-righteousness of
certainty. Yet in spite of this renunciation, or rather because of it, the
eschatology of the sacred expresses a genuine hope – hope in the ultimate
possibility of a unified or reconciled discourse. And as such, it comple-
ments critique with prophecy, suspicion with affirmation. In a rare moment
of enthusiasm, Ricoeur ventures a discreet mention of a "hermeneutics of
God's coming, of the approach of his Kingdom ... representing the
prophecy of consciousness" (*The Conflict of Interpretations*). But as prophecy, the affirmation of the sacred can never be verified. We can only hope
for something that is *not yet* given. The sacred, explains Ricoeur, is at most
that 'promised land' of a fulfilled ontology which the interpreter, "like
Moses, can only glimpse before dying" ('Phenomenology and Hermeneutics'). Because we are finite human beings, we remain within the historical
limits of the hermeneutic circle. The philosophical claim to absolute
knowledge is a false myth that must be perpetually demythologised. The
hermeneutics of affirmation must always be coupled with a hermeneutics
of suspicion. "It is because absolute knowledge is impossible", concludes
Ricoeur, "that the conflict of interpretations is insurmountable" ('Appropriation', 1981, in *Hermeneutics and the Human Sciences*).

APPENDIX:
THE HERMENEUTIC MODEL OF THE TEXT

Whereas Husserl approached meaning as an essence to be intuited (*Wesenschau*), Ricoeur approaches it as a text to be interpreted. He recognises, moreover, that every text of meaning implies an historical context. The hermeneutic model shows how the multiple meaning of words (polysemy) derives not just from the world of the text itself but from a double historical reference *both* to the original conditions of utterance or inscription (the world of the author) *and* to the subsequent conditions of reception or interpretation (the world of the addressee). As Ricoeur observes, *language always speaks to somebody about something.* This means that, at the most basic level, the meanings of language are substantially determined by their particular 'dialogical' situation. "It is with this selective function of context", affirms Ricoeur, "that interpretation, in the most primitive sense of the word, is connected. Interpretation is the process by which, in the interplay of question and answer, the interlocutors collectively determine the contextual values which structure their conversation" ('Phenomenology and Hermeneutics').

Consequently, interpretation can no longer be construed as the exclusive activity of the reflective philosopher. It is now recognised as the primordial condition of our being-in-the-world *qua* language-users. Ricoeur thus endorses the view of Heidegger and Gadamer that human existence (*Dasein*) is in and of itself language (*Sprachlichkeit*): we exist in language for we are always situated within the historical context of an intersubjective dialogue with others. (For more on this aspect of Gadamer's hermeneutic model see our chapter on Habermas in the section on *Critical Theory*).

But this dialogue, Ricoeur explains, is not reducible to the immediacy of conversation; it is more than a *face-à-face* exchange between two interlocutors whose intentional meanings could be unambiguously limited to a direct 'ostensive' reference *vis-à-vis* an actual situation here and now. The hermeneutic model of dialogue extends beyond the 'direct reference' of two interlocutors immediately co-present one to the other in a commonly identifiable situation. In a broader sense, it embraces an historical horizon where meanings can outlive the 'here and now' of interpersonal conversation and endure over time, in the written texts, documents, monuments, institutions and traditions of a culture. This historical activity of language (*Geschichtesbewirkung*), pursues Ricoeur, involves an expropriation of the author's original meaning which allows for a reappropriation of meaning by subsequent interpreters. This is what Ricoeur terms the detour through the 'long' intersubjective relation:

Conversation . . . is contained within the limits of a *vis-à-vis* which is a *face-à-face*. The historical connection which encompasses it is singularly more complex. The 'short' intersubjective relation is intertwined, in the interior of the historical connection, with various 'long' intersubjective relations, mediated by diverse institutions, social roles and collectivities (groups, nations, cultural traditions, etc.). The long intersubjective relations are sustained by an historical tradition, of which dialogue is only a segment. Explication therefore extends much further than dialogue, coinciding with the broadest historical connections. ('Phenomenology and Hermeneutics').

Ricoeur likens the transmission of meaning in historical tradition (or 'sedimentation' as Merleau-Ponty termed it) to the mediating function of the *text*. The liberation of meaning from its original range of reference is analogous to the written text where meaning endures in the absence of the original author and addressee of spoken conversation. The meaning of the text is thus granted a significant autonomy with respect to i) the author's original intention; ii) the initial situation of discourse; and iii) the original addressee. Hermeneutics approximates in this manner, to the condition of textual exegesis where meaning enjoys a certain independence from an original first order reference and opens up a 'second order reference' *in front of the text*. It is this new order of reference carried by the 'autonomous' text which invites in turn a multiplicity of readings – that is, an open horizon of interpretations.

The historical transmission of meaning thus places us in a hermeneutic circle where each interpretation is both preceded by a semantic horizon inherited from tradition and yet exposed to multiple subsequent rereadings by other interpreters. Indeed it is precisely because all interpretation places the reader in *medias res* – in a dialectical circle of intersubjectivity rather than at a fixed beginning or end – that the idealist appeal to a presuppositionless foundation is doomed to failure. To interpret history is, Ricoeur submits, to arrive in the middle of a dialogue which has already begun and in which we try to orientate ourselves in order to make some new sense of it. (A similar point was humorously expressed by T. S. Eliot in relation to literary tradition when he remarked that while immature poets 'imitate', mature poets 'steal' – his argument being that no poet can lay claim to the absolute originality of a *creatio ex nihilo*). Husserl's attempt to forego the hermeneutic circle in favour of an absolute intuition of pure self-consciousness, is thus refuted by Ricoeur's model of the text. Idealist phenomenology, declares Ricoeur, "can therefore sustain its pretention to ultimate foundation only by adopting, in an intuitive rather than a speculative mode, the Hegelian claim to absolute knowledge. But the key hypothesis of hermeneutic philosophy is that interpretation is an open process which no single vision can conclude" ('Phenomenology and

Hermeneutics,').

Accordingly, if Husserl's phenomenology was first advanced as a critique of the empirical sciences' claim to absolute objectivity, Ricoeur's hermeneutics is advanced as a critique of Husserl's and Hegel's idealist claim to absolute subjectivity. Hermeneutics proclaims the pure self-understanding of a transcendental ego to be impossible; it demonstrates that understanding always labours within the historical horizon of an intersubjective communication where we interpret meanings that have been 'distanciated' from subjective consciousness. For it is, paradoxically, in so far as we *belong* to an historical tradition that meaning is always at a *distance* from us in the immediate here and now. 'Distanciation' is the dialectical counterpart of 'belonging'. These two movements represent the twin arches of the hermeneutic bridge. The text thus becomes, for Ricoeur, the model for a belonging to communication in and through distance. In interpretation we endeavour to reappropriate those meanings that have been disappropriated from understanding. Hermeneutics, in short, is the attempt to render near that which is far – temporally, geographically, culturally, spiritually etc. It strives to recover that which has been removed.

Ricoeur fully recognises the rapport between the hermeneutic function of 'distantiation' and the controversial phenomenon of *ideology* understood as the 'alienation' of meaning from the human subject. But hermeneutics also provides the possibility of a critique of ideology in its project to restore a new form of self-understanding by means of the 'long' detour of interpretation. The 'self' thus retrieved from the ideological distantiation of 'false consciousness' is not, however, the self-identical cogito coveted by idealism. Here again the analogy of textual distanciation is rewarding. To read a text is to expose oneself to an horizon of 'other' or 'alien' meanings that exceed my subjective consciousness. The text requires the reader, just as much as the original author, to transcend his own subjective intentions. It opens us to a world of *possible* meanings, to new modes of being-in-the-world and of being-interpreted. This new world of being brought to language by the text is what Ricoeur calls the 'second order reference' which removes us from the 'first order reference' of the familiar world we inhabit here and now (i.e. prior to our exposure to the hermeneutic circle of the text).

In contrast to the idealist thesis of a self-positing subject whose world is *for itself* alone, hermeneutics divests subjectivity of its presumption to be the absolute origin of meaning. Instead it proposes subjectivity as a goal or *telos* to be reached *after* the intersubjective detour of interpretation. In the process, of course, the very concept of subjectivity is radically altered. For Ricoeur insists that it is only by means of the distancing of the self from its original self – in this intersubjective detour via meanings *other* than its own – that the interpreter can hope to recover a new sense of subjectivity: enlarged, decentred and open to novel possibilities of self-interpretation. Once more, we find Ricoeur invoking the theory of the text as his guideline:

It shows that the act of subjectivity is not so much what initiates understanding as what terminates it. This terminal act can be characterised as appropriation. [But] it does not purport . . . to rejoin the original subjectivity which would support the meaning of the text. Rather it *responds* to the matter of the text, and hence to the proposals of meaning which the text unfolds. It is thus the counterpart of the distanciation which establishes the autonomy of the text with respect to its author, its situation and its original addressee. Thus appropriation can be integrated into the theory of interpretation without surreptitiously reintroducing the primacy of subjectivity. ('Phenomenology and Hermeneutics').

To take a concrete example, if I read Tolstoy's novel *Anna Karenina*, I expose myself to an alien consciousness, time and place (i.e. the sensibility of the various characters of Russian society in the late nineteenth century described by the author). I am thus invited to extend my actual horizons of experience here and now by imaginatively reliving the world represented in Tolstoy's text. And in so doing, I am disappropriated from my given assumptions regarding my own immediate world at the same time as I seek to reappropriate this 'other' world for my contemporary understanding. But in this dialectical movement between disappropriation and appropriation what is ultimately revealed is a 'possible world' which results from the encounter between my world and Tolstoy's – a new horizon of experience which is opened up by the matter of the text itself and which exceeds both Tolstoy's original consciousness as an author and my contemporary consciousness as a reader. In this dialectical encounter in and through the text, the meanings intended by both author and reader find themselves transformed and enlarged.

Ricoeur's notion of appropriation does not then imply some triumphalist return of a sovereign subject to itself. If the goal of hermeneutics remains 'self-understanding' this must be reinterpreted in the altered sense of understanding oneself *in front of the text*. "What the interpreter says is a re-saying which reactivates what is said by the text" ('What is a Text?') What is appropriated is the matter of the text – a new horizon of possible meanings opened up by the language of the text. "But the matter of the text only becomes my own", insists Ricoeur, "if I disappropriate myself, in order to let the matter of the text be. So I exchange the *me* (*moi*), *master* of itself, for the *self* (*soi*), *disciple* of the text" ('Phenomenology and Hermeneutics').

In this way, hermeneutics may serve as a double critique. It is a critique of *egology* based on the illusion that the self can constitute itself as absolute origin. But it is equally a critique of *ideology* which rests on the obverse illusion that self-understanding has no role to play – particularly in a socio-historical or political context. The former results from the extreme of appropriation (total self-possession by the exclusion of the other), the latter from the extreme of disappropriation (the total alienation of my meaning by some impersonal or anonymous other). Hermeneutics bids us surmount these two illusions by reinstating a complementary dialectic of self and other.

Jacques Derrida

Der der, deary didi! Der? I? Da! Deary? da! Der I, didida; da dada, didideary da.
Dadareder, didireader. Dare I die deary da? Da dare die didi. Die derider! Didiwriter.
Dadadididididada. Aaaaaaaaa! Der i da.

This 'Oedipal Fragment' of deconstructive pastiche was composed by
Terry Eagleton, the avant-garde English critic, in filial disobedience to the
modern father of deconstruction, Jacques Derrida. Few modern thinkers
have generated so much international celebration or censure as this French
exponent of the 'textual revolution'. He has been both reviled and revered
for his anarchic play with the eccentric ingenuities of language. No sacred
concept of traditional thought has been spared a prod from his dissecting
scalpel. He has danced on the graves of all our hallowed certainties. To
some, he is no more than a mischief-maker, to others, he is the most
revolutionary philosopher of the twentieth century.

Derrida is a French Algerian of Jewish origin. Born in Algeria in 1931,
he moved to France as a young student and quickly acquired a reputation
for innovative thinking. He studied phenomenology in Paris with Emmanuel Levinas – who was one of the first to introduce Husserl's work to
France in the early thirties – and with Paul Ricoeur at the *Centre Phénomé-*
nologique et Herméneutique. His earliest published works were radical rereadings of Husserl's phenomenological theory of language: *Edmund Huss-*
erl's 'Origin of Geometry': An Introduction (1962) and *Speech and Phenomena*
(1967). But Derrida was always more than a brilliant commentator. In an
impressive series of original works – amongst them, *Of Grammatology*
(1967), *Writing and Difference* (1967), *Dissemination* (1972), *Margins of*
Philosophy (1972) and *Glas* (1974) – Derrida rigorously undermines traditional notions of thinking and endeavours to overcome the conventional
division between philosophical and aesthetic discourse. This division, he
argues, is ultimately determined by a 'logocentric' bias in Western metaphysics which outlaws all meaning that does not conform to a centralising
rationalistic logic of identity and non-contradiction. Against such narrow
'logocentrism', Derrida celebrates the free play of language as an endless
differance of meaning. He has taught for many years now at *l'Ecole Normale*
Supérieure in Paris and at both Yale and Johns Hopkins University in the
USA.

Not surprisingly, Derrida refuses to be definitively placed within the available philosophical categories. His influence has extended far beyond philosophy to such disparate disciplines as literary criticism, sociology, political theory, psychology, anthropology, theology and many more. But even within the realm of philosophy itself, there has been much dispute as to how Derrida's strategies of deconstruction are to be assessed. This 'undecidability' has been cultivated by Derrida himself. One of the motivating impulses of his work has been to disrupt all univocal classifications and fixed identities which he sees as symptomatic of the logocentric bias of Western thinking – the compulsion to have a central place for everything and to reduce everything to this central place. In short, Derrida's refusal to be neatly labelled is entirely consistent with his essentially anarchic position, or rather non-position.

I: BEYOND HUSSERL AND HEIDEGGER

These reservations notwithstanding, it is legitimate to point to certain intellectual fidelities in Derrida's philosophy. There can be little doubt, for example, that Derrida has much in common with the structuralist and post-structuralist efforts to dismantle the traditional metaphysical categories of subjectivity and reference in favour of the free play of language. But Derrida's programme of deconstruction derives, by his own admission, even more fundamentally from his formative studies of the phenomenological thinkers, Husserl and Heidegger. In a recent interview, Derrida acknowledges the following debt to phenomenology:

> My philosophical formation owes much to the thought of Husserl, Heidegger and Hegel. Heidegger is probably the most constant influence, and particularly his project of *overcoming/deconstructing* Greek Metaphysics. Husserl, whom I studied in a more detailed and painstaking fashion, taught me a certain methodical prudence and reserve, a rigorous technique of unravelling and formulating questions. But I never shared Husserl's pathos for, and commitment to, a phenomenology of presence. In fact, it was Husserl's method that helped me to suspect the very notion of presence and the fundamental role it played in all philosophies. My relationship with Heidegger is much more enigmatic and extensive: here my interest was not just *methodological* but existential. The content and themes of Heidegger's questioning excited me – especially the 'ontological difference', the critique of Platonism and the relationship between language and Being. (*Dialogues with Contemporary Continental Thinkers*, 1984).

The primary lesson that Derrida gleaned from the 'deconstructive' tendencies of the late Husserl and Heidegger was the impossibility of discovering a radical beginning. It was, ironically, Husserl himself who sowed the seeds of doubt. By seeking so emphatically a pure intuition of presence beyond all presuppositions of language or history, Husserl's ultimate failure to secure such an absolute beginning spelt the end of traditional metaphysics. As he was compelled to confess, almost despite himself, in a controversial appendix to *The Crisis*: "Philosophy as a rigorous science – the dream is over (*der Traum ist ausgeträumt*)". In this last work, Husserl came increasingly to recognise that the transcendental subject's world of immediate experience was in fact grounded in the historicity of a cultural life-world rather than grounding it. This failure of the phenomenological quest for an intuition of timeless essences was not lost on Derrida (though he fully acknowledged that phenomenology had become deconstruction by default rather than by design).

Derrida claims that with Heidegger the deconstructive impulse took a more explicit turn. Heidegger's critical project in *Being and Time* was guided from the outset by a resolve to overcome (*ueberwinden*) what he termed the 'ontotheological' bias of Western metaphysics – that is, a systematic prejudice against the temporal and historical character of our experience of Being. But Heidegger himself still retained a 'nostalgia' for some original and unifying word of Being which, he believed, might be restored once the 'ontotheological' scaffolding of traditional philosophy had been dismantled. As Richard Rorty, the American philosopher, has accurately remarked:

> Derrida is one of the very few philosophers, perhaps the only one so far, to go along enthusiastically and whole-heartedly with Heidegger's criticism of 'ontotheology' while still resisting the old wizard's spell. After learning all that Heidegger had to teach, he still manages to look Heidegger in the eye and stare him down. Heidegger's own writing combined enormous respect for such predecessors as Plato and Nietzsche with a fierce will to be free of them. Derrida has the same filial relation to Heidegger himself. Having done to Heidegger what Heidegger did to Nietzsche is the negative achievement which, after all the chatter about 'deconstruction' is over, will give Derrida a place in the history of philosophy ('Signposts along the way that reason went', 1984).

Derrida, in short, applies his deconstructive reading not only to Western metaphysics but also to his own phenomenological masters, Husserl and Heidegger, whom he suspects still remain, to a greater or lesser extent, enthralled by the 'logocentric' spell. (For a detailed discussion of this deconstruction of phenomenology see the Appendix to this chapter.)

But what exactly does Derrida mean by 'logocentrism'? He uses this term to characterise the recurring propensity of Western thinking to centralise or ground its understanding on notions of 'presence' (*logos*). Derrida defines the history of metaphysics, and indeed the history of the West as a whole, accordingly, as a narrative of the "determinations of being as *presence* in all the senses of the word" ('Structure, Sign and Play' in *Writing and Difference*, 1967). It would be possible, he argues, "to show that all the names related to fundamentals, to principles, or to the centre have designated the constant of a presence – *eidos, arche, telos, energeia, ousia* (essence, existence, substance, subject), *aletheia*, transcendentality, consciousness, or conscience, God, man and so forth" (*ibid.*). Derrida proposes to break with this logocentrism by rethinking its guiding concepts in such a way that the centralising notion of presence is revealed to have *never been itself.* He endeavours to expose the ruling categories of an original presence as no more than substitutes or supplements of their own absence. Like the king's new clothes they are but rhetorically present – strategic illusions to preserve the pretence of self-possession, power and authority. Once deconstruction has got to work, declares Derrida, and shown that presence as a supplementary representation does not in fact re-present anything at all, does not substitute itself for something which somehow preexisted it, then we are obliged to recognise that there never was a centre. The following passage from Derrida's seminal essay, 'Structure, Sign and Play' provides a characteristically dense formulation of deconstruction.

> It was . . . necessary to begin to think that there was no centre, that the centre could not be thought in the form of a being-present, that the centre had no natural locus, that it was not a fixed locus but a function, a sort of non-locus in which an infinite number of sign-substitutions came into play. This moment was that in which language invaded the universal problematic; that in which, in the absence of a centre or origin, everything became discourse . . . that is to say, when everything became a system where the central signified, the original or transcendental signified, is never absolutely present outside a system of differences. The absence of the transcendental signified extends the domain and the interplay of signification *ad infinitum (ibid.)*

By privileging the free play of *signification* over the presentational intentions of *perception* (favoured by Merleau-Ponty) or the representational intentions of *imagination* (favoured by Sartre), Derrida contrives to de-centre all notions of original presence. But by opening Pandora's box of free play, Derrida also deconstructs the traditional concept of signification itself. He reveals it to be a process of 'dissemination', an endless shifting from sign to sign which can never be terminated or fixed by reducing the signifying process to some transcendental starting-point or end-point. This interminable play of signs, each one substituting for the other in an infinite chain, becomes for Derrida an affirmation of the non-centre (and it does so otherwise than as the loss of a centre which might be recovered as presence). In short, signification does not present or represent some original presence; the very notion of presence is *itself* an *effect* produced by signification.

Using the more technical terms of linguistics, Derrida argues that every signifier serves as a metaphor for a signified that can never be situated outside language. And so the signified itself becomes a signifier which can only function by referring, or rather deferring, to other signifiers. There is no reference outside language. There is no *hors texte*. Even the 'things themselves', so cherished by Husserl, can no longer be construed as immediately experienced phenomena. They too are signs, 'effects' of language. "There is no phenomenality", writes Derrida in *Of Grammatology* (1967), "reducing the sign or the representer so that the thing signified may be allowed to glow finally in the luminosity of its presence. The so-called 'thing itself' is always already a *representamen* shielded from the simplicity of intuitive evidence. The *representamen* functions only by giving rise to an *interpretant* that itself becomes a sign and so on to infinity." The only legitimate hermeneutics, Derrida suggests, is *intra-linguistic*: a hermeneutics which interprets interpretations rather than things. Derrida concludes, therefore, that from the moment there is meaning there is nothing but signs: "We *think only in signs* . . . One could call *play* the absence of the transcendental signified as limitlessness of play, that is to say as the destruction of onto-theology and the metaphysics of presence" (*Ibid.*).

II: LOGOCENTRISM AND PHONOCENTRISM

One of the most effective ways in which the logocentric bias of Western metaphysics operates is in the traditional priority afforded to *speech* (*phone*) over *writing* (*gramme*). Or as Derrida puts it, logocentrism is phonocentrism. This equation is witnessed as early as Plato who spoke of truth being expressed in "a silent dialogue of the soul with itself", that is, as an immediate presence of the speaker to himself. Here, Plato believed, truth is still pure self-immediacy; it has not yet been contaminated by the risk of alienation or confusion. In silent speech meaning is still identical with itself. It is what it says and says what it is. By keeping *others* at bay, the self can here lay claim to the unadulterated sovereignty of a single truth.

The next model which, for Derrida, most approximates to this 'phonocentric' ideal of self-immediacy is that of a dialogue between two speakers who are present to each other in a shared time and place. Though no longer immediately identical with itself, meaning can still be recovered as 'presence' to the extent that both speakers in dialogue can *say exactly what they mean*. The meaning intended in their speech can be directly attested to by reference to a commonly experienced context *here and now*. Hence

Plato's preference for the format of the Socratic dialogue as exis ntial witness to the immediate experience of speech.

Writing, on the contrary, was generally treated with great suspicion by Plato. By breaking with the phonocentric model of dialogical immediacy of self to self (or of self to the other immediately present to the self), writing exposes us to the 'alienation' of meaning from itself. The inscription of meaning in signs grants it an autonomy and independence *vis à vis* the intention of the original author. It sets meaning at a distance from its original self-presence. It introduces the possibility of other interpretations, quite *different* to those originally intended. This alienation of meaning is most evident in the fact that written signs can continue to signify in the absence of the author, even after the death of the author. Thus Plato can accuse writing of a certain parricide. Written signs are like illegitimate offspring who have divested themselves of the authors who originally fathered them. In *Dissemination* (1972), Derrida offers an elaborate deconstructive analysis of Plato's hostile assessment of writing in the *Phaedrus*. In this dialogue, Plato warns against the abuses which attend upon the alienation of speech in writing. "Once speeches have been written down", Socrates argues, "they are tumbled about anywhere among those who may or may not understand them, and know not to whom they should reply, to whom not: and, if they are maltreated or abused, they have no parent to protect them; and they cannot protect or defend themselves" (*Phaedrus*, 275). To this illegitimacy of the written word, Plato contrasts the true pedigree of the spoken dialogue – "another kind of word or speech far better than this, and having far greater power – a son of the same family, but lawfully begotten . . . I mean an intelligent word graven in the soul . . . the living word of knowledge of which the written word is no more than an image" (*ibid.*)'

Plato frequently ascribes the term *pharmakon* to writing. Derrida draws our attention to the curious fact that this term is ambiguous, meaning both a 'cure' and a 'poison'. Writing for Plato is an evil disease to the degree that it corrupts meaning by removing it from the authoritative presence-to-itself of the speaker's original intention. It displaces meaning *outside* of the author, depriving it of its parental tutelage and thus exposing it to error. But meaning is also, paradoxically, a cure. It is only because meaning can be repeated and thereby recollected from oblivion that it c... remain the *same*, that is identical with itself. The ideality of the Platonic *eidos*, as Derrida observes, is its power to be repeated over time. This is why he speaks of truth as remembering (*anamnesis*). But the best aid to remembering the original utterances of meaning is, ironically, writing. For writing can cl.. to preserve the original intention of speakers which would otherwise be forgotten over time, allowing this intention to be reiterated in a quasi-timeless or eternal fashion. In short, writing is *both* the disease which alienates speech as immediate self-presence *and* the cure which permits it to achieve a durability beyond the temporal/spatial confines of its original expression.

Derrida proposes to deconstruct Platonic metaphysics in this manner by demonstrating that its most revered categories of timeless presence – *eidos*, *logos* etc. – are in fact based on a "complicity of contrary values". While it declares the phonocentric priority of speech (as an index of presence, identity, unity and immediacy) over writing (as an index of absence, difference, multiplicity and distance), Platonic metaphysics requires writing to preserve speech, to re-present its original presence in its very absence. As *pharmakon*, writing is therefore a play of irreconcilable opposites. For it alienates the invisible interiority of the soul-in-dialogue-with-itself by embodying it in visual markings and written signs outside of the soul and *at the same time* functions as a salvatory power which can reawaken the soul to forgotten truths. "If the *pharmakon* is ambivalent", writes Derrida, "it is because it constitutes the medium in which opposites are opposed, the movement of the play that links them among themselves, reverses them or makes one side cross over into the other (soul/body, good/evil, inside/outside, memory/forgetfulness, speech/writing) . . . The *pharmakon* is the production of difference. It is the *différance* of difference" (*Dissemination*)

III: THE OPERATION OF DIFFERANCE

Derrida purports to deconstruct the Platonic hierarchy of identity by disclosing how it is preceded by *différance*. Derrida often uses this neologism, differance, to denote the dual functioning of writing as both a *differing* (each sign differs from the other) and a *deferring* (the endless chain of signs postpones any termination of the chain in some original signified). The French term, *différer* carries both these senses. The metaphysical prestige of the *logos* – as a centred and centring self-identity – is subverted by the operation of *différance*.

Derrida bases his argument here on the fact that the intention (*vouloir-dire*) of speech can only presume to remain identical with itself to the extent that it is repeated at *different* times *as the same*. Consequently, the very notion of sameness as 'reiterability' presupposes the differentiating play of writing and reading. Derrida can affirm, consequently, that presence sustains itself by differing from itself; and that, as such, presence is always deferred. It becomes a goal (*telos*) rather than an origin (*arche*). But a goal, Derrida is quick to remind us, that can never be attained; for writing shows that the self-present interiority of the soul, coveted by the phonocentric preference for speech, in fact requires the exteriority of visible markings – an embodiment in written signs – so that it may be temporally repeated in a series of different readings. But this very dependence on the temporalising function of repetition, where one signifier endlessly substitutes for another, means that the play of signification can never be finalised in some *timeless* origin or end. The goal of speech as a self-presence before or beyond time can only be produced over time by the temporalising play of writing; and this very play undermines self-presence, deferring it *ad infinitum*. Presence is thus shown to be incorrigibly infested by differance. Barbara Johnson summarises Derrida's rather convoluted argumentation with admirable concision in her introduction to the English translation of *Dissemination*:

> Derrida's critique of Western metaphysics focuses on its privileging of the spoken word over the written word. The spoken word is given a higher value because the speaker and listener are both present to the utterance simultaneously. There is no temporal or spatial distance between speaker, speech, and listener, since the speaker hears himself speak at the same moment the listener does. This immediacy seems to guarantee the notion that in the spoken word we know what we mean, mean what we say, say what we mean, and know what we have said. Whether or not perfect understanding always occurs *in fact*, this image of perfectly self-present meaning is, according to Derrida, the underlying ideal of Western culture. Derrida has termed this belief in the self-presentation of meaning "logocentrism", from the Greek word *Logos* (meaning speech, logic, reason, the Word of God). Writing, on the other hand, is considered by the logocentric system to be only when speaking is impossible. Writing is thus a second-rate activity that tries to overcome distance by making use of it: the writer puts his thought on paper, distancing it from himself, transforming it into something that can be read by someone far away, even after the writer's death. This inclusion of death, distance and difference is thought to be a corruption of the self-presence of meaning, to open meaning up to all forms of adulteration which immediacy would have prevented. (*ibid.*)

Derrida's meticulous critique of the phonocentric prejudice is not confined, however, to showing how speech is differentiated by its external inscription in writing. He argues that the play of differance is *internal* to speech itself. Speech is in fact already inhabited by difference to the extent that each word or spoken sign is divided from the outset into a phonic signifer and a conceptual signified. As Derrida observes in his crucial essay on 'Differance', included as an appendix in the English translation of *Speech and Phenomena* (1967), Saussure's linguistic analysis already revealed how speech is itself a system of differences between signs rather than a collection of separate semantic units. Saussure demonstrated in his *Course in General Linguistics* that a sign cannot signify anything by itself, but only by marking a divergence or difference of meaning between itself and other signs. But precisely because the meanings of spoken signs are engendered by the differences which emerge among them, the possibility of speech as an immediacy of self-presence is ruled out from the outset. Speech can only presume to presence by repressing the differentiating structures which allow it to function in the first place.

This functioning of difference *within* speech is what Derrida calls *archi-writing*, a sort of writing before writing. *Archi-writing* cannot be objectively defined. "It is that very thing", Derrida remarks, "which cannot let itself be reduced to the form of a presence . . . [which] orders all objectivity of the object and all relation of knowledge" (*Of Grammatology*). As such, it calls for a non-logocentric linguistics – what Derrida terms 'grammatology'. This linguistics is not some new science; for the very notion of scientific 'objectivity' entails the ideal of a *repeatable* presence that in turn presupposes a temporal differentiation which subverts the very illusion of presence.

Grammatology dispenses with the idea of scientific objectivity – which is a self-contradiction – in favour of a deconstructive reading of texts. It is, in Derrida's own terms, a 'vigilant practice or exercise of textual division" (*Positions*, 1972). But Derrida's grammatology does not simply deconstruct all normative concepts of language and logic; it equally confounds all normative concepts of reality. Deconstruction dismantles metaphysical idealisms *and* realisms. It holds that our traditional notions of reality are themselves structured by the signifying practices of discourse which define or explain it. By showing that all *reference* (to reality) is predetermined by *meaning* and that all meaning is predetermined by *archi-writing*, as a differential play of signifiers, Derrida obliges logocentrism to self-deconstruct.

Grammatology thus assumes the guise of an unrelenting scepticism intent on revealing that both 'reality' and 'consciousness' are constructs of a play of multiple signification which undermines the illusion of a posterior 'objective' reference or a prior 'subjective' intention.

Grammatology shows that there is nothing before or after language. The concepts of reality and rationality are exposed as effects of figurality. Derrida unmasks the duplicitous and endlessly disseminating strategies of language thereby collapsing the logocentric rationalism of metaphysics into a carnival of figurative conceits. At this point, Derrida endorses Nietszche's observation that "truth is an illusion that has forgotten that it is an illusion . . . an army of faded metaphors".

Derrida extends his critique of the phonocentric model to a variety of other logocentric prejudices supported by the Western metaphysics of presence.

Firstly, he remarks how the *epistemological primacy* of reason and perception, as modes of presenting what is other than consciousness to itself, epitomises a sustained attempt to obviate the differentiating mediations of signs. This primacy is particularly evident in the realist notion of truth as an *adequatio intellectus et rei* (the identity of the mind and reality) or in the idealist definition of truth as the *cogito* (consciousness which is immediately present to itself).

Secondly, Derrida instances the logocentric bias manifest in the *chronological primacy* afforded by successive metaphysical systems to the timeless present, divorced from the temporally differentiated horizons of past and future. This primacy is manifest (1) in the metaphysical preference for the immortal soul over the temporal body, (2) in the definition of Transcendental Forms as eternal and immutable identities and (3) in the notion of God as a timeless present, *Nunc Stans*.

Thirdly, Derrida refers to the *sexual* primacy of male over female. This he terms the 'phallogocentric' character of logocentrism. The phallus was privileged as a symbol of sovereign self-sufficiency and self-possession. To possess a phallus was to be identical with oneself, enjoying the power of adequate presence. To lack this, to be female, was to be haunted by absence and therefore condemned to the vagaries of material desire and the temporal cycles of procreation. Intellect, spirit, reason – these were male preserves, proud sanctuaries of presence unadulterated by feminine lack or instability.

Fourthly, and perhaps most importantly, Derrida examines the *ontological primacy* of Being as pure self-presence rigidly opposed to the absences of non-being or the temporal differences of becoming. This ontological primacy of presence is one of the most salient contours of the entire history of metaphysics. Its developing lineage could be traced from Plato's celebrated model of the soul in silent dialogue with itself; to Aristotle's *telos* as 'self-thinking-thought'; to Augustine's description of the Divine Being as 'self-loving-love' (*Amor quo Deus Se Ipsum amat*); to Aquinas' notion of God as 'self-subsisting-substance' (*Ipsum Esse Subsistens*) or as Pure Act of Self-Presence beyond the 'potency' of temporal becoming (*Actus Purus non habens aliquid de potentialitate*); to the late Scholastic and Cartesian formulation of Supreme Being as a 'self-causing-cause' (*Ens Causa Sui*). All of these ontological models of presence are constructed upon figurative metaphors and temporal differentiations which they suppress in order to sustain the pretence of self-identity. It is by scrupulously unravelling such strategies of suppression and contradiction that Derrida proposes to deconstruct metaphysics.

Finally, Derrida's programme of deconstruction has, in recent times, been directed with increasing frequency and controversy to literary theory. It is probably fair to say that it is here that Derrida's thinking has exerted its most radical influence, particularly in the Anglo-American world where 'deconstructive criticism' has become almost *de rigueur* in avant-garde circles. The central thrust of such criticism is to dismantle traditional theories of the literary work as a totalised 'book' (i.e. a fixed message corresponding to the original intention and context of authorship). The death of the 'book', founded on the illusion of an original authorial and authoritative truth, heralds the birth of the 'text' as a free play of signifiers open to an infinite number of readings and rereadings. This textual revolution emancipates reading from the traditional idea of an extra-linguistic intention which would function as a 'transcendental signifier' guiding the signifers within the text and thus guaranteeing the 'correctness' of its readings. Deconstruction celebrates the endless multiplication of meaning over the spurious if comforting unity of a single correct reading. The text becomes an autonomous chain of signifers irreducible to any fixed reference (transcendental signified) or intention (transcendental signifier) outside of the text. The deconstructed text is without origin or end.

But textual deconstruction does not stop there. The discovery of textuality is not limited to novels and poems. History itself, as that which supposedly precedes or excedes language, is also exposed as text. To say, therefore, that literature somehow re-presents history, is simply to say that one kind of text refers to another kind – and so on *ad infinitum*. A fine assessment of Derrida's all-embracing theory of textuality, or rather-intertextuality, is offered by Vincent Leitch in *Deconstructive Criticism* (1983). He writes:

> Since language serves as ground of existence, the world emerges as infinite Text. Everything gets textualized. All contexts, whether political, economic, social, psychological, historical or theological, become intertexts; that is, outside influences and forces undergo textualization. Instead of literature we have textuality; in place of tradition, intertextuality. Authors die so that readers can come into prominence. In any case, all selves, whether of critics, poets, or readers, appear as language constructions – texts. What are texts? Strings of differential traces. Sequences of floating signifiers. Sets of infiltrated signs dragging along ultimately indecipherable intertextual elements. Sites for the freeplay of grammar, rhetoric, and (illusory) reference. What about the truth of the text? The random flights of signifiers across the textual surface, the disseminations of meaning, offer truth under one condition: that the chaotic processes of textuality be willfully regulated, controlled, or stopped. Truth comes forth in the reifications . . . of reading. Truth is not an entity or property of the text. No text utters its truth; the truth lies elsewhere in the reading. Constitutionally, reading is misreading. Deconstruction works to deregulate controlled dissemination and celebrate misreading. (*Ibid.*)

CONCLUSION

Let us summarise the broad outlines of Derrida's complex work of deconstruction. His oeuvre consists largely of a series of critical readings not only of his phenomenological mentors, Husserl and Heidegger, but also of such key Western thinkers as Plato, Rousseau, Nietzsche, Freud, Saussure and others. In each case, Derrida labours to show how Western thinking has been dominated by a metaphysics of presence which exercises a hierarchical preference for the one over the many, identity over difference, spirit over matter, eternity over time, immediacy over deferment, the same over the other – and perhaps most significant for Derrida's analytic purposes, speech over writing. Derrida proposes grammatology as a deconstructive science of writing which will undo such metaphysical oppositions (and not simply reverse them) by detecting the covert operations of *differance* – of difference and deferment – at the heart of metaphysical language. This involves meticulous textual disclosure of the various strategies devised by metaphysics to suppress this operation of *differance* in its search for a self-identical presence.

But Derrida is equally determined to avoid replacing one kind of logocentric certainty with another. And so he declares that even his own deconstructive terms – *differance, archi-writing, trace, supplement, palimpsest, dissemination, erasure* and indeed the very term *deconstruction* itself – must themselves be placed 'under erasure' lest a new dogmatism take the place of the old. Derrida resolves accordingly to deploy his own deconstructive terms as 'undecidables'. They are 'undecidables', he explains, precisely because they forego the fallacious claim to a single determinate meaning, cultivating instead two or more different meanings which serve to set up and undermine oppositions. Thus *differance* means both to defer and to differ; *supplement*, to increase and to replace; *pharmakon*, to poison and to cure etc. This notion of a non-logocentric thinking, which can, in James Joyce's apt phrase, have at least 'two thinks at a time', is perhaps most clearly illustrated in Derrida's account of the erasure of the 'trace' in *Of Grammatology*:

> The value of the transcendental *arche* (origin) must make its necessity felt before letting itself be erased. The concept of the arche-trace must comply with both that necessity and that erasure. It is in fact contradictory and not acceptable within the logic of identity. The trace is not only the disappearance of the origin . . . it means that the origin did not even disappear, that it was never constituted except reciprocally by a non-origin, the trace, which thus becomes the origin of the origin. (*Ibid.*)

In order to wrench the concept of the trace from the classical scheme which would derive it from an originary presence, Derrida declares it an 'undecidable' irreducible to the *either/or* logic of Western metaphysics. This logic was based on the logocentric practice of binary opposition and functioned according to three main principles: (1) the principle of identity (*A* is *A*); (2) the principle of non-contradiction (*A* cannot be non-*A*); and (3) the principle of the excluded middle (truth is either *A* or non-*A*). Derrida subverts this binary logic of *either/or* into a deconstructive logic of *both/and* – or to be more exact, of *neither/nor*. In this manner, he deconstructs decidable concepts into undecidable traces which are never identical with themselves, which harbour meanings other than themselves within themselves, thus contradicting themselves, differing from themselves, operating under erasure. Derrida speaks of setting to work within the texts of the history of philosophy 'undecidable' terms which can "no longer be included within philosophical (binary) opposition, resisting and disorganising it, without ever constituting a third term, without ever leaving room for a solution in the form of a speculative dialectics – the *pharmakon* (for instance) is neither remedy nor poison, neither good nor evil, neither speech nor writing . . . neither/nor, that is simultaneously either/or" (*Positions*).

But Derrida insists that his programme of deconstruction is not simply a nihilistic reduction of meaning to non-meaning. On the contrary, he affirms that it is a radical emancipation of meaning into a play of otherness – what he calls *alterity*. The fact that meaning always remains other than what we take it to mean does not condemn us to non-sense: such nihilism would be no more than a new form of dogmatism. What deconstruction certainly does denounce is the attempt to reduce the signifying process to a totalised system of absolute knowledge – to a meaning that could be possessed once and for all. In this respect, Derrida might be said to have developed to its ultimate consequence one of the basic discoveries of phenomenology: that meaning is always *other* than consciousness, extending infinitely beyond the self into the ever receding horizons of historical signification. By deconstructing transcendental subjectivity into the spatio-temporal play of language, Derrida does not do away with the subject altogether – as several of his critics and disciples have claimed; he simply opens the subject to its own desire for what is other than itself. The deconstructed subject is not pure negation; it is rather a ludic affirmation of self-differentiation. To those who would accuse him of annihilating the human subject or of incarcerating it within a nihilistic prison-house of language, Derrida delivers this defiant parting shot:

The subject is not some meta-linguistic substance or identity, some pure cogito of self-presence; it is always inscribed in language and this very inscription constitutes a form of liberty . . . for it shows the subject that it is not tied to a single identity or essence, but lives in language, as *differance*, and is therefore perpetually haunted by the 'other' . . . Deconstruction gives pleasure in that it gives desire. To deconstruct a text is to disclose how it functions as desire, as a search for presence and fulfillment which is interminably deferred. One cannot read without opening oneself to the desire of language, to the search for that which remains absent and other than oneself. Without a certain love of the text no reading would be possible. In every reading there is a *corps-à-corps* between reader and text, an in-corporation of the reader's desire into the desire of the text. Here is pleasure, the very opposite of that arid intellectualism of which deconstruction has so often been accused. (*Dialogues with Contemporary Continental Thinkers*).

APPENDIX:
DECONSTRUCTING PHENOMENOLOGY

In his first two major publications, *An Introduction to Husserl's Origin of Geometry* (1962) and *Speech and Phenomena* (1967), Derrida gives a deconstrucive reading of Husserl's philosophy of signification. He argues that phenomenology as a quest for radical origins and beginnings contains within itself the seeds of its own undoing – the possibility of its own self-overcoming. By indicating the structural self-conflict within Husserl's own texts, Derrida endeavours to retrieve the grammatological implications which Husserl himself often sought to suppress.

In *Speech and Phenomena* Derrida examines how the theory of meaning advanced by Husserl in the *Logical Investigations* rests upon an untenable opposition between 'expression' (*Ausdruck*) and 'indication' (*Anzeigen*). Husserl wishes to privilege expression which he relates to the models of *perception* and the *voice* as immediate intuitions of presence. To see or hear something is to intuit it in the fullness of its presence, without gaps or distances, that is, as a fulfillment of the intention of consciousness which aims at the 'thing itself'. By way of contrast, Husserl relates 'indication' to the inferior model of signification which always falls short of 'expression' in so far as the sign is an empty or non-intuitive intention (*une visée à vide*) which aims at the thing itself in its *absence*. (The sign 'table', for example, can indicate a table even if the object itself or the perceiving subject is no longer present). For the early Husserl, therefore, the pure intuition of essences requires a pure perception or expression devoid of signs which entail the function of non-presence. Language can only be intuitive to the extent that it suppresses its condition as a signifying *indication* and fulfils itself as immediate *expression*. "Signs as indicators (*Anzeichen*)", writes Husserl, "do not express anything." They are incapable of providing a pure intuition immediately present both to the object intended and the subject intending. They disrupt the pure self-identity of consciousness by introducing the indicative detour through distance and absence. The closest language can come to an intuition of the 'thing itself', according to Husserl, is by redeeming it from the written sign and restoring it to the immediacy of a self-present speech. In this respect, Husserl's hierarchical opposition of expression and indication corresponds to the tradition metaphysical opposition of the *phone* of speech and the *gramma* of writing.

Derrida claims that his own critical reading of Husserl in *Speech and Phenomena* first posed the decisive question "of the voice . . . such as it may be represented in the history of metaphysics and in the most modern critical, and vigilant form of metaphysics: Husserl's transcendental phenomenology" (*Positions*). Derrida suggests that Husserl's suspicious attitude to 'indication' as a menacing appendage to 'expression', springs from his fascination with the ideal of self-presence which he, true to the Western tradition of metaphysical idealism, locates in the silent voice (*phone*) of the transcendental subject's interior soliloquy. This self-identical voice is the ideal sign for Husserl because the "phenomenological essence of this operation [is] that *I hear and understand myself (je m'entends) at the same time that I speak*" (*Speech and Phenomena*). This operation of hearing oneself speak, of pure auto-affection, is, Derrida surmises, the basis of Husserl's ideal of transcendental subjectivity: the ideal of pure self-immediacy as absolute origin of meaning.

But Derrida argues that Husserl's own analysis occasionally undermines his priority of expression (*phone*) over indication (*gramma*). In several key passages Husserl is compelled to acknowledge that there is a sense which precedes expression, that meanings are always empty signifying intentions – indicating or aiming at presence – *before* they are fulfilled as perceptually intuited presences. Put in another way, the presence of an essential intuition presupposes an horizon of perspectival indications which aim at the still absent ideal of an invariant essence. Consequently, a phenomenology of presence requires that the *self-identity* of an 'expressive' perception be preceded by the *alterity* of an 'indicative' signification. Thus Husserl demonstrates, almost despite himself, that "non-perception precedes perception, the non-present inhabits the present" (*Speech and Phenomena*).

Signification can occur not only in the absence of the *object* it signifies (to say or write the word 'table' does not mean I actually see a table) but also of the *subject* that signifies (the word 'table' can function as a sign long after the departure or demise of myself as speaker). The transcendental ego, so cherished by Husserl as a self-identical presence, is debunked as an illusory product of a prior process of signification. Husserl's transcendental 'I' had sought to sustain itself as a timeless self-presence by constituting itself in the originary experience of a 'living present' (*Lebende Gegenwart*). But this living present cannot provide the autonomous sanctuary of pure auto-affection for, as Husserl's own phenomenological analysis showed, it is inhabited by temporal differences – that is, by the temporal 'retention' of a past trace (which is no longer) and the temporal 'protention' of a future trace (which is not yet). This temporal differentiation of the living present, as a repeatability of anterior or posterior traces, is what Derrida terms *arche-writing*. This writing 'older than speech' is defined as an inner distancing whereby each present sign is already spaced and temporalised by *other* signs. In this way, the transcendental interiority of self-presence is exploded, exteriorised, alienated from itself. Or as Derrida puts it, following the analysis of Emmanuel Levinas, self-identity is undermined by alterity.

This notion of a temporal distancing also accounts, Derrida submits, for the differential structure of *desire*. Desire implies the awareness of otherness. The desire for presence can only arise from a prior awareness of its absence, that is, from the dispersal of the self over time. The self can only attempt to be present to itself by first representing its absent past and future to itself in a 'living present' here and now. But this means that my presence presupposes the re-presentation of my absence. To try to recover ourselves from our temporal self-differentiation by the self-presence of an interior soliloquy is therefore self-defeating. For the very ideal of such 'expressive' speech in the living present already harbours within itself a temporal *differance* which possesses the alienating structure of *arche-writing*. Without this possibility of *differance*, Derrida claims, "the desire of presence as such would not find its breathing space. That means by the same token that this desire carries in itself the destiny of its own non-satisfaction" (*Of Grammatology*). We may say accordingly that *differance* produces what it forbids and forbids what it produces – that is, presence. Husserl's ideal of a pure transcendental speech, where the self could be identical with itself, is no more than a goal of endless signifying traces that can never be retraced to some original presence. It is, of necessity, a perpetually deferred goal, for self-presence is always shot through with traces of something *not-itself* – the otherness of past and future. The ideal of a timeless self-identity is a product of temporal differences. Presence, and the living present which founds it, are no more than fictions created by *differance*.

By showing how Husserl's own analysis reveals, in spite of itself, the way in which alterity and differ*a*nce is presupposed by the very notion of presence, Derrida is able to quote Husserl against himself, ruling out of order his claim that a silent interior monologue would provide a pure self-communication uncontaminated by alien signs. In this manner, he is able to conclude that Husserl's very ideal of intuitive speech is based upon the non-intuitive structure of writing:

> The absence of intuition – and therefore of the subject of the intuition is not only *tolerated* by speech; it is *required* by the general structure of signification, when considered *in itself*. It is radically requisite; the total absence of the subject and the object of a statement – the death of the writer and/or the disappearance of the object he was able to describe – does not prevent a text from 'meaning' something. On the contrary, this possibility gives birth to meaning as such, gives it out to be heard and read. (*Speech and Phenomena*).

In his polemical and pioneering *Introduction* to Husserl's *The Origin of Geometry* (appendix 6 of *The Crisis of European Science and Transcendental Phenomenology*, 1934–7), Derrida offers another deconstructive reading of his phenomenological mentor. Here he focuses less on the phonocentric essences of subjectivity than on the logocentric essences of scientific and historical traditions. In *Positions*, Derrida points out that in this *Introduction*, his first work published in 1962, "the problematic of writing was already in place . . . and bound to the irreducible structure of '*différer*' in its relationships to consciousness, presence, science, history and the history of science, the disappearance or deferral of the origin, etc.".

In *The Origin of Geometry*, Husserl had posed the problem of how the essences of geometry, as ideal scientific objectivities, first arise in history. Derrida shows that Husserl is ultimately compelled to avow, however obliquely and reluctantly, that this ideal logos is in fact *produced* by history – that is, history understood as an intersubjective process of temporal repetition which depends upon a worldly *inscription* of meaning (i.e. in documents and texts). Thus the possibility of scientific objectivity presupposes the historical activity of intersubjective reason which in turn presupposes writing as the possibility of infinite repeatability over historical time. The *logos* of reason, Derrida observes accordingly, "differs from itself in order to reappropriate itself". The *logos* cannot contemplate itself in the pure here-and-now of a Living Present; it can only hold on to itself and preserve itself by means of an historical self-differentiation which permits it to retain the past and project a future. But precisely as historical self-differentiation, the ideal *logos* of geometry is also a self-postponement. Without this consciousness of delay or deferment, geometry as the possibility of history would be impossible. There is no such thing, therefore, as some timeless or absolute origin of geometry which might be recovered in its pristine purity. The very idea of an origin which precedes history is itself a product of history, a teleological project that is perpetually deferred. "The originary

Differance of the absolute Origin", writes Derrida, "is perhaps what has always been said through the concept of the '*transcendental*' . . . this strange procession [ahead of itself] of a '*Rückfrage*' [questioning back] is the movement sketched in *The Origin of Geometry*" (*Introduction*).

Once again, we find Derrida pitting Husserl against himself. In a series of close textual readings, he shows how Husserl's attempt to locate the ideal 'origin' of objective essences – such as geometry or mathematics – in a transcendental subjectivity which antedates or transcends history is fundamentally contradictory. Husserl himself was obliged to admit that the timeless and ahistorical character of the 'universal' laws of geometry could only be assured by historical repetition (*Wiederholung*). For he acknowledged that it is only through the mediation of language – or more exactly, through the inscription of the signifying intentions of the geometer in written documents – that geometry could be supposed to transcend the signifying consciousness of the historically situated geometer in order to assume the permanent status of an essential law. By 'fixing' the signification of geometry, writing allows it to be reiterated again and again throughout history. And it is by virtue of this reiterability of the signification at different historical periods, distanced in time and space, that the signification can presume to be the same and to supersede history. In short, the essence of geometry depends upon the various re-readings and reinscriptions of different geometrical thinkers who attempted to rethink the original essence of its laws – Euclid, Copernicus, Newton, Husserl and so on. But since this history of geometry is also the history of the representation of its representations it cannot be reduced to an original presence. The ideal of a timeless origin is itself a product of temporal repetition; it is at all times dependent on an historical *Lebenswelt* which retrieves it from the past and projects it forward again into the future.

Derrida concludes accordingly that the *origin* of geometry remains for Husserl an open-ended goal which various historical consciousnesses aim at without ever realising it in a full intuitive presence. The essence of geometry is not to be found in an origin at all but in the historical repetition of the signifying projection of a *telos* – of an endlessly deferred end. Husserl's search for an absolute presuppositionless origin thus cancels itself out. The very idea of origin is shown to have presupposed its own future. Presence dissolves into its own self-postponement.

In a series of critical essays in *Writing and Difference* (1967), and *Margins of Philosophy* (1972), Derrida interprets Heidegger's project to 'overcome' (*überwinden*) metaphysics as a logical consequence of Husserl's failure to recover an absolute origin of meaning. Heidegger's practice of putting

Being under erasure (*sous rature*), particularly in late texts such as *The Saying of Anaximander* (1950), is singled out for special attention. Derrida remarks how the question of Being became for Heidegger a non-conceptualisable quest for a presence that can never be more than a self-cancelling trace of itself. The later Heidegger's strategy of crossing-out 'Being' whenever he wrote it expressed a conviction that this self-eliminating textual sign was the only means by which conceptual language could indicate presence.

The history of Being is thus read by Derrida, taking his cue from Heidegger, as a *palimpsest* whose ever-receding textual traces can never be brought to halt in an origin or end. Derrida extends this notion of metaphysics into the corresponding metaphor of a *white mythology*. Metaphysics is a white mythology, he contends, precisely because it has forgotten its own mythological derivation; because it has covered over or whitewashed those metaphorising figurations which gave rise to its concepts. And it has done this in order to present them as pure and distinct ideas capable of a direct intuition of Being. Derrida approves the Heideggerean observation that the founding concepts of Western metaphysics – *Theoria, Arche, Eidos, Eschaton* etc. – are no more than faded metaphors of reappropriation: that is, metaphors of ground-foundation or home-return which signify a desire to recover lost origins or transcend time towards a final vision of presence.

In his essay 'White Mythology' in *Margins of Philosophy* (1972), Derrida elaborates on this equation between metaphysics and worn-out metaphor. He denounces the self-concealing metaphoricity of metaphysics as a kind of usury (the French term *usure* also means to wear out) which exploits a 'linguistic surplus-value' to produce the fetish of conceptual presence. Derrida pushes Heidegger's project of deconstruction to the point where we can begin to uncover the *unthought* collusion between metaphysical suppression and covered-over metaphor. He analyses how concepts arise when metaphors fade away. Since metaphoricity is masked in the production of conceptuality, Derrida unmasks concepts so as to lay bare the hidden play of metaphors from which they first derive. He thus reveals how metaphysical idealisation results from the effacing of a prior metaphorical process. This process itself accounts for the metaphysical activity of transporting or carrying beyond (*meta-phorein*) – i.e. transporting the visible into the invisible, the sensible into the intelligible, nature into spirit, darkness into light, the immanent into the transcendent, and so on. In short, the production of metaphysical ideas requires the erasure of those figural traces which produced them. "It is metaphysics", states Derrida, "which has effaced in itself that fabulous scene which brought it into being, and which yet remains, active and stirring, inscribed in white ink, an invisible drawing covered over in the palimpsest" ('White Mythology').

On the basis of such intricate observations, Derrida concludes that metaphysics is a metaphorical cover-up. But its metaphoricity can only be metaphorically stated. We cannot have a conceptual theory of metaphor; for there is no place *outside* of metaphor which could include under its order the field to which it belongs. The foundational concepts of metaphysics – *Theoria, Eidos, Logos* etc. – are themselves metaphors. Even the concept of metaphor is itself a metaphor (*meta-phora*, to carry or transport beyond). Derrida confesses therefore that there is no 'logocentric' principle for delimiting or fixing metaphor. It is absolutely uncontrollable – a free play of figuration.

From Heidegger's equation of metaphysics and metaphoricity, Derrida learned that "language bears within itself the necessity of its own critique" (*Writing and Difference*). By detecting and unravelling the suppressed figural play of texts, Derrida turns language against itself, liberating the suppressed orders of its meaning, laying bare those gaps (*failles*) where the text transgresses its own conceptual system, where its 'linguistic unconscious' operates. Metaphysical language is a prime suspect for Derrida's detective work since it mistakes its figurative metaphors for literal concepts (thus repressing their signifying function as 'indications' of a presence through absence).

Already Heidegger had tried to deconstruct metaphysics by retracing the idea of Being to the temporalising process of signification which precedes it. He called this the hermeneutic circle where the question of Being always refers back to the trace of a precomprehension or foreunderstanding of this question. By crossing out the word 'Being' and letting both the deletion and the word stand in contradiction – B~~ein~~g – Heidegger contrived to use the language of metaphysics to overcome metaphysics. This much at least Derrida learned from Heidegger. And we find him speaking approvingly of a "discourse which borrows from a heritage, the resources necessary for the deconstruction of that heritage itself" (*Writing and Difference*). By means of this strategy, Heideggerean deconstruction had revealed the sign 'Being' to be a trace which indicates presence only in and through absence. This process Derrida refers to as *supplementarity*: 'Being' as a trace is precisely that which supplements absence in the sense of both adding to and standing in for an absence. "The indefinite process of supplementarity has already infiltrated presence", writes Derrida, "has always already inscribed there a space of repetition and the splitting of the self (over time)" (*Of Grammatology*). The placing of 'Being' *under erasure* exposes it as no more than a trace or supplement of its own absence, as an endless difference which can never be recuperated into a presence. In short, the deconstructive scruple of *sous rature* explodes the presumption that metaphysics knows the solution to the riddle or can name the unnameable differ*a*nce. Derrida's deconstructive conclusion to his reading of Heidegger in the essay 'Differance', is instructive in this regard:

> "Older" than Being itself, our language has no name for such a differance. But we "already know" that if it is unnameable, this is not simply provisional; it is not because our language has still not found or received this *name*, or because we would have to look for it in another language, outside the finite system of our language. It is because there is no *name* for this – not even essence or Being – not even the name 'differance', which is not a name, which is not a pure nominal unity, and continually breaks up in a chain of different substitutions . . . There will be no unique name, nor even the name of Being. It must be conceived without *nostalgia*; that is, it must be conceived outside the myth of the purely maternal or paternal language belonging to the lost fatherland of thought. On the contrary we must *affirm* it . . . with a certain laughter and with a certain dance. ('Differance' in *Speech and Phenomena*)

CRITICAL THEORY

Georg Lukács

Georg Lukács is generally considered one of the most significant cultural theorists of our century and perhaps the most original Marxist thinker to emerge in Europe since Marx. His intellectual formation is somewhat unique in that he was influenced by both 'Western' and 'Eastern' European movements of thought. He has received the highest critical acclaim from authors as ideologically diverse as Jean-Paul Sartre, Thomas Mann and George Steiner.

Lukács was born to an aristocratic Jewish family in 1885 in Budapest, then a powerful cultural centre of the Austro-Hungarian Empire. He obtained a doctorate in philosophy in Budapest University in 1906. His first two works – *The History of the Evolution of the Modern Drama* and *Soul and Form* – were rather romantic and esoteric exercises in philosophical aesthetics; both were originally written in his native Hungarian and published in 1911. Lukács travelled to Germany while still a young man and pursued his studies at the universities of Berlin and of Heidelberg. Most of his philosophical works after this period were written in German. It was, moreover, during these formative years in German academic circles that Lukács came under the influence of the critical philosophy of neo-Kantianism, particularly of Heinrich Rickert, and the life-philosophy (*Lebensphilosophie*) of Dilthey which was prevalent at the time. From the Heidelberg school of neo-Kantianism, Lukács learned that the fundamental questions of truth pertain to a moral and aesthetic intuition irreducible to the empirical positivism of the natural sciences. Not surprisingly this rather 'idealist' doctrine left Lukács favourably disposed to Dilthey's famous distinction between the *Geisteswissenschaften* (the sciences of the spirit – the human sciences) and the *Naturwissenschaften* (the natural sciences).

Between 1910 and 1920 Lukács also became familiar with the 'intuitionist' philosophies of neo-Hegelian and Husserlian phenomenology which enjoyed considerable favour in the German universities of the time. Both of these philosophies confirmed Dilthey's conviction that the laws of human understanding were ultimately independent of causal explanation – as practiced by the positive sciences – and required a more spiritual act of lived 'empathic' intuition. All of these 'idealist' philosophies seem to have taught Lukács at least one enduring lesson – that the history of the human spirit (*Geistesgeschichte*) could not be explained away in terms of a general methodology of neutral or ahistorical 'facts'.

The first noticeable shift in Lukács early thought came in the transition from what he described as the 'subjective idealism' of neo-Kantianism to the 'objective idealism' of Hegelian phenomenology. This latter position held that our objective knowledge of reality is constituted by a dialectical act of consciousness governed, in turn, by the historical experience of Spirit. It was this initial transition which paved the way for his first internationally renowned work on literary theory, *The Theory of the Novel* (1920). This book contained an incisive critique of the decadence of bourgeois liberalism and already signalled the second major shift of Lukács' thought, in the twenties, to an original sythesis of left-wing 'realist' Hegelianism and Marxist humanism – a philosophical synthesis best represented by his monumental *History and Class Consciousness* (1923). Lukács subsequent and final commitment to a Marxist theory of art and culture resulted in a series of radically innovative works ranging from *The Historical Novel* (1955) to *The Meaning of Contemporary Realism* (1958).

But Lukács' intellectual career was equally informed by the concrete political experience of his early years. This impressed upon him that 'contemplation' and 'speculation' were not in themselves enough; that spiritual liberation had to be accompanied by a correlative material liberation from the constraints of social oppression. Profoundly disillusioned with the failure of the Western bourgeois intelligentsia to respond to the crisis in European society which gave rise to the First World War, Lukács saw the Russian Revolution of 1917 as offering the possibility of a new beginning. He joined the Communist Party of Hungary in 1918 and served as a Deputy People's Commissar for Education in Béla Kun's Hungarian Soviet Republic in 1919. After the rapid collapse of this socialist government, Lukács was compelled to seek exile in Austria, Germany and later in the Soviet Union. From 1930 to 1944 he worked at the Marx-Engels Institute in Moscow and remained an exponent of communist ideology, though at times his thinking brought him into conflict with the orthodox Stalinist party. Lukács returned to Budapest and gave spirited support to the short lived revolution of 1956–7, serving as a Minister of Culture. On account of this involvement, he subsequently forfeited his chair at the University of Budapest and was expelled from the Communist Party. Exiled in Roumania for a short time, Lukács returned to Budapest and died there in 1971.

I

It was during his period of exile in Vienna in the early twenties that Lukács completed his celebrated studies in Hegelian Marxism collected under the general title of *History and Class Consciousness*. Lukács' experience of the Russian Revolution and of Béla Kun's Hungarian uprising had convinced him of the central Marxist principle, enunciated in the eleventh thesis on Feuerbach, that men are not only the 'interpreters' of history – as the idealist philosophers believed – but the 'makers' of it. It was appropriate, therefore, that Lukács' first work of political theory should seek to identify the guiding laws and forces which enabled men to make their own history rather than merely suffer it as passive or manipulated victims. Here Lukács endorsed Marx's belief that class consciousness and class struggle are the living forces of historical transformation and that the privileged agency of such transformation is the proletariat. The originality of Lukács' approach was to reinject a strong dose of left-wing Hegelian dialectics back into Marxist theory, then in danger of becoming a positivist system akin to that of the natural sciences.

Lukács was critical of Engels' positivist reading of Marxism in the *Anti-Duhring* and later in his career took a decisive stand against the determinist orthodoxies of what he called the 'official Marxism' promoted by Stalin and Zhdanov. He believed that these reductionist versions of Marxism ignored the creative role of human consciousness and decision and thus deformed the original insight of Marx into the dynamic relationship between theory and practice. This deformation represented what Lukács termed a 'second crisis' *internal* to Marxism and comparable to the first crisis of capitalism which was external to it. In an inteview entitled 'The twin crises', published in 1970 just one year before his death, Lukács spoke of his life work from the 1920s onward as a contribution to the 'struggle for the renewal of Marxism'. This struggle aimed at a 'transition from a non-democratic Stalinist system to socialist democracy' and depended on a 'revival of Marxist theory' based on a refusal of the orthodox 'economism' which reduced Marx to a 'professional economist'. Enlisting Lenin's and Rosa Luxemburg's emphasis on the active role of human will and intervention, Lukács confirmed the view expressed in the former's *What is to be Done?* that there can be no revolution without a *theory* of revolution. Indeed Lukács maintained that without a 'renewal' of Marxist theory the problems of modern capitalism in the advanced industrial countries of the West, as well as the problems in the post-revolutionary socialist countries of the East, would remain unresolved. 'Without the necessary renewal of theory', Lukács wrote, 'there can be none of practice'

('The Twin Crises' in *Marxism and Human Liberation*, 1973). He thus laid one of the keystones of the intellectual movement of the 'New Left'.

Lukács held that this great renewal could be assisted by forming a new alliance between the dialectical insights of Hegel (whom he described as the 'last great bourgeois thinker') and the revolutionary insights of Marx (the first great post-bourgeois thinker) into the historical reality of class struggle. In this way, Lukács endeavoured to transmute Hegel's dynamically unfolding World-Spirit into a Marxist dialectic of historical transformation which would unite the subjective virtues of consciousness and freedom with the objective laws of man's socio-economic condition. Inspired by such a renewed understanding of historical reality, the revolutionary class-consciousness of the proletariat overcomes the age-old metaphysical oppositions between subjectivity and objectivity, mind and matter, theory and practice.

Lukács wrote *History and Class Consciousness* to retrieve dialectical materialism from the positivism which dominated European thinking, East and West, at the turn of the century. It has been hailed by the New Left critic, Lucien Goldmann, as a 'major event in the evolution of Marxist thought'. In this work, Lukács argued that meaning is *neither* something simply created by the human subject over and against the real objective world (as the transcendental idealism of Kant maintained), *nor* something determined by anonymous laws of natural causality, but a 'potential' for human praxis and consciousness residing within this world as *history*. Lukács held that Marx's most valuable discovery was that history is a mediating dialectic capable of conjugating human understanding and the concrete world of praxis. Parting company with the phenomenologists, Lukács declared that everything that men do is 'historical'; and that they do it not just as isolated 'authentic' individuals but as a 'collective subject' whose commitment to the 'objective possibility' of historical liberation derives from their social consciousness of being a universal class – that is, the proletariat. Lukács was developing here, of course, Marx's definition of the proletariat as "a class which is the dissolution of all classes . . . which has a universal character because its sufferings are universal . . . and which can only redeem itself by a total redemption of humanity" (*Contribution to the Critique of Hegel's Philosophy of Right*).

Repudiating those who reduced Marxism to a dogmatic system of empirically determined facts, Lukács sets out in *History and Class Consciousness* to redefine Marxism as a 'dialectical method' which permits theory to become a 'material force' of practice. The essential aim of dialectical materialism is, he maintains, 'to convert theory into a vehicle of revolution'. But this should not be misinterpreted as a blind, irrational surrender to some inevitable law of historical progress. If theoretical consciousness requires to be translated into practice, the reverse is equally necessary. Lukács affirms this to be the meaning of Marx's enigmatic statement in a letter to Ruge that "reality must also strive towards thought" and that "it will then be realized that the world has long since possessed something in the form of a dream which it need only take possession of consciously in order to possess it in reality". Lukács contends, therefore, that it is only when consciousness discovers itself (as 'subjective possibility') in reality (as 'objective possibility') that theory and praxis can at last be reconciled.

Consequently, if the Hegelian dialectic must be superseded because of its 'idealist' emphasis on the autonomous powers of consciousness, the 'scientistic' dialectic of Engels must also be superseded in so far as it suspends the role of the subject altogether and sponsors a rigid causality which ignores the interaction of subject and object as dialectical counterparts of the historical process. In other words, while metaphysical idealism failed to 'change reality' by confining the transformative power of theory to a purely subjective consciousness, positivistic Marxism fails to provide the key to changing reality by assuming that it unfolds according to its own determinist laws independently of human initiative or intervention. In both cases, the dialectical method is betrayed in that theory and praxis remain radically divorced.

The so-called 'facts' of history are for Lukács, never simply 'pure data' for scientific observation and computation. They are always already invested with human consciousness and labour, that is, 'interpreted' in the light of the 'totality' of human relations with reality – a totality which is none other than the 'historical dialectic' itself. The dialectical concept of 'totality' was one of Lukács' most crucial contributions to the Marxist debate. "The blinkered empiricist", writes Lukács, "believes that every piece of data from economic life, every statistic, every raw event already constitutes an important fact. In so doing, he forgets that however simple an enumeration of 'facts' may be, however lacking in commentary, it already implies an 'interpretation' " (*History and Class Consciousness*). By drawing a sharp dividing line between the isolated facts of 'objective' science, on the one hand, and the images and ideas of 'subjective' consciousness, on the other, idealists and postivists alike fail to appreciate the dynamic transformative tendencies with which the factual world is charged. Thus, for example, we find the 'facts' of the capitalist system being regarded fatalistically as *what is given*; and in this way reality is divested of its human potential for historical change or revolution. "In the teeth of all these isolated and isolating facts and partial systems", counters Lukács, "dialectics insists on the concrete unity of the whole" (*History and Class Consciousness*). For it is only in a dialectical context which recognises the autonomous facts of our world as *interrelated* aspects of a socio-historical process, thereby integrating them into a dialectical totality, that "knowledge of the facts becomes knowledge of *reality*". For Lukács reality is dialectical precisely because it is a synthesis of diverse elements. He invokes here Marx's dictum that 'the relations of production of every society form a whole'. The dialectical materialism of Marx, he insists, departs from all previous forms of materialism by affirming that material reality is not some static impersonal object but a dynamic human activity. And by the same token, Lukács is determined to distinguish this dialectical materialism from the 'vulgar Marxism' practised by many of Marx's successors.

II

One of the major obstacles to the dialectical process is what Lukács calls the phenomenon of 'reification'. This involves the practice of reducing men to the condition of 'things' (*res*). Though the term 'reification' is original to Lukács, he maintains that its sense ultimately derives from Marx's sketch of 'commodity fetishism' in the opening chapter of the first volume of *Capital*. Marx critically exposed the fetishisation of commodities which takes place in capitalist societies where the creative labour of men is alienated in their 'expropriated' produce. This alienation occurs to the extent that man's produce is artificially removed from its origin in the human *value* of labour and presented in the market place by exploitative employers as some quasi-magical 'merchandise' – commodities whose only recognized value is that of *exchange*. Commodities are fetishised therefore – that is, assume a quasi-magical character – because they appear to generate relations amongst themselves in the realm of exchange. And by the same token, the economic laws of exchange displace and disguise the *real* relations of workers with consumers, with one another and with the available productive resources. Man – both as producer and consumer of commodities – thus becomes passive before the laws of the economy.

The fetishisation of commodities parallels the transposition of real human value into imaginary money value. Or as the young Marx puts it in his *Paris Manuscript* (1844) on 'Money', we are involved here with an inversion of the true relationship of things, for money acts as a magico-mystical alchemy which makes 'impossibilities fraternise' (e.g. through money the ignorant man can presume to buy himself wisdom, the ugly man to buy himself a beautiful wife and so on). Fetishisation involves the analogous translation of the real value of human labour into the imaginary value of commodities. In this way human beings are alienated from the fruits of their labour, which now appear as 'things in themselves' – as if they had originated from nowhere or simply dropped out of the skies onto the market place.

Lukács developed Marx's seminal sketch of 'fetishism'. He took it to be a generalisable category for the fate of consciousness under a capitalist economy where the human *quality* of labour is treated solely in terms of numerical *quantity*. Lukács' use of the term 'reification' refers indirectly to the fetishisation of market commodities and directly to the alienation of human consciousness as it becomes something abstracted, isolated, frozen, dehumanised – a passive spectator of its own alienated labour, bereft of its productive rapport with the social totality. When the commodity is *fetishised*, consciousness is *reified*. Capitalism contrives, accordingly, to isolate both the commodity and consciousness in order to deny their dialectical interaction in the totality of social relations. Once this interaction is exposed then so also is the manipulative exploitation and alienation of the capitalist system. Fetishism and reification are two sides of the same capitalist coin (the former emphasising the false elevation of things to the condition of human consciousness, the latter focusing on the false reduction of human consciousness to the condition of things). And Lukács observes that this reciprocal process of falsification is increasingly evidenced in the growing quantification, specialisation and division of labour in advanced industrial society.

In *History and Class Consciousness* Lukács outlines a detailed dialectic between 'real consciousness' (which he defines as the actual self-awareness of an individual or group within the practical limits of a particular class) and 'possible consciousness' (which refers to a class's collective consciousness of its 'objective possibilities' of historical realisation). Real and possible consciousness coalesce in the praxis of the proletariat and thereby surpass the false consciousness of ideology towards a dialectical consciousness of the *social totality*. Lukács charts here a series of evolving gradations of 'totality' ranging from the 'relative totality' of the existing relations between classes as a social process, to the larger 'historical totality' of the relations between this relative totality itself and the nature of reality as a whole. Lukács' category of 'totality' is intended, therefore, not as some homogenous totalitarian system, but as a dynamic dialectic of structuration and destructuration ceaselessly evolving towards the global socialist goal of history.

Not surprisingly, Lukács was denounced by the Soviet Stalinist party as a 'revisionist'. He was accused of trading in progressive 'scientific' Marxism for an anthropological pseudo-Marxism of left-wing Hegelian provenance.

In short, the Stalinists saw Lukács as transposing Marxism back into a dialectical idealism which amounted to little more than 'utopian activism' – a term used by the 'official' Marxists for *petit-bourgeois* anarchism. Lukács suffered bitterly from these condemnations by the Communist Party; but despite several rather clumsy attempts to 'recant' – as in his half-hearted 1967 preface to *History and Class Consciousness* where he reproached his earlier 'subjectivism' – Lukács was to remain at heart an Hegelian Marxist to the last. (Though it is true that his rejection of the early claim that the proletariat represents the identical subject-object of history was due more to his reading of Marx's *Paris Manuscript*, first published in German in the thirties, than to any external political pressures). His mature book on Hegel, published as late as 1948, took a firm stand against the prevailing orthodoxy – first promoted by Zhdanov – by arguing for a direct continuity between Hegel and Marx.

Perhaps Lukács' single most original contribution to the whole Marxist debate, and certainly the one which made him most enemies on both sides of the ideological divide, was his contention that the philosophical truth of the dialectical method transcended the old antithesis between idealism and materialism. The highest form of historical consciousness – ushered in by the revolutionary proletariat who had become masters of their own labour productivity and intellectual creativity – must, Lukács believed, surpass all such rigid and absolutist oppositions. Otherwise, Marxism could not overcome the traditional forms of historical alienation; nor could it lay claim to the status of a 'dialectical synthesis' representing what Lukács termed the 'concrete totality of history'. It is in the name of such a dialectical synthesis that we find Lukács denouncing *both* the mechanistic materialism of the Soviet positivists *and* the decadent bourgeois idealisms of Western existentialism and modernism.

III

Though Lukács' initial celebrity as an intellectual was occasioned by the publication of *History and Class Consciousness*, he is arguably more reputed today for his writings on literature and culture. This is particularly so in the West where his reputation as an aesthetic theorist has flourished in recent years.

Lukács' early romantic idealist works – most notably *Soul and Form* (1911) – expressed a belief that there existed an incorrigible disjunction between art (as meaningful) and life (as meaningless). This attitude was radically revised, however, after his conversion to Marxism. In his Marxist writings on aesthetics, published after 1920, Lukács insists that art's role is essentially 'realist', reflecting the intrinsic patterns and possibilities of historical action. Common to both art and life, claims the mature Lukács, is the power to transform the events of our social experience into explicit 'narrative' sequences. Art is now seen as a forceful reminder that man has the power to tell a story and thus interpret his own creative role in the total process of history. Lukács' dialectical theory of literature maintains that narrative forms both reflect existing social structures and project alternative ones. The primary aim of literary form, it contends, is to heighten our consciousness of (i) social praxis and (ii) of the teleological-revolutionary project of integrated narrative unity between man and nature which motivates such praxis.

Lukács believed that the work of art goes beyond both religion and science by virtue of its progressive powers of 'mediation' – that is, its capacity to mirror and prefigure a possible synthesis between the traditional divisions of subject and object, man and nature, consciousness and reality, the individual and society. His commitment to the idea of a dialectical rapport between consciousness and reality, for example, is witnessed in his revision of Aristotle's notion of art as imitation (*mimesis*). In the *Poetics*, Aristotle had defined art as the 'imitation of an action'. This signified a mode of representation which augments and redescribes the 'universal' dimension of the contingent particularities of history. Lukács reinterprets this model as a dialectical *practice* that reconciles the subjective consciousness of the maker with the objective realities latent in nature. He dialectises the realist mode of *mimesis*. And the resulting 'realist dialectics' is clearly evidenced in such aesthetic writings as *Theory of the Novel* (1920), *Studies in European Realism* (1935–39) and *The Meaning of Contemporary Realism* (1958).

In *Theory of the Novel*, Lukács traces the way in which the 'mimetic' relationship between the art work and society – or what he alternatively calls 'essence' and 'life' – originated in the aesthetic forms of ancient Greece and subsequently evolved in dialectical fashion. He identifies three principal genres of Greek art: (i) the *epic* genre in which 'essence' as artistically represented, and 'life' as concretely experienced, are considered to be one continuous whole; (ii) the *tragic* genre in which the aesthetic essence and social existence are experienced as separate and even opposed phenomena, e.g. when the hero's moment of insight proffers a brief glimpse of some 'fulfilment' or 'truth' which society and nature refuse him; (iii) the *Platonic* genre in which the rupture between the meaninglessness of existing material reality and the meaning projected by our aesthetic and spiritual intuitions of truth, becomes an unbridgeable divide – the latter being consigned to a transcendent otherworld of immutable Ideas.

Lukács considers the modern 'realist' novel as an attempt to recover the narrative continuity between spiritual essence and material life which Greek epic enjoyed in a primitive and limited way. The fundamental difference between the epic and novelistic vision of continuity, however, is that in the latter it is no longer the gods but men who seek to secure the unity of essence and life. The narrative of the realist novel represents a quest structure without the guaranteed resolution of a providential deity. The hero must invent meaning *ex nihilo*, as it were, drawing from the sole resources of his own consciousness and desire; he can no longer expect to receive it as a pre-established gift from the gods. In fact, the novel as narrative is a *formal* act of creation whose *thematic* content is precisely the quest of a hero to invent narrative coherence for his solitary and fragmented existence in a society devoid of meaning. The great realist novels, Lukács argues accordingly, are attempts to reconcile, in fiction at least, the disjunction between subjective consciousness and objective reality – a disjunction which the history of class-division, particularly acute in the capitalist era in which the novel genre arises, has brought about.

Lukács analyses how 'realist' novels characteristically begin with a description of actual social alienation which the individual hero desires to overcome by discovering the possibility of a new 'reconciled' order. The novel thus unfolds as an open-ended quest which moves toward the *goal* of unified experience (an experience presupposed by the primitive epic as its *starting point*). While the epic saw unity as an objective property of a divinely orchestrated cosmos, the novel portrays it as a subjective project of human consciousness which is never fully realised. But where the heroes and heroines of novels fail to reconcile consciousness and reality, the novelist succeeds in partial manner. For the novelist achieves a *formal* narrative reordering of real experience. In this respect, Lukács emphasises the 'utopian' character of all great 'realist' novels. Thus in later works, he will argue that such exercises in narrative ordering constitute a structural *anticipation* of a coalescence of consciousness and life; and that as such, they prefigure that historical unity of experience which may ultimately be realised through the revolutionary praxis of the proletariat. The conflict of the novel is, so to speak, an exercise in shadow-boxing which prepares us for the real revolutionary struggle to come.

Lukács outlines a typological classification of the novel in terms of three main categories. First, there is the novel of *abstract idealism*. Lukács cites Cervantes' *Don Quixote* as an example. Here the hero still inhabits a quasi-metaphysical world of magic and superstition and he embarks on a series of picturesque adventures through the objective spatial world of nature, assuming that meaning can be found in the *here and now*. Second,

we have the novel of *romantic disillusionment*. This category is best represented by Flaubert's *Education Sentimentale* where the hero seeks his
solution in a wish-fulfilling journey through subjective time, harkening
back to a past world that no longer exists or forward to a future world that
does not yet exist. Either way, the romantic novel works towards a transcendence of the here and now. The action takes place within the contemplative
or confessional consciousness of the hero or heroine. Lastly, there are
novels which approach the category of *social realism*. Here the quest
through subjective time is presented as a reflection of historical time, that
is, of the collective shared time of mankind. Lukács cites instances of this
kind of dialectical mediation between individual and universal values –
surpassing the limits of naive idealism and romanticism – in certain works
of Tolstoy, Goethe and Dostoyevsky. Moreover, Lukács argues that in
'realist' novels there is the suggestion that the ultimate form of neo-epic
reconciliation between the human spirit and nature is attainable through
the dialectical process of history. But this final unity of 'essence' and 'life',
Lukács insists, can only be achieved in historical reality by transforming not
just the narrative form of fiction but the very productive forms and forces of
society itself.

Lukács first adumbrates the 'utopian' perspective of the realist novel in
Theory of the Novel. But it is in later writings such as *The Historical Novel*
(1955) or *The Meaning of Contemporary Realism* (1958) that he spells out its
implications. In his famous essay on Dostoyevsky, for example, Lukács
praises his depiction of 'the psychological and moral dialectic of concrete
actions' (e.g. the violence and deprivation of his angst-ridden heroes) as a
utopian protest against the alienation of bourgeois society. Approving the
quest-motivation of Dostoyevsky's characters – 'they are all as if at a railway
station' – he goes on to affirm that while Dostoyevsky was the first to portray
'the mental deformations that are brought about as a social necessity by life
in a modern city', his real genius consisted 'precisely in his power of
recognizing and representing the dynamism of a future social, moral and
psychological evolution from germs of something barely beginning'.
Lukács can conclude, therefore, that Dostoyevsky 'does not confine
himself to description and analysis . . . but offers also a genesis, a didactic
and a perspective'.

The later Lukács characterises narrative plots and styles as 'realist' to the
extent that they reflect both the determining social forces during a certain
historical period and the dynamic tendencies implanted in the social
environment by human praxis. 'Realist' works penetrate deeper than the
contingent appearances of our alienated world in order to represent the

potential of society for historical transformation. Thus nineteenth-century realist authors such as Balzac or Tolstoy are thought by Lukács to contribute to the overall project of 'dereifying' human consciousness, permitting us to acknowledge our creative capacities for political liberation.

In *The Historical Novel*, Lukács establishes a 'typology' which defines 'realist' characters, such as Goethe's Werther or Dostoyevsky's Raskolnikov, as dialectical mediations between concrete psychological individuality and a universal essence which 'imitates' the collective consciousness of mankind. The 'significant forms' of a realist novel will thus correspond in some 'typical' way to the social consciousness, real or virtual, of the class ideology which it 'reflects' – the bourgeoisie for Balzac or Scott, the peasants for Tolstoy, the dispossessed or disaffected criminals for Dostoyevsky and so on. The genuine function of the arts, Lukács contends, is the reflection of the 'objective truth' of any given historical period; and the task of the literary theorist is to clarify 'the relation between ideology (in the sense of *Weltanschauung*) and artistic creation'.

Lukács' notion of 'realism' draws from both the Eastern model of 'socialist realism' and the Western model of 'critical realism'. As such it has nothing to do with photographic naturalism or the allegorical representationalism of a crude one-to-one correspondence between character and stereotype. These are deformations of realism which Lukács criticises in Zola and again in modernist authors such as Joyce and Kafka (where reality is reduced to the random impressions of a decadent bourgeois consciousness). For Lukács the characters of a genuinely realist work are 'typical' only in the sense that they mirror the ideological forces of social change prevalent in a particular moment of historical transition. Thus, Tolstoy's Anna Karenin, to take a favourite example, lives out in a coherent if tragic manner, the covert social contradictions of her class at a decisive historical juncture.

This definition of historical realism accounts for Lukács' deep antipathy towards the modernist practice of symbolism. He denounced this modernist strategy for emptying characters and events of their real historical substance, fetishising them as autonomous signs of some ineffable meaning. Lukács holds that the effect of such symbolising practices in the work of Gide, Lawrence or Joyce is to drain reality of its dialectical content and transform it into a nihilistic allegory whose final end is an impotent solipsism of absolute subjectivity. Thus in his controversial essay on 'The ideology of modernism' in *The Meaning of Contemporary Realism*, we find Lukács castigating modernism as a decadent contemplation of nothingness. He locates its philosophical expression in the existentialist pessimism of philosophers such as Heidegger and the early Sartre – thinkers who assumed that the ontological constitution of human subjectivity condemns us to perpetual alienation irrespective of the historical evolution of society. Taking its cue from such an existentialist ideology, modernism totally ignores the fact that human anguish is a symptom of the decadent phase of capitalism. Whether it is aware of doing so or not, it seduces its readers into a reactionary contemplation of nothingness and despair.

Modernist literature represents, for Lukács, a regression to the metaphysical and ahistorical universe of 'abstract idealism' – with the singular difference that now the gulf separating the 'essence' of consciousness from the 'life' of social reality is deemed insurmountable. Reality becomes synonymous with absurdity; and spirit becomes synonymous with endless self-frustration. The very quest structure which underwrote the possibility of socially meaningful narrative – that is, of the dialectical rapport between narration and the social totality of history – is radically undermined. Lukács sees the work of Beckett, Tom Wolfe, Joyce and Kafka as signalling the demise of the quest novel and the emergence of a nihilistic anti-novel. In these works, the realist criterion of art as 'imitation of action' is no longer possible, Lukács charges, for *action* is no longer possible. The modernist anti-novel gravitates towards static paralysis, towards silence. And in the process, the 'objective' world of history is annihilated and replaced by a cult of subjective disaffection and despair. As Lukács remarks: "Lack of objectivity in the description of the outer world finds its complement in the reduction of reality to a nightmare. Beckett's *Molloy* is perhaps the *ne plus ultra* of this development . . .". With the arrival of modernism the only subject left to writing is, paradoxically, the impossibility of writing!

Lukács thus contrasts the literature of realism, which aims at a 'truthful reflection of reality' by mirroring the 'interaction of character and social environment', with modernist literature where man is presented as 'being by nature solitary, asocial and unable to enter into relationships with other human beings'. This modernist tendency is exemplified, according to Lukács, in Musil's notion of 'existence without quality'; Joyce's 'incoherent stream of consciousness'; Gide's 'action gratuite'; and Kafka's and Beckett's obsession with metaphysical absurdity – all of which epitomise the disintegration of narrative objectivity and the dissolution of the real world into the abstractions of subjective interiority.

Lukács rejection of the ideology of modernism is largely moral in nature. His critique is motivated by a conviction that the modernist ethos closes off the historical project of a better future. By obliterating history, Lukács observes, modernist man comes to experience an 'intoxicated fascination for his own forlorn condition'. Modernism 'worships the void created by God's absence' and cultivates the virtues of madness and eccentricity. This cult of literary 'psychopathology' denies the fact that abnormality is very often socially conditioned. It leads to the glorification of an 'undisguised antihumanism' which expresses itself in an 'experimental' free-play of stylistic distortion. Lukács writes:

> Distortion becomes as inseparable a part of the portrayal of reality as the recourse to the pathological. But literature must have a concept of the normal if it is to 'place' distortion correctly; that is to say, to see it *as* distortion. . . . Life under capitalism is, often correctly, presented as a distortion (a petrification or paralysis) of the human substance. But to present psychopathology as a way of escape from this distortion is itself a distortion. We are invited to measure one type of distortion against another and arrive, necessarily, at universal distortion. There is no principle to set against the general pattern, no standard by which the petty-bourgeois and the pathological can be seen in the social context. And these tendencies, far from being relativized with time, become ever more absolute. Distortion becomes the normal condition of human existence; the proper study, the formative principle, of art and literature ('The ideology of modernism' *op.cit.*)

It is with a similar scruple of moral reprobation that Lukács berates Kafka's 'mood of total impotence in the face of the unintelligible power of circumstances'; or deplores Musil's remark that 'if humanity dreamt collectively it would dream Moosbrugger' (a mentally retarded sexual pervert with homocidal tendencies). What Lukács most abhors in modernism, in short, is the simultaneous abandonment of *human normality*, *historical reality* and *collective responsibility* – values which he considered the very foundation-stones of a Marxist humanism. Lukács candidly admits the overriding ethical motivation of his theory of art in the following passage from *The Meaning of Contemporary Realism*:

> Underlying the problem of (historical) perspective in literature is a profound ethical complex, reflected in the composition of the work itself. Every human action is based on a presupposition of its inherent meaningfulness, at least to the subject. Absence of meaning makes a mockery of action and reduces art to naturalistic deception . . . Modernism means not the enrichment but the negation of art. (*ibid.*)

IV

But if Lukács disapproved of modernism as a symptom of the ideological decadence of the West, he was equally disapproving of the fact that 'official' Marxism, particularly during the Stalinist period, should have dismissed *all* Western thinking as decadent, thus isolating itself completely from non-

Soviet developments of thought. Lukács charged that such an attitude of doctrinaire puritanism was profoundly mistaken. And also 'un-Marxist', for Lukács was quick to recall how Marx and Lenin always kept abreast of the latest findings in contemporary philosophy and scientific theory and frequently incorporated such findings into their own thinking. (Marx, for example, was influenced by the work of Darwin, Morgan and Mauser, not to mention Hegel). In his 1970 interview, 'The twin crises', Lukács argues that we should return to the 'real methodology' of Marxism in order to understand the history of the era *after* Marx – both capitalist and communist. Such redeployment of Marx's dialectical method of analysis requires, he holds, that we operate in a spirit of openness to other – i.e. pre-Marxist or post-Marxist – intellectual discoveries. The philosophies of Aristotle and Hegel in particular represent, for Lukács, fundamental contributions to the development of human understanding *before* Marx. And similarly, the radical changes in both Western and Eastern society *since* Marx, demand not just a shift in practical strategy but in critical theory. As Lukács points out: "This has yet to be worked out from a theoretical Marxist standpoint. It is one of the greatest sins of Marxism that there has been no real economic analysis of capitalism since Lenin's book on imperialism – which was written in 1916. Likewise, there is no real historical and economic analysis of the development of socialism. Hence the task that I see for Marxists is that they should examine critically what we can learn from Western writing" ('The twin crises').

Lukács himself practised what he preached. His philosophical borrowings from such 'unorthodox' thinkers as Hegel or Benjamin and his familiarity with recent developments in phenomenology, existentialism and structuralism, for example, are evidence of a definite critical freedom. His final works on aesthetics and ontology – still not fully assimilated in philosophical circles in the English-speaking world – will no doubt provide further testimony to his critical freedom. Lukács ultimately believed that the renewal of the foundation of Marxist theory, which he sought so relentlessly throughout his career, could only be achieved if Marx's own work was approached not as some unalterable sacred dogma but as a dialectical method open to new interpretations and capable of responding to the changing circumstances of each new historical crisis.

Walter Benjamin

Walter Benjamin slips through every net of critical identification. He carries about him an aura of anomaly. He is a Marxist and a mystic, an advocate of dialectical materialism and a theologically-obsessed aesthete who professes the virtues of popular culture. For Benjamin, hashish or the Holy Talmud are as much a part of the revolutionary baggage as the striker's manual. Fidelity to the fruits of the earth is no longer considered incompatible with the claims of messianic eternity; it is recommended as its dialectical precondition.

Benjamin was born to a family of assimilated Jews in Berlin in 1892. At twenty one years of age, he was leader of the left-wing Free Student Association, a sympathiser of the Zionist movement in Berlin and had already begun a life-long friendship and intellectual correspondence with the Jewish biblical scholar, Gershom Scholem. Benjamin's subsequent affiliation with the Frankfurt School and working relationships with such Marxist thinkers as Brecht and Lukács, did not prevent him from continuing to adduce the prophets of Israel with as much enthusiasm as Marx or Lenin. Indeed in his 'Critique of violence' (1921), Benjamin argues that even the most valid form of legal violence – the general workers' strike – must ultimately remain answerable to the Fifth Commandment. Similarly, Bejamin's innovative essay, 'On language as such and on the language of men' (1916), anticipates some of the radical discoveries of Chomsky or the structuralists on the sole authority of the Adamic 'naming' episode of the first book of Genesis. Little wonder that Brecht threw up his hands in dismay when Benjamin informed him in 1938 that he had been writing and reflecting on the Marxist revolution for over twenty years without ever having read the *Capital!*

I

It was also a conjunction of material and spiritual idioms which so attracted Benjamin to Baudelaire and the surrealists. He revered Paris – the surrealist headquarters which offered him refuge from both the Weimar and Hitler regimes – for having initiated him into the secrets of the 'art of wandering'. Baudelaire, one of the progenitors of surrealism, was for Benjamin the wanderer or *flâneur* par excellence. The *flâneur* is someone whose indolence is creative, whose lack of any set direction or design is visionary. The ostensible aimlessness of Baudelaire's *flâneur* disposes him to discern 'correspondances' between seemingly random and unconnected objects, correlating their spiritual and material resonances, transfiguring the ordinary into the extraordinary. Moreover, the *flâneur* flourishes in certain historical circumstances, e.g. the transitional period of early Western capitalism where the urban system of interlocking arcades was replaced (as in Paris, for example) by a system of open boulevards. Baudelaire taught Benjamin that to stray through a city was to discover how meaning is less a matter of temporal progress (*chronos*) than of spatial placement (*topos*). Any preoccupation with revolutionary history requires therefore a corresponding concern for revolutionary topology – a curious conviction expressed, for example, in Benjamin's fascination for photography as a means of capturing moments in spatial images or icons.

Benjamin hailed surrealism as an aesthetic attempt to transmute time into space, to transform the inelecutable flux of history into a world of mystical presents. He held that while in *time* man is determined to be what he actually is or has been, in space the imagination can move its elbows, spread out in all directions, spatialise the single self into many selves – each one sur-real but no less significant for being so. Nonetheless, because the surreal continually falls outside of reality, it is condemned to a certain practical failure. But Benjamin celebrated this 'purity and beauty of failure' in his essays on the surrealists and on Baudelaire, Kafka, Proust and Kraus. He compared the world to a city of ruins which bears witness to a meaning which as fled and never returned. Each piece of broken arch or irongrid in the city serves as a vestigial reminder of a lost and not yet rediscovered paradise. Everything present testifies to an absent truth and offers itself to the critical eye as a *sign* to be interpreted. Or to put it in another way, everything real points to a sur-real level of meaning beyond itself. 'Ambiguity displaces authenticity in all things', writes Benjamin in characteristically cryptic fashion. The world can no longer be taken for granted as a universal given; it is now exposed as an *allegory* with a complex of meanings open to a wide range of implicitly related readings. Benjamin never forgot the cabalistic teaching that there are at least forty-nine levels of meaning to everything! There is no absolutist dogma and we are all refugees who – like Benjamin himself – choose our meanings as we choose our place of provisional abode. This is perhaps why Benjamin endorsed *irony* as the 'most European of all accomplishments'. For irony is the ability to stand at the crossroads of a disintegrating culture, to see reality from different angles at once, to keep all the conflicting options open.

Benjamin liked to portray cities as 'little worlds' where history's meanings were miniaturised in a collage of physical objects. He wrote of the revolutionary import of urban mundanities, translating street gossip into radical aphorism, deciphering the potential epiphany lurking within each *objet trouvé*. Thus the traditional notion of sacred illumination gave way in Benjamin to the more democratic notion of illumination as *profane* – or more correctly, as both sacred and profane. Benjamin called for a mode of attention and a method of reading as intense and as scrupulous as that demanded by the sacred, but applied to mundane or profane existence. In this way the sacred would be revealed in the profane and the profane in the sacred. There is probably no more crucial idea in Benjamin's work. He saw it as entailing a heuristic endeavour 'to establish the image of history even in its most inconspicuous fixtures of existence, its rejects'. And this is perhaps why Benjamin devotes so much of his writing to random memories of childhood or to casual discarded experiences in Marseilles, Naples, Moscow, Berlin, Paris and other places where he found temporary asylum from the momentous march of time. It also explains his passion for 'minute things'. His friend, Scholem, speaks, for instance, of how Benjamin became enchanted by two grains of wheat in the Jewish section of the Musée de Cluny in Paris 'on which a kindred soul had inscribed the complete *Shema Israel*'. Furthermore, Benjamin haboured an ambition – or so Adorno suggests – to write a book made up entirely of quotations. And his writings display a singular obsession with what he termed 'thought fragments' – frequently expressed in proverbs, maxims and lapidary phrases.

Benjamin regarded this 'fragmentary' approach as fulfilling his desire for an 'intentionless speech', that is, a speech free from the means–end pragmatism of normal discourse. He saw himself as a collector of words and things. And he compared the vocation of the collector to that of the revolutionary. Both, Benjamin maintained, dreamt their way "not only into a remote or bygone world, but at the same time into a better one in which, to be sure, people are not provided with what they need any more than they are in the everyday world, but in which things are liberated from the drudgery of usefulness' (*Schritten I*, 1955). Traditionally this role of disinterested contemplation was fulfilled by the religious 'cult' of sacred objects or art works which provided things with an 'aura' of other-worldly difference. Capitalism, as Marx perspicaciously observed, exploits this role by 'fetishising' the commodities of the market place. In contrast to both these attitudes, Benjamin sees the collector as redeeming objects from utilitarian routine for their own sake. Hannah Arendt comments on this striking aspect of Benjamin's thinking in her remarkable introduction to the

English translation of *Illuminations* (1968):

> A collected object possesses only an amateur value and no use value whatsoever
> . . . And inasmuch as collecting can fasten on any category of objects (not just art
> objects, which are in any case removed from the everyday world of use objects
> because they are 'good' for nothing) and thus, as it were, redeem the object as a
> thing since it now is no longer a means to an end but has intrinsic worth,
> Benjamin could understand the collector's passion as an attitude akin to that of
> the revolutionary . . . Collecting is the redemption of things which is to comple-
> ment the redemption of man. (*ibid.*)

But Benjamin recognised that the hermeneutic practice of reading
existence as a collector's allegory, also runs the risk of esotericism. 'The life
of letters', he warned, can become 'existence under the aegis of mere mind
as prostitution is existence under the aegis of mere sexuality.' And it was
just this solitary confinement to the surreal world of the imagination, with
its attendant abandonment of the historical world, that Benjamin saw as
one of the great temptations of modernity. Taken to its extreme, this
tendency issues in suicide. 'The resistance which modernity offers to the
natural productive élan of a person is out of proportion to his strength',
Benjamin comments. 'It is understandable if a person grows tired and takes
refuge in death.' Under the sign of modernity suicide is often 'an act which
seals an heroic will'. While trying to flee from France into Spain in 1940,
with the Nazis in pursuit, Benjamin discovered the border temporarily
closed and took his own life. So perturbed were the border guards by
Benjamin's suicide that they allowed the other refugees accompanying him
to pass through to safety.

If suicide was the extreme option of the alienated individual, terrorism
was, for Benjamin, the desperate modern equivalent of the alienated
community. Benjamin held that both responses expressed a certain apocalyptic pessimism. These arresting lines from a study entitled 'The destructive character' written in 1931, prophetically anticipate the rise of 'terrorist'
movements in recent times:

> No vision inspires the destructive character. He has few needs, and the least of
> them is to know what will replace what has been destroyed. First of all, for a
> moment at least, empty space, the place where the thing stood or the victim lived
> . . . The destructive character does his work, the only work he avoids is being
> creative. Just as the creator seeks solitude, the destroyer must be constantly
> surrounded by people, witness to his efficacy. The destructive character is a
> signal. Just as a trigometric sign is exposed on all sides to the wind, so he is to
> rumour. [He] has no interest in being understood. Attempts in this direction he
> regards as superficial. Being misunderstood cannot harm. On the contrary he
> provokes it . . . The destructive character lives from the feeling, not that life is
> worth living, but that suicide is not worth the trouble. (*Ibid.*)

Perhaps by taking the trouble, in his own final encounter with the blank wall of contemporary despair, Benjamin chose what he deemed to be the nobler response.

II

We have already adverted to Benjamin's abiding passion for Jewish theology and mysticism. This passion dates from his friendship with Scholem, begun in 1915, and his marriage to Dora Kellner, daughter of a prominent Zionest leader, in 1917. Although Benjamin resisted Scholem's pleas to join him in Palestine in the early twenties, the influence of the latter's rather unorthodox religiosity remained a constant feature of Benjamin's entire intellectual career. Unlike Erich Fromm and other Jewish critical theorists in the Frankfurt School who showed interest in a humanist religious anthropology – often akin to Buber's and Landauer's work in the neighbouring Frankfurt Lehrhaus – Benjamin always preferred Scholem's emphasis on the more esoteric writings of the Jewish Cabala. Indeed Benjamin has stated that his own unusual approach to literary allegory and symbolism in his first major work, *The Origin of German Tragic Drama*, was directly inspired by the cabalistic practice of exegesis which read sacred texts in terms of multiple meanings. As he candidly explained in a letter in 1931, 'I have never been able to do research and think in a way other than, if I may so put it, in a theological sense – namely, in accordance with Talmudic teaching of the forty-nine levels of meaning in every passage in the Torah'. Moreover, this quasi-mystical model of exegesis was already outlined in his definition of communication in the 1919 study entitled 'On language as such':

> Things have no proper names except in God. For in his creative word, God called them into being, calling them by their proper names. In the language of men, however, they are overnamed. There is, in the relation of human languages to that of things, something that can be approximately described as 'overnaming': over-naming as the deepest linguistic reason for all melancholy ... It is certain that the language of art can be understood only in the deepest relationship to the doctrine of signs ... For language is in every case not only communication of the communicable but also, at the same time, a symbol of the noncommunicable ... Man communicates himself to God through name, which he gives to nature and (in proper names) to his own kind, and to nature he gives names according to the communication that he receives from her, for the whole of nature, too, is imbued with a nameless, unspoken language, the residue of the creative word of God, which is preserved in man as the cognizing name and above man as the judgment suspended over him. The language of nature is comparable to a secret password that each sentry passes to the next in his own language, but the meaning of the password is the sentry's language itself. All higher language is a translation of

those lower, until in ultimate clarity the word of God unfolds, which is the unity of this movement made up of language. (*ibid.*)

But Benjamin's belief in the 'ultimate clarity' of the divine word was qualified by his conviction that this word remains inaccessible to human knowledge. In fact, Benjamin's theological musings go hand in glove with a thoroughgoing scepticism which stresses that the 'signs' to be found in this finite, historical world are more often 'allegories' that bear oblique witness to some absent meaning than 'symbols' incarnating some romantically redemptive presence. This distinction between allegory and symbol first emerges in Benjamin's early work on the origins of German baroque tragedy (*Der Ursprung des deutschen Trauerspiels*, 1928). Whereas symbol is predicated upon the experience, or at least the possibility, of *continuity* (the reconciliation of man, God and nature), allegory is predicated upon a form of experience haunted by death, anguish and alienation – in short, by *discontinuity*. For symbolism the divine is immanent; for allegory it is radically transcendent, a perpetual absence, a *Deus Absconditus*. Benjamin saw the baroque use of allegory as an uncanny prefiguration of the modernist condition. He maintained that the baroque writer and modern writer are both anti-romantic in their pessimistic conviction that meaning has fled from the earth and left behind only the 'signs' of things unreadable – a script we can no longer decipher with confident clarity. He writes:

> Where the symbol as it fades shows the face of Nature in the light of salvation, in allegory it is the *facies hippocratica* of history that lies like a frozen landscape before the eye of the beholder. History in everything that it has of the unseasonable, painful, abortive, expresses itself in that face – nay rather in that death's-head. And while it may be true that such an allegorical mode is utterly lacking in any 'symbolic' freedom of expression, in any classical harmony of feature, in anything human – that which is expressed here portentously in the form of a riddle is not only the nature of human life in general, but also the biographical historicity of the individual in its most natural and organically corrupted form. This – the baroque, earthbound exposition of history as the story of the world's suffering – is the very essence of allegorical perception; history takes on meaning only in the stations of its agony and decay. (*Schriften I*)

Kafka was for Benjamin the modernist epitome of the 'allegorical' author. He identified with Kafka as a solitary and largely misunderstood writer who was, like himself, a German-speaking Jew endeavouring to read the indecipherable brail of modern existence. But what most drew Benjamin to Kafka was the 'simple recognition that he was a failure'. This also explained the allegorical character of the Kafkaesque vision; for, as Benjamin puts it, 'once he was certain of eventual failure, everything worked out for him as in a dream'. Benjamin speaks of the 'purity and beauty' of Kafka's failure as an emblem of the modern condition of homeless, wordless destitution which, in spite of all, never relinquishes the impossible quest for a language of universal communication. Kafka's 'Jewishness' probably served to further accentuate the 'alien' quality of the language he wrote in. In one of his letters, Kafka himself had remarked on how, as a German-Jewish writer, he felt a double impossibility of writing and of not writing. His use of the German language was experienced, accordingly, as a "self-lamenting usurpation of an alien property . . . which remains someone else's possession even if not a single linguistic mistake can be pointed out" (Quoted in Arendt's Introduction to *Illuminations* (1968)).

Authors like Kafka served for Benjamin to highlight what was in fact the general predicament of modern European man: the struggle for creative expression despite the loss of that shared language of counsel and tradition which, in his remarkable essay on Leskov, Benjamin described as the very basis of storytelling. The anonymous folktale, argues Benjamin, presupposed a communicability of experience based on a common sense of inherited 'wisdom' which has almost disappeared from the modern world. This 'epic' function of storytelling was itself dependent upon historically determinate models of production which Benjamin identifies with the medieval guild and artisanal culture. If seafaring merchants and sedentary peasant cultivators were the originators of tales, it was the traditional life of the artisan system which enabled them to flourish. "The sedentary master and the wandering apprentice", Benjamin observes, "worked together in the same room; indeed, every master had himself been a wandering apprentice before settling down at home or in some foreign city. If peasants and sailors were the inventors of storytelling, the guild system proved to be the place of its highest development. In it the lore of distance, as the traveller brought it back, combined with that lore of the past that most fully reveals its riches to the stay-at-home" ('The storyteller: reflections on the works of Nikolai Leskov', 1936 in *Illuminations*).

The rise of the novel in the modern era of spiritual subjectivism, bourgeois individualism and Cartesian idealism, betokens the loss of the 'epic' sense of harmony between man, God and nature. The modern novel is, for Benjamin, an allegorical sign of the forlorn contemporary individual seeking a universal language which is either irretrievably past or inaccessibly future. Benjamin sums up his argument as follows:

> The art of storytelling is reaching its end because the epic side of truth, wisdom, is dying out . . . The earliest symptom of a process whose end is the decline of storytelling is the rise of the novel at the beginning of modern times . . . What can be handed on orally, the wealth of the epic, is of a different kind from what constitutes the stock in trade of the novel. What differentiates the novel from all other forms of prose literature – the fairy tale, the legend, even the novella – is that it neither comes from oral tradition nor goes into it. This distinguishes it

from storytelling in particular. The storyteller takes what he tells from experience – his own or that reported by others. And he in turn makes it the experience of those who are listening to his tale. The novelist has isolated himself. The birthplace of the novel is the solitary individual, who is no longer able to express himself by giving examples of his most important concerns, is himself uncounseled, and cannot counsel others. To write a novel means to carry the incommensurable to extremes in the representation of human life . . . The legitimacy it provides, stands in direct opposition to reality. ('The storyteller'.)

Thus in Kafka, as the modernist logical conclusion of this tendency in the novel form, we find Joseph K or the other questing heroes of his novels, being haunted by the alphabet of a wisdom which they cannot interpret. Drawing on the Jewish distinction between the *Halakah* as revealed truth and the *Haggadah* as the historical tradition which transmits truth from generation to generation by means of parable and interpretation, Benjamin describes Kafka's work as a desperate and paradoxical attempt to preserve the *transmissibility* of truth without truth:

It is this consistency of truth that has been lost. Kafka was far from being the first to face this situation. Many had accommodated themselves to it, clinging to truth or whatever they happened to regard as truth and, with a more or less heavy heart, forgoing its transmissibility. Kafka's real genius was that he tried something entirely new: he sacrificed truth for the sake of clinging to its transmissibility, its haggadic element. Kafka's writings are by their nature parables. But it is in their misery and their beauty that they had to become *more* than parables. They do not modestly lie at the feet of the doctrine, as the Haggadah lies at the feet of Halakah. Though apparently reduced to submission, they unexpectedly raise a mighty paw against it. This is why, in regard to Kafka, we can no longer speak of wisdom. Only the products of its decay remain. There are two: one is the rumour about the true things (a sort of theological whispered intelligence dealing with matters discredited and obsolete); the other product of this diathesis is folly – which, to be sure, has utterly squandered the substance of wisdom, but preserves its attractiveness and assurance, which rumour invariably lacks . . . Thus, as Kafka puts it, there is an infinite amount of hope, but not for us. This statement really contains Kafka's hope; it is the source of his radiant serenity. ('Max Brod's Book on Kafka', 1938 in *Illuminations*).

Benjamin sees in Proust another emblematic symptom of the modernist discrepancy between the aesthetic world of dream and the material world of life. Whereas Kafka's characters respond to the absence of meaning by aspiring towards some impossible revelation in the future, the Proustian narrator does so by trying to recollect lost harmonies from the past. For both, however, the present is experienced as irredeemably discontinuous, out of joint with itself. The important thing for a 'remembering author', observes Benjamin in his study of Proust, is not what he encounters in the here and now, 'but the meaning of his memory, the Penelope work of recollection . . . for an experienced event is finite – at any rate confined to one sphere of experience; a remembered event is infinite, because it is only a key to everything that happened before it and after it' ('The image of Proust', 1929). In other words, the material discontinuities of the historical present are only redeemable through the spiritual continuities of literary *remembrance*. The fact, however, that Proustian continuity is obtained at the expense of historical actuality means that discontinuity haunts the entire work and makes it essentially 'allegorical' in form. This is why Benjamin endorses Max Unold's description of Proust's oeuvre as a series of 'pointless stories', an endless parodic play with styles. He characterises Proust as an iconoclastic 'connoisseur of ceremonies' mercilessly deglamourising the bourgeois hypocrisies of egocentric courtship and morality. 'The overloud and inconceivably hollow chatter which comes roaring out of Proust's novels', Benjamin comments, 'is the sound of society plunging down into the abyss of this loneliness.' Proust's writing thus minutely records the maladies and misunderstandings of contemporary society, converting his own personal experience as Jew and asthmatic into the exquisite torments of his literary impersonations. For Proust, as for Kafka and Benjamin, *le temps* is always irrevocably *perdu*.

III

Benjamin's analysis of modernist culture testifies to his conviction that the dehumanising material conditions of contemporary capitalist society can only be overcome, if at all, by combining a messianic theology of redemption (whose mystical *Jetztzeit* – timeless moment – turns the bourgeois notion of time as a linear, continuous progress upside down) with a Marxist notion of historical materialism (whose model of revolution also implies an upheaval of natural 'empty' time). Benjamin portrays his characteristic alliance of mysticism and Marxism in the following cryptic opening to his 'Theses on the philosophy of history' (1950):

> The story is told of an automaton constructed in such a way that it could play a winning game of chess, answering each move of an opponent with a countermove. A puppet in Turkish attire and with a hookah in its mouth sat before a chessboard placed on a large table ... Actually, a little hunchback who was an expert chess player sat inside and guided the puppet's hand by means of strings. One can imagine a philosophical counterpart to this device. The puppet called 'historical materialism' is to win all the time. It can easily be a match for anyone if it enlists the services of theology, which today, as we know, is wizened and has to keep out of sight. 'Theses on the Philosophy of History' in *Illuminations*).

It may be more than a coincidence that Benjamin frequently referred to himself as 'the hunchback' in several letters and personal reflections.

While Adorno and the Frankfurt School remained sceptical of Benjamin's theological penchant, they were supportive for the most part of his revisionist reading of Marxism. Benjamin's colleagues in the Frankfurt School were largely responsible for arranging his escape from the Nazi authorities in France (which ended so tragically at the Spanish border) and for collecting, editing and publishing his work after his death. Adorno and Horkheimer were particularly enthusiastic about Benjamin's thesis that historical materialism 'brushes history against the grain', rereading the events that have made us what we are, salvaging repressed lineages of struggle, and reminding us that 'there is no cultural document that is not at the same time a record of barbarism' ('Theses on the philosophy of history.').

Benjamin's enigmatic theses were seen to extend the Frankfurt School's repudiation of the positivistic interpretation of Marxism as a scientific economism which reduces history to a system of mechanical laws. Against Engel's *Anti-Duhring* and Stalin's dogmatism, Benjamin argued that the revolution is without guarantee; he repeatedly affirmed that every phase of history is incomplete and open to a multiplicity of readings which subverts any pretention to certainty. Not only the past but the present must be brushed against the grain so that we may 'explode the continuum of history' – that is, the illusion that it is one continuous whole. In this way, Benjamin refutes all attempts to exploit the model of dialectic for the purposes of ideological domination. His own idiosyncratic interpretations of history would appear to logically demand a form of non-doctrinaire experimentation. And to this end, Benjamin advanced a hermeneutic model of tentative exploration. 'For successful excavation a plan is needed', he writes, 'Yet no less indispensable is the cautious probing of the spade in the loam; it is to cheat oneself of the richest prize to preserve as a record merely the inventory of one's discoveries, and not this dark joy of the place of the finding itself. Fruitless searching is as much a part of this as succeeding, and consequently remembrance must not proceed in the manner of a narrative or still less of a report, but must . . . assay its spade in ever new places and in the old ones delve to ever deeper layers' ('Theses on the philosophy of history'). Benjamin believed that such an open-handed procedure of interpretation would liberate us not only from the reifying predeterminism of historicism, which construes history in terms of inexorable progress, but also from the modernist excesses of arbitrary discontinuity which presuppose an absolute disjunction between the literary world of signs and the material world of concrete praxis. Such a hermeneutic procedure also enables Benjamin to tolerate certain fundamental tensions – some would say contradictions – in his work: most notably, perhaps, the tension between his fidelity to theology and to dialectical materialism.

Benjamin realized that the orthodox interpretations of history are very often those which serve the prejudices of the ruling class. He insisted in the 'Theses' that 'in every era the attempt must be made to wrest tradition away from the conformism that is about to overpower it. The Messiah comes not only as a redeemer, he comes as the subduer of the Antichrist'. According to Benjamin, historical materialism offers the possibility of such a revision of history in so far as it attends to the silenced voices of the past, to the 'courage, humour, cunning and fortitude' of those who struggled for happiness and justice, and lost. This requires that we recollect the 'inconspicuous transformations' of history erased from the official annals of the ruling classes; that we pay as much heed to the 'anonymous toil' of the oppressed as to the 'great minds and talents'; and that we recognise the sad truth that every 'document of civilisation is at the same time a document of barbarism'. Only in this way, can we remain faithful to that 'secret agreement' between the generations of the past and the present, which Benjamin sees as the hope of redemption.

Historiography is not some neutral science of facts which could presume to record the 'way it really was' as Ranke held. It is a battleground of conflicting interpretations. Among the most insidious of such interpretations is the historicist belief in the inevitability of progress. This reduces history to a continuum of 'homogenous empty time'. Benjamin counters this notion in his portrait of the redemptive angel in the 'Theses on the philosophy of history':

> This is how one pictures the angel of history. His face is turned toward the past. Where we perceive a chain of events, he sees one single catastrophe which keeps piling wreckage upon wreckage and hurls it in front of his feet. The angel would like to stay, awaken the dead and remake what has been smashed. But a storm is blowing from Paradise, it has got caught in his wings with such violence that the angel can no longer close them. This storm irresistibly propels him into the future to which his back is turned, while the pile of debris before him grows skyward. This storm is what we call progress. (*ibid.*)

Benjamin counsels a messianic Marxism whose task it is to 'fight for the oppressed past'. Such a hermeneutic model divines the messianic dimension of each 'now' (*Jetztzeit*) and so recovers the discarded fragments of genuine human experience from the 'homogenous course of history'. The revolutionary potential of every historical moment is thus salvaged from the indifference of 'empty time' and recognised as the 'strait gate through which the Messiah might enter'. Such a view, Benjamin argues, is shared by both the Jew and the revolutionary. "The historical materialist", he writes, "leaves it to others to be drained by the whore called *Once upon a time* in historicism's bordello. He remains in control of his powers, man enough to blast open the continuum of history" (*ibid.*)

Benjamin draws a sharp distinction in the 'Theses' between *vulgar Marxism*, which conforms to the historicist illusion that progress entails an increasingly technocratic exploitation of nature, and *messianic Marxism* which takes its inspiration from utopian socialists like Fourier. Against the 'positivistic conception' of the vulgar-Marxists, Benjamin celebrates Fourier's often ridiculed fantasies of efficient co-operative labour resulting in four moons illuminating the night, ice receding from the poles, sea water transformed into drinking water and beasts of prey into friends of man. "All this", concludes Benjamin, "illustrates the kind of labour which, far from exploiting nature, is capable of delivering her of the creations which lie dormant in her womb as potentials" (*ibid.*) This kind of unexpected or eccentric reading of political theory – brushing the new as well as the old orthodoxies against the grain – is typical of Benjamin's style of thinking.

IV

Benjamin's interest in Marxist dialectics was, to speak in general terms, less 'economic' than 'cultural'. In this he was influenced not only by the Frankfurt School – he first had contact with Adorno in 1923 – but also by his acquaintance with Ernst Bloch, the 'theologian of the revolution', first begun in 1918, and with the Russian poet Mayakovsky whom he met during a visit to Moscow in 1926. Benjamin appears to have been somewhat divided, however, between his professional fidelity to his Frankfurt School colleagues – one of his principle sources of income after 1935 was a substantial stipend from the Institute, then in exile in the United States – and his rather tumultuous personal fidelity to his close friend, the revolutionary playwright Bertolt Brecht. Adorno and Horkheimer had warned Benjamin against what they considered to be Brecht's 'unmediated' materialism, and particularly his recommendation that art be used as a direct propaganda weapon of Communist ideology. The Institute members favoured a more 'dialectical' and flexible understanding of the complex relationship between the infrastructures of historical materialism and the superstructural role of art and philosophy. They saw the latter's function as primarily one of critical *negation* (of present historical conditions) and *transcendence* (towards images of 'other' historical possibilities). Theorists like Adorno and Marcuse, for example, wished to preserve the critical potential of such categories as 'subjective interiority' or 'individual consciousness' and strenuously argued that they not be rejected in the name of some crude 'collective' system or mass movement. At most, they argued, these categories should be both partially overcome and partially retained (*aufheben*) in a higher and more inclusive form of dialectical consciousness.

On occasions, the influence of the Frankfurt School appears to gain the upper hand. It has been suggested that one reason for this was that Benjamin's failure to secure an academic post in Germany after the rejection of his doctorate – on the origins of German tragedy – at the University of Frankfurt made him dependent on the Institute not only for his financial subsistence but also for publication. (Two of his major studies were published in the Institute's *Zeitschrift* in the thirties – the essay on 'Certain motifs in Baudelaire' and on 'The work of art in the age of mechanical reproduction'). Indeed in 1935 Benjamin confessed that 'there is nothing so urgent to me as connecting my work as tightly and productively with the Institute as possible'. However, the Brechtian connection continued to manifest itself in various aspects of Benjamin's writing and was the source of protracted disagreements with Adorno concerning the editing of several of his essays for the *Zeitschrift*. Adorno disapproved of Brecht's 'crude thinking', especially in his occasionally impassioned defences of the Soviet system. But we have it on the authority of Hannah Arendt, who knew Benjamin in Paris in the thirties, that it was precisely the non-Hegelian character of Brecht's understanding of the revolutionary struggle which attracted Benjamin in a curious way. He was never wholly at ease with the neat dialectical jargonising of the Hegelian Marxists and admired Brecht's rather brazen ability to use plain, everyday language and populist proverbs in order to communicate his message to as wide an audience as possible. Benjamin was also influenced by Brecht's optimistic attitude to popular culture and the mechanically reproduced plastic arts (for example, cinema and other technologically innovative mass media). This attitude was in marked contrast to the fundamental distrust displayed towards the mechanical arts by Adorno and Marcuse. The general view of the Frankfurt School was that popular culture was basically anti-art and thus corrosive of the dialectical powers of critical negation and transcendence which characterised the genuine aesthetic consciousness. Not surprisingly then, Brecht's practice of mixing the idioms of drama, cinema newsclips, street song and political sloganising was looked at askance!

Benjamin found himself vacillating between the opposing views of Brecht's populism and the Institute's elitism. This was particularly evident in his celebrated study on 'The work of art in the age of mechanical reproduction' first published in the *Zeitschrift* in 1936. The conclusion to this essay was a cause of controversy between Adorno and Benjamin. Benjamin had stated that while 'fascism rendered politics aesthetic, communism responds by politicizing art'. Adorno objected to the suggestion not only that art in the modern era be considered exclusively in its technological, mechanically reproducible aspect, but also that, as such, art be construed as a politically progressive weapon once it is governed by the right ideology i.e. communism.

Throughout the essay itself, Benjamin interrogates two kinds of art – 'auratic' and 'mechanical'. He writes with considerable sympathy of the traditional and now disappearing role of art as 'aura'. Traditional art, he argues, possessed an 'aura of authenticity' which surrounded the original – non-mechanically reproducible – *oeuvre*, endowing it with qualities of 'uniqueness', 'distance' and 'otherness'. These auratic qualities of the original, humanly-crafted art work elicited a meditative response in the onlooker which enabled him to transcend time and to perceive the 'beauty' of the work as a quasi-eternal 'moment of completion'. Benjamin traces this auratic dimension of art back to its magico-cultic origins of primitive history. At times during the essay, he appears to invoke the theological idea of a collective psyche (*anima mundi*) which could generate recurring 'archetypal' images and thereby transcend the limits of normal time. Benjamin identifies these auratic images with Goethe's *Urphänomene* (eternal forms that recur throughout history), Baudelaire's *correspondances* (an aesthetic conflation of spiritual and material meanings) and Leibniz's *monads* (the idea that each autonomous consciousness somehow precontains the totality of experience within itself in crystallised form). "In the beautiful, the ritual value of art appears", remarks Benjamin in his Baudelaire essay (1939). 'The *correspondances* are the data of remembrance – not historical data, but data of prehistory. What makes festive days great and significant is the encounter with an earlier life' (*ibid.*).

Benjamin's distinction between auratic and technological art is expressed in two different kinds of experience: 'auratic' *Erfahrung* or integrated narrative experience; and 'technological' *Erlebnis* or atomised, discrete, fragmented experience. The former, observes Benjamin – with Proust, depth-psychology and Jewish mysticism in mind – "is indeed a matter of tradition, in collective existence as well as private life . . . a convergence in memory of accumulated and frequently unconscious data" ('On some motifs in Baudelaire', 1939). On the other hand, *Erlebnis* typifies the modern loss of a sense of traditional wisdom and communal narrative. The rise of radio and the electronic mass media spells the kiss of death to linear, narrative coherence (e.g. storytelling or even the classical bourgeois novel) by promoting a form of dislocated information and simulation which communicates in isolated sensory moments – in 'shocks of novelty', as Benjamin described it – subversive of the auratic qualities of contemplative distance and uniqueness. Whereas the authentic aura of the work of art depended on its being imbedded in the fabric of sacred tradition, the technologically reproduced work demands an immediate accessibility, Benjamin writes:

> The social bases of the contemporary decay of the aura ... rests on two circumstances, both of which are related to the increasing significance of the masses in contemporary life. Namely, the desire of contemporary masses to bring things 'closer' spatially and humanly, which is just as ardent as their bent toward overcoming the uniqueness of every reality by accepting its reproduction. Unmistakeably, reproduction as offered by picture magazines and newsreels differs from the image seen by the unarmed eye. Uniqueness and permanence are as closely linked in the latter as are transitoriness and reproducibility in the former ... The adjustment of reality to the masses and of the masses to reality is a process of unlimited scope, as much for thinking as for perception ('The work of art in the age of mechanical reproduction', 1936 in *Illuminations*)

Despite a certain sympathy for the psychosocial critique of mass culture advanced by the Institute, there are passages in the 1936 essay where Benjamin appears to subscribe to Brecht's view that traditional art is dead and gone and must now be replaced by a technological art geared to revolutionary purposes. In such passages, Benjamin suggests that any aesthetic attempt to restore the traditional experience of integrated narrative unity is likely to result in a conservative, perhaps even reactionary position. For in most instances, such an aesthetic refuses to admit that the historical conditions of contemporary alienation and barbarism no longer allow for the possibility of a genuine 'auratic' experience. This coincides, in the case of fascism, with a perverted exploitation of the aesthetic 'aura', witnessed in a regressive cultism which feeds on ritualistic repetitiveness. Fascism 'aestheticizes politics', Benjamin claims, in the form of secularised ceremonials and rites – e.g. the Nazi use of racial myths and mass rallies, stylised goosestepping, salutes and fetishised insignia etc. So doing, fascism depoliticises consciousness; it replaces critical historical awareness with a mystificatory cult of power. Fascism, for Benjamin, represents a cancerous expansion of the magico-religious potency of the 'aura' beyond the individual artwork, where it traditionally belonged, into the arena of political totalitarianism. Fascism, in short, is the mutual contamination of a corrupt art and a corrupt politics. It was when faced with this extreme malady of modern political life that Benjamin proposed the extreme cure of a revolutionary politicisation of art. The sentiment guiding Benjamin's thinking seems to have been that if art can no longer be separated from politics in the modern era, then it should be allied to a political project that aims to dramatically improve the human condition – i.e. communism.

V

Benjamin concedes, rather reluctantly, that the modern age of mechanical reproduction has ushered in the end of genuine 'auratic' experience. The imminent demise of authentic *Erfahrung* appears to be a matter of historical fact. So one *either* nostalgically bemoans the loss – as Adorno does when he ruefully doubts whether poetry can ever be written again after Auschwitz – *or* one resolves to take political and aesthetic advantage of it – as does Brecht when he employs new technological media for progressive revolutionary ends. Benjamin was poised somewhere between the two positions. The eclipse of the 'aura' in mechanically-produced art led Benjamin to conclude in his 1936 essay that as soon as the criterion of authenticity ceases to apply to artistic creation, 'the total function of art is reversed. Instead of being based on (religious) ritual, it begins to be based on another practice – politics'. Thus with radio and cinema, for example, Benjamin finds the replacement of the traditional experience of sacramental 'distance' with one of immediate fusion between author and audience, between what is represented and the sensory reception of the viewer or listener. Everyone can participate. Limits, confines, boundaries and distances disappear. As Benjamin comments, the newsreel – to take just one instance of the electronic media – 'offers everyone the possibility to move from passer-by to movie extra'.

While modernist 'high culture' appeals to the anguished subjectivity of the alienated individual, the technologically-produced arts sponsor a more democratic 'popular culture' based on mass response. Where the former tends toward intellectual contemplation (e.g. the novels of Thomas Mann, Samuel Beckett or J.–P. Sartre), the latter solicits an attitude of emotional and often unconscious 'distraction'. In contrast, therefore, to the Frankfurt School's critique of mass culture as a one-dimensional experience which supports the status quo by fostering an attitude of passive conformism or uncritical 'mob rule', Benjamin held that mechanically-reproduced art, if infused with a progressive political aim, could appeal to and alter the response of the masses in a revolutionary way. As he observed in the 1936 essay: "the reactionary attitude toward a Picasso painting changes into the (liberating) reaction toward a Chaplin movie". Mechanical reproduction emancipates the work of art from its traditional dependency on 'authentic originality', and excludes no-one from the art of communication. By dispensing with the idea of a single 'original', the photographic print or film reel – any number of which can exist – makes cultural experience available to anyone who wishes to participate:

> The technique of reproduction detaches the reproduced object from the domain of tradition. By making many reproductions it substitutes plurality of copies for a unique experience. And in permitting the reproduction to meet the beholder or listener in his own particular situation, it reactivates the object reproduced. These two processes lead to a tremendous shattering of tradition which is the obverse of the contemporary crisis and renewal of mankind. Both processes are intimately connected with the contemporary mass movements. Their most powerful agent is the film. Its social significance, particularly in its most positive form, is inconceivable without its destructive, cathartic aspect, that is, the liquidation of the traditional value of the cultural heritage. ('The work of art in the age of mechanical reproduction'.)

Benjamin was impatient with modernists like Mallarmé who advocated a 'negative theology of art' which denied any social function or political content whatsoever. He preferred the more nuanced attitude of Valéry which he cites as an epigraph to his 1936 essay. Valéry acknowledged that profound changes were impending in the 'ancient craft of the beautiful' and affirmed that we must expect "great innovations to transform the entire technique of the arts, thereby affecting artistic invention itself and perhaps even bringing about an amazing change in our very notion of art" (*ibid.*). But while Benjamin fully accepted that the function of art was historically situated, he remained extremely critical of the many abuses of technological art in our times. He especially abhorred the view advanced by Marinetti and the Futurists that modern man is self-alienated to the point where his own destruction becomes an 'aesthetic pleasure of the first order'. Marinetti celebrated war as providing 'the artistic gratification of a sense perception that has been changed by technology'. In the 1936 essay, Benjamin quotes with some horror the following passage from Marinetti's Futurist manifesto:

> War is beautiful because it establishes man's dominion over the subjugated machinery by means of gas masks, terrifying megaphones, flame throwers, and small tanks. War is beautiful because it initiates the dreamt-of metalization of the human body. War is beautiful because it combines the gunfire, the cannonades, the cease-fire, the scents, and the stench of putrefaction into a symphony. War is beautiful because it creates new architecture, like that of big tanks, the geometrical formation flights, the smoke spirals from burning villages, and many others . . . Poets and artists of Futurism! . . . remember these principles of an aesthetics of war so that your struggle for a new literature and a new graphic art . . . may be illumined by them! (*ibid.*)

Beyond the alternatives of romantic 'auratic' art and 'aura-less' mass culture, Benjamin seems to have personally favoured a third kind of modern aesthetic form – the 'allegorical' form. We have already mentioned Benjamin's manifest enthusiasm for writers like Kafka, Proust and Baudelaire whose works register a search for 'auratic' cyphers of transcendence which is never fulfilled but is never completely abandoned either. These works are 'allegorical' in the sense that they refuse to serve either as fetishised commodities of mass consumption or as integrated narratives of 'auratic' experience. They aspire to 'moments of completion' while describing how such moments are impossible in this alienated modern world from which meaning has fled. They remind us, in short, that meaning today can only be given in hints and guesses, in signs that point to other possibilities of experience, in allegories of absence. Benjamin's particular fondness for such works bespeaks a deep nostalgia for lost things, for *le temps perdu*. But this very nostaligia is itself an indication of how Benjamin remained convinced that aesthetic perception is bound to historical conditions. It is an honourable nostaligia for our times. As Frederick Jameson remarks, "there is no reason why a nostalgia conscious of itself, a lucid and remorseless dissatisfaction with the present on the grounds of some remembered plenitude, cannot furnish as adequate a revolutionary stimulus as any other: the example of Benjamin is there to prove it" (*Marxism and Form*, 1971).

VI: CONCLUSION

Benjamin was a critical theorist of many colours. He was at once a poetic theologian, an historical materialist, a metaphysical linguist, a politically committed *flâneur* – and many other things besides. He felt his time to be out of joint and felt out of joint with his time. A Jew in Nazi Germany, a mystic in Moscow, a sober German in jovial Paris, he was forever homeless, stateless and jobless – an *homme de lettres* whom the academies refused to acknowledge as one of their own. The fact that everything he wrote turned out to be *sui generis*, as his exiled compatriot and Paris acquaintance Hannah Arendt observed, characterised him as one of those 'unclassifiable ones' whose work "neither fits the existing order nor introduces a new genre that lends itself to future classification . . . Often an era most clearly brands with its seal those who have been least influenced by it, who have been most remote from it, and who therefore have suffered most" ('Introduction' to *Illuminations*). If Benjamin continued to hope during his own lifetime – despite countless personal failures and the horrors of Nazi barbarism – for a cultural and political renewal of modern man, it was in the manner of his favorite maxim: 'only for the sake of those without hope have we been given hope'.

Antonio Gramsci

"Reality does not exist on its own, in and for itself", wrote Gramsci in *The Prison Notebooks*, "but only in an historical relationship with the men who modify it." Gramsci was one of the first critical thinkers of this century to reread Marx in the light of the changing circumstances of advanced industrial capitalism. Born in Sardinia in 1891, Gramsci's writings criticised 'scientific' Marxism for reducing social philosophy to an exclusively economic analysis. He realized that such a restrictive analysis was incapable of responding to the 'ideological' challenge of bourgeois revisionism. Over and against the determinist materialism of Plekanov, Kautsky and the Second International, Gramsci sought to reintroduce a human 'philosophy of praxis' which would prise the historical dialectic free from mechanistic models of interpretation.

I

Curiously, it was Gramsci's practical commitments as a young activist in the Turin factory strikes and trade council movements between 1916 and 1919 and subsequently as both a founder-member of the Italian Communist Party (*CPI*) and its newspaper *Ordine Nuovo*, that convinced him of the necessity for a more *theoretical* analysis of the role of Marxism in Western industrial society. Without such a critical-theoretical reappraisal of revolutionary strategy, Gramsci believed that what he called the 'hegemony' of bourgeois values would continue its covert 'counter-revolution' and thereby effectively forestall attempts to overcome the capitalist system.

That the economic 'infrastructure' had to be appropriated and transformed by the proletariat, Gramsci did not doubt. What he did doubt and question, however, was *the way in which* this revolutionary appropriation might be achieved and, furthermore, the *reasons for which* it should be achieved. In short, Gramsci acknowledged that the class war in twentieth-century Europe was being fought not just at the level of socio-economic infrastructures but also, and sometimes even more effectively, at the level of cultural–ideological 'superstructures'. Or to put it another way, the proletariat's appropriation of the 'means of production' must include not just the means of *labour* but also of *information*, not just the running of factories and farmyards but also the modes of producing and diffusing knowledge – the systems of education, propaganda, art, the media and so on. In this respect, Gramsci was among the first European thinkers – along with Lukács – to call for a 'readaption' of Marxism to the altered historical conditions of this century. He was almost certainly the first to argue that 'cultural production'was as fundamental an issue in the class struggle as 'commodity production', and that political revolution could not succeed without radical changes in the overall ideology of a society.

It has sometimes been suggested that Gramsci's active involvement in practical politics obstructed or compromised his freedom of thought. There is, in fact, little evidence for this. What is sure, however, is that Gramsci's commitment to revolutionary praxis, especially prior to his imprisonment by Mussolini in 1926 – he died eleven years later, one week after his release – lent a quality of concrete immediacy to his analysis, a quality sometimes lacking, for example, in the more abstract theorising of the Frankfurt School. The experience of the failure of the German revolution in 1917 appears to have instilled a deep sense of political disillusionment and even pessimism in thinkers like Marcuse and Horkheimer; and this may partially account for the fact that both of them fought shy of any direct party political *engagement*. Marcuse and his colleagues were certainly effected by the political implications of the second world war or, more positively, of the student revolts of the 1960s. But such exposure to the harsher weathers of history, did not fundamentally *condition* their critique as it did in Gramsci's case. Indeed, the events of 1968 for example may be said to have confirmed Marcuse's model of revolt rather than to have occasioned it. The theory preceded the praxis. Or as Martin Jay rather contentiously observed in his history of the Frankfurt School, there was often an option for "the purity of theory over the affiliation that a concrete attempt to realise it would have required" (*The Dialectical Imagination*, 1973). With Gramsci the reverse was the case. His most comprehensive and influential work was written in the form of prison notebooks *after* the battle. His reflections followed on the heels of his political activity. And such activity included being elected secretary of the Italian communist party and also a member of the Italian parliament in 1924, two years before his arrest by the Fascists. Nor should one underestimate, in this regard, the lasting impact of Gramsci's extremely poor working-class upbringing in Sardinia (he was only able to study in the University of Turin thanks to a scholarship) – another factor which distinguishes him from the Frankfurt school theorists who were almost invariably from a highly cultured bourgeois background.

Gramsci made an important distinction between the 'traditional intellectual,' divorced from the immediate social struggles of history, and the 'organic intellectual' who emerges from the midst of such struggles. Gramsci claims that "by intellectual is meant not only those strata commonly understood by the denomination, but in general the whole social stratum that exercises organisational functions in the broad sense, both in the field of production, and in the cultural one, and in the politico-administrative one" (*Prison Notebooks*). Intellectuals are not some autonomous group removed from history but an organic offshoot of a social group. "Every social group", writes Gramsci, "coming into existence on the original terrain of an essential function in the world of economic production creates together with itself, organically, one or more strata of intellectuals which give it homogeneity and an awareness of its own function not only in the economic but also in the social and political fields" (*ibid*). Thus, for example, the capitalist entrepreneur creates alongside himself the industrial technician, the specialist political economist and other organisers of a new legal cultural system. And the working class produces its own 'organic intellectuals', who are indispensable to its organisation and expansion since, as Gramsci observes, "in the political party the elements of an economic social group get beyond the moment of their historical development and become agents of more general activities of a national and international character" (*ibid.*) The transition to socialism involves therefore not just the substitution of communist entrepreneurs for capitalist ones but a new relationship between the producers and the social organization of knowledge. To create a new stratum of intellectuals it is necessary, insists Gramsci, to critically elaborate "the intellectual activity that exists *in everyone* at a certain degree of development", on the basis of their productive and practical experience, in order that it may become "the foundation of a new and integral conception of the world" (*ibid.*). Gramsci identifies this conception with Marxist humanism whose ultimate goal is to unite humanity now divided into corporate groups and classes. The role of Gramsci's 'new organic intellectual' is neither elitist and authoritarian, nor servile and passive; his aim is the ultimate unity of theory and practice. "The mode of being of the new intellectual," he writes, "can no longer consist in eloquence, which is an exterior and momentary mover of passions, but in active participation in practical life, as constructor, organiser, permanent persuader and not just orator" (*ibid.*).

However, Gramsci shared with the Frankfurt School philosophers the belief that the concept of revolutionary struggle needed to be given a wider berth. He readily agreed that the contemporary revitalisation of Marxism could only take place by advancing a new perspective which would make intelligible the subtle and often covert rearrangements of class politics in advanced industrial societies. This led in turn to a recognition of the crucial role played by 'ideology' and of the need, accordingly, for a radical *cultural* critique.

The shift towards a more cultural–philosophical reassessment of Marxism was perhaps facilitated in Gramsci's case – as also in the case of Lukács, Bloch and the Frankfurt School – by the fact that his intellectual formation was coloured at an early stage by the tradition of philosophical idealism, and particularly by the neo-Hegelian idealism of his intellectual compatriot, Bernadetto Croce. This formative interest in liberal idealist philosophy in the prewar years, may go some way to explaining Gramsci's resistance to the orthodox 'scientific' Marxism approved by the Second International and his eagerness to push historical materialism in the direction of a critical humanism. It would appear, therefore, that it was as much Gramsci's early philosophical investigations – written under the influence of a Crocean idealism and published in the Italian journals *Il Grido del Populo* and *Avanti* – as his early trade union and political activism, that gave his work its particularly undogmatic (some would say 'unscientific') character of radical exploration. Moreover, this flexible model of Marxist interpretation explains why Gramsci's work has proved so attractive to both the New Left movement in the Anglo-American world, where he was comprehensively translated in the sixties and seventies, and to various national liberation struggles in the Third World. Though concretely situated in the specific context of the Italian Left, the theories advanced by Gramsci in his *Prison Notebooks*, have lent themselves to a internationally wide range of diverse cultural and historical contexts. In a passage from 'The Modern Prince', Gramsci points to the necessity of reassessing the Marxist legacy in terms of the broad intellectual currents of modern culture:

> Marxism has been a potent force in modern culture and, to a certain extent, has determined and fertilized a number of currents of thought within it. The study of this most significant fact has been either neglected or ignored outright by the so-called orthodox (Marxists), and for the following reasons: the most significant philosophical combination that occurred was that in which Marxism was blended with various idealist tendencies, and was regarded by the orthodox, who were necessarily bound to the cultural currents of the last century (positivism, scientism), as an absurdity if not sheer charlatanism (*ibid.*).

II

If Lukács is best known for his analysis of *reification*, the most pivotal notion in Gramsci's work is undoubtedly that of ideological *hegemony*. The centrality of this notion expresses Gramsci's conviction that the positivistic model of Marxist economism was insufficient and required a broader appreciation of the strategies of revolution at the level of a culture's 'mass consciousness'. In order to propagate his analysis of the political role of ideology (initially developed during his involvement in the Turin experiments), Gramsci launched a journal in 1918 called the *Ordine Nuovo*. He edited this publication off and on until his arrest in 1926. It was here that Gramsci first advanced his critique of contemporary capitalist consciousness and outlined his blueprint for an alternative revolutionary consciousness. The early Lukács, as we noted, had also written about the cardinal role of political consciousness in the dialectical advancement of historical revolution, but his subsequent experiences of doctrinaire Stalinism – particularly in Moscow – may have accounted for his turn to more 'literary' considerations in later writings. Gramsci too spent time in post-revolutionary Moscow. However this was during the more benign reign of Lenin and he never received the censorious reaction to his innovative theories that Lukács had later to endure.

It was primarily in the thirty-two prison notebooks, written during his incarceration in Turin between 1926 and 1937, that Gramsci recorded his most comprehensive description of the struggle for revolutionary consciousness in advanced industrial capitalism. *The Prison Notebooks* spell out in detail what Gramsci means by 'ideological hegemony'. He defines it as a phenomenon whereby a dominant class contrives to retain political power by manipulating popular opinion (or what Gramsci refers to as the 'popular consensus') in civil society rather than simply by the crude military intervention of the state. Gramsci argued that 'ideological hegemony' is often most effectively sustained through the clever exploitation of religion, education, or popular national cultures.

Gramsci first introduced this concept of 'ideological hegemony' to explain what he considered to be the flexible dialectical relation between base (the economic infrastructure) and superstructure (the realm of 'psychological' motivation, be it political, religious, aesthetic, mythic, tribal etc., which predisposes people to acquire a particular kind of consciousness or to undertake a particular kind of action). Gramsci rejected the orthodox Marxist view that cultural and philosophical superstructures are no more than passive 'reflections' of what is taking place at the level of the economic base. Indeed, to hold such a position, he claimed, is implicitly to deny the fact that Marxism itself was first expressed in the superstructural form of a theoretical analysis. And it is also to underestimate the complex cultural factors which 'motivate' the revolutionary transition from one kind of society (e.g. capitalist) to another (e.g. socialist).

To affirm an absolute causal priority of material base over ideological superstructure is to reduce history to an *undialectical* system of mechanical determinism. And so we find Gramsci arguing in the *Prison Notebooks* and elsewhere that in certain circumstances the ideas, symbols and emblems which organise the attitudes of a society can be just as 'material' as the economic conditions of production. Labour production is not the only field of human expression subject to class exploitation. Our ideas too, especially under the contemporary reign of bureaucratisation and mass media manipulation, can become part and parcel of the ruling class's 'hegemonic' power. In other words, the ideological control of mass consciousness has become quite as decisive a factor in the strategy of class domination as the physical control exerted by legal and military coercion. Ideology organises the way in which 'civil society' *represents itself to itself*; it determines the overall cast of mind of any given culture – the system of images, myths and moral values a people identifies with – both publicly at the level of national self-representation and privately at the level of personal or family self-presentation. Gramsci maintains, in short, that the idioms of power extend beyond the state apparatus to the general 'ethos' of the national community which imbues every area of our social experience from church to school to family.

The function of critical theory for Gramsci is to expose the manner in which this process of ideological persuasion translates itself from a cultural invention into a natural assumption. This requires that we interrogate the ways in which the masses come to internalise the ideological hegemony of the ruling class as their own value system, as part of their 'national outlook' or native 'common sense' (even though it goes against their own class interests). In exposing the complex devices whereby a dominant *culture* is converted into *nature* and thus surreptitiously 'legitimated', Gramsci anticipated both the structuralist semiotics of Barthes' *Mythologiques* and the critical hermeneutics of Habermas's *Legitimation Crisis*.

III

Gramsci's account of how *class* interests mask themselves as *cultural* values, which in turn mask themselves as *natural* instincts, represents arguably his most significant contribution to contemporary Marxist theory. This account enabled him to explain how the widespread proletarian uprising predicted by Marx failed to materialise not just because of insufficient 'objective contradictions' in the economic structures of capitalism, but because capitalism stage-managed another kind of 'legitimacy' by manipulating the more 'subjective' motivations of the national psychology. If the crisis of capitalism in Italy, for example, ultimately gave rise to even stronger forms of bourgeois control rather than to a successful communist revolution, the reasons for this – at the outset at any rate – had as much to do with the domination of consciousness as with the domination of physical force. To understand this phenomenon Gramsci emphasised that it was important to place the 'popular consciousness' of the entire Italian people in the witness box along with the more specifically 'bourgeois conscious-ness' of the ruling class.

A hegemonic consensus was achieved by the bourgeoisie of advanced industrial societies not primarily by explicit military coercion but by incul-cating in the masses a fatalistic and ultimately passive attitude to those in power. Gramsci deems it an urgent task of Marxist theory to demystify the prestige of such ideological authority; and this necessitates the creation of a new popular consensus motivated by the genuinely universal goal of 'liberty for all'. Gramsci unequivocally opposed the notion of a *comintern* or *reign of terror* as a reactionary means towards a revolutionary end.

Gramsci affirms, accordingly, that the class war is not determined solely by scientifically computable 'facts' but by ethical–political 'values'. A state experiences crisis as soon as its 'spiritual prestige', sustained by ideological mystification, has been stripped away; for then it is exposed in the naked oppressiveness of its 'economic-corporate' existence. Moreover, it is gene-rally when a state is deprived of its ideological support in the 'popular opinion' of civil society that it has recourse to force. The deployment of military aggression to prop up a regime is already symptomatic of the breakdown of its 'ideological hegemony'.

In this context, Gramsci sees the role of critical theory as twofold. It must serve as an iconoclastic demystification of the old system of values; and it must propose a new system of values. In this respect, the revolution requires both a negation of authoritarian ideology and the creation of liberating alternatives. This latter project of liberation cannot be predeter-mined in the form of 'text-book' solutions. It is to be specifically character-ised in each instance by the particular national experiences and traditions of each society. Gramsci observes that the 'ideological hegemony' of the bourgeois class has been preserved in Italy, for example, largely due to the influence of the Catholic Church whose centralised policies and clerical hierarchies endorsed a cult of 'otherworldly' power and a conservative resistance to social change. In the Nordic and Anglo-Saxon countries by contrast, the ideological hegemony of the bourgeoisie has been shored up, in part at least, by the culture of Protestantism whose emphasis on puritani-cal self-abnegation, predestination and salvation by works, led to a repress-ion of sexual and creative energies in the name of a highly rationalised pragmatism. Taking a cue from Max Weber's *The Protestant Ethic and the Spirit of Capitalism*, Gramsci argued that the Protestant cultivation of an individualistic and sexually restrictive 'ethos' extending from the public factory floor to the private home, served as one of the most efficient 'co-optative' mechanisms of advanced capitalism. By imbuing the entire fabric of civil society with an ethos of privatised spirituality, legalistic bureaucracy and high-performance technology which segregates and depoliticises its citizens, the advanced capitalist state can uphold its 'legitimacy' without recourse to arms.

Gramsci considered this process of 'ideological hegemony' to be especially effective in the United States, for there the bourgeois–capitalist–Protestant hegemony was able to progress untramelled by ideological opposition from residual medieval–feudal structures or indeed from radical socialist movements. The dominant culture of what Gramsci called 'Americanism' evolved from pioneer Protestant individualism in the eighteenth century to a corporate–state bureaucracy in the twentieth century – epitomised by the scientific 'management' of industry and everyday social life. This evolution culminated in a specific form of rationalised (e.g. conveyor belt) capitalism which Gramsci refers to as 'Taylorism' or 'Fordism'. A new secular theology of technological pragmatism, he points out, produced a 'national–popular consciousness' that was itself highly standardised. A consequence of this was that American workers were offered fewer occasions for critical thinking and became increasingly blind to the realities of class domination. Their entire intellectual, emotional and moral consciousness was being drained of radical protest and transmuted into obedient conformism. The United States, Gramsci concludes, thus produced the most sophisticated model of corporate–liberal capitalism by identifying the value system of the *state* with that of *civil society* in all of the latter's multiple expressions – the home, education, religion, law, the media etc. 'Americanism' is an ideological hegemony that is efficient because all pervasive – i.e. its value system of technological rationalism is shared by both the ruling classes and the ruled (against the better interests of the latter).

Gramsci saw the emergence of fascism in Europe as yet another attempt to superimpose the corporate–bureaucracy of the state on the ideological structures of civil society. Americanism and fascism were considered as two major obstacles to the advancement of revolutionary consciousness in the contemporary era of rationalised capitalism. While invoking different priorities – Americanism the priority of individual freedom, fascism the priority of collective authority – both served to prolong the reign of capitalism in readjusted form. Gramsci concluded that the question of state domination cannot be adequately resolved without addressing the question of the ideological direction of society as a whole. In other words, the ideological motivations of conservative capitalist societies must be analysed and deciphered before a new 'integrated' culture with liberated social relations can emerge.

Gramsci held, accordingly, that the violent and immediate overthrow of the corrupt Russian state by the Bolsheviks could not serve as an adequate model for the revolutionary struggle in the Western nations of advanced capitalism. For whereas in the former the state was everything and civil society nothing, in the latter the bourgeoisie had succeeded in appropriating the 'popular consciousness' of civil society and had divided not only worker against worker but even each worker against himself. Consequently, Gramsci counselled an 'organic' rather than 'catastrophist' movement of revolt in the West; since he believed that the structures of civil society had become so intrinsically adapted to the rule of advanced capitalism that they could effectively resist or 'co-opt' any direct assault on the institutions of state power. In short, Gramsci predicted that the reversal of 'ideological hegemony' would be a long hard battle with 'popular consciousness' as the most decisive battleground.

IV

But Gramsci's analysis was not confined to critical *negation*. It also emphasised the creative role played by human consciousness in the transformation both of the ideological structures of society and of the economic infrastructures they safeguarded. In the first major introduction in English to Gramsci's political philosophy, Carl Boggs highlights this aspect of his thinking:

> Gramsci was above all a *creative* Marxist who never failed to seize upon the active, political, or 'voluntarist' side of theory in contrast to the fatalistic reliance upon objective forces and scientific 'laws' of capitalist development that had been central to the Marxist tradition. Gramsci was convinced, after witnessing the failure of the Second International, that socialist revolution would not come mechanically from the breakdown of the capitalist economy but would have to be *built*, that is won through purposive human action within a wide range of historical settings. The transition to socialism could not be expected to follow any unilinear pattern . . . Gramsci argued that such a realisation necessitated a new (reconstituted) philosophical foundation for Marxism which would restore the subjective dimension to socialist politics and place human actors at the centre of the revolutionary process. (*Gramsci's Marxism*, 1976)

By thus acknowledging the capacity of revolutionary consciousness to transform society, Gramsci was in turn able to stress the importance of theoretical strategy as a guiding force in revolutionary practice. Like his Hungarian counterpart, Lukács, he laid great emphasis upon the need to conjugate theory and practice in a dialectical reciprocity which would overcome the old metaphysical oppositions between our intellectual and material existence. He recognised that the weapons of class war today are not just military and mechanical but perhaps more significantly cultural. This explains why, for instance, Gramsci deemed his extended critique of the influential role of the Catholic Church in Italy to be quite as relevant as his detailed empirical description of industrial conditions in Turin in 1918.

A radical theory of advanced capitalism, Gramsci contended, must begin with what he termed a programme of 'counter-hegemonic consciousness transformation' (or what in the Latin American movements of liberation has been termed 'conscientisation' – see, for example, Paulo Freire's *Pedagogy of the Oppressed*, 1972). This programme would take full account of the formative role of the particular traditions of belief or value in each specific culture. Without such an awareness, it would be virtually impossible to explain, for example, why certain 'working classes' in certain societies at certain moments in modern history have opted to put nationalist or tribal interests before class ones: e.g. in Hitler's Germany, Thatcher's Britain–Falklands débâcle or in Paisley's Ulster (in particular the loyalist workers' strike in 1973 which brought down the power-sharing Sunningdale executive). Cognisant of such complex factors, Gramsci argued for a correlative, and where possible simultaneous, transformation of both the superstructures and infrastructures of advanced capitalism. Only such a transformation, he insisted, could permit an 'integrated' culture to emerge organically *within* each particular society rather than be imposed from *without* by an abstract scientific model (*à la* Kautsky) or by a naive spontaneous one (*à la* Rosa Luxemburg).

Gramsci's regard for the *specificity* of each revolutionary situation – what he called its 'national–popular' character – enabled him to readapt Marx's critique of nineteenth-century industrial England and Lenin's critique of pre-industrial Russia, to the unique conditions of the contemporary Italian proletariat, divided as it was between the industrialised northern population and the more rural southern population. While their economic plight was substantially different, both northern and southern workers shared a common tradition of ideological assumptions determining their social relations; and it was this latter 'ensemble of relations' which constituted an ideological hegemony exerting its influence over rural peasant and factory labourer alike. Gramsci's idea of a 'national–popular' totality of relations, particular to each national culture, enabled him to demarcate the differences between revolutionary strategy in the third world and in the advanced world. It also set a precedent for the independent stance taken by the modern Italian Communist Party *vis-à-vis* its Soviet counterpart, establishing some of the broad outlines of what has come to be known as 'Eurocommunism'. Such a flexible approach to Marxism is one of the most conspicuous legacies of this Italian thinker who was convinced that an understanding of indigenous cultural phenomena (such as the Risorgimento or the Vatican or Machiavellianism) was as significant for the revolutionary struggle in his country as a thorough knowledge of the writings of Marx and Lenin.

The readaption of Marxism to the 'national–popular' character also involved for Gramsci a more sophisticated approach to bourgeois culture. Gramsci pointed out that certain elements in bourgeois culture can 'anticipate' the socialist struggle for liberty and should not be repudiated out of hand. It was for this reason that he became extremely impatient with the 'puritanism' of absentionist socialists who preferred to wash their hands of all political involvement, Pontius Pilate fashion, than to share power within existing bourgeois institutions. This absolutist stance came to be popularly known by the Gramsci neologism *pontiuspilotisimo*. Bourgeois culture, Gramsci remained convinced, is capable of occasionally expressing progressive forms of moral protest against injustice and inequality and this 'native' tradition of protest should be fostered by socialism rather than summarily dismissed.

It was in the sense, therefore, of both a philosophical openness to certain unorthodox ideas and a political openness to changing circumstances that Gramsci proposed his model of popular cultural revolution. He declared that the revolution can begin here and now in the fledgling protests of local councils, communal soviets, trade unions, avant-garde cultural movements etc. Otherwise, the organically developing moments of struggle will be sacrificed for the sake of some centrally dictated state overthrow bereft of popular support. Moreover, the fragmentary and exploratory nature of Gramsci's writings may well be due to his sense that theory must continually revise its own premises and keep itself open to new modes of understanding, lest it fail to adequately respond to the unique historical context of each individual culture. Indeed, it was by rejecting the Jacobin–dogmatic model of revolution that Gramsci became one of the first twentieth century thinkers to proclaim the compatibility of Marxism with genuine participatory democracy.

It may well have been this same scruple for intellectual flexibility which prompted Gramsci to reintegrate into revolutionary theories certain aspects of Crocean idealism. Gramsci recognised here a strong weapon against the orthodox dogmas of 'mechanistic Marxism'. By reincorporating the 'subjective' dimensions of will, freedom, responsibility and action into the historical dialectic, Gramsci endeavoured to counteract the doctrinaire view that history unfolds according to 'objective' laws of economic evolution irrespective of human intervention. Gramsci denounced this latter doctrine as a threat to the very idea of revolutionary praxis in so far as it encouraged attitudes of anti-humanism and acquiesence. As such, he believed that it produced little more than another brand of 'sterile mysticism' which deemed the human subject impotent and history an ineluctable law. Such a positivistic version of Marxism could only serve to hinder the 'intellectual–moral renewal' – a renewal which Gramsci remained certain would lead to the new age of socialism, just as the philosophical renewal of the Enlightenment resulted in the French Revolution of 1789. Ideas are for Gramsci an indispensible force of historical change. "Man", he conceded, "is above all else – mind".

V

Gramsci saw it as his vocation to salvage the 'political philosophy' of Marx ignored by mechanistic Marxism. The genuine task of Marxism, he maintained, is not to substitute empirical materialism for speculative idealism, but rather to transcend both extremes in the form of a new dialectical relationship between matter and mind. Without such a dialectical mediation, idealism becomes an 'empty metaphysics' and materialism a 'flat determinism'. Both of these extreme positions remain the preserve of what Gramsci referred to as 'Byzantine theorists' – intellectuals who persist in interpreting history in terms of fixed, abstract categories (purely subjective in the case of idealism or purely objective in the case of materialism).

Refusing the dogmatic opposition between scientific objectivism and metaphysical subjectivism, Gramsci advocated a non-doctrinaire Marxism. It is significant that he praised the Bolshevik revolution of 1917 not only for overcoming the Tsarist regime of feudal fatalism but also for demonstrating that historical change is brought about by *human praxis* as well as by economic laws. Similarly he approved Lenin's view that it is the actions of men that *change* the course of history rather than being simply determined by it. As Carl Boggs observes: "The Russian upheaval, in Gramsci's opinion, constituted in many significant respects a revolution *against Marx's Capital*, which had become an abstract, mechanistic treatise lacking any active political content ... In one historic episode the

Bolshevik revolution dramatically repudiated the entire body of elaborate, self-confident predictions based upon the 'laws of *capital*', overturning with it the mythical powers of economic determinism. For Gramsci, Lenin and the Bolsheviks could be defined as *living* rather than *abstract* Marxists who seized historical initiative through self-conscious action, who acted upon the actuality of the revolution instead of waiting for material conditions to 'ripen'. Political action had outstripped the lifeless, positivist Marxism that was supposed to serve as a framework for revolutionary praxis" (*Gramsci's Marxism*). In short, Gramsci saw the Russian revolution as confirmation of his view that the progress of history is propelled less by mathematically computable laws than by a dialectical interplay between the material conditions of production and the free decisions of the human producers themselves. Against the practice of sociological determinism which 'depoliticises' people by making them submissive to the laws of history, Gramsci argued that the true role of socialism was to rouse men and women from their dogmatic slumbers and remind them that history was of their own making.

But while Gramsci approved Lenin's hostility to positivistic interpretations of Marxism, he remained suspicious of the 'voluntaristic' excesses of some of his doctrines – and particularly his view that the elite 'vanguard party' should rule the 'masses' for their own good, rooting out all impure tendencies, until such time as they are ready to take power into their own hands. Gramsci glimpsed here the danger of a new kind of dogmatism. He warned that the exercise of decision-making should not become the prerogative of some centralised and supposedly 'enlightened' party elite. It must remain the rightful property of the social mass to be democratically expressed in self-governing councils and soviets.

This 'democratisation' of decision-making also necessitates a 'democratisation' of knowledge. Gramsci maintained that 'concepts' are not formal structures in some self-contained system (as Althusser was to argue) but flexible strategies which develop from one historical tradition to the next as *willed* human responses to the changing social environment. To confine the endless transformations of intellectual history within a closed system of homogenous relations is to put a straitjacket on the dialectic. Each individual consciousness, Gramsci affirms in the *Prison Notebooks*, "is the synthesis not only of existing relations, but of the history of these relations". To properly appreciate, therefore, the radical implications of Marx's 'historical materialism', we must place the emphasis on the term *historical* (which introduces the novel idea of dialectical change) rather than exclusively on the term *materialism* (which taken in isolation simply connotes an obsolete metaphysical teaching). "The philosophy of praxis", Gramsci bravely asserts, "is absolute historicism . . . an absolute humanism of hist ry" (*Prison Notebooks*). Once Marxist theory is sundered from its d ectical mooring in the history of human consciousness, it produces its o. .1 brand of mystification. And when this happens history becomes a caricature of itself, the manipulandum of an anonymous System.

It is against the backdrop of such philosophical debate, that we must understand Gramsci's repeated appeals in *The Prison Notebooks* for a 'critical theory' which would profile the irreducible role of man's *conscious* motivation in the revolutionary struggle. "The existence of objective conditions, of possibilities of freedom is not yet enough", he writes, "it is necessary to 'know' them, and know them to use them. And to want to use them" (*Prison Notebooks*). Predictably, Gramsci was denounced by some Marxist critics for his leanings towards the bourgeois philosophies of 'humanism' and 'historicism'. There is certainly evidence to suggest that Gramsci subscribed to Croce's belief that one of the primary 'motivations' of history was of an 'intellectual–moral' nature and that this required a philosophical evaluation of alternative ways of perceiving and expressing the world. But it must be added that in contrast to Croce, Gramsci insisted that this philosophy must be one of *praxis*, applying human creativity not just to a speculative dialectic but to a concretely realisable one. Thus while Gramsci declared that Marxism needed to cultivate a critical theory over and above the calculations of empirical science, he disagreed with such 'dialectical idealists' as Hegel and Croce that theory constituted some privileged realm of inspired genius. One of the most original ideas canvassed by Gramsci was that philosophy (while often originating in individual minds) was ultimately a *mass* phenomenon, in the sense that the highest mode of achieving truth is through the collective self-consciousness of a people as it comes to realise itself through historical action. To regard illumination as the special preserve of exceptional individuals is to revert to a kind of religious fetishism which takes the dialectical risk out of history. Indeed, Gramsci leaves us in little doubt as to his own views on this question when he satirises Croce as the 'high priest of contemporary historicist religion'. In short, even though he appropriated the Crocean concept of 'ideological hegemony' as a crucial motivating agency of historical consciousness, he rebuked Croce for ignoring the fact that such motivation, while causally undetermined, is nonetheless situated within the material parameters of the class struggle. Gramsci ultimately recommended that we replace Croce's 'speculative historicism' with a concretely situated historicism devoid of theological mystique.

The contradictions of the dialectic are not autonomous occurrences to be impassively contemplated by academic philosophers. They are not laboratory specimens for disinterested spectators. The truly committed thinker is, for Gamsci, one who posits these contradictions as an integral element of his own historical experience in order to "elevate this element to a principle of knowledge and therefore of action" (*Prison Notebooks*). In this way, the quest for critical self-consciousness ceases to be the privilege of a few rarefied spirits and becomes instead the vocation of each member of human society. This, in the final analysis, is the revolutionary import of Gramsci's oft-quoted maxim that '*all* men are philosophers'.

APPENDIX: THE POLITICAL ROLE OF THE INTELLECTUAL

Gramsci differs from many traditional Marxists in claiming that the transformation from capitalism to socialism requires not just an analysis of economic structures but of the relations between rulers and ruled (i.e. between leaders, the party and the mass of the population). If the revolution was to be successful, he was convinced, it must represent the *whole* people and demonstrate that the exploiter class are in fact a minority – contrary to the views propagated by the bourgeois ideology. This raised the vexed question of hegemony, that is, of securing the consent of the majority of the population. Gramsci was under no illusion that one of the primary reasons the bourgeois state had survived this long was because it had preserved its hegemony by disguising the sectional class interests of one particular group (the bourgeoisie) behind a banner of 'universal consensus' – to which other opposing groups gave consent often against their own class interests. Gramsci writes:

> The development and expansion of the particular group (those in power) are conceived of and presented as being the motor force of a universal expansion, of a development of all the 'national' energies. In other words, the dominant group is coordinated concretely with the general interests of the subordinate groups, and the life of the state is conceived of as a continuous process of formation and superseding of unstable equilibria (on the juridical plane) between the interests of the fundamental group and those of the subordinate groups – equilibria in which the interests of the dominant group prevail, but only up to a certain point, i.e. stopping short of narrowly corporate economic interests. (*Prison Notebooks*)

Gramsci maintains that in a genuinely socialist society, the consent of the majority would be won in a democratic and participatory fashion; in other words, the consensus required for a new hegemony would *really*, and not just supposedly, reflect the universal interests of the working class. In order to achieve such a consensus the role of the intellectual is indispensable.

Here Gramsci goes beyond Lenin's thesis in *State and Revolution* which limits the political to the state, thereby underestimating the pivotal role played by ideology at a 'national–popular' level. Gramsci believed this role was crucial both in the transition from a capitalist to a socialist state and in the eventual 'withering away of the state'. In order to forge a new 'historic bloc' where different aspects of social reality – economic, cultural, political etc. – can be grouped together to form a new alliance of interests, Gramsci pointed out that careful attention must be paid to the *specific national context* in which the emerging revolutionary movement aims to establish an alternative form of leadership or hegemony. This requires that the new 'organic' intellectuals of the working class be able to identify, articulate and organise the real needs and aspirations of the mass of the population in the light of their particular historical circumstances. The role of national traditions therefore, as expressive of the people as a whole, is integral to the project of a revolutionary transformation of society, rather than marginal as traditional Marxism believed. A proper understanding of the 'national–popular' will enable a variety of groups to join with the working class in the creation of a new historic bloc (or alliance of interests) capable of transcending narrow sectional interests. This approach always involves a certain degree of dialogue and compromise, a factor which may explain why many regard Gramsci as a 'Euro-Communist' *avant la lettre*.

Gramsci believed that the failure to achieve such a popular consensus leads to 'Statology' or 'Caesarism': the quasi-religious belief in the state's power to effect social transformation independently of the active participation of the mass of the population. Gramsci's wide-ranging studies of the actual institutions, customs and conventions of real states compelled him to recognise that the state is not only the instrument of a class but a complex web of relationships; and that it is at the level of these relationships of ideological dominion and consensus that each state seeks to derive its authority. Thus while Gramsci acknowledged that the power of the state is fundamentally related to the economic base (and the specific class interests of ownership), he denies that it reflects it in terms of a mechanical one-to-one correspondence, as orthodox Marxism held. For Gramsci the relation between the state and the economically dominant class is neither simple nor causally linear. It is mediated by a complex of ideological relations in which the intellectual (as mediator between rulers and ruled) plays a decisive role. The creation of a socialist society is, consequently, less a matter of dramatically replacing one dominant group with another – however progressive – than of establishing a 'new organization of knowledge' by the mass of the people.

A proper appreciation of the role played by intellectuals in achieving a new 'national–popular' consensus is particularly urgent in view of Gramsci's central distinction between 'war of movement' (a frontal and usually violent confrontation between the working classes and the state as in the October Revolution in Russia) and 'war of position' (a complex and protracted struggle more appropriate to the modern conditions of advanced industrial societies where government authority is based on some degree of mass consent as a result of state interventionism in civil society at large and collective–national organisation at social and cultural levels). The effective strategy of 'war of position' is described by Gramsci as the "most important question of political theory that the post-war period has posed" (*Prison Notebooks*). He defines the significant differences between the conditions of revolution in the East and West as follows:

> In Russia the State was everything, civil society was primitive and gelantinous; in the West, there was a proper relation between State and civil society, and when the State trembled a sturdy structure of civil society was at once revealed. The State was only an outer ditch, behind which there stood a powerful system of fortresses and earthworks: more or less numerous from one State to the next, it goes without saying – but this precisely necessitated an accurate reconnaissance of each individual country. (*Ibid.*)

Gramsci argued that a 'war of position' must always *precede* a 'war of movement' if the notion of democratic revolution is to be sustained; and it must also continue *after* the transfer of state power for as long as a new society is in the process of construction. Hence Gramsci insisted that the revolutionary transfer of state power (as one aspect of a wide variety of 'hegemonic' influences) needs to be accompanied by an 'intellectual and moral' revolution. Such a revolution calls for a radical change in the people's entire 'conception of the world' (on a par with the kind of change brought about by the Enlightenment or the Protestant Reformation for example), that is, in their perception of the relations of individuals to each other, to the productive forces of the economy, to the organisational institutions of politics and to religion, the nation, folklore and other cultural traditions. In the absence of such an 'intellectual' revolution, the working-class movement fails to adequately respond to the vital problem of leadership on the basis of consensus. As Gramsci remarked, the working class must "*already* exercise leadership before winning governmental power (this indeed is one of the principal conditions for the winning of such power); it subsequently becomes dominant when it exercises power, but even if it holds it firmly in its grasp, it must *continue* to 'lead' as well . . . one should not count only on the material force which power gives in order to exercise an effective leadership" (*Prison Notebooks*). The intellectuals, as organisers of the new consensus and of the relations between rulers and ruled, have an essential part to play in such leadership.

Gramsci's recognition of the necessity for an intellectual renewal of 'national–popular' traditions, departs from the view that revolution represents some absolute rupture with the past by creating a new society *ex nihilo*. Here Gramsci advances the model of 'revolution as process', as a continuum which begins with the old society and continues on after the transfer of power. For Gramsci the actual transfer of state power is just one moment – albeit a crucial one – in the continuous organic struggle of the masses to overcome capitalism. This approach was, of course, further supported by Gramsci's conviction that the model of the October Revolution ('war of movement') is no longer feasible in the advanced industrial societies and must be replaced by a strategic 'war of position' which operates at all the levels of civil society – and not just at the level of state or corporate power. In the twentieth century, Gramsci realised, the ruling classes in the West govern less by explicit force or coercion than by a 'hegemonic' manipulation of mass opinion.

A genuine socialist revolution cannot, therefore, be brought about by a small elite but only by the mass of the population motivated by a new intellectual 'conception of the world'. For the transition to socialism involves overcoming not just the capitalist system of State domination but also its apparatus of ideological hegemony which controls the values, aspirations, fidelities and understanding of the people as a whole. This requires for Gramsci full democratic access to knowledge and science. The working class cannot properly appropriate the means of technological production, for example, without an adequate understanding of advances in modern science. But Gramsci was far from convinced that such access had been achieved in the Soviet system where scientific research was bedevilled by bureaucratic practices:

> . . . a critical point of view which requires the utmost intelligence, open-minded-ness, mental freshness and scientific inventiveness has become monopolized by narrow-minded wretches who manage, due only to their dogmatic position, to maintain a position with the bibliography of science rather than in science . . . An ossified form of thinking is the greatest danger in these questions: a certain chaotic disorder is preferable to the philistine defence of pre-constituted positions. (*Prison Notebooks*)

The alternative to the intellectual democracy of a 'revolution as process' is what Gramsci describes as 'passive revolution': a form of historical change which originates 'on high' (i.e. from the elite rulers of the state) without the active initiative of the population and consequently without a substantial alteration in the fundamental relation of power. This phenomenon of 'passive revolution' – originally derived from Burke and the conservative tradition – was witnessed, says Gramsci, in the establishment of the Italian nation-state, in the introduction of 'scientific management' and 'rationalised production' in the US (what he calls 'Taylorism', 'Fordism' or 'Americanism') or most drastically in the modern rise of fascism. Gramsci maintained that 'passive revolution' was one of the most effective means devised by modern capitalism to preserve control within the hands of a small group by instituting modest economic or political reforms which expanded the base of popular support without actively engaging the conscious will of the people. As Gramsci observed in Notebook 22, fascism is the most explicit "form of passive revolution belonging to the twentieth century just as liberalism had been in the nineteenth".

The ultimate answer to the reactionary ploys of 'passive revolution' lies, according to Gramsci, at the level of hegemony. For the most basic problem of hegemony is not how revolutionaries come to power but how they come to be accepted as genuine leaders or guides by the mass of the people. Thus revolutionaries must consider the joint dilemma of (i) how they can win the intellectual assent of the people and (ii) how and when they should actively assume leadership in terms of power. Eric Hobsbawm offers some concrete contemporary examples of this dilemma:

> The Polish communists in 1945 established their power and were ready to exercise hegemony, but were probably not then accepted as a hegemonic force in that country. The German social-democrats in 1918 would probably have been accepted as a hegemonic force, but refused to accept that responsibility. Therein lies the tragedy of the German revolution. The Czech communists might have been accepted as a hegemonic force both in 1945 and in 1968, and were ready to play this role, but were not allowed to do so. The struggle for hegemony before, during and after the transition remains crucial in all circumstances. Power alone, even revolutionary power, cannot replace it. ('Gramsci and Marxist political theory' in *Approaches to Gramsci*, ed. A. Sassoon, 1982)

Gramsci was extremely sensitive to this dialectic of continuity and revolution. He recognised that revolution is both the negation and fulfilment of a people's past history; that it not only changes the existing 'national–popular' ideology of the people but also conserves it in important ways. And, as already noted, Gramsci was the first Marxist theorist to fully appreciate that capitalism had survived into the twentieth century not simply by means of economic and political domination but because it had succeeded in masking the class interests of its rulers behind those of the nation as a whole. Only this practice of hegemony – e.g. the ideological identifications of class and nation – could properly account for the numerous cases of rulers and ruled overcoming class differences in defence of such 'national–popular' notions as the Motherland or King and Country etc. Even the *Paris Commune* was in large part motivated by revolutionary patriotism. Thus Gramsci acknowledged that the role of the 'national-popular' consensus can be reactionary or progressive. It can lead to either 'bureaucratic centralism' (where the individual or group identifies with the totality of the state or nation in a passive, indirect way) or to 'democratic centralism' (where the consent of individual groups takes the form of active, direct participation).

Not surprisingly, Gramsci was suspicious of any utopian vision which ignored the organic relationship between the project of a socialist future and the pre-socialist past or present which it aims to replace. Socialism, he held, could not be achieved or sustained simply by securing a socially owned economy and controlling the forces of production in terms of five year plans. The goal of socialist production cannot be isolated as a purely technical problem of economics. It requires a transformation of (1) all the ideological institutions of society – legal, political, cultural etc.; and (2) of the entire relationship between leaders, party and masses in order to cultivate a 'collective will' based on the 'active and conscious co-partici-pation' of the people. Revolution must be conceived consequently not just as an instrumental transformation of the means of production but as an intellectual transformation of human potential which issues in a new consciousness. Gramsci insists, therefore, that a revolutionary party – what he called the 'Modern Prince' or 'Collective Intellectual' – can only become a genuine historical movement to the extent that it is the operative expression of a 'national–popular collective will'; that is, "the proclaimer and organizer of an intellectual and moral reform, which also means creating the terrain for a subsequent development . . . towards the reali-zation of a superior, total form of modern civilization" (*Prison Notebooks*)

The most immediate task of the revolutionary movement, Gramsci argued, is to expand its basis of popular consent by embarking on a process of democratic intellectual reform. For as he observes in his prison writings, "a human mass does not 'distinguish' itself, does not become independent without, in the widest sense, organising itself, and there is no organisation without intellectuals" (*Prison Notebooks*). The unity of theory and practice enunciated by historical materialism, demands the construction of an 'intellectual-moral bloc' capable of involving the "progress of the mass and not only of small intellectual groups" (*ibid.*). Gramsci concluded accordingly that the most important question facing the new organic intellectuals of the revolutionary movement is the following: ". . . is it the intention that there should always be rulers and ruled, or is the objective to create the conditions in which this division is no longer necessary? In other words, is the initial premise the perpetual division of the human race, or the belief that this division is only an historical fact, corresponding to certain conditions?" (*ibid.*). Gramsci's answer to this question is clear.

In the light of the above analysis, we may perhaps better appreciate why Gramsci conceived of his major work, *The Prison Notebooks*, as an inquiry into the contemporary political role of intellectuals in the wake of the Russian revolution, the defeated workers' movement in Western Europe (and in particular Turin), the rise of fascism and the general reorganisation of capitalism in advanced industrial countries (typified by the phenomenon of 'Fordism'). In the eighth notebook, Gramsci provided a summary index of all the major subjects of his prison research under the significant heading: *Scattered Notes and Comments for a History of the Italian Intellectuals.*

Ernst Bloch

Ernst Bloch was born to Jewish parents in Ludwigshaften, Germany in 1895. Like so many of the radical German thinkers of his generation, he was deeply marked by his personal experience of the Social Democrat Revolution of 1917 and, of course, the Russian Revolution. Bloch was foremost in the vanguard of humanist Marxists who believed that the socialist revolution aimed at a utopian liberation which could not be contained within the narrow limits of scientific socialism – or what came to be known as 'vulgar Marxism'.

Bloch shared with his close friend, Walter Benjamin – another German Marxist of Jewish origin – a desire to combine a revolutionary commitment to dialectical materialism with a future-oriented 'hope' which, he believed, was expressed by certain cultural, religious and metaphysical traditions. Indeed Bloch's insistence that the 'utopian' kernel of religion and art be restored as an historical 'horizon' of dialectical Marxism earned him the nickname of 'the theologian of the revolution'. One of Bloch's earliest works was a study of the messianic socialism of the German peasant revolt in the eighteenth century, entitled *Thomas Muenzer as Theologian of Revolution* (1921). The titles and preoccupations of his other major publications also point in this direction, e.g. *Spirit of Utopia* (1918), *The Principle of Hope* (1959) and *A Philosophy of the Future* (1963).

Bloch frequently expressed the conviction that unless the revolution incorporated a radical understanding of the spiritual experiences of human transcendence, mystery, hope and a moral critique of purely technical ratiocination, it would degenerate into a soulless dogmatism. Not surprisingly, Bloch was denounced by the intellectual right as a 'renegade communist' and by the Stalinist left as a 'bourgeois humanist'. Though he emigrated to the United States in 1938, he returned to Communist East Germany after the war where he occupied the chair of philosophy at Leipzig's Karl Marx University for several years. But he moved to West Germany when he was forced to retire from Leipzig University – shortly after the erection of the Berlin Wall in the late fifties – because of the authorities' increasing displeasure with the 'theological' bent of his writing and teaching. It was as an unorthodox Marxist emigré in the West, therefore, that Bloch completed his monumental three-volume work, *The*

Principle of Hope, and became involved in numerous intellectual controversies of the New Left. In the sixties and seventies, Bloch was translated extensively into English and proved a guiding inspiration for both the student revolts and the theologies of liberation.

I

Bloch's most original contributions to Marxist theory were in the field of cultural history rather than of economic science in the strict sense. He believed that the 'infrastructural' analysis of orthodox Marxism needed to be supplemented by a critical analysis of the dialectical workings of such 'superstructures' as art, religion and philosophy. He did not deny the validity of a political economy based on the principles of dialectical materialism. He simply affirmed that this was not *all* there was to Marxist theory. The antagonism between the forces and relations of production (between the proletariat and capital) remained for Bloch the *source* of the revolutionary struggle; he acknowledged it as the efficient cause. But the *direction* of the revolution involved another dimension of Marxist analysis – the dimension of a final cause. This is what traditional metaphysics referred to as 'teleology' and what theology referred to as 'eschatology': the science of the 'last things' or the coming of the Kingdom. Bloch calls it 'utopia'.

Bloch invariably placed the focus on the philosophical rather than the positivist aspects of Marxism. In this respect, he became a fellow-traveller of the new humanist movement in Marxist theory advanced by Lukács, Brecht, Benjamin and the Frankfurt school with whom he engaged in fruitful critical dialogue from the thirties onwards.

But if Bloch's thought is characterised by a distinctively 'messianic' perspective, it is also profoundly committed to 'secular' concerns. Bloch celebrated the theological dreams of a perfect kingdom of justice, for he was convinced that without such paradigms of hope in future possibilities of 'newness' (*novum*) and 'otherness' (*plus ultra*) there would be less reason to resist the alienating conditions of the present. He insisted that just as theology needs dialectical materialism to bring it back to this world, dialectical materialism needs a theology of hope in order to keep open the futural horizon of transcendence, as a sort of spiritual leaven to the ongoing revolutionary struggle. Once the revolution erases the spiritual future from its conscience, it betrays itself and ceases to be *historical* materialism.

The overriding preoccupation of Bloch's 'polyrhythmic' *oeuvre* – numbering some twenty major works ranging from philosophy to cultural and political theory – remains throughout utopia. The 'critical-utopian' project is for Bloch a perennial witness to the human aspiration for a radically transformed world. This is a universal project in which the dreams and images of all human cultures, however diverse, can participate. And it is for this reason that in a work like *The Philosophy of the Future*, Bloch has no compunction about juxtaposing quotations from the Bible, Virgil's *Aeneid*, Goethe's *Faust* or Hegel's *Phenomonology of Spirit*, with passages from Marx on political history. Time and again in his writings, Bloch instances 'prefigurations' of the utopian dream which he believes it is the duty of Marxist theory to reappropriate and restore to its true historical meaning. Indeed, one of Bloch's favourite and oft-quoted maxims was, not surprisingly, the comment by Marx to Ruge in 1843: "For a long time the world has dreamt of that which we must understand clearly if we are to possess it in reality. It will become evident that it is not a question of a rupture between past and future, but of a realisation of the projections of the past.'

Bloch sought a philosophical fusion between the most venerable traditions of the 'metaphysics of desire' – extending from Plato to Hegel and the German Idealists – and the new dialectical materialism of revolutionary Marxism. He strove to materialise idealism and to idealise materialism. This dual fidelity to traditionally opposed philosophies was not, of course, without its difficulties and even contradictions. One need only cite Bloch's tortuous attempts, on occasion, to reconcile certain doctrinal principles of the Communist Party (even though he himself never became a member) with the innovative 'experimentalism' of his own writings (Benjamin hailed Bloch as a master of the German avant-garde essay). Like almost everything in Bloch's intellectual project, the ultimate resolution of the conflict between Marxist materialism and the spiritual yearnings of traditional idealisms, remained to the end a *utopian possibility* rather than an established fact.

Marx's famous statement that we must not only *interpret* the world as the philosophers had done, but *change* it, was understood by Bloch to mean not the end of philosophy *per se* but the translation of abstract speculation into a project of historical action. In other words, dialectical materialism retained for Bloch the status of a 'philosophy' but one which endeavoured to understand the world as a possibility of radical transformation. He resisted all reductionist readings of Marx's manifesto. It was not, he claimed, a summons to abandon imaginative and intellectual exploration in favour of a cheerless pragmatism. Bloch argued consistently that the 'facts' of history could only make sense if considered in the dialectical terms of a *total* historical perspective. And this required that as much attention be paid to the forgotten horizons of the past and undiscovered horizons of the future as to the immediate present.

Because he affirmed the need to reinsert Marxist theory into a historical dialectic of ongoing change, Bloch is often portrayed as an 'Hegelian Marxist' in the mould of Lukács or the Frankfurt school. Indeed Bloch himself pointed out to the American critic, Dick Howard, that his first work, *Spirit of Utopia* (1919), was as much indebted to the early Lukács as was Lukács' *History and Class Consciousness* (1923) to many of his own early writings. Both of these Marxist thinkers hailed originally from the common philosophical tradition of German idealism – a tradition which counted Goethe, Kant and Hegel amongst its luminary pioneers and which, Bloch and Lukács believed, found its true complimentary expression in the dialectical 'materialisation' which Marxism brought about. Both thinkers wrote of history as a dialectical category of mediation between consciousness and matter, labouring to overcome the idealist dualism of subject and object. Similarly, both exploded the static category of a reified present which had dominated traditional metaphysics and positivism. As Bloch remarked in his review of Lukács' *History and Class Consciousness*, the *now* could only be understood dialectically in terms of those "tendencies from whose opposition it can create the future . . . the birth of the *new*".

Bloch parted company with Lukács, however, on the question of the determining role of class consciousness. He accused the latter of a 'sociological homogenization' of history which promoted premature party-line solutions to the problems of human experience and thereby underestimated the need to remain open to the 'qualitative leap of the new'. Lukács, it is true, had scant regard for that 'sense of the incidental' which Bloch and Benjamin so cherished as an epiphany of the 'secrets of the world'. And while Lukács became a party member and displayed a certain willingness to accommodate theory to the pragmatic necessities of historical circumstance, Bloch refused to do either. Like Benjamin, Bloch felt he could best serve Marxism by remaining a critical nomad forever wandering 'through the desert' (a favourite Blochian motif and in fact the title of another early work published in 1923).

The disagreement between Bloch and Lukács also expressed itself in their conflicting concepts of 'contradiction'. Lukács viewed 'contradiction' as an immediate condition of actual class struggle. By contrast, Bloch spoke of a 'temporality of contradiction' which viewed present socio-political contradictions as being determined, in part at least, by non-contemporary contradictions derived from past or future tendencies of historical development. Such an analysis would, Bloch held, permit Marxist theory to reactivate the 'unfulfilled intentions' of the forgotten past – that is, the various projections of a just, harmonious and non-alienated society recorded in the social and cultural visions of former generations – and at the same time, preserve the present historical struggle as 'an open system of experimentation' directed toward the still possible horizon of the 'not-yet' (*Noch-Nicht*). Bloch maintained, accordingly, that the revolutionary intellectual must continue to respect 'the unfulfilled fairy tale of the good old times, the unresolved myth of the mysterious old being or of nature'. Far from signalling a regressive nostalgia, this critical attention to the utopian anticipations of such by-gone myths sustain a consciousness of dialectical *continuity* with the present.

But Bloch remained equally suspicious of any simplistic notion of history as an inevitable linear progress. Such notions, he insisted, merely reduce the dialectic to a means–end rationalistion where the future can be scientifically predicted. They invariably result in a narrow ideology of pseudo-utopias. Against this Bloch argued for the *unpredictable* character of history; he continually affirmed its latent potential for 'qualitative leaps' towards the New. The past and the future are not abstract grammatical tenses to be passively contemplated or technically computed; they act as the critical consciences of today, functioning, respectively, as active memory and active vocation. A Marxist science which analyses the conditions of labour and production in the empirical present is of course necessary; but it is not sufficient. *Science*, as an empirical critique of alienated labour, and *utopia*, as a non-empirical projection of the 'Kingdom of Feedom', need each other. For without such a dialectical relationship between the contemporary and the non-contemporary, the old opposition between reason and hope, Bloch asserts, cannot be overcome.

Bloch has been accused of committing the unforgiveable sin of 'subjective idealism'. Habermas, for example, referred to him as a 'Marxist Schelling' suffering from an overdose of messianic mysticism. Other Marxist commentators have looked with scepticism at his manifest enthusiasm for Bruno, Nicholas of Cusa and several Christian mystics who equated the kingdom of God with a divine *potential* for transcendence latent within history. But such critics fail to fully appreciate the essentially 'dialectical' nature of Bloch's thought as it swings between materialism and mysticism, political commitment and philosophical distance, seeking out the possible points of *mediation*.

II

The concept of 'possibility' plays a pivotal role in Bloch's work. In *The Principle of Hope*, he outlines two main categories of the possible. Firstly, there is the 'subjective possibility' of human consciousness; this expresses itself pre-eminently in the superstructural symbolisms of religion, art, metaphysics and political theory. Secondly, there is 'real-objective possibility' which resides in nature itself as the material basis of historical change. History is the creative dialectic which results from the interchange between these two horizons of the possible; and as such it enables man and nature to become 'co-producers' of the future.

The 'real-objective possibility' is sometimes described by Bloch as a seed within the material order which, under appropriate circumstances, may unfold into a 'resurrection of nature'. And, by extension, this as yet unfulfilled potency of nature can combine with the similarly unfulfilled intentions of human consciousness to realise the 'Novum still far away'. Block defines the *Novum*, accordingly as the 'realisation of hope according to the prefigurations of the possibility of its realisation'. But in contrast to the Hegelian-idealist definition of the essence of history as that which has been (*das Wesen ist gewesen*), Bloch offers an Hegelian-Marxist redefinition of this essence as that which has not yet been (*noch nie so gewesen*). The authentic function of the critical mind must be construed, therefore, not as some platonic quest for otherworldly solutions but as a 'maieutic' deliverance of the virtual potencies of both objective nature and subjective consciousness; that is, as the creative labour of historical praxis. Interpreting the world so as to change it means that philosophy discovers its ultimate vocation as Marxist midwifery.

The dialectical category of the 'possible' does not require a negation of the real as the idealists, Sartre or even Adorno, maintained. Nor can it be adequately comprehended as a retrospective illusion of the real in the past, as Bergson held. The 'possible' for Bloch is the *prefiguration* of the real, the anticipation (past or present) of the futural reality of the *Novum*. Thus Bloch can write in *On Karl Marx* (1968) that "human life is primarily a process of transcendence, of stepping beyond the given . . .". But this notion of transcendence in no way implies an evasion of the material conditions of history. It does indeed turn determinism on its head; and as such, it refutes both the metaphysical materialism of Democritus and the scientistic materialism of Engels. But this transgression of historical determinism does not deny the historical conditioning of consciousness by the socio-economic determinants of labour and class. What Bloch's theory of the 'possible' in fact signals is a dialectical interplay between such historical conditions and the powers of utopian consciousness which can transcend and ultimately transmute these historical conditions into a Kingdom of Freedom. Here again Bloch invokes the great works of art as evidence of such creative transcendence. In the following polemical passage from *A Philosophy of the Future* (1963), he states his own view on this subject in opposition to Lukács' more sociological approach which, he

believes, unduly limits the meaning of an art work to the ideological and
social context in which it was first produced:

> A *significant* work of art does not perish with the passing of time; it belongs only
> ideologically and not *creatively* to the age in which it is socially rooted. The
> permanence and greatness of major works of art consists precisely in their
> operation through a fulness of pre-semblance (*Vor-schein*) of realms of utopian
> significance . . . driving forward and soaring towards a goal . . . In these cases a
> *cultural surplus* is clearly effective: something that moves above and beyond the
> ideology of a particular age . . . And a combined application of sound economic
> analysis and sociologistic-schematic blinkers, even in the form of Georg Lukács'
> theory of literature, merely obscures the utopian perspective of every work of art.
> (*ibid.*).

Where Lukács diagnosed the 'despair' of such modernist authors as
Beckett and Kafka as a symptom of decadent nihilism, Bloch reads it more
sympathetically as a paradoxical *via crucis* of hope. Bloch argues that the
'angst' of modernist writing or expressionist painting epitomises a revolt
against alienation which bears witness to a longing for better things.
Indeed, his overall analysis of art in the utopian perspective of *final causality*
rather than the reductive perspective of *efficient causality* – where the
'negativity' of an artwork is explained in terms of the 'negative' socio-political conditions which predetermined the artist's class allegiance – evinces a
curious blending of Marxist and phenomenological idioms. At times,
Bloch's theoretical appraisal of the role of symbolism, for example, actually
seems closer to the phenomonenological hermeneutics of Heidegger or
Ricoeur than to the materialist hermeneutics of Lukács or Lenin. Like
Ricoeur, he prefers a 'hermeneutic of affirmation' which deciphers symbols *prospectively* in terms of the 'possible worlds' they open up, to the
'hermeneutic of suspicion' practiced by 'vulgar' materialists and narrow
Freudians who analyse symbols *retrospectively*, reducing their content to the
anterior causes of their constituent parts. Far from being a passive mirror of
the ideological bias of class interests, the artwork is, as Bloch puts it in *The
Principle of Hope*, 'at once the laboratory and the carnival of possibilities'.
This metaphor of the laboratory is particularly interesting in that it
expresses Bloch's view that art is also part of the 'labour' process of history,
albeit the most exploratory and experimental part. The metaphor of the
carnival, on the other hand, suggests that aesthetic productions are
fundamentally playful in the sense of liberating us into an experience of
novelty, strangeness and wonder. In other words, the 'appearance' (*Schein*)
of the art form at once reflects the historical conditioning of its production
and surpasses this conditioning by way of an 'anticipation' (*Vorschein*) of
alternative possibilities of experience. On the basis of such an analysis,

Bloch has far less difficulty than someone like Lukács in squaring the exigencies of a modernist revolution in literature with a Marxist revolution in politics.

III

Bloch's investigation of utopian possibility does not, however, limit itself to aesthetic considerations. It also embraces works of science. The rigid distinction between the arts and sciences is declared untenable for a truly dialectical understanding. All the great scientific discoveries of men such as Galileo, Kepler or Newton presuppose the creative imagining of what Bloch calls 'objectively new possibilities'. These imaginings do not unfold, to be sure, as religious aspirations or aesthetic forms, but as 'ideal types of supposition'. The discoveries of physicists, for example, began as exploratory hypotheses directed beyond the empirical givens towards a future horizon of novel evidence. What is now a proven fact was once an imagined possibility. Or as Bloch states in *A Philosophy of the Future*, scientific inventions involve "anticipatory traces (*Spuren*) of an essence which can never be reduced to already existing facts"; and this for the reason that the "direction of its postulative *ideal types* . . . rectifies itself only in *fieri*, in *process*, and therefore not – in its being other than factual truth – by *the fact of that which is the case*". Consequently, while science deals with the material world, it can only evolve as such to the extent that it creatively experiments with the 'tendency of the process and the latency of objective-real possibility'. This means that science is essentially motivated by a methodological *plus ultra* which never allows it to stagnate into a 'reified system of facts'; and which, furthermore, ensures that every *attribute-definition (definitio)* of experimental observation presupposes an *orientation-definition (destinatio)*. Thus science is also enlisted into the service of disclosing those objective-real possibilities (*objectiv-real Mögliche*) which orient the utopian horizons of the dialectic. Bloch describes this utopian role of scientific investigation, accordingly, as "the world experimenting with itself and creating its own possible forms in a process . . . of historical *fieri*" (*A Philosophy of the Future*).

All of man's cultural projections – scientific, artistic, religious and philosophical – share a common horizon of teleological possibility. Perhaps Bloch's most detailed account of this 'tendential-anticipation' of the possible is contained in a study entitled 'The category of the possible' in *The Principle of Hope*. Here Bloch suggests that our various cultural works disclose a 'being-according-to-the-possible' (*chata to dunamaton*) which guides our approach, both theoretical and practical, to the material world while being simultaneously guided by the 'being-in-possibility' (*to dunamei on*) of the material world. In this manner, Bloch proposes a Marxist–Hegelian reading of Aristotle's notion of the possible (*dunamis*) in the *Physics*. He relocates the Aristotelian discovery of the 'dynamic' character of material potency in a properly historical perspective. For Aristotle the final goal (*telos*) of the striving of all potency was a Divine Self-Thinking-Thought of eternal and immutable actuality, radically transcendent of historical time and matter. For Bloch, by contrast, the ultimate *telos* is the possibility of a future 'kingdom of liberty' to be realised on this temporal and material earth. Bloch argues that this utopian goal motivates both a subjective possibility of mind and an objective possibility of nature. Hence his declaration that "theory and praxis are intimately linked to the interrogation of the modes of objective–real possibility" (*ibid.*).

The possibility of the *Telos* or *Novum* – as Bloch also calls it – takes the form of a virtual free space inhabiting reality; as such it keeps history out-of-joint with itself, non-identical, non-contemporary, open to change because turned towards what is not yet. Such a *telos* for Bloch is not some abstract speculative fixity; it is the very "womb of fertility from which all the figures of our world emerge . . . showing the face of hope in real possibility" (*ibid.*) Once comprehended in terms of the Marxist-Hegelian dialectic, utopia reveals not just *mind* but *matter* itself as an indispensable factor of historical transcendence. But this kind of comprehension calls for a new relationship between the epistemological categories of subjectivity and objectivity. And Bloch maintains that nothing short of a radically dialectical cosmology can succeed in providing the basis for such a revision of our traditional notions of subject and object:

> The subjective factor here represents our inexhaustible capacity to change the course of things; and the objective factor is the world's inexhaustible potentiality to undergo change . . . The subjective potency coincides not only with the forces which alter the direction of history but also with that which realizes itself in history – and this coincidence increases as men become the conscious producers of their history. Similarly, the objective potency coincides not only with that which is changeable but also with what realizes itself in history; and here again this coincidence increases as the external world – outside of man – comes more and more into mediation with man. (*The Principle of Hope*)

Without such a dialectical cosmology, the project of utopian freedom which motivates man's historical struggle for a better world, would be no more than an illusory or 'negative' possibility. So that while Bloch asserts that the meaning of human history resides in the active construction of the 'Commonwealth of Freedom', he is insistent that "without a positively-possible meaning in the surrounding cosmology which all historical events ultimately merge with, the progress of this historical process might as well never have happened' (*A Philsophy of the Future*).

In this manner, Bloch advances a critical hermeneutic capable of discriminating between (1) the empty utopias of solipsistic fantasy and (2) authentic utopias whose ideal possibility finds an objective correlative in the real possibilities of revolutionary history (*das sachhaft–objectgemäss Mögliche*). To divest utopia of this tendential grounding in the 'real-objective possibility' of matter, is to condemn human action to a directionless voluntarism. The critical category of the possible sponsored by Bloch functions, therefore, in a dual capacity. It serves as both a critical *limit* of meaning (what Bloch calls the 'world-according-to-possibility') and as a critical reminder of the *limitless* dynamism of meaning (what he calls the 'world-in-possibility'). As such, this category dispels traditional notions of history as an arbitrary chaos, an eternal repetition of static sameness, or a pre-established harmony ineluctably unfolding according to mechanistic laws. Such notions are inherently reactionary in so far as they deny the revolutionary intervention in history of free human praxis. Utopia, Bloch suggests, is better understood as a *May-Be* (*Kann-Sein*) latent in material nature, a possibility which cannot be realised without the transformation of history by human consciousness and labour.

This critical–utopian analysis of the relationship between human foresight (*Vor-sicht*) and material progress, implies that cultural works become historical at the same time as history itself becomes a cultural work. In other words, utopian possibility requires of its actualisation both the partial conditionality of material history and the partial unconditionality of aesthetic or 'superstructural' consciousness. In contrast to the neo-Kantian *Gestandstheorie*, therefore, Bloch construes the category of the possible not as an *a priori* structure of formal knowledge but as the very precondition of historical salvation.

Here we meet with Bloch's most conclusive definition of the possible as the concept of salvation (*der Heilsbegriff*). The truth of man's redemption from alienation, he emphasises, is no longer to be sought in metaphysical notions of suprahistorical self-sufficiency – e.g. the *ens causa sui, ens realissimum* or *a se esse*. Such notions, if taken as realities rather than as prefigurations (*Vor-bildungen*), simply prolong human alienation, as Marx acknowledged when he spoke of religion as the opium of the people. Redemption must be reinterpreted according to the model of dialectical materialism as a Kingdom of Liberty whose historical realisation – and there is no other kind – depends on man's free decision to make the revolutionary possibilities latent in history *real*. "The interdependence", writes Bloch, "is here such that without the potentiality of the *power-to-become-other*, the capacity of the *power-to-make-other* would have no space in which to operate; just as without man's *power-to-make-other* the world's *power-to-become-other* could not be meaningfully mediated by human action. Consequently, the principle of possibility can only reveal itself as it is ... thanks to the active intervention of man in the domain of the transfigurable – the concept of salvation" (*The Principle of Hope*).

The coming of the Kingdom on earth is contingent upon the creative initiatives of man. "What is possible", Bloch concludes, "can as easily sink into nothingness as realise itself as the Kingdom." It is for this reason that Bloch strenuously resists the efforts of traditional metaphysicians and logicians to eliminate the dynamic character of the possible by interpreting it retroactively as that which has already been realised in the past. He opposes all attempts to reduce truth to some absolute Being which might be *recollected* in its aboriginal oneness (e.g. Plato's notion of *anamnesis* or Hegel's notion of *Erinnerung*). Instead, Bloch reinterprets the category of the possible as a future-oriented determination (*zukunfttragende Bestimmtheit*) – one which delivers past and present being into utopian becoming. Thus he replaces the old static ontologies with a dialectical ontology of endless, revolutionary movement:

> Possibility no longer resides in a ready-made ontology of being as that-which-has-been-up-to-now, but in an ontology which is to be forever refounded on the being-of-that-which-is-not-yet, an ontology which discovers the future even in the past in the totality of nature ... The category of real possibility is the category of that space which opens up before the movement of matter as a dialectical process: it is the specific property of that dimension of reality which is situated *in front of* its unfolding. (*The Principle of Hope*)

CONCLUSION

Bloch's work has been summed up by one commentator, Maynard Solomon, as a 'Talmudic socialism'. This description suggests that Bloch – along with Benjamin, Marcuse and certain other twentieth-century Marxists of Jewish origin – continued a messianic strain of socialism which surfaced from time to time in such pioneering reformers as Joachim of Fiori, Thomas Münzer, the Paraguayan Jesuits, Albert Schweitzer and so on. Indeed, Bloch's theology of revolution is fundamentally ecumenical in that he focuses on the eschatological goal of history which, he claims, is the common horizon aspired towards by all genuine messianic religions – Jewish, Christian or otherwise. The real genesis, as Bloch remarked in *The Principle of Hope*, is not at the beginning but at the end.

Bloch believed that Marxism should take seriously Marx's own proposed alliance between 'the poor and the thinkers'. Such an alliance implies that the hope for an emancipation of the dispossessed also finds blueprints of future fulfilment in the great spiritual movements and minds of the past. In other words, Marxism and theology can make common cause in their respective projects of liberation. For as Bloch maintains, 'the place into which the gods were imagined' is the same potential space of utopian hope which motivates the communist revolution and provides its ultimate *raison d'être*. Without such a spiritual (or superstructural) motivation Bloch feared that Marxism can easily degenerate into a mechanistic materialism "fixated on an atheistic *status quo* that offers the human soul nothing but a more or less eudaimonistically furnished heaven on earth . . ." (*Man on His Own*, 1970).

The theological project of a future Kingdom of Freedom is, for Bloch, a necessary reminder to Marxists that the revolution is not yet complete in the here and now of a purely economic–political system. This project prevents us from making peace with the world as it *is*, keeping us open to the future – the world as it *might be* – by revealing a perpetual dissatisfaction with the present state of things. Once deprived of such a theology of utopia, the revolution risks succumbing to the constraints of ideology. For while ideology seeks to conserve and consolidate what has already been achieved, utopia makes us aware that the age-old dreams of a better world are *still* unfulfilled. Only that which has never yet come to pass, asserts Bloch, never grows old. Unlike ideologies, authentic utopias do not vindicate the interests of the ruling class –the ideological status quo – of a society.

The 'Heaven on Earth' which Bloch sponsors is a *potential* space which 'lies ahead' and which may only be realised if and when a socio-political liberation of the material forces of production coincides with a spiritual liberation of the human heart, mind and imagination. And in similar fashion, Bloch would insist that a theology of the Kingdom simply degenerates into passive submission unless its 'collective dreams' of a messianic era are translated daily into the concrete social objectives of an ongoing revolutionary commitment. "It is precisely hope", writes Bloch, "to the extent that it is joined to a world that does not surrender, that neither falls into despair nor sinks into quietist confidence" (*Man On His Own*).

But Bloch's messianic socialism participates in an open-ended utopian project in more than a theological sense. Alongside the messianic images of the Judaeo-Christian biblical tradition – e.g. Paradise, the resurrection of the body, the Coming of the Kingdom, the Land of Milk and Honey, the Age of Redemption when the Lion lies down with the Lamb etc. – Bloch lists the utopian images of various secular cultural works. Here he includes the archetypal representations of utopian transcendence to be found in great works of art – Blake's Jerusalem, Cervantes' Cave of Montesinos Mozart's Magic Flute, Defoe's Island of Crusoe/Man Friday fraternity, Beethoven's Ninth Symphony and so on. But Bloch's cultural analysis of utopian archetypes is not confined to works of 'High Art'. It also embraces myths, folktales and fairy stories of popular culture – such as the Golden Age, El Dorado, Atlantis, the Islands of Eternal Youth, the Happy Hunting Ground, the Eternal Feminine, the Big Rock Candy Mountain or Robin Hood's refuge at Sherwood Forest. So that while Bloch may be said to privilege images of a utopian *future*, it is significant that he finds most of his examples in the cultural and religious expressions of the *past*. In other words, the utopian foreward-look implies not a rupture with the traditional representations of our collective childhood but a recovery of these age-old memories. As Bloch explains in *The Principle of Hope*, when man eventually comes to self-realisation and grounds "his life in real democracy without renunciation and estrangement, then there will arise in the world something which appears to us all in childhood, and in which none of us yet was – home".

Herbert Marcuse

Herbert Marcuse was undoubtedly the most renowned representative of Critical Theory. His hotly debated analysis of the ideological underpinnings of advanced industrial society became a spawning ground for revolutionary ideas amongst the young generations. An influential and long-serving member of the Frankfurt Institute of Social Research, he is still considered by many to have been the key philosophical catalyst of the New Left.

I

The reasons for Marcuse's celebrity are not difficult to identify. Firstly, his thought is uncommonly *synthetic*. It represents an open-ended, inclusive exploration drawing freely from a wide variety of intellectual movements. Marcuse abhorred cliques and orthodoxies. In his writings, Marx, Freud, Heidegger, Hegel and the German idealists sit together with unprecedented ease. Marcuse did not hesitate to take on board what he considered to be the major modern contributions to critical thinking, ranging from the dialectical critique of historical consciousness to the phenomenological critique of existential consciousness and the psychoanalytic critique of the libidinal unconscious.

Marcuse's international reputation also owes much to the fact that – unlike such critical theorists as Lukács, Gramsci or Benjamin – he spanned the divide between the Continental and Anglo-American worlds of thought. A native of Germany – he was born in Berlin to a bourgeois Jewish family in 1898 – Marcuse fled the Nazi regime in the thirties and settled in the United States, together with his Frankfurt School colleagues Horkheimer and Adorno. Here he lived, wrote and taught (in the universities of Columbia, Brandeis and California) until his death in 1979.

But Marcuse always remained an intellectual emigré. He never subscribed to the 'positivism' which was at one time almost *de rigueur* in the American university system. On the contrary, he clung to the virtues of what he termed '*negative* thinking', intent on subverting the 'one-dimensional' ideologies of technological rationality which underwrote the system of advanced capitalism. Throughout his mature career, Marcuse applied the dialectical methods of Critical Theory to modern Western society. He never ceased to challenge the ruses of the latter's '*affirmative* culture' whose aim was to 'contain' the human need for freedom and happiness within the strict limits of a repressive consumer society and manipulative mass media. Marcuse promoted the idea of a 'great refusal' which would encourage people to think critically for themselves and thereby combat the blind belief in the inevitability of technical progress. His various analyses of the 'one-dimensional' mentality served to introduce the trojan horses of Hegel, Marx and Freud into the contemporary citadel of uncritical positivism.

Marcuse's work, while complex, was popular because it was at all times relevant. It refused to keep philosophical inquiry within safe academic confines. In this respect, it was intended to be, and was perceived as being, 'dangerous thinking'. Time and again, Marcuse was denounced by the American press as a communist subversive or, at best, as an eccentric *provocateur* of the 'looney left'.

Marcuse remained faithful to Marx's basic insight that theory should never be divorced from a critique of man's historical and social condition. But he was never a doctrinaire or card-carrying Marxist. Unlike Lukács or Gramsci, he declined to join the Communist Party. Indeed his detailed study of bureaucratic socialism, *Soviet Marxism: A Critical Analysis* (1958), was an uncompromising attack on the attempt to subordinate the radical humanism of Marx's writings to the simplifications of an orthodox party ideology. Marcuse maintained that such an attempt was no more than a disguised version of 'state capitalism' in the service of another brand of technical rationality. In totalitarian communism the *critical* aspect of Marxism – which for Marcuse represented its radicality as a project of emancipation – was betrayed.

Marcuse called for a new interpretation of Marx capable of sustaining a more flexible rapport between the exigencies of reason and imagination, equality and freedom, happiness and justice. He argued that the liberation of man from the alienating conditions of advanced industrial society required a reappropriation not only of the economic means of production but also the cultural means of experience and expression. The revolutionary potential of labour as a transformative agency of history needed to be complemented by the critical potential of the creative imagination – what Marcuse referred to as the 'aesthetic dimension'.

Marcuse's ideas became an inspirational guide for the emerging New Left in the sixties. One of their catchcries – *l'imagination au pouvoir* – was a summary account of his 'aesthetic' critique. Indeed, as the Paris students joined forces with the striking workers in May '68, they marched to the concerted chant of 'Marx, Mao, Marcuse'. And while Marcuse was surely sceptical of such rhetorical slogans, he could not but have been a little pleased with the knowledge that his work had proved relevant to the dissenting modern generation, transcending the limits of theoretical discussion to solicit a movement of practical revolt.

II

Marcuse's first philosophical project was to reconcile the existential philosophy of concrete subjectivity with the dialectical theory of historical materialism. From an early age Marcuse had been involved in radical student politics. He participated in the Social Democratic revolution in Berlin in 1917 and familiarised himself with Marx's writings. But his philosophical career proper began when he went to work with Martin Heidegger at Freiburg University in 1928. In 'Contributions to a phenomenology of historical materialism' (1928), his first important philosophical publication, Marcuse hailed Heidegger's *Being and Time* (1927) as that 'turning point in the history of philosophy' where bourgeois thought 'transcends itself from within' paving the way for a new 'concrete' mode of thinking. Marcuse recalls this formative period of his intellectual development in an interview with Frederick Olafson in 1977:

> We saw in Heidegger what we had first seen in Husserl, a new beginning, the first radical attempt to put philosophy on really concrete foundations – philosophy concerned with the human existence, the human condition, and not with merely abstract ideas and principles ... At the same time I wrote articles of Marxist analysis for the then theoretical organ of the German Socialists, *Die Gesellschaft*. So I certainly was interested, and I first, like all the others, believed there could be some combination between existentialism and Marxism, precisely because of their insistence on concrete analysis of the actual human existence, human beings and their world. (*ibid.*)

Marcuse believed that Marxism provided the correct analysis of the material causes of contemporary alienation under capitalism. But he maintained that the revolutionary transformation of society could not take effect without the free critical consciousness of those oppressed by capitalism. For in the period of 'high capitalism' – that is, organised industrial capitalism – it was not just the socio-economic institutions that were held in bondage but also the existential life of each individual being (*Dasein*). One of the most pernicious features of 'high capitalism', Marcuse always held, was the manipulative erosion of the personal sphere of critical experience.

Marx's 'scientific' analysis of the laws of economic production was not sufficient in itself to account for how human consciousness could go beyond these laws in order to change them – in order to redirect history towards the goal of liberation. The young Marcuse claimed that Heidegger's 'concrete philosophy' of 'historicity' (*Geschichtlichkeit*) as an authentic 'being-with-others' (*Miteinandersein*), offered the possibility of a new 'revolutionary beginning' which might save Marxist theory from the dogmatic scientism of the Second International with its subordination of conscious political action to the impersonal dictates of historical laws. In short, while Marx had accurately diagnosed the material forces governing the reification of social relations under capitalism, Heideggerian phenomenology advanced a model for understanding the fundamental ways in which this reification effected the existentially lived experience of each human being. Martin Schoolman has suggested that Marcuse's use of such Heideggerian terms as 'authenticity', 'human existence', 'being-with-others' and 'historicity' in his early writings, was primarily intended to free the notion of individual consciousness from the narrow ideological moorings of social alienation:

> Although capital invades and subjects to its rule the social forms of human existence, the existential inclination or fundamental human striving toward these forms endures because it is an essential attribute of each individual. Basic dispositions toward love, friendship and community are increasingly denied and limited as their areas of expression are annexed by a commodity economy. Yet, as these inclinations constitute the individual, it not only remains possible but also is necessary to speak of an individual living apart from and against the reified world of affairs, even though this individual now views this world in fetishized terms. Within the extended framework, the individual is understood to be *constrained* to view the world ideologically but not *determined* to do so. And constraints can be shattered. (Martin Schoolman, *The Imaginary Witness: The Critical Theory of Herbert Marcuse*, 1980)

Marcuse sought to 'radicalise' Marxism by supplementing the Marxist critique of the social conditions of alienation with a concrete analysis of how consciousness may *transcend* these conditions in order to liberate itself. Such a category of transcendence implies a permanent and irreducible human disposition toward freedom in spite of the ideological impositions of capitalist society. It was just such a 'trans-historical' potency for historical freedom which Heidegger's existential descriptions disclosed.

Hence Marcuse's view that the administrative suppression of the economic structures of monopolistic exploitation is a necessary but not sufficient condition of liberation. For the revolution to succeed, a properly *philosophical* appreciation of the essential structures of concrete individual experience is also required. The traditional Marxist emphasis on the theoretical category of class – even as expressed in as subtle a thinker as Lukács – is not enough. The notion of 'class consciousness', particularly as formulated by scientific Marxism, is too abstract to properly account for the significant potential for radical dissent in the existential situation of each living, concrete individual. In an early study entitled 'On the problem of the dialectic' (1930), Marcuse goes so far as to declare that a doctrinaire insistence on 'correct class consciousness' as the sole possessor of genuine revolutionary theory, is "a violation of the dimension of historicity, a fixation *outside* of what happens from whence an artificially abstract connection with history must be produced". And in another seminal article, written about the same time, 'On concrete philosophy' (1929), Marcuse is even more emphatic in his preference for the existential category of the reflective individual – as a projection of authentic possibilities of being – over the scientific concept of an impersonal class:

> The meaning of philosophizing, though not completed in the 'individual person', can be fulfilled only through each individual person *and thus has its basis in the existence of each individual person*. The concreteness of philosophy, in the existence of each individual person, must never be relegated to an abstract subject, to a 'one', for this would mean relegating decisive responsibility to some arbitrary universality. (*Ibid.*)

Marcuse, it must be noted, did not see this emphasis on the existential dimension of consciousness as signalling a departure from Marx. On the contrary, he believed that it was in fact more faithful to Marx's assertion in *The German Ideology* that the premises from which he begins are "the real individuals, their activity and the material conditions under which they live, both those which they find already existing and those produced by their activity". Marcuse's reading of Marx's *1844 Paris Manuscripts* – discovered and published in the early thirties – confirmed this 'humanistic' tendency of analysis. So that while the young Marcuse employed existential phenomenology to compensate for some of the inadequacies of 'scientific Marxism', it was never a question of abandoning Marx for Heidegger. It was, more exactly and characteristically, a question of *synthesis*. Without the Marxist commitment to revolutionary praxis based on a critique of the material constraints imposed upon human existence by capitalism, phenomenology would remain little more than a hazy and ineffectual idealism. Marcuse proposed accordingly a 'dialectical phenomenology' which would overcome the limitations of both Marxist dialectics and Heidegger phenomenology while combining their respective strengths. For where phenomenology penetrates to the underlying existential structures of human experience, historical materialism grasps the material conditions of its historical configurations. In other words, if dialectical theory must become more concretely existential, phenomenological theory must become more concretely committed. Marcuse sums up his initial philosophical project as follows:

Thus, on the one hand we demand that Heidegger's phenomenology of human existence be driven to dialectical concreteness so that it can be fulfilled in a phenomenology of concrete existence and of the historically concrete act demanded of it. And, on the other hand, the dialectical method of knowing must go the other way and become phenomenological so as to incorporate concreteness in a complete account of its object. In the analysis of the given, it must not simply locate it historically, or indicate its roots in a historical situation of human existence. It must also ask whether the given is thereby exhausted, or whether it contains an authentic meaning which, although not ahistorical, endures through all historicity . . . Only a unification of both methods, a dialectical phenomenology as a method of continuous and radical concreteness, can do justice to the historicity of human existence. ('Contributions to a phenomenology of historical materialism')

III

But Marcuse's 'radicalisation' of Marx drew from other disciplines besides that of phenomenological existentialism. Hegelian dialectics, modern aesthetics and psychoanalysis also played a decisive role in the Marcusian model of Critical Theory.

Marcuse's reading of Hegel impressed upon him the necessity of restoring Marxism to its original understanding of history as a 'dialectical' interchange between the dynamism of Spirit (*Geist*) and the material conditions of reality. From his early work, *Hegel's Ontology and the Foundations of a Theory of Historicity* (1932) to his mature work, *Reason and Revolution: Hegel and the Rise of Social Theory* (1941), Marcuse remained, broadly speaking, an 'Hegelian-Marxist'. In Hegel's recognition of the dialectical surplus of the 'essential' categories of Spirit over the 'actual' categories of social alienation, Marcuse saw the theoretical basis for a 'permanent revolution' against the repressive conditions of established society. Or to put it in another way, the Hegelian model of 'dialectic' offered Marxism – its intellectual offspring – an *ontological* foundation of critical transcendence which might enable it to fulfil its goal of a liberated social existence.

Marcuse believed that by resituating the 'two-dimensional' division between subject and object in a dialectic of 'being-in-motion', Hegel had pushed bourgeois idealism beyond the limits of a static dualism and pointed to the possibility of historical emancipation. Affirming that the discontinuity between the 'potential' and 'actual' dimensions of being is not some irrevocable destiny but an historical phase which can be understood and eventually surmounted, Hegelian dialectics revealed history as a teleological project whose 'end' (*telos*) is Freedom. The existing alienation of bourgeois civilisation was no longer, therefore, to be passively

contemplated or accepted as a *fait accompli*. But while Marcuse acknowledged that Hegel's dialectical 'spirit of contradiction' provided the ontological basis of a Great Refusal, he insisted that without Marxism this
theoretical model of 'negation' could never be translated into a concrete
programme of political revolution.

Marcuse's abiding preoccupation with the critical power of *aesthetic imagination* revolved around similar considerations. Though he remained a
committed socialist throughout his life, Marcuse never renounced his
youthful conviction – dating from his 1922 doctoral thesis on *The German
Artist Novel* – that certain aesthetic ideals of bourgeois culture could furnish
a critical refuge from the repressive practices of bourgeois society. Rather
than dismiss romantic or modernist literature as reactionary obscurantist
nihilism – after the fashion of Lukács and the Socialist Realists – Marcuse
stressed the manner in which such literature could offer asylum from the
dehumanising structures of capitalism, cultivating 'utopian images' of past
or future worlds in opposition to the tyranny of the present.

Marcuse first identified this capacity of art to 'presage possible truths' in
his analysis of the German artist novel (*Künstlerroman*). This literary genre
was characterised by the narrative efforts of isolated individuals to construct a private vision of beauty in the face of prevailing social alienation.
The artist-novel described the evolution of a dissenting spirit beyond naive
despondency to a mature consciousness of new possibilities of meaning. It
recorded an 'interior journey' of self-reconstruction in response to the
modern experience of crisis resulting from the collapse of traditional forms
of community. "The tearing-asunder of a unified life-form, the opposition
of art and life and the separation of the artist from the surrounding world",
observes Marcuse, "is the presupposition of the artist-novel, and its problem, the suffering and longing of the artist, his struggle for a new community" (*The German Artist-Novel*, 1922). Otherwise put, when meaningful
experience is no longer to be found in the existing social relations, it seeks
an alternative expression in art. The artist-novel is thus defined by Marcuse as an attempt to resolve the problems of alienation in an aesthetic form
removed from the life-form of the surrounding society. The heroes of the
German *Künstlerroman*, from Goethe's Werther to Mann's Von Aschen-
bach, are self-conscious artists living in a state of perpetual estrangement.
But this experience of estrangement is not mere escapism; it can also serve
to *remind* us that there existed certain ancient cultures – Marcuse mentions
pre-Socratic Greece – where art and reality could be represented as a
unified whole. And by the same token, suggests Marcuse, the modern
aesthetic of estrangement *anticipates* the possibility of surpassing our

present experience of dislocation toward a utopian future. This critical consciousness of existing 'between two worlds' – one recollected and the other projected – is what Marcuse terms 'anticipatory memory' (*Die vordeutende Erinnerung*).

Marcuse also adverted to this utopian function of 'anticipatory memory' in the poetic works of Baudelaire and the surrealists (authors equally beloved of his fellow Marxist critic, Walter Benjamin). Marcuse disapproved of Lukács' tendency to connect literary works 'externally' with social relations, preferring to trace these social indices in the formal, and frequently anti-political aspects of the oeuvre. He agreed with Benjamin and Bloch that it is often in the 'sur-real' style and sensual experience of the work that a protest against the existing political order may be best expressed. In other words, art resists the monopolistic control of social reality under capitalism precisely by resorting to utopian images of past or future which preserve the desire for liberation. In this respect, Marcuse invoked Baudelaire's definition of poetry in *Invitation au Voyage*: "Poetry has a great destiny! As joy or as lament, it carries forever within itself a divine utopian character. As soon as it ceases to contradict the world of facts, poetry ceases to be poetry". In his last work, *The Aesthetic Dimension* (1977), Marcuse returns to the poetic function of 'anticipatory memory' as utopian witness:

> The utopia in great art is never the simple negation of the reality principle but its transcending preservation in which past and present cast their shadow on fulfillment. The authentic utopia is grounded in recollection. All reification is forgetting. Art fights reification by making the petrified world speak, sing, perhaps dance. Forgetting past suffering and past joy alleviates life under a repressive reality principle. In contrast, remembrance spurs the drive for the conquest of suffering and the permanence of joy . . . The horizon of history is still open. If the remembrance of things past would become a motive power in the struggle for changing the world, the struggle would be waged for a revolution hitherto suppressed in the previous historical revolutions. (*Ibid.*)

IV

The collapse of the German revolution of 1917, the betrayal of Soviet socialism under Stalin and the rise of fascism in Europe, all confirmed Marcuse's view that there existed a radical disjunction between the project of liberation and the existing orders of social reality. It was in 1933, when the Nazi takeover of his native Germany had brought home to Marcuse the massive degree of opposition to human freedom, that he decided to join the programme of Critical Theory recently inaugurated by Horkheimer and Adorno at the Frankfurt Institute of Social Research.

During his time with the Institute between 1933 and 1941 (most of it spent in exile in the US), Marcuse developed a highly sophisticated socio-historical analysis of the workings of ideology. This analysis reinforced his belief in the indispensable role of critical negation and confirmed his suspicion of any attempt to subordinate this role to the exigencies of an 'unmediated' political program. In contrast to Lukács, who became a member of the Communist Party in 1918, Marcuse followed the example of his Frankfurt School colleagues and retained his political independence. Indeed, he was to remain a partisan of the 'homeless' or non-party left throughout his intellectual career. It was Marcuse who was largely responsible for the Institute's rejection of the common tendency to reduce the revolutionary project to a tactical pragmatism. The pragmatist approach, he felt, could only lead to a betrayal of the revolution and the execution of its intellectuals (e.g. Rosa Luxemburg, Leon Trotsky etc.). At all times, Marcuse fiercely defended the need for a *theoretical* reflection on the universal project of liberty as a perpetual negation of repression – under whatever ideological guise it might appear.

The first 'co-operative' work of the Institute in which Marcuse participated was a study of the social and psychological sources of 'authoritarianism' – a factor which was considered one of the main reasons for the successful rise of fascism in Germany. Marcuse and his colleagues related the ideological underpinnings of National Socialism to the monopolistic stage of 'state capitalism' defined as a 'total-authoritarian' control of both the public and private spheres of existence. Fascism signified not the end of capitalism but the transition from one kind of capitalism (bourgeois liberalism) to another (state authoritarianism). In the famous series of studies on 'Authority and family', published in the Institute's *Zeitscrift* in 1936, Marcuse – together with Horkheimer and Fromm – investigated the pivotal role played by the Germanic institution of the family in rendering individuals passive before the rule of authority. These studies had a particularly significant influence on Marcuse's intellectual formation in that they impressed upon him the fruitfulness of a multidisciplinary approach drawn from psychoanalysis, sociology, political theory and the history of ideas. As such, this approach served to expose the limits of positivist social science which collaborated in the preservation of the 'existing state of affairs' by confining research to the so-called 'objectivity' of empirically observable facts. Critical Theory, by contrast, sought to challenge this repressive state of affairs by acknowledging a dialectical tension between critical reason and the reality of existing social oppression – a tension which kept alive the possibility of a revolt against this reality. In short, the dialectical critique advanced by Marcuse and the Frankfurt School demanded that an empirical description of the material conditions of existence under capitalism be oriented by an analysis of the complex 'ideological' factors which produce and are produced by these conditions. Barry Katz offers the following useful summary of the distinctive character of this kind of critique in his intellectual biography of Marcuse:

> The dominant concepts of modern thought and ideology were dismantled, traced back to the material circumstances in which they originated (characteristically as the progressive requirements of an ascending middle class), and then systematically reconstructed so as to reveal their changed political functions in new circumstances. The truth as well as the falsehood of the concepts that guide philosophy, science, and social *praxis* is thus exposed, and their ideological hold is loosened. (Barry Katz, *Herbert Marcuse: Art of Liberation*, 1982)

Critical Theory criticised the ideology of positivism as a 'rationalised irrationalism'. In reducing the life of reason to a purely instrumental or 'technological' rationality, positivism denies the dialectical tension between the actual and the potential, the present and the future (or past), and thereby encourages conformity to the existing structures of repression. Already in the 1936 studies on authority, Marcuse had pointed to the hidden complicity between positivism and authoritarianism in so far as both solicit an uncritical compliance with the 'objective' order of things. But it was in a later and more comprehensive study of the ideology of advanced individual society, *One-Dimensional Man* (1964), that Marcuse spelt out the full implications of the positivist mentality. Demonstrating how positivism replaces critical rationality with technological rationality, Marcuse argues that it serves as a crucial ideological ally of the new 'one-dimensional' society. Positivism precludes the possibility of critical transcendence which Marcuse holds to be the true vocation of philosophical consciousness; it dismisses as 'non-sensical' all alternative modes of thought which contradict the established universe of facts:

> The contemporary effort to reduce the scope and the truth of philosophy is tremendous . . . It leaves the established reality untouched; it abhors transgression . . . One might ask what remains of philosophy? What remains of thinking, intelligence, without anything hypothetical, without any explanation? . . . What is involved is the spread of a new ideology which undertakes to describe what is happening (and meant) by eliminating the concepts capable of understanding what is happening (and meant) . . . But this radical acceptance of the empirical violates the empirical, for in it speaks the mutilated, 'abstract' individual who experiences only that which is *given to him*, who has only the facts and not the factors, whose behaviour is one-dimensional and manipulated. By virtue of the factual repression, the experienced world is the result of a restricted experience, and the positivist cleaning of the mind brings the mind in line with the restricted experience. (*One-Dimensional Man*)

The transformation of critical into 'positive' thinking is epitomised by a reactionary resolve to 'leave everything as it is'. This also expresses itself in the neo-positivist repudiation of philosophical 'universals', on the pretext that they do not conform to the analytic purity of formal logic or the exactness of empirical verification. In this rejection of all those elements of thought or speech – metaphysical, poetic, dialectical etc. – which transgress the accepted system of validation, Marcuse sees a fundamental hostility to non-conformist critical consciousness for while the particular 'facts' of ordinary discourse and behaviour are indeed reducible to the immediate data of observation and measurement, the 'factors' which cause these facts and govern their social interrelation are not so reducible. Even though it often presumes to expose the 'mystifying' character of metaphysical universals, positivist analysis in fact serves to "mystify the terms of ordinary language by leaving them in the repressive context of the established universe of discourse" (*ibid.*). Marcuse concludes, accordingly, that the positivist cult of ordinary language and behaviour curbs the capacity for change. "Multi-dimensional language," he observes, "is made into one-dimensional language, in which different and conflicting meanings no longer interpenetrate but are kept apart; the explosive historical dimension of meaning is thus silenced" (*ibid*).

V

Faced with the reductive ideology of one-dimensional society – powered by a 'technological rationality' which subjects human needs to the industrial apparatus of commodity production and consumption – Marcuse called for the establishment of a 'critical rationality' capable of transforming submissiveness into revolt. But he believed that theory must extend its 'negative' critique of ideological falsifications into a 'creative' critique of those hidden desires and drives for a liberated existence.

In *Eros and Civilization: A Philosophical Inquiry into Freud* (1955), Marcuse attempts to combine these two aspects of 'negative' and 'utopian' critique. This work explores how our unconscious libidinal energies (*eros*) express an instinctual dynamic which tends toward a non-repressive order which the contemporary practice of 'social engineering' attempts to repress. This repression is most evident, Marcuse argues, in the economic management of sexuality which manipulates erotic needs for the purposes of unlimited technique productivity and progress.

Marcuse defines *eros* as a creative life-instinct (or 'Pleasure Principle') which seeks fulfilment in a transformed order of social relations (or 'Reality Principle') where the genuine demands of happiness and freedom, sensuousness and reason may be reconciled. These conditions can only be met, Marcuse argues, in a non-repressive order where alienating work is transformed into play. But the domination of contemporary society by technological rationality (or the 'Performance Principle') resists any such transformation. Such rationality merely exploits instinctual desires for its own ends of increased productivity and consumption. Indeed the Performance Principle which governs advanced industrial societies goes so far as to invent new (unnecessary) needs as soon as the old (necessary) ones are satisfied. This manipulation of instinctual desire in order to extend the domain of commodity production and technical control results in a 'surplus repression'; and its eventual consequence is the replacement of the life-instinct (*eros*) by a destructive death-instinct (what Freud referred to as *thanatos*).

Since the Pleasure Principle is incompatible with the prevailing Reality Principle – dominated as it is by the Performance Principle of technological rationality – it seeks refuge in the unreal, that is, in the *imaginary* world of dream, art and myth. Marcuse speaks accordingly of the image of life without oppression as the 'truth value of phantasy'. Here once again Marcuse employs the notion of critical memory in reinterpreting the mythological images of Orpheus and Narcissus as archetypal projections of a non-repressive harmony between man and nature. In the retrieval of these lost cultural images, Marcuse sees a new role for Freud's recognition that imagination can preserve certain truths which are refractory to the dictates of a repressive reason:

> Phantasy is cognitive in so far as it preserves the truth of the Great Refusal, or, positively, in so far as it protects, against all reason, the aspirations for the integral fulfilment of man and nature which are repressed by reason. In the realm of phantasy, the unreasonable images of freedom become rational, and the 'lower depth' of instinctual gratification assumes a new dignity. The culture of the performance principle makes it bow before the strange truths which imagination keeps alive in folklore and fairy tale, in literature and art. (*Eros and Civilization*)

Marcuse describes how the myths of Orpheus and Narcissus symbolise possibilities of experience suppressed in our advanced industrial society. These archetypal figures represent the Pleasure Principle of sensuousness, play and song. They prefigure a life lived in attunement with nature (the trees and animals respond to Orpheus' language; the forest and the spring respond to Narcissus' desire). Marcuse maintains, therefore, that the Orphic and Narcissistic *eros* "awakens and liberates potentialities that are real in things animate and inanimate, in organic and inorganic nature – real but in the un-erotic reality suppressed" (*ibid.*). Put in another way, the Orphic–Narcissistic images represent a non-repressive mode of sublimation which hints at the possibility of a libidinal transformation of this world (where subject and object are radically opposed) into a new mode of being (where they might be dialectically united).

In this respect, Marcuse revolutionises Freud's notion of 'primary narcissism' as a preconscious integration of the ego with the objective environment. He concludes that the Orphic and Narcissistic *eros* points to a utopian mediation between the Reality Principle of history and the Pleasure Principle of phantasy; for it recalls "the experience of a world that is not to be mastered or controlled but liberated' (*Ibid.*). In so doing, it negates the present order of manipulative sexuality (what Marcuse calls 'repressive desublimation') in the name of a new erotic order of beauty and contemplation. And by thus reviving the repressed memories of libidinal gratification – in opposition to the hierarchical genital sexuality of the Performance Principle – Narcissus and Orpheus serve as dissenting 'cultural heroes' heralding the metamorphosis of a purely functional labour into a creative sexuality of play (what Marcuse refers to as 'polymorphus pregenital erotism'). The best prospect for utopia in our time, Marcuse suggests, is through a reactivation of these prehistoric and childhood drives which reside as innate, albeit suppressed, archetypes in the human unconscious:

> The Orphic Eros transforms being; he masters cruelty and death through liberation. His language is *song*, and his work is *play*. Narcissus' life is that of *beauty*, and his existence is *contemplation*. These images refer to the *aesthetic* dimension as the one in which their reality principle must be sought and validated (*ibid.*).

Marcuse acknowledges, consequently, that Critical Theory is not just a critique of ideological distortion but also a positive recovery of the utopian aspirations of the past – aspirations which have been censored by the technological rationality of the established present but retained in the aesthetic unconscious of our cultural heritage and also in the unconscious memory of each individual's childhood desires. This accounts for Marcuse's rather enigmatic statement that under the contemporary conditions of social alienation, 'critical theory must concern itself to a hitherto unknown extent with the past – precisely in so far as it is concerned with the future' ('Philosophy and Critical Theory', 1938). The cultural experience of a Greek myth or statue, of a classical concerto or romantic poem, or indeed any other genuine recollection of *le temps perdu*, can offer a 'foretaste of the potentialities' of a liberated and as yet unrealised utopia.

VI

Marcuse thus recognised that the realm of freedom envisioned by the imagination lies beyond the realm of necessity characterised by the laborious 'struggle for existence'. The procurement of the necessities of life is, he believed, the prerequisite but not the ultimate goal of a free society. Such a society can only fully exist when the principle of unproductive and useless 'play' has cancelled the exploitative nature of labour. While our advanced industrial society has today reached a stage where 'abundance' is a possibility for all, it manages to devise new modes of 'surplus repression'. Commodities are manufactured with a 'built-in obsolescence' to ensure their rapid replacement by newer and better models (this phenomenon is particularly widespread in the automobile industry, for instance). Entirely new needs of consumption are fabricated by the market system in order to further extend its functional potential. And this emergence of a mass consumer culture – powered along by streamlined commercials and media promotion – signals an additional invasion of human liberty; for, as Marcuse pointed out, it means the expansion of repressive manipulation beyond the purely economic sphere to the most private sphere of man's unconscious desires. Marcuse foresaw that the union of productivity and destruction in the name of limitless technological progress would not easily be broken. New and more sophisticated forms of social control were being mobilised daily. As he remarked in his famous 1966 Preface to *Eros and Civilization*:

The very forces which rendered society capable of pacifying the struggle for existence served to repress in the individuals the need for such a liberation. Where the high standard of living does not suffice for reconciling the people with their life and their rulers, the 'social engineering' of the soul and the 'science of human relations' provide the necessary libidinal cathexis. In the affluent society, the authorities are hardly forced to justify their dominion. They deliver the goods; they satisfy the sexual and the aggressive energy of their subjects. Like the unconscious, the destructive energy of which they so successfully represent, they are this side of good and evil, and the principle of contradiction has no place in their logic. As the affluence of society depends increasingly on the uninterrupted production and consumption of waste, gadgets, planned obsolescence, and means of destruction, the individuals have to be adapted to those requirements in more than traditional ways. The 'economic whip', even in its most refined forms, seems no longer adequate to insure the continuation of the struggle for existence in today's outdated organization, nor do the laws and patriotism seem adequate to insure active popular support for the ever more dangerous expansion of the system. Scientific management of instinctual needs has long since become a vital factor in the reproduction of the system: merchandise which has to be bought and used is made into objects of the libido; and the national Enemy who has to be fought and hated is distorted and inflated to such an extent that he can activate and satisfy aggressiveness in the depth dimension of the unconscious. Mass democracy . . . not only permits the people (up to a point) to choose their own masters and to participate (up to a point) in the government which governs them –

it also allows the masters to disappear behind the technological veil of the productive and destructive apparatus which they control, and it conceals the human (and material) costs of the benefits and comforts which it bestows upon those who collaborate. The people, efficiently manipulated and organized, are free; ignorance and impotence . . . is the price of their freedom. (*ibid.*).

In short, the manipulative requirements of the market economy, based on the dehumanising strategies of profit and affluence, have managed to distort the erotic energies of the life-instict. Through a process of 'repressive desublimation', *eros* is perverted and eventually replaced by the destructive drives of *thanatos*. Marcuse is compelled to conclude accordingly that the very development of technical productivity and economic surplus in advanced industrial society – to a level at which the masses can participate in its benefits – has at the same time suppressed the agent of revolution: the critical historical subject himself. Thus even though liberation ostensibly represents a materially realisable possibility for the affluent society, it equally represents the 'most rationally and effectively repressed – the most abstract and remote possibility' (1966 preface to *Eros and Civilization*). The question that haunted Marcuse in his later years was this: how it is that the subjective needs of happiness and freedom are becoming increasingly repressed in that very modern civilisation which offers the most advanced objective conditions for their fulfilment?

Marcuse surmised that it may well be those who remain free from the economic and corporate blessings of advanced industrial society that possess the best chance of 'turning the wheel of progress in another direction' (*ibid.*). Since the majority of the people in the affluent society are now on the side of the *is* (the status quo) rather than the *might be* (the project of revolution), Marcuse looks to the 'refugees of defamed humanity' – the oppressed Third World, the intellectual dissidents, the disenchanted students or protesting youth – for the rebirth of a new consciousness, a new instinctual refusal. In today's civilisation of administered repression 'the fight for Eros is the political fight' (*ibid.*). If this fight is abandoned, or simply fails, then Marcuse warns that "the second period of barbarism may well be the continued empire of civilisation" (*One-Dimensional Man*).

CONCLUSION

Marcuse's hopes were, no doubt, partially realised in the student revolts which swept through America and Europe in the late sixties. But only partially. The absence of any organised movement of critical reflection left the protest hopelessly divided. Its spontaneous activism – while responding to the criterion of instinctual revolt – neglected a coherent intellectual critique which might have extended the rebellion into a sustained historical project. Not surprisingly, the revolutionary *élan* of the protesting youth was either co-opted or compromised by the increasingly advanced affluence of the technocratic counter-revolution. The rebels of yesterday became the conformists of today.

In the face of such disappointments at the level of political *praxis*, Marcuse returned in his last years to the 'aesthetic' project of critical refusal. His biographer, Barry Katz, has aptly described the intellectual mood of the mature Marcuse as one of 'cheerful pessimism'. In *The Aesthetic Dimension* (1977), published shortly before his death, Marcuse contended that art is perhaps the last remaining refuge for two-dimensional experience in our one-dimensional society. Against those who argue for a direct equation of artistic imagination and political reality, Marcuse counsels caution. He defends art's 'distance from actuality' and invokes Stendhal's definition of beauty as the *'promise* of happiness' rather than its immediate *possession*. Contesting both the socialist realism of orthodox Marxism and the naturalist realism of bourgeois conservatism, Marcuse calls for a renewed appreciation of the radical estrangement or transcendence of art. This he refers to as an irreducibly 'aesthetic dimension' which negates our actual experience of repression in the name of a potential experience of freedom. He writes:

> The radical qualities of art, that is to say, its indictment of the established reality and its invocation of the beautiful image (*schöner Schein*) of liberation are grounded precisely in the dimension where art *transcends* its social determination and emancipates itself from the given universe of discourse and behaviour . . . The world formed by art is recognized as a reality which is suppressed and distorted in the given reality. This experience culminates in extreme situations (of love and death, guilt and failure, but also joy, happiness and fulfilment) which explode the given reality in the name of truths normally denied or even unheard. The inner logic of the work of art terminates in the emergence of another reason, another sensibility, which defy the rationality and sensibility incorporated in the dominant social institutions. (*The Aesthetic Dimension*)

By refusing to conform to the conventional order of perception, art – particularly when it is innovatory or experimental – does not 'represent' the contemporary social environment, it revolts against it. Art is radical when it exposes the familiar as unfamiliar, challenges our preconceived assumptions and invites us to apprehend the world in a new way. Poetry or painting creates its own language – a language of otherness and inwardness which illuminates the repressed potentialities of historical experience and thus keeps alive the utopian aspiration. Even esoteric literature, notes Marcuse, can contain a form of protest to the degree that it takes its leave of the 'normal' universe as standardised communication and behaviour. By contrast, the art work that seeks above all else to popularise itself by capitulating to an immediately identifiable social discourse, forfeits its emancipatory impact and risks becoming, often despite itself, an additional instrument of ideological conformity. For this reason Marcuse remains suspicious of attempts by anti-art and popular-art movements to jettison aesthetic form for the sake of immediate accessibility. Divesting literature or visual art of its 'estranging' power, such movements also deprive it of its critical, and by extension liberating, potential. Though they often claim to be politically radical, they are usually the opposite; for in subordinating aesthetic strangeness to everyday familiarity the artist ceases to protest against the *way things are*. Marcuse insists that when art abandons the 'aesthetic dimensions' of formal autonomy and spiritual inwardness altogether, it surrenders to the formless and spiritless reality it seeks to indict; it issues in a further banalisation of experience.

The last hope of critical theory, Marcuse concludes, lies in the Great Refusal of art – or more exactly, of that art which refuses to negate itself as art by conforming to the oppressive constraints of existing reality. The antagonistic conflict between the interiority of art and the exteriority of social reality must not be suspended. To do so, Marcuse asserts, is to eradicate revolutionary hope, for it means reducing the *possible* worlds of liberty to the present world of domination. "The basic thesis that art must be a factor in changing the world", writes Marcuse, "can easily turn into its opposite if the tension between art and radical praxis is flattened out so that art loses its own dimension for change . . . The flight into inwardness and the insistence on a private sphere may well serve as bulwarks against a society which administers all dimensions of human existence. Inwardness and subjectivity may well become the inner and outer space for the subversion of experience, for the emergence of another universe' (*The Aesthetic Dimension*). Marcuse's final work perfectly examplifies that subtle dialectical balance between critical negation and utopian affirmation which is perhaps the most distinctive hallmark of his entire critical project.

Jürgen Habermas

Jürgen Habermas is the most distinguished 'second generation' disciple of the Frankfurt School. In the early sixties, he took over the chair of Philosophy and Social Science at Frankfurt University and relaunched the project of Critical Theory inaugurated by Horkheimer, Adorno and Marcuse in Germany in the late twenties and thirties. From his mentors Habermas inherited the view that the Marxist critique of capitalism needed to be revised and readapted to the radically altered conditions of our modern technological society. Where traditional Marxism had focused on the *economic* control of the means of production, Habermas switched the emphasis to the *ideological* control of the means of communication. Taking up the analysis of the betrayal of reason under contemporary advanced capitalism – as outlined by Adorno and Horkheimer in the *Dialectic of Enlightenment* (1947) – Habermas applied this analysis to the role of the social sciences and systems theory.

I

Before proceeding to discuss Habermas's own distinct application of Critical Theory to the social sciences, it might be useful to give a brief account here of the seminal 'Frankfurt School' arguments advanced by Adorno and Horkheimer (though several of these will have been briefly touched on in our chapter on Marcuse). The authors of *Dialectic of Enlightenment* held that the modern reign of technological rationality reduced the vocation of reason to a utilitarian calculus of means and ends, to a purely instrumental function. A main source of domination in advanced state capitalism – which Adorno and Horkheimer, like Marcuse, identified with both fascist and Soviet totalitarianism – was the authoritarian distrust of critical questioning and dissent. This distrust often expressed itself in the state having recourse to terror and coercion to enforce its programme of 'progress', based on the demands of technocratic pragmatism. Adorno and Horkheimer protested strenuously against this blind belief in historical progress.

Such protest assumed the form of a plea for critical consciousness to combat the crude anti-intellectualism characteristic of both totalitarian leaders and the populist masses they led. (Adorno and Horkheimer observed, for instance, that in Chaplin's *Great Dictator*, the barber and the dictator were one and the same man.) In the reign of technological rationality, man has become a machine of repetitive production and consumption. Man's social existence, be it work (mass production) or leisure (mass consumption), is regulated in all its details: humanity is dissolved into administration.

The authors of *Dialectic* saw this impoverishment of experience as a direct consequence of the enlightenment cult of rational progress. In the new society life is discontinuous, alienated, atomised, isolated. A mass culture has emerged which thrives, paradoxically, on the complete privatisation of experience, that is, on the divorce of the individual from genuine social participation in a concrete historical situation.

This accounts for the anti-populist streak in the *Dialectic*, the deep suspicion of what the authors refer to rather contemptuously as the 'culture industry'. Whereas art had once served to register protest (e.g. the classical genre of tragedy), in modern popular culture it is increasingly reduced to an agency of one-dimensional consumerism whose primary aims are consolation, resignation and conformity. By falsely and prematurely harmonising the particular and the universal – whose very antagonism had exposed the social contradictions in previous societies – the technological society employs mass culture to seduce its consumers into a state of passive acquiescence. Thus the power of 'negation' which the Frankfurt School equated with the potential for revolutionary resistance is substantially eroded. The mass submissiveness induced by modern popular culture was, for Adorno and Horkheimer, the logical counterpart of the domination implicit in the work ethic of instrumental rationality bequeathed by the enlightenment.

Dialectic of Enlightenment was largely composed during the Second World War while its authors were still in exile in the USA (it was first published in German in 1947). The overall analysis was informed by a profound sense of disillusionment resulting from the collapse of genuine class solidarity, witnessed in the rise of fascism in Europe, of totalitarianism in the Soviet Union and of a conformist mass culture in the industrial West, particularly in America. The authoritarian technological society had now become, it was argued, a global phenomenon whose real origins could be traced back to the enlightenment division between man and nature, evidenced as far back as the Cartesian dualism of subject and object and the Newtonian separation of spirit and matter. The massive development of the positive sciences had objectified nature and by the same token had made man into an object of instrumental exploitation. Consequently, knowledge was made to serve the dominant means of production which in advanced industrial society became identical with a repressive, omnipresent technology devoted to interests of mastery and control. The original enlightenment over-emphasis on man's autonomy (*vis-à-vis* nature) had finally led to man's total submission to a denatured technocracy, the human spirit being reduced to a mere functional thing among things.

But Adorno and Horkheimer argued that the calculating formal rationalism advanced by the enlightenment was in fact a travesty of the true character of dialectical reason (*Vernunft*) whose purpose it is to critically negate the conditions of historical alienation and to project utopian possibilities of reconciling man and nature. Martin Jay, in his history of the Frankfurt School entitled *The Dialectical Imagination*, sums up the main arguments of Adorno and Horkheimer as follows:

> The Enlightenment, for all its claims to have surpassed mythopoeic confusion by the introduction of rational analysis, had itself fallen a victim to a new myth. This was one of the major themes of the *Dialectic*. At the root of the Enlightenment's program of domination, Horkheimer and Adorno charged, was a secularized version of the religious belief that God controlled the world. As a result, the human subject confronted the natural object as an inferior, external other . . . Industrialism objectified spirits . . . The instrumental manipulation of nature by man led inevitably to the concomitant relationship among men. The unbridgeable distance between subject and object in the Enlightenment world view corresponded to the relative status of rulers and ruled in the modern authoritarian states. The objectification of the world has produced a similar effect in human relations. (*ibid.*).

The ultimate legacy of the enlightenment was the equation of rationalisation with reification. In the face of such a legacy, which had issued in the tyranny of scientific positivism and the terrors of totalitarian inhumanity in our century, Adorno and Horkheimer insisted that the best option for dialectical reason was to preserve the principle of 'negation' as the only means of salvaging truth from the pervasive technocratic control of man's contemporary existence. It was against this rather pessimistic background of last ditch migration, that Habermas moved to restore the social project of Critical Theory.

II

In *Knowledge and Human Interests* (1968), Habermas investigates the covert 'logic of the social sciences', exposing its frequent recourse to strategies of domination. In *Technology and Science as 'Ideology'*, published in the same year, he declares the urgent task of 'critical theory' to be a 'critique of ideology' – ideology being understood as a 'false consciousness' which distorts communication and conceals the exercise of domination.

Habermas argues that a radical critique of ideology requires that we go beyond the limits of romantic hermeneutics. This latter conception ultimately serves to rehabilitate certain reactionary notions of *prejudice, tradition* and *authority* – notions which Gadamer in *Truth and Method* (1960) had deemed essential for the retrieval of a genuine sense of 'belonging' (*Zugehörigkeit*) to history. Habermas endeavours to steer a medial course between the Scylla of romantic hermeneutics which celebrates a mythic past of empathic fellowship and the Charybdis of positivistic rationalism devoted to an abstract system of technological administration. Whereas Gadamer and Heidegger had spoken of the pre-judicial structure of a 'hermeneutic circle' of consciousness, Habermas promotes a model of 'interest' (*Anteil*) along the lines of the dialectical consciousness advocated by Lukács and the Frankfurt school.

Habermas's model of 'interest' rests upon the conviction that all authentic human discourse aims at a regulative ideal of universal, unrestricted communication; and that ideology understood as the systematic deformation of communication by the covert operations of force, represents the betrayal of such an ideal. Thus in addition to the phenomenological hermeneutics of tradition which invokes the priority of the '*human* sciences' as a means of disclosing the fundamental structures of knowledge in our pre-understanding (*Vorstrucktur des Verstehens*), Habermas calls for a critique of ideology which appeals to a 'critical *social* science' committed to the exposure of the traditional institutional reifications of meaning.

Habermas characterises romantic hermeneutics as a 'relative idealism' which treats language as a transcendental absolute and thereby ignores the 'objective contexts' of technical and political domination which constrain our 'communicative competence' as social actors. Gadamer's uncritical affirmation of 'tradition' as a linguistic body of commonly shared assumptions, takes no account, says Habermas, of how 'public opinion' can be manipulated to secure a 'false consensus' – that is, a consensus not willingly or consciously assented to but passively accepted by a 'depoliticised' public. Habermas proposes instead a *critical* 'comprehension of cultural tradition'; for this alone would be capable of identifying the ideological underpinnings of 'systematically distorted communication' which prevents social groups from recognising and pursuing their own emancipatory aims. He argues that the norms of social action cannot be naively taken for granted but must be subjected to a 'consensual discourse' by means of which social actors can ascertain which norms genuinely serve their interests.

The stated aim of *Knowledge and Human Interests* is to 'recover the forgotten experience of reflection'. Habermas interrogates the failures and successes of knowledge by analysing how the critical subject has been threatened by the modern rise of positivism. However, in contrast to the 'structuralist' antipathy toward the 'humanist' notion of a reflective human subject, Habermas considers the history of philosophy as a series of progressive attempts to radicalise the reflective task. This history of radicalisation reaches modern fruition in the successive discoveries of the Kantian transcendental subject, the Fiction ego and the Hegelian *Geist*, culminating in the Marxist synthesis of critical reflection with productive praxis – a dialectical synthesis which aims to resolve the traditional opposition between idealism and materialism. Within this critical perspective, Habermas maintains that Marx's *Critique of Political Economy* plays the same role in historical materialism as did Hegel's *Logic* in metaphysical idealism. Both works served, from different angles, to advance the cause of critical reflection.

With Marxism, man, as a social being was provided with the possibility of becoming the subject of critical reflection. But Habermas demonstrates how Marxism has also – often despite its original project – contributed to the movement of positivism by laying inordinate stress on the purely instrumental dimensions of human labour and production. Hence Marxism too, even though it opens up one of the most advanced horizons of critical reflection to date, must itself be subjected to critical reflection if it is not to become just another ideology of dogmatic control – as happened, for example, in the Soviet system. In other words, even Marxism as the critique of ideology must submit itself as an ideology for critique.

For Habermas there is no philosophy that is above critique. There exists no transcendental plane of timeless certitude, no place where a *disinterested* consciousness could detach itself from all historical and ideological concerns and thereby lay claim to some absolute knowledge. All theories, and particularly those which present themselves as perfectly neutral and objective, are ideologies concealing their own vested interests by dressing them up in the guise of an ahistorical rationalisation. The overall task of critical theory is, therefore, to disclose those interests which lie behind the various exercises of knowledge.

There exists, Habermas argues, a *pluralism* of interests. These he groups under three main categories: (i) *instrumental interest* (ii) *practical interest* and (iii) *the interest in emancipation*.

The instrumental interest is the perspective which motivates the allegedly neutral 'emprical–analytic sciences'. This perspective limits meaning to empirical facts whose validity depends, in turn, on their technical exploitability within a utilitarian system of behaviour. The criterion invoked here is that of a means/end pragmatism of 'purposive-rational action'; it is epitomised in the contemporary ideology of scientific technology. Habermas defines it as 'the cognitive interest in technical control over objectified processes', otherwise known as *positivism*. Habermas readily concedes that the instrumental interest has its valid place as one interest amongst others. He criticises it, however, as soon as it presumes to be the only or the all-englobing interest.

The second category of interest, the practical, favours a model of *communicative action*. Practical interest refers to a field of intersubjective action. This, for Habermas, is the domain of the 'historical–hermeneutic sciences'. It endeavours to understand the inherently *human* dimension of meaning achieved through the interpretation of messages exchanged in everyday language. Here we are concerned with the 'symbolic interaction' of human meanings transmitted by the texts of our cultural traditions and embodied in our social norms and institutions. Habermas believes that Marx recognised a distinction between technical and practical interests when he separated the 'relations of production' (which under capitalism operated as ideological domination and class division) and the 'forces of production' (that is, the labour of human action which sought to express the 'generic essence' of man). Indeed the very possibility of a critique of ideology depends upon a recognition of the split between the technical–analytic interest and the practical–communicative interest. But it is just this split which Marxism itself conceals, as soon as it is acknowledged, by ultimately subsuming both the interests of *relation* and *force* under the same 'scientific' category of 'production'. Consequently, the recognition of the difference between the opposed orders of interest which made possible the Marxist critique of ideology in the first place is undermined by the Marxist claim to scientific positivism. In reminding us of this crucial difference between the interests of technical control and practical communication, Habermas endeavours to restore the possibility of genuine Critical Theory.

The third category of interest is what Habermas terms the 'interest in emancipation' or 'critical self-reflection'. He identifies this with the project of a 'critical social science' modelled on the Critical Theory of the Frankfurt School and Institute for Social Research. Whereas the technical–analytic sciences had denied the 'critical instance' altogether and whereas the 'hermeneutic-human sciences' had subordinated it to the pre-understanding of traditional heritage, Habermas asserts the ultimate superiority of critical self-reflection which opens up a project of emancipation. The critical social sciences enable the forgotten interests of knowledge to become conscious of themselves. They dispel the positivist illusion of 'disinterestedness' and unmask the ideological interests at work in those institutionalised regularities of behaviour which the 'empirical–analytic' sciences mistook for 'objective social laws'. Acknowledging its own guiding interest in emancipation, critical social science shows how this same interest has motivated all of the great philosophies – even though it is only when philosophy reaches the stage of critical self-understanding that it can liberate itself from those dogmatisms which construe meaning as something metaphysically preestablished rather than as a dialectical project of historical interests. While the 'critical instance' does not lay claim, therefore, to some dis-interested vantage point uncompromised by institutional constraints, it can nonetheless work from within the limits of an historically situated consciousness to dissolve such constraints and point towards an *ideal space of free communication*.

Habermas' main concern is to demonstrate that *all* knowledge is ultimately guided by interest. This represents a direct challenge to modern positivism, obsessed as it is with a totally detached, impersonal and value-free system of 'objectivity'. Behind this 'objectivist illusion', Habermas discerns a concealed vested interest: the attempt to subordinate the *practical* domain of human interaction and communication to the *technical* requirements of industrial and technological administration. Habermas argues that it is only by exposing this conflict between practical and technical interests, covertly at work in the functioning of human knowledge, that we can become reflectively aware of the third and ultimately most positive form of cognitive interest – the interest in emancipation as a basic human need for autonomy, responsibility and justice. 'Knowledge–constitutive interests' are not therefore, as the positive sciences assume, negative influences to be eliminated for the sake of the objectivity of truth. Rather they determine the aspects under which reality is accessible to human experience. The diagram opposite offers a summary of Habermas' threefold categorisation of the interests of human knowledge.

III

Perhaps Habermas' most important contribution to the development of Critical Theory is his notion of an 'ideal speech situation' as the regulative goal of human existence. It certainly represents his most signal advance beyond the pessimistic conclusions of Adorno and Horkheimer. By means of systematic self-reflection, Habermas hopes to diminish the existing

Knowledge-constitutive interests	The different sciences	Forms of social action
(1) *Technical:* concerned with control and survival	Empirical-Analytical sciences	Labour
(2) *Practical:* seeking mutual understanding within a common tradition.	Historical-Hermeneutical sciences	Social interaction
(3) *Emancipatory:* Freedom from a dogmatic and controlling past.	Socially critical sciences	Communication via the ideal speech situation

(From Dermot Lane, 'Habermas and praxis' in *Foundations for a Social Theology*, 1983)

obstructions to the realisation of genuine social relations. He calls in particular for a critique of the dominant illusions that currently inhibit equal communicative exchange between social actors. But such a critique must be motivated, he suggests, by an ideal speech situation where these illusions would no longer operate. This regulative ideal represents a democratic system of communication where there would exist a symmetrical distribution of chances to choose and apply speech-acts in an undistorted manner. It would be fulfilled when all possible participants in discourse possess an equal opportunity to initiate communication and become transparent by their words and actions. To date, communication has been distorted by unequal distribution of dialogue opportunities which sustain privileged positions. The 'ideal speech situation' serves for Habermas as a critical standard which enables us to identify and eventually dismantle the barriers which prohibit symmetrical communicative exchange. He writes:

> The idea of a true consensus, implies the idea of a true existence . . . Only the formal anticipation of the idealized dialogue, as a form of life to be realized, guarantees the ultimate, counterfactual agreement that already unites us and which allows us to criticize any factual agreement, if it is a false one, as such. ('The hermeneutic claim to universality', 1971)

Habermas endorses Marcuse's view that the Marxist critique of ideology (as distortion of communication) needs to be supplemented by a psychoanalytic critique of those unconscious subterfuges which social agents deploy to hide from themselves the repressive strategies of power – e.g. authority, censorship and violence. Psychoanalysis offers Critical Theory as a method of unmasking the deforming uses of language which reflect and often condition the dialectical rapport between action and authority, praxis and power, the forces and the relations of production. Just as the psychoanalytic subject resists facing up to his unconscious desires by rationalising' the distortions of his dream-illusions, so too ideology serves, at the broader level of social interaction, to 'rationalise' the power-ploys of domination by retrospectively rearranging and justifying its motivations. In both cases, we are confronted with a 'systematic distortion of communication' which requires to be deciphered and dismantled.

Habermas defers here to Lorenzer's model of psychoanalysis as *Sprachanalyse* (the analysis of speech). This model involves a 'meta-hermeneutic' or 'depth-hermeneutic' (*Tiefenhermeneutik*) capable of disclosing the subject's quest for self-understanding through a process of desymbolisation and resymbolisation. Such a critical meta-hermeneutic, Habermas believes, can transcend the romantic or purely phenomenological hermeneutics which rests upon a spontaneous recovery of intersubjective dialogue. Where Gadamer sought to overcome misunderstanding by means of a question-and-answer retrieval of some original dialogical understanding, Habermas opts for a more arduous detour through a critique of ideology which leads beyond the structure of transcendental consciousness (the phenomenological heritage) to the socio-historical structure of praxis and liberation (the Marxist heritage). Such a critique claims that non-meaning is not simply a fall from some originally 'pure' dialogue but the inevitable starting point of all language. We begin with ideologised speech and require a critique of ideology to open up the possibility of genuine language. The notion of an unrestricted and unconstrained communication remains, therefore, for Habermas a utopian or regulative idea *à la* Kant. Such an ideal speech situation has *never yet existed*, for our inherited 'communicative competence' is intrinsically deformed by the hidden interests of domination and power.

The meta-hermeneutic model of *Sprachanalyse* aims to 'reconstruct' the 'primitive scenes' of desymbolisation so that we may explain the 'why' – that is, the socio-political motivations – of the ideological 'symptoms'. Only such a method can enable a community to reflect upon itself, to achieve genuine critical independence (*Selbständigkeit*) by exposing the genesis of its distorted speech in and through ideological desymbolisation. Thus exposing the genetic origin of 'non-meaning' as a strategy of domination, Habermas projects the possibility of a resymbolisation of genuine speech based on the principles of liberty and consensus – understood in a real rather than an illusory manner.

It is in the light of the above analysis that Habermas criticises traditional hermeneutics for ignoring the socio-political dimension of misunderstanding. He disapproves of Gadamer's tendency to approach language on an exclusively poetic and ontological plane, as if a consensus of dialogical communication could be achieved by naively recovering our traditional 'belongingness' to Being. For Habermas the construction of genuine consensus cannot dispense with a project of historical action. Hence where the romantic hermeneutic spoke of a *retrieval* of lost meaning (the model of recollection), Habermas speaks of an *anticipation* of possible meaning (the model of emancipation).

In contrast to Gadamer's view that misunderstanding presupposes a prior understanding, Habermas insists that where there is misunderstanding there may exist a posterior understanding if and only if we first undertake a critique of those ideological distortions which reside at the origin of this misunderstanding. What is given is always already deformed communication. The language we inherit has 'dirty hands'. In other words, Habermas wishes to 'dialectise' the hermeneutic model of *Sprachlichkeit* in order to show that the ideal of communicative competence is not an ontologial *precondition* of understanding but an historical *possibility* yet to be achieved by a commitment to the 'interest in emancipation'. Only in this manner, he believes, can we reconcile the philosophers who *interpret* the world and the social actors who *change* it. Thus Habermas' critique becomes what Paul Ricoeur calls 'an explanatory science of distortion . . . an eschatology of non-violence (which) forms the ultimate philosophical horizon of a critique of ideology. This eschatology, close to that of Ernst Bloch, takes the place of the ontology of lingual understanding in a hermeneutics of tradition' ('Hermeneutics and the critique of ideology', 1973).

IV

In *Knowledge and Human Interests*, as we have seen, Habermas addressed the problem of ideology from the point of view of scientific methodology. In later works he endeavours to apply his theory to some of the more concrete social conditions of contemporary western capitalism. Perhaps the most impressive example of such 'applied' Critical Theory is *Legitimation Crisis* (1973), a work which analyses the workings of ideology in the advanced industrial societies of 'late capitalism'.

Habermas endorses the view, originally canvassed by Marcuse and the Frankfurt School, that one of the primary tasks of Critical Theory in the twentieth century is to challenge the hegemony of scientific technology.

Habermas argues that societies have always solicited the support of ideologies to justify the interests of the ruling elite. In primitive societies this ideology took the form of a magico-totemic mystification. In the late Middle Ages and the Renaissance it assumed the guise of a more enlightened religious or political philosophy. And in the bourgeois society of early 'liberal capitalism' – which Marx himself experienced -- ideology played a more explicitly economic role in protecting the interests of the employer and propertied classes (thereby concealing the real origin of wealth – i.e. the exploitation and expropriation of the labour 'surplus-value' of workers – behind a discourse of *laissez-faire* liberalism and upward social mobility).

Under late capitalism, however, ideology is not so easily identifiable. The primary source of domination in today's society, Habermas contends, is the *productivity of rationality itself*. The social process has now become a self-regulating technological system whose overriding purpose is its own preservation:

> Since the end of the nineteenth century ... the development tendency characteristic of advanced capitalism has become increasingly momentous: the scientization of technology. The institutional pressure to augment the productivity of labour through the introduction of new technology has always existed under capitalism. But innovations depended on sporadic inventions, which, while economically motivated, were still fortuitous in character. This changed as technical development entered into a feedback relation with the progress of the modern sciences. With the advent of large-scale industrial research, science, technology, and industrial utilization were fused into a system. Since then, industrial research has been linked up with research under government contract, which primarily promotes scientific and technical progress in the military sector. From there information flows back into the sectors of civilian production. Thus technology and science become a leading productive force, rendering inoperative the conditions for Marx's labour theory of value. It is no longer meaningful to calculate the amount of capital investment in research and development on the basis of the value of unskilled (simple) labour power, when scientific–technical progress has become an independent source of surplus value, in relation to which the only source of surplus value considered by Marx, namely the labour power of the immediate producers, plays an even smaller role ... This technocracy thesis ... becomes a background ideology that penetrates into the consciousness of the depoliticized mass of the population, where it can take on legitimating power. It is a singular achievement of this ideology to detach society's self-understanding from the frame of reference of communicative action and from the concepts of symbolic interaction and replace it with a scientific model. Accordingly the culturally defined self-understanding of a social life-world is replaced by the self-reification of men under categories of purposive–rational action and adaptive behavior. (*Technology and Science as 'Ideology'*, in *Towards a Rational Society*, 1968)

Thus the former ideological conflict of classes is today replaced by another less recognisable form of conflict – that between the self-justifying ideology of technological domination (which serves to 'legitimate' late capitalism) and a critical movement which refuses that very ideology in the interest of emancipation. The new ideology subordinates all spheres of communication to the single sphere of the *instrumental*. This gives rise to the reign of technical reason. Only that which is functional, consumable, computable and therefore 'rationalisable' within the instrumental system of technical positivism is considered 'legitimate'.

And so technological science itself becomes the ideological system which underwrites the productive system of technological science. In this way, capitalism has recourse to an anonymous ideological system which dispenses with the reflective subject. It becomes a structure which structures itself, a reason which rationalises itself, a language which speaks itself, a legitimacy which legitimates itself. This ideologisation of science is for Habermas the major source of the 'legitimation crisis' in modern society. He explains:

> The expression 'traditional society' refers to the circumstance that the institutional framework is grounded in the unquestionable underpinning of legitimation constituted by mythical, religious or metaphysical interpretations of reality – cosmic as well as social – as a whole. 'Traditional' societies exist as long as the development of systems of purposive rational action keeps within the limits of the legitimating efficacy of cultural traditions ... The capitalist mode of production can be comprehended as a mechanism that guarantees the *permanent* expansion of subsystems of purposive–rational action and thereby overturns the traditionalist 'superiority' of the institutional framework to the forces of production. Capitalism is the first mode of production in world history to institutionalize self-sustaining economic growth. It has generated an industrial system that could be freed from the institutional framework. (*Technology and Science as 'Ideology'*)

In the first part of *Legitimation Crisis*, Habermas identifies the ways in which advanced capitalism contrives to legitimate itself through the ideological 'misrepresentations' of the social system. Unlike an animal organism whose crisis is one of biological survival or death, the recognition of a crisis in society presupposes a *theoretical distance* which permits a critical explanation of the causes and motivations of social development. Capitalism seeks to deflect such a critical exposure by a counter–critical ideology (i.e. the 'technocracy thesis') which protects the status quo. Such an ideology claims, for example, that late capitalism has successfully resolved the problems of contemporary social change and overcome the class divisions which Marx decried.

But this ideological 'legitimation' involves several contradictions. It in fact turns science against itself by elevating one specific kind of science – the analytic–empirical science of positivism – at the expense of others (e.g.

the critical social sciences). However, the technocratic invocation of democratic pluralism and the freedom of research, obliges it to tolerate a certain minimum of critical reflection – which in turn threatens to expose its hegemonic control of knowledge. This ideology of late capitalism may ultimately be said to involve a *contradictory* project; for while it *functions* as a class system of domination and constraint, it *represents* itself as a society of freedom, democracy, equal opportunity and progress for all.

The main concern of Habermas's critical project is to combine a theoretical analysis of the 'logic of the social sciences' with a concrete 'praxeology' of the strategies of political change. He believes that both are necessary if a genuine dialectical balance between theory and practice is to be achieved. The goal of this combined analysis is a sort of Marxian enlightenment of liberty.

Even though Habermas shared Marcuse's sympathy for the student revolts of the sixties against the 'ideology of achievement', he expressed reservations about their precipitate willingness to abandon theoretical rigour for the sake of spontaneous action. Such uncritical voluntarism, he claimed, runs the risk of degenerating into an impotent anarchy which can be recuperated within the 'accommodating' ideology of late capitalism. It might be noted, in addition, that Habermas was also fervently opposed to the Leninist brand of voluntarism which dispensed with the need for democratic self-reflection by arrogating to the vanguard party the sole right of legitimation. He saw this as resulting in but another form of ideological violence (especially under Stalinism) mirroring its capitalist adversary.

V

Habermas supports the Frankfurt School's original project of an alliance between scientific research and socio-cultural interpretation. He maintains that without a critical investigation of the social structures of communication operative in late capitalism, it is impossible to initiate an enlightened programme of political emancipation. But what exactly does Habermas mean by 'late capitalism'? His works tend to employ this term in a broad connotative fashion rather than clearly define it. In his detailed commentary on Habermas in *The Marxian Legacy* (1977), Dick Howard offers the following useful summary:

> Descriptively, it points to the increased role of organisation through the intervention of the state in all areas of life. This occurs because of a high degree of capitalist concentration, multinational corporate activity and an ever more controlled and manipulated market. The increasingly restricted private sphere and

minimisation of the market as a form of social distribution imply a change in the class stratification which creates a variety of new forms of social behaviour. The increased application of science and technology changes the work process and affects the profit and investment choices of the giant corporations, as well as the options for government spending. Mechanised farming and greater urbanisation create new social problems that take on a political expression outside of the traditional scheme of party democracy. Mass media and the theoretically equal chance of all for education affect the socialisation process and role conceptions. Scarcity is no longer immediately physical . . . it is nature itself, and a meaning for social existence which have become the scare resource. What is needed here is not a description of the changes, but a theoretical guideline to make sense of and differentiate this complex of phenomena. Habermas proposes a systems theoretical approach articulated in terms of the question of crisis" (*ibid.*).

Habermas argues that the crisis of late capitalism manifests itself in efforts to justify its 'rationality of administration' by reconciling its 'system of production' with a 'system of interpretation'. This justification functions at three main levels: the political, the economic and the socio-cultural. To critically explain these *crises of legitimation* within capitalism's efforts to represent itself, Habermas declares that 'systems theory' which deals with the synchronic structures of contemporary capitalism, must be accompanied by a theory of 'social evolution' which explains how one system of 'social formation' evolves into another. In particular, Habermas resolves to analyse how capitalism continued to produce new self-adaptive mechanisms in order to perpetuate itself and offset those 'internal contradictions' which Marx predicted would bring about its imminent collapse. Habermas shows how the *economic* order attempts to solve the contradictions caused by the fall in the profit rate and surplus value by resorting to new *political* strategies of state administration and intervention. In this way, capitalism seeks to alter the economic laws by changing the administrative laws which, for example, govern the banking system, the building industry, public transport, natural resources and education. One might also cite here the 'rationalisation' programme introduced by the modern welfare state and evidenced in its urbanisation schemes, tax concessions, ecological and trade union reforms, subsidies for ailing production industries, the massive extension of service industries and so on. 'Rationality problems' arise here from the fact that governments try to plan unplannable economies – that is, conceive of them as predictable structural systems – and invariably end up resorting to some kind of 'crisis management.'

But in thus altering the traditional forms of our political existence in order to control its inherent economic contradictions and class tensions, late capitalism is now confronted with the *socio-cultural* problem of how to legitimate its motivations. This legitimation problem leads beyond both the purely economic crisis of production and the political crisis of administration to the socio-cultural crisis of *identity*. To unmask this last crisis, which capitalism astutely essays to conceal, it is necessary to expose the continuing if latent existence of class tensions in late capitalism – and particularly the fundamental tension which exists between the class whose interest is domination and the class whose interest is emancipation. "Because the activity of the state follows the declared goal of directing the system by avoiding crises", observes Habermas, "and because the class relation has thus lost its unpolitical forms, the class structure *must* be affirmed in struggles for the administratively mediated division of the social productive growth" (*Legimation Crisis*).

In times of severe recession and rising unemployment, the compensatory reforms of the welfare state, which presuppose economic prosperity and surplus for their effective functioning, no longer suffice to camouflage the division inherent in late capitalism – even in its revamped form. But what the system forfeits at the economic level it seeks to recover at the ideological level. This requires a program of propaganda to try to surmount the 'motivational crisis' of its citizens (e.g. why should they go on supporting this system where they are asked to make personal sacrifices – higher taxes and inflation rates coupled with restraint in wage demands – for the ultimate good of the state?). In short, ideology is deployed to resolve the growing discrepancy between the demands of the state administration and the needs of each individual social agent.

The 'motivational crisis' to which ideology seeks to respond, operates at the normative level of cultural self-representation. It becomes manifest in those collective symbols, norms or images by means of which a society represents itself to itself in order to legitimate the control of the means of production and communication. The 'empirical logic of economic' is not adequate to this task. It requires that capitalism has recourse to the 'motivational' potencies of socio-cultural experience. But the sense of crisis heightens as capitalism discovers that these very potencies have already become saturated by the system of technical exploitation which is showing strains at the properly economic level. Obvious examples of this contamination of the 'motivational' (practical) interest by the 'utilitarian' (technical) interest are the administrative 'commodification' of interpersonal relations in the service of industrial productivity; the commercialisation of political and cultural discourse as marketable values (e.g. in the popular media); the curricular bureaucratisation of education; and even the clinical scientisation of psychological and family life. Capitalism often finds, accordingly, that it has already converted into the technical currency of instrumental interest, those very cultural deposits of 'motivation' which its recourse to ideology seeks to exploit. The legimation crisis of late capitalism thus reaches its ultimate expression in an unresolvable conflict between problems of system (instrumental–economic) and problems of motivation (socio-cultural).

VI

In response to this stalemate of late capitalism, Habermas proposes a *praxeology* capable of conjugating the radical principles of dialectical materialism with a critical theory of social evolution. The aim of such a praxeology is to secure an open system of communication enabling each subject to become self-reflective and thereby enlighten itself as to its potentially liberating role in the dialectical process of history. Without such self-reflection it is impossible to envisage alternative modes of relation between institutions and individuals. As Habermas puts it, critical theory must be both a changing weapon of critique and a critique of the weapons of change.

A theory of social evolution is crucial to Habermas' critical reinterpretation of historical materialism for it ensures that the project of social praxis is guided by a discursive quest for 'universal' consensus – the indispensable criterion of genuine legitimation. The ultimate goal of Habermas' social theory is, as we noted, a universal ideal of undistorted communication for all. But he insists that this ideal represents an ongoing 'process of enlightenment', one which requires the free participation of individual subjects responding to concrete social situations. The universal cannot be realised without the individual – contrary to the counsel of vulgar or positivistic Marxism. If man is indeed a social being whose work and speech is determined by empirically situated institutions, he is also a reflective individual capable of transcending these determining structures. Moreover, if such reflective transcendence were not possible, Critical Theory itself would have to be abandoned. Habermas resolves, therefore, to show how an enlightened interest in emancipation can supersede the limits of 'instrumental' interest and thereby inaugurate a universalisable project of radical political change. As soon as one abolishes the critical interest in universal emancipation for the sake of crude instrumental efficacity, history becomes a matter of the blind leading the blind, a directionless dance of reflex actions.

While Habermas subscribes then to the Frankfurt School view that Marx's critique of political economy needs to be supplemented by a more contemporary critique of the role of instrumental reason in advanced industrial society, he disassociates himself from the apocalyptic pessimism of Adorno and Horkheimer as expressed in the *Dialectic of Enlightenment*. For Habermas the enlightenment ideals of practical rationality and liberty are not dead letters, vague abstractions travestied beyond redemption by the technological domination of the modern era. One does not have to resort to the sanctuaries of religious spirituality (the later Horkheimer) or aesthetic formalism (the later Marcuse and Adorno) to retrieve some hope of universal freedom. Such freedom is attainable, Habermas insists, *within* the social praxis of history. A rational society characterised by universal and unrestricted communication remains for Habermas a realisable ideal. And such an ideal necessitates that we forego both the nostalgic quest for lost traditions (romantic hermeneutics) and the naive belief in a spontaneous activism of the present (revolutionary anarchism) in favour of a critical deciphering and reconstruction of language aimed at an ideal speech situation where each individual may freely participate in social interaction.

Without this normative 'linguistic universal' to guide us, Habermas warns that the individual appeal to a reflective critical rationality cannot hope to combat the self-perpetuating system of distorted communication which prevails in late capitalism. Individual reflection must always be social, Habermas declares, and social reflection must always be individual.

VII: CONCLUSION

The dialectical social critique proposed by Habermas is intended to counteract the dominating influence of the 'behaviourist' approach to the social world – an approach which reduces human consciousness to a series of adaptive reflexes and thereby sustains the technocratic programme of 'human engineering.' Habermas seeks to restore the project of a practical questioning of our social existence in the face of the pervading growth of technically conditioned behaviour. He points to the necessity of combating the new positivistic way of thinking, articulated in the technocratic consciousness, which has become a substitute ideology for the demolished bourgeois ideologies and which suppresses the possibility of both ethical and political critique. This substitute ideology is denounced as follows:

> Technocratic consciousness reflects . . . the repression of 'ethics' as such as a category of life. The common positivistic way of thinking renders inert the frame of interaction of ordinary language in which . . . the conditions of distorted communication can be reflectively detected and broken down. The depoliticization of the mass of the population, which is legitimated through technocratic consciousness, is at the same time men's self-objectivication in categories equally of both purposive-rational action and adaptive behavior. The reified models of the sciences migrate into the sociocultural life-world and gain objective power

over the latter's self-understanding. The ideological nucleus of this consciousness is the *elimination of the distinction between the practical and the technical*. It
reflects, but does not objectively account for, the new constellation of a disem-
powered institutional framework and systems of purposive-rational action that
have taken on a life of their own. (*'Technology and Science as 'Ideology'*.).

The main aim of Habermas' work is, accordingly, to analyse the ways in
which the new ideology violates our practical and emancipatory interest in
forms of communication free from domination. It demonstrates (1) how the
technocratic ideology works against the creation of an intersubjectivity of
mutual understanding; and (2) how its sole concern is the expansion of the
sphere of technical manipulation. The technocrats of both capitalistic
planning and of bureaucratic socialism, Habermas concludes, often share a
common objective – to bring society under control by restructuring it
according to self-regulated systems of instrumental action.

Habermas distinguishes finally between two types of 'rationality'. On the
one hand, there is the scientific–technical rationalisation of society which,
taken to its extreme, amounts to a "cybernetic dream of the instinct-like
self-stabilisation of society". On the other hand, there is what Habermas
describes as a practical rationalisation "*at the level of the institutional
framework* [which] can occur only in the medium of symbolic interaction
itself, that is, through *removing restrictions on communication*". Of this second
positive kind of rationalisation, he writes:

> Public, unrestricted discussion, free from domination, of the suitability and
> desirability of action-orienting principles and norms in the light of the socio-
> cultural repercussions of developing subsystems of purposive-rational action –
> such communication at all levels of political and repoliticized decision-making
> processes is the only medium in which anything like 'rationalization' is possible
> . . . Such a process of generalized reflection . . . does not lead per se to the better
> functioning of social systems but would furnish the members of society with the
> opportunity for further emancipation and progressive individuation. (*Technology
> and Science as 'Ideology'*.)

But since advanced capitalism is dependent on a depoliticised public
realm, it strongly resists the move towards unrestricted communication. It
seeks instead to immunise itself against any questioning of its 'technocratic
background ideology'. And so a 'new conflict zone' emerges – the public
sphere of mass media and communication systems – in place of the old
class antagonisms explicit in liberal capitalism. Habernas notes how, at the
level of the public administration of communication, capitalism contrives to
suppress the difference between the 'technical' interest in instrumental
control and the 'practical' interest in a radical transformation of the institutional framework which determines the possibility of social interaction.

The publicly administered definitions of our depolitised culture under capitalism "extend to *what* we want for our lives, but not to *how* we would like to live if we could find out, with regard to attainable potentials, how we *could* live" (*Technology and Science as 'Ideology'.*). The ultimate task of Habermas' Critical Theory is therefore to predict and devise ways of *repoliticising* the dessicated public sphere of communication.

Habermas aims to rehabilitate a substantive theory of critical reason against the prevailing extremes of positivist rationalism and romantic irrationalism. This necessitates a reappreciation of the role of the reflective subject and a new interpretation of historical materialism clearly at odds with the orthodox tenets of traditional Marxism (e.g. the determining role of the proletariat, class struggle and the material economic base). Against the end-of-subjectivity thesis – which flourishes in much Marxist and structuralist thinking – Habermas contends that the fundamental questions of 'meaning', 'value' and 'truth' cannot be dispensed with in the name of a scientific system of anonymous laws (be they historical or structural). True to the basic humanist inspiration of Critical Theory, Habermas holds fast to the notion of the human subject – albeit a radically politicised subject – as the irreducible source of both theoretical and social transformation.

STRUCTURALISM

Ferdinand de Saussure

Structuralism embraces a wide variety of intellectual disciplines. It has found influential exponents in linguistics, anthropology, psychoanalysis, sociology, aesthetics and political theory. Above all, structuralism is a *method*. Its aim is to analyse isolated events or meanings in terms of their underlying structural laws. It seeks to comprehend *particulars* by describing their interrelationship within the totality of *general* codes which govern them. It looks for the deep and often hidden structures beneath the surface manifestations of meaning.

Ferdinand de Saussure is generally recognised as the founding father of the structuralist method of analysis. Born in Switzerland in 1857, Saussure studied at the University of Leipzig before going on to teach linguistics in Paris and Geneva. In his *Course in General Linguistics*, published in 1916, three years after his death, Saussure outlined the principles of a new linguistic theory which came to be known as 'semiology'. (The English translation of this work was first published in 1959). Semiology means a science (*logos*) of signs (*semeia*). The great originality of Saussure's approach was to treat language as a self-regulating rather than referential system of signs. In other words, he argued that language should be analysed in terms of its internal *structures* (what language is *in itself* as a formal system of relations) and not, as had traditionally been the case, simply in terms of its *content* (what language is about, that is, what it refers to). This radical shift of focus from traditional to modern linguistics is neatly summed up in Saussure's famous maxim: 'language is a form not a substance'.

I

Saussure – whose specialist expertise was in phonology (the study of language as a system of sounds) – insisted that linguistics must transcend its habitual confinement to the study of grammar and philology. Whereas the latter sciences had tended to concentrate on empirical instances of spoken language as it evolves historically (e.g. nineteenth century historicism), Saussure's structuralist model sought to identify the formal laws of the total language system which ultimately structure the utterances of spoken language. He claimed that a structural analysis of spoken language could disclose its operations as a network of permutations *between* signs made possible by the linguistic system which usually remains concealed. The primary task facing modern linguistics, he believed, was to describe the workings of this hidden or unconscious system thus making it available for scientific investigation.

In the course of his formulation of a new science of linguistics, Saussure proposed a series of important distinctions – between *langue* and *parole*, signifier and signified, system and realization, semiology and semantics, paradigmatic and syntagmatic, synchrony and diachrony etc. These distinctions were to inform the basic method of structuralist analysis as it was variously employed by such thinkers as Lévi-Strauss, Lacan, Barthes, Foucault and others. Saussure's writings are, for the most part, highly technical. This is not surprising since his primary interest was one of method. In so far as subsequent 'structuralists' succeeded in *applying* his linguistic method to more concrete forms of discourse – the discourse of myth (Lévi-Strauss), of literature and ideology (Barthes), of the unconscious (Lacan) and so on – the practical implications of Saussure's discovery of structural analysis become more obvious and more accessible. But before we proceed to examine these various applications of the method – in the following chapters of this section – it is necessary to outline the central features of Saussure's own pioneering groundwork.

II

In seeking to provide his new theory of linguistics with a rigorous scientific basis, free from the narrow positivism of previous 'empiricist' approaches, Saussure proferred his now celebrated distinction between *language* and *speech*. This distinction serves as the cornerstone of structuralist linguistics. Language or *langue* is defined as the systematic totality of all possible linguistic usages. Speech or *parole*, by contrast, refers to any particular act of language; it is the actual manner in which we realise the possibilities of the abstract language system in our everyday concrete utterances. So that while language is a universal and timeless system, speech belongs to the here and now. It is therefore at the secondary level of speech that 'humanistic' questions of style or originality – the ways in which we use language for a particular practical purpose or to express our sense of individuality, etc. – enter into consideration. Saussure did not deny the importance of these historical dimensions of speech. He simply affirmed that they were not primary. They do not ultimately determine the laws according to which language works. More simply stated, if *langue* is the whole of language, *parole* is the part (or multiplicity of parts) which operates within the whole.

Saussure's study of language may be termed 'structuralist', accordingly, to the degree that its emphasis falls not on the empirical content of words – as traditional linguistics held – but on the structural interrelationships which obtain between part and whole. This is what Saussure means when he declares that the meaning of a sentence is not to be found in its substance but in its structure.

Saussure gives priority to *langue* over *parole*. He affirms that the individual act of uttering or understanding a sentence can have no meaning in itself, but only within the framework of the overall language system. Sassure's model of *langue* must not, however, be confused here with, for example, Jung's psychological notion of a 'collective psychic unconscious'; nor with Durkheim's notion of a 'collective social consciousness' (though he was strongly influenced by Durkheim's sociology); nor indeed with the old Platonic notion of transcendental, otherworldly essences. *Langue*, as Sassure understands it, is a formal system of signs which makes no claim to refer to anything outside of itself. *Langue* has no substantial existence either in an empiricist sense (for language does not exist as some objective entity in the real world) or in an idealist sense (it does not exist as some subjective entity in the collective or individual mind). Similarly when Saussure tells us that language *precedes* the particular occasions of its usage (as *parole*), he does not intend this priority to be understood in the conventional sense of the combined classifications of dictionaries and grammers. (For here language is no more than the abstract sum of its articulated parts). In fact, Saussure understands *langue* as the totality of the coexistence of its potential parts. It is neither the *a posteriori* sum of its parts, nor some *a priori* metaphysical Idea from which all the parts could be deduced.

The totality of language remains intangible from the point of view of direct empirical access. Saussure describes it as an 'inner storehouse' which escapes immediate observation in any particular word or sentence. But precisely as such, *langue* is what is both implied and presupposed by every single tangible utterance as *parole*. Moreover, because *langue* constitutes a self-regulating system of signs, irreducible to any manifestation external to language, it is complete in itself. One cannot say what language is in any terms (e.g. empirical or metaphysical) other than its own. Language functions always within its own self-referential limits. As Saussure explains: "Language is a system of inter-dependent terms in which the value of each term results solely from the simultaneous presence of the others" (*Course in General Linguistics*). This is why Saussure insisted that a properly scientific study of the determining laws of language would have to prize linguistics free from its traditional subordination to other related sciences, such as psychology or history. Only by so doing can we begin to understand what language is in itself. This new understanding would, Saussure believed, be made possible by the new linguistic model of 'semiology'.

Saussure's method makes it possible to determine the linguistic code which gives a specific structure to each of the languages spoken by different linguistic communities. He believed that the 'system' of language (*langue*) could be made into an autonomous object of scientific investigation, even though it had been virtually ignored by classical philosophies. Saussure was less concerned with the particular messages (*paroles*) of individual speakers than with the linguistic set of codes which constituted the basis for such messages. While the message is individual and intentional (it is 'meant' by someone), the code is collective, anonymous and, as it were, 'unconscious' (not in the Freudian sense of libidinal energies or desires but in the broad sense of a cultural–structural unconscious). Having established this distinction between the operations of *parole* and *langue*, Saussure was able to argue that the latter was more suitable for rigorous scientific scrutiny since it functions at the quasi-algebraic level of combining the phonological, lexical and syntactical capacities of the language system. Unlike *parole* which is amenable to semantic change and contingency – thus involving the researcher in a wide variety of disciplines, e.g. history, psychology, philology and so on – *langue* constitutes the object of a single science: structural linguistics. In short, by bracketing the intentional message for the sake of the structural code, Saussure resolves to set linguistics on a firmly scientific footing.

III

Traditional linguistics had advanced 'referential' models of language which construed the sign as a *name* referring to a *thing*. By contrast, Saussure defines the sign as a relation between a *form* or acoustic image expressed by the human voice (what he called the 'signifier') and a *concept* or mental idea (what he called the 'signified'). This model of material signifier and mental signified gave rise to two rival interpretations of Saussure; 1) the 'materialist' which saw Saussure as privileging the phonetic dimensions of language and 2) the 'rationalist' which claimed that he gave priority to the conceptual dimensions of language as an abstract system. Indeed this basic difference of emphasis was to inform subsequent interpretations of the active structuralist movement.

One of the most controversial – if not unprecedented – aspects of Saussure's model was its insistence that this structural relation between 'signified' and 'signifier' is *arbitrary*. In other words, the relationship between a sign and that which it signifies is not natural. It is not determined, founded or guaranteed by any natural law – ontological or divine. It is a matter of social and cultural convention. Let us take some obvious examples. There is nothing bearlike about the word bear. There is nothing large about the word large. Likewise, liquid semi-vowels cannot simply be equated with water; or open vowel sounds with objects that are heavy or loud. Many who wish to support the view that the choice of words to designate things is not arbitrary, cite the example of onomatopoeia (when the signifier sounds like the signified, e.g. cuckoo) Saussure points out, however, that not only are onomatopoeic formations very limited in number, but they are never organic elements of a linguistic system. Saussure thus rejects the onomatopeic theory of the origin of language. He writes:

> Words like French *fouet* 'whip' or *glas* 'knell' may strike certain ears with suggestive sonority, but to see that they have not always had this property we need only examine their Latin forms (*fouet* is derived from *fagus* 'beech-tree', *glas* from *classicum* 'sound of a trumpet'). The quality of their present sounds, or rather the quality that is attributed to them is a fortuitous result of phonetic evolution. (*Course in General Linguistics*)

Saussure goes on to observe that even authentic onomatopoeic words such as *glug-glug* or *tick-tock* are also chosen somewhat arbitrarily, for they are in fact only approximate and more or less conventional imitations of certain sounds. Furthermore, such onomatopoeic terms, once introduced to a language, undergo the same evolution (in both sound and form) as other terms – e.g. the evolution of the vulgar Latin term, *pipio*, into the modern word *pigeon*. In other words, even those rare cases of authentic onomatopoeia tend to ultimately lose their original character in order to assume that of the linguistic sign in general, which is un-natural in the sense of being *unmotivated*. The linguistic sign is arbitrary, in short, because it is not motivated by any natural bond between signifier and signified. Saussure offers the following explanation:

> The idea of 'sister' is not linked by any inner relationship to the succession of sounds s-$\ddot{o}$-r which serves as its signifier in French; that it could be represented equally by just any other sequence is proved by differences among languages and by the very existence of different languages: the signified 'ox' has as its signifier b-$\ddot{o}$-f on one side of the border and o-k-s on the other. (*ibid.*)

But to declare that there is no natural motivation in our choice of signifier (e.g. the combination of the six English phonemes in 'sister') to signify a signified (the mental concept of a female sibling) is not to imply that this choice is left to each speaker. On the contrary, Saussure suggests that once a sign has become established in the linguistic community, no individual can wilfully change it. The linguistic system determines individual utterance rather than being determined by it. Indeed, this aspect of Saussure's linguistic model was to become a central premise of the entire structuralist movement. It implied a fundamental rejection of the romantic and existentialist doctrines that the individual consciousness or 'genius' is the privileged locus of the creation of meaning. In answer to Sartre's view, for example, that each individual existence is what each individual makes of it, the structuralist replies that the meaning of each person's *parole* is governed by the collective and pre-personal system of *langue*. This conflict of views represents one of the most fiercely debated issues of modern Continental philosophy.

But Saussure's structural linguistics is not merely in dispute with existentialism. It also involves a refutation of metaphysical or mystical theories about the origin of language. This attitude is quaintly summed up in Boehme's belief in the 'signatures of things', in a 'language of nature . . . which is a mystery granted by the grace of God'. According to this view, nature is a script written by God and first articulated by Adam when he identified the proper name for each of the animals of God's creation. It follows from such a premiss that there is a 'natural' signifer for each 'natural' signified which ultimately corresponds to the original signature of its Divine Creator. The task of a metaphysical inquiry into language is to penetrate beneath the confusions of our everyday discourse in order to rediscover the original correspondence which exists between word and thing.

The originality of Saussure's position was to argue that the meaning of language is generated *within* language itself, that it is not derived from some prior reality existing independently of language – be it God's metaphysical creation or man's subjective consciousness. A primary tenet of structuralism is consequently that signs are not given by divine or natural experience, but constitute arbitrary functions within a purely formal system. (This view would be corroborated by Jakobson and the 'formalist' school of linguistics which also exerted a profound influence on post-Saussurian developments in structuralism). Saussure affirms that signs relate primarily not to things in the world but to other signs within the language system. In other words, the origin of meaning resides neither in God nor Man, but in language itself. One can see here the germ of the oft-quoted conviction that structuralism implies the demise of God and of Man; and that as such it involves a refusal of both Deism and humanism.

IV

Saussure's approach is also innovatory in that it locates the primary intralinguistic relations betweens signs at the level of sound i.e. the acoustic dimension of language which he calls the *signifier*. He appears to re :rse the traditional priority given to the signified over the signifier. He sets the signifier free, as it were, providing it with a certain autonomy. But Saussure is quick to point out that the acoustic properties of signifiers do not generate meaning as *isolated* sound-objects (*phonetics*); they do so only by means of structural relations between acoustic 'differences' (*phonemes*). It is not, he insists, the material substance of individual words which makes them properly linguistic, but their relationship to other words in the non-material or abstract system of signs. A sign never operates in splendid isolation. As a pure physical sound, totally divorced from other contrasting sounds, it signifies nothing at all. The sign only signifies in so far as it *differs* from other related signs. Its *intralinguistic* context in the overall system of signifiers is essential.

Saussure thus records his revolutionary discovery that the meaning of a sign is engendered by the differences or oppositions which appear between signs within language. He affirms that language is most properly understood as a verbal chain of self-differentiation which works by means of 'phonemic' oppositions (e.g. cat is neither hat nor mat; free is neither tree nor spree and so on). Without this initial and remarkably simple act of acoustic difference between the sounds of signifiers, it would be quite impossible to attribute different meanings to different words.

This basic premiss of structural linguistics may be summarised as follows: the lateral opposition between one signifier and another (cat and mat) serves to demarcate phonemic divergences which ultimately allow for the subsequent relation of the signifier, as an acoustic phenomenon, to its signified (its conceptual meaning). This relation between signifier and signified is, as we saw, arbitrarily determined by the various linguistic conventions which obtain in different cultures – e.g. 'child' in English is '*kind*' in German and '*enfant*' in French etc. No one of these terms can lay claim to a natural privilege *vis-à-vis* the others. So that it would not be Saussure's concern, for instance, to chart some genealogical chain to ascertain which term existed first and thus approximated most closely to some pure etymological origin (e.g. some 'original' Indo-European language). For Saussure there are no corrupt languages because there is no pure language bestowed on us by God, Nature, Race or Reason. Language works not by virtue of a vertical descent from or ascent to a pre-established system of correspondences. It works horizontally within a differential system of phonemic signifiers. This is what Saussure is getting at when he declares that the internal articulation of meaning *between* signs precedes the external representation of meaning *by* signs. For the structuralist, the door into language opens from within. And in this respect, language may be compared to a game of charades: it is only comprehensible through the interaction of signs, any one of which taken separately is incomprehensible. A sign cannot signify unless it is combined or contrasted with other signs.

A number of important consequences ensue from this structural understanding of linguistics. It is, for example, because each acoustic signifier operates differentially in relation to other signifiers (which it is *not*), that we can distinguish the specific grammatical function of one word (e.g. a singular noun) from the contrasting functions of other words which it is *not* (e.g. plural nouns or pronouns, verbs, prepositions and so on). Moreover, while it is true that these differences may be first identified at the level of individual utterance (*parole*), they only become meaningful in terms of the structural contrasts which the overall system of *langue* imposes on them. In other words, acoustic differences cannot generate and distribute meaning between signs outside of the predetermining structures of *langue*. Indeed, as Jakobson and Lévi-Strauss were to remark, without the linguistic capacity for paired or binary oppositions within a system, it would not be possible for the child to order its world, or for mankind to undergo its decisive transition from *nature* (where the world is experienced as an indiscriminate chaos) to *culture* (where the world is experienced as an ordered set of distinctions). For Saussure, as for Jakobson and Lévi-Strauss, *langue* is a universal property of mankind. "Whether we take the signified or the signifier", writes Saussure, "language has neither ideas nor sounds that existed before the linguistic system, but only conceptual and phonic differences that have been issued from the system" (*ibid.*)

V

Saussure elaborates this point by formulating another important distinction, that between *syntagmatic* and *paradigmatic* modes of signification. The relation between signifiers functions syntagmatically when it operates as a differentiation between contiguous terms. In the sentence 'the blue bird sings', for example, the noun relates back to an adjective which precedes it and forward to a verb which follows it. The paradigmatic relation, by contrast, operates by virtue of association rather contiguity. Here the noun 'bird' receives its signification by means of an implied phonetic opposition to other associated terms in the total language system from which it is differentiated: 'bird' is *not* 'birth' or 'burn', it is *not* 'curd' or 'third' etc. Indeed this discovery of the paradigmatic functioning of signs, leads to the curious observation that it is in fact an implied or presupposed association (contrast or comparison) with *absent* words (e.g. 'birth') which constitutes the meaning of the actual word *present* in the spoken or written sentence ('bird'). (The difference between a syntagmatic and paradigmatic reading is comparable to the two ways in which we might read a menu. To read it syntagmatically would be to move horizontally from one course to the next – e.g. *entrée, main course, dessert*; whereas to read it paradigmatically would be to move vertically down the possible alternatives within any single course – e.g. pâté, soup, seafood cocktail and so on under the heading of *entrée*.)

Here once again, Saussure's 'structuralist' preferences are in evidence. He appears to privilege the paradigmatic mode of signification in so far as it is governed not by sequential operations (of noun and verb, subject and predicate etc.) apparent on the surface of the sentence (*syntagma*), but by deep structural laws of association which relate each manifest signifier to the other 'potential', but not actually present, signifiers within the total system of language. Words signify then both by virtue of 'associated' phonetic differences and by virtue of their 'contiguous' differences to other words in the same sentence which, in turn, signifies by virtue of its difference to other sentences in the system of language as a whole. "In language", as Saussure puts it, "there are only differences without positive terms".

These considerations lead finally to Saussure's celebrated distinction between *diachrony* and *synchrony*. Whereas most linguistic studies before Saussure had emphasised the 'historical' or *diachronic* dimension of language – questions of its philological genesis and development etc. – Saussure concentrates upon the 'a-historical' or *synchronic* character of language. The commonplace diachronic approaches had focused on the changes and particularities of language as it progressed from one historical period to the next. Saussure, by contrast, argues that language, taken as an autonomous synchronic system, must be understood in its totality at every moment, as a sort of timeless present, regardless of what came before or after. This emphasis on synchrony would assist the scientific requirement of maximum unity and coherence. The history of language, in so far as Saussure considers it at all, is treated as a series of complete systems – each constituting a perpetual present, as it were, with all the possibilities of meaning implied in every moment.

The business of the linguist, it appears consequently, is not to try to assume the status of some spectator outside of the totality of language, to arrive at some transcendental vantage point from which the historical alterations and developments of language could be identified. For structuralism this is impossible. There is no outside to language. The totality of language (*langue*) is not something that can become an object for a subject; it is already there in all of its parts, in each of its manifestations in history; it is virtually present, as it were, in each *parole* which it alone makes possible.

Saussure suggests accordingly that it is language which enables us to articulate the meanings of history: The meaning of history is not merely disclosed by language, it is determined by it. Thus structuralism challenges all linguistic models which construed language as a collection of independently exisiting word-units, each with its own specific meaning attached to it, developing diachronically in historical time according to observable laws of change. The operations of language are not simply dependent on historical causes existing beyond language – e.g. changing economic conditions, demographic shifts, or geographical variations. Moreover, most people, Saussure pursues, use language without being aware of the historical origin or evolution of its individual parts. And here, Saussure's linguistic model finds common cause with Durkheim's sociology and Malinowski's anthropology as a reaction against nineteenth century historicism. Saussure does not, of course, deny that such empirical changes occur in history. He simply affirms that it is not the *system* of language as *langue* that is determined by them, only the specific actualisations of its parts as *parole*. In short, the history of *parole* presupposes the ahistory of *langue*. Language does not unfold within history. History unfolds within language. (In general, however, Saussure himself remains rather vague about history. It was for subsequent structuralists to spell out the implications of this complex rapport between structure and history).

Such considerations lie behind Saussure's favourite comparison between language and a game of chess. It can be played by many different people in many different places at many different times; and on each occasion it can undergo different combinations of moves and countermoves – but it remains throughout the *same* game. However much the surface moves (*paroles*) of the game may vary, the underlying structural rules (*langue*) are invariant. It is true, of course, that these rules only acquire concrete manifestation in the relationships that unfold between the chess pieces in particular games. But, by the same token, the very fact that the laws of *langue* preexist each manifestation of *parole*, means that they ultimately precondition each of these manifestations. The synchronic system of the game is presupposed by the diachronic moves within it.

VI: CONCLUSION

Saussure may be considered the major forerunner of modern structuralism (if one can speak in such teleological terms) in so far as he uncovered the systematic codes which govern the workings of language. His scientific investigation was less concerned with *what* meaning is than with *how* it is produced by the structural operations of sign systems; he placed the emphasis on the structural rather than the empirical dimensions of language. This led to the revolutionary discovery that the linguistic system as a whole precedes the particular workings of signs and ultimately determines their capacity to generate meaning. Saussure did not preoccupy himself with 'epistemological' questions of whether this or that meaning is true or false. He suspended, as it were, the complex problem of *reference* (i.e. of how words refer to empirical or ontological truths outside of language) in order to highlight what he deemed to be the more fundamental problem of how meaning originates within the formal operations of language itself.

This shift of attention amounted to a radical revision of traditional approaches to linguistics. It sponsored the view that reference is dependent on meaning, rather than the reverse; and furthermore that meaning as such is derived from a structural system of signifying relationships internal to language. This claim issued in the general principle – which was to become a cornerstone of the entire structuralist edifice – that what we call 'reality' or 'truth' is in fact a construct of the language employed to describe it. At its simplest level, such a principle would account for the fact that different linguistic cultures have different ways of understanding the natural environment, the colour spectrum or social and economic institutions, because they deploy different signifying practices to explain their world.

Saussure fully recognised the innovative implications of this new structural linguistics for a scientific study of the life of signs within society. He asserted that "semiology would show what constitutes signs, what laws govern them", while adding that "since the science does not yet exist, no one can say what it would be . . ." (*Course in General Linguistics*). Saussure took the first pioneering steps in the formulation of this science. But he remained for the most part at the technical level of methodological analysis. With some rare exceptions – as when towards the end of his life he began to investigate the use of anagrams and proper names in poetic discourse – Saussure himself did not *apply* his structural method to the many concrete instances of signifying discourses. He analysed how they *could* work rather than how they actually *did* work. The work of 'application' would be reserved for those who came after him.

Combining the linguistic methodology of Saussure with other critical developments of modern thought (e.g. psychoanalysis, Marxism or the formalism of Propp and Jakobson), the subsequent structuralists demonstrated in more precise terms just what the 'study of the life of signs within society' could achieve. They did this in a wide variety of ways showing how cultural meanings relate to the hidden discourses of (1) power and knowledge (Foucault); (2) the psychic unconscious (Lacan); (3) myth, kinship and symbol (Lévi-Strauss); (4) political ideology (Althusser); and (5) literature and mass culture (Barthes). But however varied the content of their investigations, what these 'structuralist' critics all agreed upon was that first, language comprises a system of signifying operations which ultimately predetermine our modes of experiencing our world; and that second, such operations are irreducible either to some 'subjective' private reference prior to language or to some 'objective' empirical reference beyond language. Finally, the different developments of structuralist analysis after Saussure were motivated by the conviction that the theoretical requirements implied by his linguistic model could be extended to cultural and social codes – such as myths, literary texts or the popular media – codes which are larger than the linguistic units (phonetic or lexical) of a sentence. Saussure blazed the trail. It was for his disciples to stake out the hitherto unexplored territories which his structural method of linguistics opened up.

Claude Lévi-Strauss

If Saussure sketched the map of linguistic structuralism, Lévi-Strauss was the first to occupy the terrain by attempting a structuralist analysis of social anthropology. Lévi-Strauss' prolific work demonstrated the potential of the Saussurian model of language for a new understanding of man's cultural expressions. He applied the structuralist method to a systematic investigation of mythic, symbolic and kinship codes, thereby helping to establish it as one of the most influential theoretical tools of modern European thought.

I

Lévi-Strauss was born in Belgium in 1908. He taught in various universities and scientific institutes throughout the world, including the University of Sao Paulo in Brazil, the New School for Social Research in New York, the Laboratory of Social Anthropology at the University of Paris and later at the Collège de France in Paris. Lévi-Strauss' international repute was largely due to his ability to employ the structuralist methods of research in order to reorganise the basic materials of social anthropology (with which his Brazilian travels in particular had made him familiar) along new scientific lines.

Lévi-Strauss was by no means the first scholar to investigate the area of social anthropology. Sir James Frazer had studied the anthropological foundations of primitive societies from the perspective of human psychology. Bronislav Malinowski and his followers had carried out impressive research into anthropological customs and rites (in particular the Melesian) in terms of a functional sociology. But the singular success of Lévi-Strauss' approach was to have set the whole basis of such scholarship onto a new footing by interrogating the hidden logic of 'deep structures' which underpinned the operations of social cultures. Far from dismissing the important discoveries made by Frazer and Malinowski at the psychological and sociological levels, Lévi-Strauss provided such discoveries with a rigorously scientific grounding by uncovering the universal and timeless structures of human society, and, by extension, of the human mind. This new science he called 'structural anthropology'.

Taking his methodological cue from Saussure, Lévi-Strauss proposed to identify the 'synchronic' structures of human society which prescind from or precede 'diachronic' development over historical time. More simply put, he looked to those mythic or ritual structures of societies which did *not* undergo change. These he termed 'cold' societies in opposition to 'hot' societies – usually of European provenance – which were typified by notions of historical evolution or transition. Because of their resistance to the relativism and contingency of historical time, 'cold' societies preserved the most explicit evidence for the permanent structures of human thinking – what Lévi-Strauss would refer to as *la pensée sauvage*. In the myths and social customs of the South American Indians, Lévi-Strauss believed he had found powerful illustrations of this *pensée sauvage*. Here he discovered 'cold' societies which had remained largely unaffected by Western culture's obsession with progress and change. In 1938, several years after he had arrived in Brazil to take the Chair of Sociology at the University of Sao Paulo, Lévi-Strauss organised an expedition to live with and study the Amazon Indians. This was to prove a decisive event in his career, furnishing him with some of the key insights for his later works, in particular *Anthropologie Structurale* (1958), the four volume *Mythologiques* (1964–1972) and *La Pensée Sauvage* (1962).

Other formative influences on Lévi-Strauss were what he described in *Tristes Tropiques* as his 'three mistresses' – geology, psychoanalysis and Marxism. What interested him in these disciplines was less their literal content than their common resolve to disclose *hidden universal strata of meaning* which lie beneath the rapidly changing surface phenomena of our world: the strata, that is, of earth formations (geology), of the unconscious (psychoanalysis) and of socio-economic relations (Marxism). "All three", observed Lévi-Strauss, "showed that understanding consists in the reduction of one type of reality to another; that true reality is never the most obviously real". Even 'economic history', as he argued in his introduction to *Structural Anthropology*, though ostensibly preoccupied with empirical facts and statistical data, "is by and large, the history of unconscious processes". The task of the social anthropologist is, therefore, to dig beneath the upper layers of historical particulars to those universal strata which most political and economic histories simply ignore – so bent are they on stringing together details of wars and dynasties on a chronological thread of secondary rationalisations. Lévi-Strauss approves the historian's desire to come to terms with the meaning of the past; but he insists that this desire needs to be complemented by the anthropologist's search for those vertical structures which subtend the linear transitions from one historical happening to another. He writes:

> They (the historian and the anthropologist) have undertaken the same journey on the same road in the same direction; only their orientation is different. The anthropologist goes forward, seeking to attain, through the conscious, of which he is always aware, more and more of the unconscious; whereas the historian advances, so to speak, backward, keeping his ι, ςς fixed on concrete and specific activities from which he withdraws only to consider them from a more complete and richer perspective. A true two-faced Janus, it is the solidarity of the two disciples that makes it possible to keep the whole road in sight. ('History and anthropology': introduction to *Structural Anthropology* 1958)

II

But if Lévi-Strauss had intellectual allies, he also had intellectual adversaries. He dismissed existentialism, for instance, as a 'shop-girl's philosophy'. His major criticism was that it laid inordinate emphasis on non-scientific experiences of a purely personal and subjective nature. Against this intellectual fashion particularly prevalent in post-war France Lévi-Strauss promoted a science of the logical structures of kinship and taxonomy (classification systems) which would enable the researcher to freeze the anecdotal and impressionistic experience of existential transience into a 'still life' of timeless space where permanent truths could be identified. While existentialist and historicist philosophies had focused almost exclusively on the characteristics of each individual culture as it evolved or differed from another, Lévi-Strauss turned our attention to the unchanging *collective* properties of human culture.

Sartre argued that every human subject is responsible for what he makes of himself. We are each one of us a free consciousness which chooses its nature and identity as it progesses in time. Lévi-Strauss, by contrast, insists that while it is true that man has made our social culture what it is, the term 'man' must be understood here not as some isolated individual but as a collective mind which does not know at a conscious level how it has organised its world or by what laws it has effected such organisation. In other words, the logic by means of which our human societies and cultures have been structured is one which remains largely 'unconscious'. What is important to explain, as Lévi-Strauss points out in *Le Cru et le Cuit*, is not how individual men think in myths but how 'myths think in men, unbenownst to them'.

This explains Lévi-Strauss's clear preference for Freud and Marx over Sartre. Where Lévi-Strauss may be said to *differ* from Freud and Marx is in affirming that the collective logic which predetermines our social experience is not just a materialist law of economic production nor a biological law of libidinal instinct, but a structural law of language itself. And here we return to Lévi-Strauss' ultimate debt to the Saussurian model. For Lévi-Strauss, man "equals" society and society "equals" language. So understood, language is the most formative feature of human culture. It is what distinguishes us from the animal order and preconditions the various relations which obtain in our social, religious or aesthetic life (what may be called the 'symbolic order' in the broad sense in which Lévi-Strauss understands this term). This primary linguistic character of our mental life or 'mind' provides the basis for all subsequent cultural patternings – even where these appear to be of a totally non-linguistic nature e.g. marriage ceremonies, curative rites, political hierarchies, kinship laws, sexual taboos, totemic practices, cooking or economic customs and so on. Just as language is made up of a system of 'phonemic differences', as Saussure and Jakobson discovered, so too several 'cold' societies were shown by Lévi-Strauss to be coordinated by an integrated system of kinship elements which operate according to a hidden logic of binary oppositions (as we shall see in greater detail below). The same goes for myth. Here the elementary structures – what Lévi-Strauss calls 'mythemes' by analogy with 'phenomenes' – conjoin or contrast to make up a meaningful whole. And likewise in cooking practices Lévi-Strauss is able to identify basic distinctions between edibles and inedibles, for example, or between raw and cooked edibles etc – what he terms 'gustemes' – which are, once again, governed by laws analogous to the differential correlation of phonemes.

Lévi-Strauss' highly diversified anthropological researches all corroborate Saussure's insight that the *parts* must be understood, not atomistically or in isolation, but within the overall signifying system as a *totality*. The traditional 'item-centred' approach which emphasised the primary importance of disparate empirical contents is replaced by what Lévi-Strauss describes as the 'relational' approach of structural linguistics. Moreover, it is not just a question of the various laws of a culture – kinship, marriage, cuisine etc. – functioning internally on the basis of binary oppositions (e.g. 'gustemes' differing from each other within the systematic whole of 'cuisine'). These various cultural systems themselves represent partial sub-systems within the entire totality of human culture or *l'esprit humaine*.

It is not surprising therefore to find Lévi-Strauss declaring in a key passage of *Structural Anthropology* that the numerous sub-systems combine within the totality of a culture to permit "the establishment between individuals and groups, of a certain kind of *communication*". For Lévi-Strauss the most universal trait of human culture is the desire to signify. This is why we find many primitive societies asking whether something is 'good to symbolise' (*bon à symboliser*) *before* they ask, for example, whether it is 'good to eat' (*bon à manger*). The human need for communicational exchange through signs would appear to precede even the most material needs of biological usage. Accordingly, marriage regulations and kinship arrangements should, Lévi-Strauss suggests, be considered primarily as a set of coded relations of exchange which perform as a *language system* (in the most general sense of a signifying system of communication). He writes: 'That the mediating factor, in this case, should be the *women* of the group, who are circulated between classes, lineages, or families, in place of the words of a group which are circulated between individuals, does not at all change the fact that the essential aspect of the phenomenon is identical in both cases' (*Structural Anthropology*). By thus equating the codes of kinship or marriage systems (as an exogamous exchange of women – or by extension, of other symbols of 'property' or 'prestige' – between different tribes) with the codes of a linguistic system (as an interrelationship between phonemic units), Lévi-Strauss relocates the structural origin of the commercial and sexual behaviour of primitive societies in the infrastructure of language itself.

III

Although Lévi-Strauss first became acquainted with the methods of structural linguistics through the mediation of Roman Jakobson, whom he met at the New School for Social Research in New York in the forties, it was not really until he wrote the bestselling *Tristes Tropiques* in 1955 and *Structural Anthropology* in 1958, that he successfully demonstrated the radical implications of the structuralist methodology for the social sciences. For Lévi-Strauss the two most significant contributions made by this new method were: (i) the shift from the study of conscious linguistic phenomena to the study of their unconscious deep structure; and (ii) the refusal to treat elements as independent entities, reinterpreting them instead in terms of their relations within a global system which operates according to generalisable laws. While insisting that his structural anthropology was 'scientific', Lévi-Strauss understood this term in the contemporary Continental (e.g. Saussurian) sense of systematic organisation, rather than in the more Anglo-American sense of empirical verification.

As we have already noted, Lévi-Strauss at all times stressed the necessity to penetrate beneath the observable surface data to the usually ignored deep-strata of the human mind. He affirmed, for example, that kinship attitudes cannot be properly comprehended on the positivistic basis of empirical observation of the 'facts', but must be construed as symbolic expressions of underlying mental structures. The apparent chaos of nature, as we superficially experience it, is always pre-patterned by a covert order of culture. Man's experience of nature does not precede culture; it is produced by it. In this respect, Lévi-Strauss' *oeuvre* may be seen as constituting a kind of 'culture analysis' which disputes the procedures of both empiricism and naturalism. It reveals that a society, like a language, is not as it *seems* but as it is *structured*. The primary task of the structural anthropologist is therefore to "grasp, beyond the conscious and always shifting images which men hold, the complete range of unconscious possibilities" ('Introduction' to *Structural Anthropology*). And for Lévi-Strauss, this totality of unconscious possibilities is equivalent to that synchronic whole which Saussure called *langue*.

To illustrate more concretely how Lévi-Strauss develops this analogy between structural anthropology and structural linguistics, it may be useful to examine in some detail his treatment of (i) kinship and (ii) myth.

(1) Kinship systems

In a study entitled 'Structural analysis in linguistics and in anthropology', Lévi-Strauss offers the following blueprint of his method:

> In the study of kinship problems (and no doubt the study of other problems as well), the anthropologist finds himself in a situation which formally resembles that of the structural linguist. Like phonemes, kinship terms are elements of meaning; like phonemes, they acquire meaning only if they are integrated into systems. 'Kinship systems' like 'phonemic systems' are built by the mind on the level of unconscious thought. Finally, the recurrence of kinship patterns, marriage rules, similar prescribed attitudes between certain types of relatives, and so forth, in scattered regions of the globe and in fundamentally different societies, leads us to believe that, in the case of kinship as well as linguistics, the observable phenomena result from the action of laws which are general but implicit . . . Although they belong to *another order of reality*, kinship phenomena are *of the same type* as linguistic phenomena. (*Structural Anthropology*)

Lévi-Strauss concludes this analogy by asking whether the anthropologist, "using a method analogous *in form* (if not in content) to the method used in structural linguistics, [can] achieve the same kind of progress in his own science as that which has taken place in linguistics?". He answers in the affirmative.

In a seminal study, *Elementary Structures of Kinship* (1949), Lévi-Strauss argued that laws of kinship constitute one of the earliest attempts by the human mind to found a social order by distinguising between different classes of human relations. He reveals how even the most basic of human relations is structured by laws determining whom one is or is not permitted to marry. By forbidding men to marry their sisters, for example, and by recommending that they marry other specified categories of women – e.g. 'matrilateral cousins' (daughters of the mother's brother) – an elementary kinship structure is established. It is such elementary structures which provide the systematic classification of marriage laws. The disclosure of these structures enables us to recognise that what seemed like contingent or arbitrary laws of marriage are in fact governed by a 'small number of simple principles' (analogous to phonemes) which permit societies to coordinate a diverse mass of ritual practices, customs and taboos into a highly organised system. Thus kinship rules are shown to ultimately furnish societies with a symbolic system of differences, a system whose logic of binary opposition is also manifest in other realms of social relation – religion, art, cuisine, folklore or the institutions of work and ownership. Taken together, these social systems of relation make up a 'cultural totality'.

Lévi-Strauss maintains that the elementary laws of kinship manifest three universal principles of the human mind: (i) the 'principle of a rule' as a means of differentiation and order; (ii) the 'principle of reciprocity' as a means of reconciling the opposition between the self and others; and (iii) the 'synthetic principle of the gift' which in marriage, for instance, allows for the transfer of a 'valuable' person or property (in what Lévi-Strauss terms the 'circulation of women') from one individual or family unit to another. These three principles account for the possibility of an ordered transition from social conflict to 'partnership'.

Lévi-Strauss believed that the discovery of this correspondence of the three principles of kinship with three universal principles of the human mind, would counteract the 'cultural relativism' of much contemporary anthropology. He concluded that his researches into the elementary structures of kinship demonstrated that cultures organise themselves not just as behavioural reactions to *external* stimuli in the empirical environment, but in accordance with *internal* structures of universal reason.

(2) Mythic systems

Concentrating on 'societies with no history' – and particularly those of the Brazilian and Northern American Indians who regarded their culture as a timeless reality whose past is present and vice versa – Lévi-Strauss was in a position to interrogate the varying systems of myth within an homogenous 'synchronic' whole. He was convinced that he had found here a primordial logic or *pensée sauvage* shared by *all* human minds.

We in the West, he submits, have become oblivious to the existence of this *pensée sauvage* as our European culture became increasingly dominated by notions of technological progress and technical superiority. But while advanced Western societies have forced this mythic mode of thinking underground, they have not obliterated it. It lives on in our unconscious, though it is often only when we come into contact with the myths and rituals of 'cold' or so-called 'primitive' societies that we find an opportunity to explicitly acknowledge its workings and subject it to scientific analysis. This is an important point. For myth, according to Lévi-Strauss, is not a matter of irrational fantasy. Myth possesses its own kind of reason which operates according to a logic of unconscious symbolism quite as rigorous as scientific logic. Indeed without the former logic it is debatable whether the latter logic would ever have existed.

Lévi-Strauss claims that while the surface contents of myth often appear trivial or confusedly repetitive, they in fact function in terms of collective 'codes' which communicate unconscious messages. Myths are not just fanciful fairy tales recounted for the sake of leisurely distraction. They are crucial attempts to resolve the fundamental but unpalatable contradictions of human existence – for example, the contradictions between life and death, between self and other, culture and nature, time and eternity and so on. Lévi-Strauss' meticulous investigations into the logic of myths reveals them to be highly structured *strategies* whose purpose it is to permit the *symbolic* expression of unconscious aspirations which are incompatible with the *real* world of our conscious experience.

IV

Lévi-Strauss provides a powerful illustration of this strategic functioning of myth in his structural analysis of the Oedipus legend. He demonstrates that the Oedipus myth comprises a series of recurring oppositions – revolving round the structural antithesis of *underrating* or *overrating* blood relations. Far from being haphazard events, these oppositions undergo specific patterns of transformation according to highly organised rules. A primary purpose of this oppositional/tranformational logic in the Oedipus myth is to reconcile (1) the cultural desire of man to escape from his 'autochthonous' (i.e. earthly) origins by overcoming monsters (the Kadmos-dragon or the Oedipus-sphynx) and (2) the awareness of the difficulties imposed by nature on the realisation of such a desire (expressed by Oedipus' physical handicaps: he is swollen-footed and is eventually blinded). The logic of myth, in other words, mediates the contradictory relationship between *nature* and *culture*. It suggests that even if nature (e.g. monsters) can be overcome, culture continues to feel the pressure of nature (e.g. club-foot, blindness).

If examined solely at the level of content, many myths might appear to be without logical rhyme or reason. But Lévi-Strauss' structural analysis shows that while the isolated, statistical 'items' of a myth (i.e. the 'mythemes' or 'shortest possible sentences') are quite arbitrary when taken in themselves, the relations between these 'mythemes' are meaningfully structured within a synchronic whole (see the table below). As Lévi-Strauss explains in 'The structural study of myth': "If there is a meaning to be found in mythology it cannot reside in the isolated elements which enter into the composition of a myth, but only in the way these elements are combined' (*Structural Anthropology*). This accounts for Lévi-Strauss' deep-seated opposition to the Jungian attempt to establish direct connections between the content and meaning of myths, that is, between isolated mythological 'archetypes' and specific unconscious messages. Lévi-Strauss replaces such a semantic approach to the interpretation of myth with the semiological approach of Saussure. Myth, he insists, is not only structured *like* language (in terms of oppositional relations between 'mythemes' analogous to the differential relations between 'phonemes'), it *is* language. "Myth is language", writes Lévi-Strauss, for "to be known, myth has to be told; it is part of human speech" ("The structural study of myth' in *Structural Anthropology*).

Lévi-Strauss' structural interpretation thus develops Saussurian linguistics into an anthropological science of myth which provides (i) economy of explanation; (ii) unity of solution; and (iii) the ability to reconstruct the whole from the fragment, as well as later stages of a myth from previous ones. But while analysis of myth is based on the methods of structural linguistics it also goes beyond it. It breaks new ground. It extends the semiological range of application beyond the 'phoneme' as the basic unit of the language sentence to the more elaborate unit of the 'mytheme' (which contains within itself the structural play of phonemes while functioning within a new system of structural play larger than the units of a sentence). As Lévi-Strauss puts it: "Myth is language functioning on an especially high level where meaning succeeds practically at *taking off* from the linguistic ground on which it keeps on rolling" (*Ibid*).

To explain more clearly what Lévi-Strauss is getting at here, let us briefly return to his detailed interpretation of the Oedipus myth. He divides the narrative of this myth into the following four vertical columns or 'mytheme-units' (see table):

(1) *Overrating of blood relations*	(2) *Underrating of blood relations*	(3) *Slaying of monsters*	(4) *Difficulties in walking*
Cadmos seeks his sister Europa, ravished by Zeus			
		Cadmos kills the dragon	
	The Spartoi kill one another		
			Labdacos (Laios' father) = lame?
	Oedipus kills his father, Laios		Laios (Oedipus' father) = left-sided?
		Oedipus kills the Sphinx	Oedipus=swollen foot?
Oedipus marries his mother, Jocasta	Eteocles kills his brother, Polynices		
Antigone buries her brother, Polynices, despite prohibition			

The first column has as its common feature the *overrating of blood relations*. The second column inverts this by expressing an *underrating of blood relations*. The third refers to the *slaying of monsters* (representing our earthly origins). While the fourth column contains the common reference of the surnames in Oedipus' father-line to *difficulties in walking and standing straight*. Lévi-Strauss argues that these constituent units cannot be coherently explained in isolation – that is, in terms of their literal-semantic content which quite evidently lacks any sustained or universal significance – but only in terms of their structural relation to each other. Thus, for example, while the third column is composed of a 'bundle of relations' which commonly refer to the *denial* of the autochthonous origin of man (the killing of monsters), the fourth column points to the *persistence* of the autochthonous origin of man (moreover, Lévi-Strauss maintains that in mythology it is a universal characteristic of men born from the earth that at the moment they emerge from the depths they cannot walk properly). Lévi-Strauss offers this summary explanation of the structural logic at work in these 'mythemic' oppositions:

> We thus find ourselves confronted with four vertical columns each of which includes several relations belonging to the same bundle. Were we to *tell* the myth, we would disregard the columns and read the rows from left to right and from top to bottom. But if we want to *understand* the myth, then we will have to disregard one half of the diachronic dimension (top to bottom) and read from left to right, column after column, each one being considered as a unit . . . The myth has to do with the inability, for a culture which holds the belief that mankind is autochthonous . . . to find a satisfactory transition between this theory and the knowledge that human beings are actually born from the union of man and woman. Although the problem obviously cannot be solved, the Oedipus myth provides a kind of logical tool which relates the original problem – born from one or born from two – to the derivative problem: born from different or born from same? By a correlation of this type, the overrating of blood relations is to the underrating of blood relations as the attempt to escape autochthony is to the impossibility to succeed in it. (*Ibid.*)

In other words, the central conflict which the Oedipus myth tries to resolve is that between autochthony (born of one and the *same* principle: the earth) and bisexual reproduction (born of two *different* parents: father and mother). Lévi-Strauss claims, furthermore, that once we analyse such structural relations within the total system of comparative mythology, we discover that the task of a great number of myths is to reconcile the opposition between unity and difference. In short, myth is ultimately defined by Lévi-Strauss as a process of *problem-solving*. It attempts to find solutions at a structural level of logic for problems which remain insoluble at the empirical level of experience.

A less intricate example of such problem solving cited by Lévi-Strauss is that of the 'trickster' in the mythology of North American Indians. The mythic role of the 'trickster' serves as a kind of messianic mediation between apparently irreconcilable oppositions. Observing that the 'trickster' is frequently compared to a coyote or a raven in many North American Indian tales, Lévi-Strauss points out that both of these creatures are 'carrion-eaters' and, as such, function as totemic symbols which mediate between the opposed orders of the herbivorous animals of agriculture (associated with life) and the carnivorous beasts of prey of hunting (associated with death). Carrion-eating animals are at once like beasts of prey in that they eat animal food *and* like food-plant producers in that they do not kill what they eat. Lévi-Strauss further consolidates his thesis by

demonstrating how this mediational function also extends to other analogous orders. For example, the coyote (as intermediary between herbivorous life and carnivorous death) is, in turn, compared (i) with mist (as
intermediary between sky and earth); (ii) with garments (as intermediary
between nature and culture); (iii) with ashes (as intermediary between the
vertical roof or chimney and horizontal hearth or ground); and (iv) with
androgenous sexual figures (as intermediary between male and female).

Lévi-Strauss concludes that the essentially ambiguous character of the
'trickster' figure perfectly corresponds to the structural role of mediation
between opposed sets of terms. He affirms, moreover, that this mediational
function is a universal property of mythic figures the world over. One finds
countless examples of mythological systems where the same god or hero is
simultaneously endowed with contradictory qualities – e.g. divine and
human, benevolent and malevolent, earthly and heavenly and so on. Indeed
these mediating paradigms find parallels, Lévi-Strauss claims, in such
familiar Western figures as Cinderella, a personage who serves to straddle
the gulf separating the orders of male and female, low class and high class
etc. But here Lévi-Strauss leaves the research to those more expert in the
mythological workings of the 'hotter' European cultures.

V

Unlike most traditional studies of comparative mythology, Lévi-Strauss'
approach is not concerned to establish the 'true' or 'authentic' version of
any given myth. A myth, he maintains, consists of *all* of its available
variations. There is no one authentic original of which all the others would
be derived or distorted copies. Every version as it emerges 'diachronically'
in history is a sort of mythic *parole* which unfolds within the synchronic
system of the mythic *langue*. And this means that the elementary structures
of myth are basically trans-cultural and trans-historical. The myths of
yesterday are as valid as those of today; and vice versa. Questions of the
chronological priority of one version of a myth over another are therefore
quite irrelevant. Even Freud's modern interpretation of the Oedipus story,
for instance, provides admissable evidence for a 'structuralist' account of
this ageless myth. For each variational difference of a myth can ultimately
be combined with other 'differences' in such a way that the logical classification of the 'totality' results not in a cluster of contingent irregularities but
in an internally coherent structural system.

One would be quite mistaken to regard the mythic and symbolic structures of *la pensée sauvage* as some kind of inferior archaism which modern
reason has totally replaced or 'gone beyond'. *La pensée sauvage* is no

antiquarian museum piece of the ancient past. What we have here is a timeless 'science of the concrete' which operates according to a structural logic quite as sophisticated as that which obtains in our contemporary 'science of the abstract'. Lévi-Strauss contends that *la pensée sauvage* is an 'unchanged and unchanging power' of the human mind. "The kind of logic in mythical thought", he writes, "is as rigorous as that of modern science . . ." (*Structural Anthropology*).

While it is true that myth functions on a symbolic level, comparable in some respects to that of magico-religious rites, and first manifests itself to us emotionally, its essential power remains *intellectual*. At its deepest level, myth endeavours, as we saw, to intellectually resolve (in the order of 'mythemic' signifiers) the conflicts and contradictions of our everyday experience (the order of the signified). Lévi-Strauss affirms consequently that it is only a structural analysis of the symbolic function in all its most primordial aspects (myth, magic, shamanistic practices, art, sorcery, dreams etc.) which can enable us to understand the intellectual condition of the human mind as a *surplus of the signifier over the signified*. The surplus expresses the fact that "the universe is never charged with sufficient meaning", and that the "mind always has more meanings available than there are objects to which to relate to them" ('The sorcerer and his magic' in *Structural Anthropology*).

This discrepancy or excess of intellectual meaning over empirical experience not only explains the ultimate *raison d-être* of myth but also the rich multiplication of different versions of the same myth. This propensity of myth to repeat and reduplicate itself epitomises for Lévi-Strauss the indefatigable efforts of the human mind to provide logical solutions to the irresolvable contradictions of the real world. Myth is a sort of intellectual *non serviam*. It is a refusal to accept things as they are, to be content with what is given (*positum*) in the here and now. It proposes to solve in narrative what is not solved in practice. The very fact that a theoretically infinite number of different versions of a myth can be generated is proof for Lévi-Strauss, if proof were needed, of the inexhaustible richness and complexity of the human intellect. The structural study of myth is, in short, a powerful reminder of the irreducibility of the mind to the 'facts' of the empirical world, of culture to nature. In this respect, structuralism is profoundly opposed to positivism.

This opposition between 'structuralist' and 'positivist' approaches to science is a crucial one. Not only would the positivist scientist abhor Lévi-Strauss' choice of shamans, sorcerers, tricksters or *bricoleurs* (handimen) to exemplify the constructive 'problem-solving' powers of the human mind;

they would be equally hostile to his suggestion that such powers ultimately devolve from a surplus of meanings over facts.

But in spite of widespread condemnation from the *doyens* of the positive sciences, Lévi-Strauss remained undaunted in his assertion that mythic thinking is capable of employing a scientific system of logical relations which harmonises conflicting elements of experience. Referring at one point in *Structural Anthropology* to the magical healing rites of a certain Indian medicine man who transposed his patient's suffering from the real world of pain to a symbolic world of painlessness by means of a fictional reconstruction of the origin of the illness, Lévi-Strauss makes the following highly significant comment: "He did not become a great shaman because he cured his patients; he cured his patients because he had become a great shaman". In other words, the shaman succeeds because he makes the patient believe in the superiority of mind over matter; and he does so by conjuring up a surplus world of 'familiar' or ritualised symbolic meanings where the 'alien' problem of illness (the strange disease which has invaded the patient's body), unmanageable at the level of real experience, can be intellectually or psychologically resolved. The fact that the symbolic world of monsters, gods and heroes which the shaman invokes to narrate and explain the illness, does not correspond with objective reality, does not impede the cure. It actually makes it possible. What is essential is that the ill person, and by extension the society to which this person belongs, *believes* in this mythic universe.

Lévi-Strauss draws a parallel here between the logic at work in shamanism and in psychoanalysis. In both cases the purpose of the 'talking cure' is to bring to a comprehensible level conflicts and resistances which have remained intractable or suppressed. The primary move for the shaman, as for the analyst, consists in rendering acceptable to the mind sufferings which the body refuses to tolerate. In the following passage from 'The effectiveness of symbols', Lévi-Strauss offers a lucid account of how the shaman's cure actually works:

The sick woman believes in the myth ... The tutelary spirits and malevolent spirits, the supernatural monsters and magical animals, are all part of a coherent system on which the native conception of the universe is founded. The sick woman accepts these mythical beings ... What she does not accept are the incoherent and arbitrary pains, which are an alien element in her system but which the shaman, calling upon myth, will reintegrate within a whole where everything is meaningful. Once the sick woman understands, however, she does more than resign herself; she gets well. But no such thing happens to our sick when the causes of their diseases have been explained to them in terms of secretions, germs, or viruses. We shall perhaps be accused of paradox if we answer that the reason lies in the fact that microbes exist and monsters do not.

And yet, the relationship between germ and disease is external to the mind of the patient, for it is a cause-and-effect relationship; whereas the relationship between monster and disease is internal to his mind, whether conscious or unconscious: It is a relationship between symbol and thing symbolized, or, to use the terminology of linguists, between sign and meaning. The shaman provides the sick woman with a *language*, by means of which unexpressed, and otherwise inexpressible, psychic states can be immediately expressed. And it is the transition to this verbal expression – at the same time making it possible to undergo in an ordered and intelligible form a real experience that would otherwise be chaotic and inexpressible – which induces the release of the physiological process, that is, the reorganization, in a favourable direction, of the process to which the sick woman is subjected (The effectiveness of symbols' in *Structural Anthropology*).

The same kind of reasoning obtains at the collective level of social ideals and ideologies. As Lévi-Strauss observes in *Tristes Tropiques*, many of our myths, both ancient and contemporary, are the "fantasy production of a society seeking passionately to give symbolic expression to the institutions it *might* have had in reality", had the socio-political conditions of that society been capable of solving its internal contradictions. But since "on the social level, the remedy was lacking", the society finds itself impotent to realise its desired goals and so begins "to dream them, to project them into the imaginary" (*ibid.*).

VI: CONCLUSION

Lévi-Strauss has been accused of being over-theoretical, of revising French rationalism under the guise of structuralism. It has been suggested that his anthropology is at best an abstract text-analysis of ethnographers' writings which fails to deal adequately with first-hand empirical material. And in this respect, his relative lack of concrete fieldwork and his excessive preoccupation with logical and mathematical systems of classification has been held against him. On the other hand, Lévi-Strauss has also been condemned as a Rousseauesque romantic who concentrates exclusively on the timeless models of 'primitive thinking' at the expense of a concrete understanding of history. (This question comes to the fore, for example, in his dispute with Sartre on the myth of the French Revolution in *The Savage Mind*, where he clearly favours the Saussurian model of structure over the existentialist model of historicity).

Lévi-Strauss' critics often fail to appreciate, however, the ultimate motivation of his work: the search for a method which would adequately identify the hitherto neglected logic of the 'savage mind' which is presupposed by the historical mind of modern Western man. Just as Saussure reacted against the nineteenth-century histories of language, so too Lévi-Strauss reacts against the apparently endless accumulation of ethnographies which adduced masses of empirical data without any overall system. Lévi-Strauss' major concern is to demonstrate how the *pensée sauvage* of myth and symbol unfolds according to a 'logic of analogy' which permits the mind to hold together disparate orders of meaning – e.g. human, divine, animal, vegetal – in a 'reciprocity of perspectives'. This kind of logic is capable of thinking one thing (e.g. death) in terms of another (e.g. life), or of thinking one set of oppositions (life/death) in terms of another (e.g. herbivorous/carnivorous). One of the earliest and most explicit examples of such a logic of structural relation, is to be found in the practice of 'totemism', that is, the representation of men as animals. Another is religious mythology where the gods can be represented as man and vice versa.

This power to establish equivalences between 'systems of difference' is, for Lévi-Strauss, at bottom an attempt to come to terms with the two great contradictions of human existence – the contradiction between the one and the many and the correlative contradiction between timelessness and time. While the *pensée sauvage* of mythic logic deals primarily with temporal oppositions (that is, conflicts which we experience in our everyday existence in time), it strives towards a formal condition of timeless unity (synchronic totality). Thus Lévi-Strauss can conclude that the primary purpose of the symbolic analogies which this logic generates in art, religion, magic or myth, is to function as 'machines for the suppression of time'. What remain irreconcilable contradictions at the level of our empirical *experience* become harmonised pairs of oppositions at the level of the logical *structure* of our myths. What cannot be resolved in fact we attempt to resolve in fiction.

Jacques Lacan

Jacques Lacan was born in Paris in 1901. He extended the frontiers of structuralism by demonstrating how the Saussurian model of linguistics could be used, with highly original if controversial results, to radicalise our understanding of psychoanalysis. The basic premiss of Lacan's programme is expressed in his famous maxim that the 'unconscious is structured like language'.

I

Lacan drew an analogy between the linguistic relation of *langue/parole* and the psychological relation of unconscious/conscious. He believed that this analogy had far-reaching implications for a true understanding of Freud's discovery of the reality of the unconscious – which he referred to as a Copernican revolution in psychology. Traditional psychology gave priority to the scientific rationality of consciousness and either ignored the world of the unconscious or else dismissed it as some kind of irrational quagmire of animal instincts. Freud reversed this priority and showed that the unconscious possesses its own rationale, its own logic of reality. It is this hidden logic which structures the desires and fantasies of the unconscious in a language-like fashion. The life of the unconscious is thus shown to be structural not instinctual. And this is why Lacan is convinced that the discoveries of Freud and Saussure overlap and complement each other. Where Freud had disclosed the language of the unconscious, Saussure had disclosed the unconscious of language.

Lacan saw the Continental model of structuralist linguistics as providing the most appropriate method for a proper appreciation of Freud's novel insights. He felt that these insights had been betrayed by the Anglo-American model of behavioural science whose blind worship of the experimental methods of positivism – or what Lacan called 'scientism' – reduced Freud's psychology of the unconscious to a narrow psychology of the ego.

One of the main targets of Lacan's attacks was Heinz Hartman's book, *Ego Psychology and the Problem of Adaptation*, which had an enormous influence on the orthodox psychoanalytic movement in the States when published there in the fifties. Hartman sought to render Freud inoffensive by accommodating his theories to the scientific methods of biology and the physical sciences. This encouraged the view that the basic problems and anxieties of the individual result from an inability to 'adapt' to the environmental conditions of his social surroundings. But for Lacan this was a travesty of Freud's discovery that it is a psychical rather than merely a physical reality that is at stake. If the external environment is hostile this is not always and only a *biological* matter of behavioural adaptation but a *symbolic* relation between the individual and his projected fears or desires. Moreover, orthodox psychology championed the ego of rational adaptation – what Lacan refers to as the cult of the 'normal man' – against the non-conformist desires of the unconscious. This model reduced psychoanalysis to a school of 'human engineering' whose primary purpose was to produce eminently adaptable citizens with reinforced cognitive egos that are virtually autonomous (see Lacan, 'function and field of human language' in *Ecrits*).

But where orthodox psychoanalysis saw a strong ego as a good thing, Lacan sees it as the essence of Narcissism, the most basic object of self-love which is the seat of denial and resistance to unconscious desire. For Lacan, the most authentic ego is not an autonomous self-identity but an alienated self-division. For only the latter can remain attuned to the secret language of the unconscious and accept that the human subject is not only permanently divided against his environment but also against himself. Thus while ego psychology 'teaches' the subject how to overcome unconscious desires in the name of a 'rational' consciousness, Lacan argues that the most profound significance of Freud's discovery was to 'unteach' the subject, as it were, to dissolve his conscious illusions so as to recover the liberating language of the unconscious. Lacan resists therefore the tendency to equate psychoanalyst and teacher (as the one who knows all). And, by the same token, he is radically opposed to the conception of a 'cure' defined in terms of an 'identification' of the subject with either the analyst as educator or with the dominant institutions of the social environment. It is essential, claims Lacan, to recognise the 'boundary between analysis and re-education'.

Lacan's differences with the conservative mainstream of Anglo-American psychoanalysis came to a head in the 1950s when he broke from the International Psychoanalytic Association and delivered his famous attack in the *Discourse of Rome* (1953). Here Lacan accused the orthodox Freudians of having medicalised psychoanalysis into a mechanical causal behaviourism. He furiously denigrated this 'reductionism' of Freud, insisting that our understanding of the psychoanalytic project be rescued from biological determinism and be reinterpreted in terms of a larger 'cultural' model which would recognise the properly *linguistic* structures of the unconscious. Only in this way could the 'genuine' Freud be rediscovered.

Psychoanalysis must be 'demedicalised', affirmed Lacan (himself a medical psychiatrist), and enter into open commerce with such non-medical disciplines as literature, philosophy, mathematics, anthropology and political theory. Indeed, it is interesting to note that when Lacan came to characterise psychoanalysis as a discipline in 'The neurotic's individual myth' (1953), he chose to refer to it as a 'liberal art'. "It is not erroneous", he explains, "if you use this word *art* in the sense in which it was used in the Middle Ages to speak of the liberal arts – that series going from astronomy to dialectic by way of arithmetic, geometry, music and grammar . . . they maintain in the foreground what might be called a fundamental relation to human proportions." Not surprisingly, many traditional Freudians were horrified to find Lacan mixing empirical evidence drawn from his clinical practice as an analyst (though he never actually published a case study) with citations not only from Saussure and Lévi-Strauss but also from Rimbaud, Joyce, Catherine of Siena, Hegel, Heidegger and the Hindu Uphanishads! But Lacan's main purpose here was not to shock his more narrow-minded colleagues but to show how the old *scientistic* approach to Freud, based on the 'objectifying' empirical data of psychiatry could be opened up to a more *conjectural* exploration of the structural language of the unconscious.

To recognise that psychoanalysis is above all else a practice of language, is to extend its sphere of influence and understanding from biology to the human sciences as a whole. In this, Lacan did not see himself as engaging in a kind of Freudian 'revisionism'. He believed that this enlarged frame of reference was a faithful response to Freud's own claim in *The Question of Lay Analysis* that the future of psychoanalysis would depend upon its capacity to "include branches of knowledge which are remote from medicine and which the doctor does not come across in his practice: the history of civilisation, mythology, the psychology of religion and the science of literature". Lacan believed that Saussure's structural linguistics – particularly as it was developed by Lévi-Strauss – provided the most fitting method for such a rapprochement between the science of psychoanalysis and the humanities. He often suggested, indeed, that if Freud had known of Saussurian semiology he would have made great use of it in his own writings. What is certain is that Lacan's synthesis of Freud and Saussure not only transformed psychoanalysis into an influential intellectual movement in France from the fifties onwards, but also transformed structuralism into a more relevant and practical method of inquiry.

II

But if Lacan succeeded in making structuralism more relevant it was not thanks to his mode of writing. Lacan's style is tantalisingly obscure. And it is intentionally so. Not so as to guard the method of structuralist psychoanalysis as some inaccessible preserve of an elite priesthood (though Lacan has frequently been accused of this by his Anglo-American critics); but so as to convey the need for a new mode of thinking and talking which results from the discovery of the hitherto unexpressed workings of the unconscious. In an effort to resist the pat formulae of scientistic Freudianism, Lacan developed new rhetorical idioms which he believed more accurately reflected the hidden structural logic of the unconscious.

It is important to appreciate therefore that Lacan's frequent use of puns, conundrums and epigrams or his linguistic play with habits of parapraxis (slips of the tongue) is not just whimsical obscurantism. It is carefully and strategically designed to show the reader that misunderstanding is, paradoxically, an integral part of understanding; that what we *seem* to say and what we *really* say are not always the same; that our conscious expression of things is forever shot through with unconscious associations of which we remain unaware. In this manner, the Lacanian practice of employing ambiguous turns of phrase and veiled allusions, poses a direct challenge to the presumed sovereignty of consciousness which seeks to reduce all experience, unconscious or otherwise, to the immediate transparency of clear and distinct ideas.

Lacan claimed that this practice of linguistic play was a fruitful response to Freud's discovery that the desires of the unconscious have their own language which is not easily translatable into the conventional rationale of linear thinking and talking. The language of unconscious desire, which expresses itself in dreams and symptoms, works dialectically in terms of riddles. Freud himself explicitly acknowledged this when he compared the structure of dreams to the structure of a rebus (an enigmatic representation of words by pictures suggesting its syllables). Since this comparison plays a crucial role in Lacan's notion of the unconscious being structured like language, it may be useful to cite here Freud's original formulation:

Suppose I have a picture-puzzle, a rebus, in front of me. It depicts a house with a boat on its roof, a single letter of the alphabet, the figure of a running man whose head has been conjured away, and so on. Now I might be misled into raising objections and declaring that the picture as a whole and its component parts are nonsensical. A boat has no business to be on the roof of a house and a headless man cannot run. Moreover, the man is bigger than the house; and if the whole picture is intended to represent a landscape, letters of the alphabet are out of place in it since such objects do not occur in nature. But obviously we can only form a proper judgment of the rebus if we put aside criticisms such as these of the whole composition of its parts and if, instead, we try to replace each separate element by a syllable or word that can be presented by the element in some way or other. The words which are put together in this way are no longer nonsensical but may form a poetic phrase of the greatest beauty and significance. A dream is a picture-puzzle of this sort. (*The Interpretation of Dreams*, 1900)

This model of the rebus lies at the root of Lacan's conviction that the psychic world of the unconscious is logical (in the sense that it structures its materials into the logic of the rebus); and that this kind of structural logic is refractory to the so called 'rationalistic' logic of our normal consciousness. As Lacan puts it: "The trade route of truth no longer passes through thought . . . Rebus, it is through you that I communicate" ('The Freudian thing' in *Écrits*, 1966).

Lacan maintains that American psychology, both behaviourist and humanist, ultimately ignored the rebus-logic of the unconscious, so intent was it on bolstering up the 'American way of life' by retrieving the conscious *ego* from the subversive desires of the unconscious *id*. American psychoanalysis aimed to produce good citizens capable of performing their social and economic functions without confusion or contradiction. And it sought to justify this practice of adapting the individual to the social environment, by a simplistic reading of the more ego-centred psychology of the late Freud (as formulated, for example, in *The Ego and The Id*, 1925). By contrast, Lacan took his model of linguistic or structural psychology from such early works as *The Interpretation of Dreams* (1900) and *The Psychopathology of Everyday Life* (1901). Here he found a radical alternative to ego psychology. He argued that Freud's most radical breakthrough – in these formative studies of the more 'linguistic' dimensions of the human psyche – was to have given priority to the unconscious language of the Id (which he compares to Saussure's *langue*) over the conscious discourse of the individual Ego (which he compares to Saussure's *parole*). Returning to Freud's famous maxim: 'Where the Id is, there I will be' (*Wo es war, so will Ich werden*), Lacan takes it to mean that the self-contained conscious Ego (*Ich*) should come to recognise its origins in the self-dissolving unconscious Id (*Es*). He offers the following translation: *Là où fut ça, il me faut advenir* ('*I must arrive there where the Id has been*'). This reading – sometimes referred to as 'pre-Socratic' – reverses the orthodox interpretation of Freud's phrase as meaning that the Ego should triumph over and replace the Id.

Lacan thus refuses the orthodox view of psychology as a form of 'soul management' which strives to make the Ego invulnerable, self-secure and transparent to itself. He argues that the true function of psychoanalysis is to challenge such 'humanist' notions of the individual as an autonomous identity or 'total personality' and to lead us back to the unconscious depths of language whose structural play of plural meanings precedes all ego-formations at the conscious level. The business of the analyst is not, he holds, to fortify the patient's sense of narcissistic identity but to subvert it, to remind him that he is a split-subject, whose conscious images of self-identity are perpetually de-centred by unconscious desires. There are no 'individuals', insists Lacan, only 'dividua' or 'divided ones'. In the following passage from the 'Agency of the letter in the unconscious', Lacan explains his position:

> If we forget the self's radical ex-centricity to itself with which man is confronted, in other words, the truth discovered by Freud, we shall falsify both the order and the methods of psychoanalytic mediation; we shall make of it nothing more than the compromise operation that it has, in effect, become, namely, just what the letter as well as the spirit of Freud's work most repudiates ... The radical heteronomy that Freud's discovery shows gaping within man can never again be covered over without whatever is used to hide it being profoundly dishonest. ('Agency of the letter in the unconscious' in *Ecrits* 1966).

Lacan's position, it might be noted, also has far-reaching political implications – though Lacan himself was always slow to spell them out. Quite clearly his attack on the American use of psychology to transmute 'ab-normal' citizens into well-functioning, streamlined, tranquilised members of the modern society of efficient production and self-achievement, endeared him to left-wing intellectuals. He not only received the favourable notice of the 'structuralist' Marxist, Louis Althusser, but also served as an inspiration for the 1968 students who saw his writings as a new critical weapon against the ideology of advanced industrial capitalism.

III

Lacan traces the formation of the ideal ego back to the earliest period of child development which he calls the 'mirror phase'. Between the ages of six and eighteen months, the child experiences its body as 'fragmented', that is, in terms of biological insufficiency and lack of cohesion. To overcome this lack of unity, the child contrives to replace the incomplete self with an ideal unified self or *imago*. This *imago* is, therefore, an imaginary projection in response to a real lack. It results from the child's passionate need to produce an imagined double of himself as 'he will have been' (when unity has eventually been achieved).

Let us examine Lacan's rather complex analysis of this 'mirror phase' in some detail. The small child, perceiving its body in a reflected image outside of itself, seeks to compensate for its sense of anatomical inadequacy by identifying with this image of integration and sufficiency. This formative process gives rise to what Lacan calls the 'specular ego'. The child imagines a future self-identity which it is *not*, which is *other* than what it is in the present. Or as Lacan remarks, the child constructs its *imago* 'like another'. Moreover, there is a further complication in that the desire realised in the form of the mirror image is not necessarily the child's desire only, but that of the mother – what the mother wishes him to be.

The child's passionate identification with this ideal stable ego is the basis of 'narcissism'. But the originality of Lacan's explanation of narcissim is to suggest that the initial project of self-sufficiency does not precede the relation to the other-than-self, but is in fact produced by it. The conscious ego, of course, denies this and clings to the illusion of the primacy of the self over the other, resisting aggressively any attempt to disturb this illusion. This obsessional narcissistic fixation on the idealised *imago* is by no means confined to childhood. It continues into adult life and produces what Lacan calls the unconscious world of the 'imaginary'. This 'imaginary' is the ultimate source of the illusions and deceits of the ego. Humanistic psychology fails to recognise this, however, and often serves to reinforce the narcissistic impulse by promoting psychic ideals of 'identity', 'integrity', 'harmony', 'selfhood' and so on. As such, it confirms rather than confronts the modern cult of 'humanistic man'.

Lacan maintains that this humanistic tendency in psychology is at odds with the original insight of Freud. The true task of psychoanalysis, he submits, is to dismantle the reified *imago* of the ego, to free the subject from the fixation with itself in order that it may acknowledge its more fundamental relation to the other. This relation with the other is what Lacan calls 'language'; it is 'symbolic' rather than 'imaginary'. Psychoanalysis, in other words, must aim to release the patient from the 'imaginary' order of self-obsession into the 'symbolic' order of language as an open dialectic between the subject and the other. For it is only in the symbolic order that the subject can recover the language of desire as 'desire of the other'.

The primary object of psychoanalysis is, therefore, to remind us that the *imago* of self-identity presupposes a dialectic of self-differentiation. The self is in truth always different from itself in so far as it it is beholden to the other. The conscious ego which declares '*c'est moi*' is in reality split and divided, for it is constructed out of an unconscious relation to the other which it cleverly conceals from itself. *The I is other*, declares Lacan (echoing Rimbaud's phrase '*ce je est un autre*').

This experience of difference, division, alienation and death, which the ego suppresses from consciousness, is intimately related to our first separation from the mother – both during the weaning process and during the initial Oedipal conflict when the father enters the relationship between child and mother and forbids the possibility of fusion. Ross Skelton describes Lacan's reading of this Oedipal drama of separation and death as follows:

> What the mother desires is the phallus, so if the boy desires her, he desires to be the object of her desire which is the phallus. His desire is to *be* the phallus where the phallus symbolizes fusion with the mother. What he will come to realize eventually, is that the mother does not have a phallus and that he is not it! What the father demands is that this fusion be dissolved and for the child this separation from the mother enforced by the father means Death, it evokes the earlier death experienced in weaning. ('Lacan and the rational ego', 1985)

This drama of separation and death is relived in the psychoanalytic relation between analyst and analysand. "The art of the analyst", says Lacan, "must be to suspend the subject's certainties until their last mirages have been consumed" ('Function and field of speech and language' in *Ecrits*). Even if it communicates nothing, the discourse between analyst and analysed represents the existence of communication, of a relation to the other. This discourse allows the *imaginary ego* to dssolve so that a *symbolising subject* may emerge, a subject who realises that the truth of desire resides in the intersubjective space between self and other. Thus we may recognise that "man's desire finds its meaning in the desire of the other . . . because the first object of desire is to be recognized by the other" (*ibid.*). In other words, it is only by dispelling our imaginary 'objectifications' of self-certainty that we re-enter the language of ongoing dialectic whose end is the other.

Far from reinforcing the sense of a unified 'self', as humanist psychology attempts, Lacanian analysis seeks to undermine it by encouraging utterances of unconscious desire which contain several contradictory or 'split' meanings. It allows the logic of the rebus to speak. It reveals that behind the apparent unity of meaning lies a diversity of meanings.

But it is not only our normal patterns of speaking and thinking that Lacanian analysis disturbs; it is also our normal sense of 'clock time'. Whereas orthodox analysts used a set time period, say one hour, for sessions with patients, Lacan introduced the controversial practice of 'flexible time', which could be anything as short as five minutes. The intention behind this was to frustrate the conscious preparations of the ego, to throw it off balance and upset its defences, thus allowing the unconscious to speak. As a 'practitioner of the symbolic function', the analyst cannot be bound by the predictable punctuation of the clock. For the clock seeks to organise the flow of time just as the *imago* seeks to organise the flow of the unconscious. Lacan insists that the experience of the unconscious operates in terms of a 'synchronic' time (where past, present and future can interrelate and overlap in all kinds of unpredictable ways) rather than in the 'diachronic' linear time of sequential punctuation. The end of analysis, or of any particular session of analysis, is not a goal to be consciously anticipated or predicted. Were this not so, the unconscious might never catch the conscious ego off guard and so never come to express itself.

For similar reasons, Lacan discouraged the notion that the patient should identify with the analyst. He rejected the orthodox practice of establishing the analyst as some sort of superior knower or guru who would somehow bring the disciple to perfect self-knowledge. On the contrary, the relationship between analyst and analysand should itself be dialectically flexible and reversible, so that the rehearsed patterns of pedagogy and power-play be avoided. The analyst should not present himself as a model of emulation as in ego psychology. For to do so would be to support the illusion that the analyst represents the idealised *imago* which each ego seeks to possess. It would be to falsely suppose that "the truth is already given in the (analyst) and that he knows it in advance" (*Ibid*).

To off-set such suppositions, Lacan suggests that the analyst preserve a certain sense of distance, absence or even silence, so that the patient may be disoriented, 'de-centred', and thus come to an awareness of itself as a 'split-I' (*Ich-Spaltung*). This decentring of the self allows the self to return to the suppressed language of the unconscious. It permits the subject to rediscover that absence at the heart of itself, that *lack* which is the desire of the other. This is what Lacan means when he declares that "the unconscious is the discourse of the other". It is a discourse which *dispossesses* us of our imaginary sense of self-completeness.

IV

We are now perhaps in a better position to assess the 'structuralist' implications of Lacan's claim that the 'unconscious is structured like language'. What he is in fact suggesting here is that human desires and fantasies operate in and through linguistic structures. But these structures are not themselves visible at the conscious level of the individual speaker's utterance (*parole*). They function as an invisible and unconscious *langue* which is 'transindividual' and which reveals itself less in *what* the speaker explicitly says than in the *way* he implicitly says or manages not to say something else. This is why Lacan argues that the analyst should never take what the speaker says at its face value but should attend instead to the various lapses of tongue, silences, equivocations, omissions, misremem-berings and so on. It is in the *faults* of communication rather than in its *fitness* that our unconscious is revealed, for this unconscious, as Lacan notes, "is that part of the concrete discourse, in so far as it is transindivid-ual, that is *not* at the disposal of the subject in reestablishing the continuity of his conscious discourse" ('Function and field of speech and language'). Or to put it another way, if the unconscious is the 'censored chapter' of language, our conscious discourse is the abridged or officially approved version. Consequently, "in order to free the subject's speech, we reintro-duce him into the language of desire, that is to say, into the *primary language*, in which, beyond what he tells of himself, he is already talking to us unknown to himself . . . in the symbols of the symptom" (*ibid.*).

In typical structuralist fashion, Lacan thus shifts the emphasis from the *content* to the *structure* of speech. By attending exclusively to the 'messages' conveyed by words, traditional analysts tended to ignore the 'foundations of words' which are the very precondition of such messages being expressed in the first place; and which reveal, furthermore, that these messages often serve as disguises of what the unconscious really desires. Lacan argues that we should treat fantasies and dreams as *signifiers* that cannot be reduced to some fixed or identifiable *signified*. The real meaning of each signifier must be sought in its relation to other signifiers within the sychronic system of our unconscious language. The dream, as Lacan remarks using Saussurian terms, has "the structure of a form of writing, which . . . reproduces the simultaneously phonetic and symbolic use of signifying elements" (*ibid.*). Each dream must be seen therefore as a signifying chain which is so structured that it is possible to use words to signify something quite other than what we actually appear to be saying in our conscious speech (e.g. when the individual gives an account or explanation of his dream).

Lacan maintains accordingly that it is at the level of a 'free association' between one signifier and another, whose random and irregular character disrupts the linear continuity of our conscious narrative (the 'language of culture'), that we are most likely to detect the hidden structures of uncon-scious language (the 'language of desire'). For Lacan the symbolic order of *langue*, which is intersubjective, precedes the order of *parole*, which is subjective. It is not the individual consciousness which speaks language but unconscious language which speaks through individual consciousness. As this structuralist premiss makes plain, the presumption that the ego could ever have full mastery over the unconscious is an illusion.

Invoking structural linguistics in rather a free manner, Lacan proceeds to equate Freud's notions of 'defence mechanism' with rhetorical devices (e.g. catachresis, litotes, periphrasis, elipsis and so on). He also employs the literary terms of 'metonymy' and 'metaphor' to define the workings of our unconscious language. "The symptom *is* a metaphor", he writes, "as desire *is* a metonymy, however funny people may find the idea" ('Agency of the letter in the unconscious' in *Ecrits*).

As these two terms are central to Lacan's overall analysis of the language of the unconscious, it may be useful to briefly explain the technical details of their functioning.

Metonymy, he maintains, refers to the 'syntagmatic' rapport between one unconscious signifier and another. It brings different signifiers together in a relation of horizontal *contiguity*. Thus, just as the sail is a metonymic sign for the ship (in that it is close to it, beside it, without actually resembling it in any way), so too desire establishes a metonymic relation between one signifier and another which does not depend on likeness or any immediate semantic correspondence. As Proust realised, for example, desire can become unconsciously associated with a particular tune, odour, taste or phrase to which it was contiguously related in space or time. Hence the odour of Cattley orchids which Odette wore serve as a metonymic signifier of Odette. The odour in no way resembles Odette but is identified with her because of their frequently experienced proximity. Desire is metonymic to the extent that there is no 'natural' or 'fixed' relationship between it and any given object. In this respect, it differs sharply from *need* which Lacan equates with predictable biological appetites. Desire, unlike need, can move freely from one signifier to another; its range of possible signifiers is almost infinite. Desire becomes problematic however whenever it becomes 'fixated' upon one single signifier which serves as 'fetish' or delusory 'imago'. It is the task of analysis to reactivate desire as a dynamism of endless displacement.

Metaphor, by contrast, operates according to the 'paradigmatic' laws of association by similarity. It functions in terms of a vertical relation between signifiers whereby one signifier is selected from a whole range or 'storehouse' of similar signifiers. So that if I use the term 'time flies' I choose the signifier 'flies' from a series of related signifiers e.g. passes, runs, crawls and so on, which could have functioned as the verb in the sentence. It is in terms of such a metaphorical relationship of association by similarity, Lacan suggests, that symptoms refer to the hidden traumas of the unconscious.

To sum up: A sign is metonymic when it relates syntagmatically to other signs present in the linear sequence of a sentence. It is metaphoric when it relates paradigmatically to other signs *not* present in the sentence, but available within the rest of language and capable of serving a similar function (in that particular place in the sentence *qua* noun or verb etc.)

While the unconscious operation of 'condensation' works by a metaphorical mode of signification, 'displacement' works by a metonymic one. In this manner, Lacan proposes to classify all of the symptoms and desires of the unconscious according to a linguistic set of relations. Malcolm Bowie offers the following summary of Lacan's classification:

> The psychical mechanism by which neurotic symptoms are produced involves the pairing of two signifiers – unconscious sexual trauma and changes within, or actions by, the body – and is thus metaphorical; whereas unconscious desire, indestructible and insatiable as it is, involves a constant displacement of energy from object to object and is thus metonymic. An arrest of the metonymic function produces not a symptom but a fetish ('Jacques Lacan' in *Structuralism and Since*, 1979).

By employing a system of linguistic units to organise the mass of clinical data which psychoanalytic practice throws up, Lacan provided a structural economy for the unconscious while at the same time responding to Freud's early intuition concerning the symbolic ordering of dream material in terms of an 'equivalence of contraries'. In this manner, Lacan was able to use the methods of structuralist linguistics to articulate Freud's psychoanalytic discoveries in much the same way as Lévi-Strauss did with Frazer's anthropological discoveries. And, furthermore, Lacan's analysis of the structural laws of the unconscious was able to dispel the prejudicial assumption of traditional psychology that the 'Id' constitutes a den of unruly animal drives without rhyme or reason. His analysis demonstrated that the order of unconscious desire unfolds according to a language which is even more sophisticated and structured than the discourse of our conscious intelligence.

V

One of the most interesting consequences of Lacan's analogy between the language of unconscious desire and the language of poetics or literary rhetoric, was the call for a rediscovery of the inventive power of *play*. Lacan championed a language of free association which exults in double and multiple meanings, in puns and paradoxes which defy the repressive practices of our normal speech (which tries to tie each signifier down to a single signified). A poetics of witticism (*jeu d'esprit*) and jokery (*calembour*), it is argued, is the most effective means of giving voice to the hidden desires of the unconscious. Thus Lacan endorses the "challenge of non-sense, where humour, in the malicious grace of the mind free from care symbolises a truth that has not said its last word" ('Function and field of speech and language' in *Écrits*). The following list of typically Lacanian puns illustrates his approach: *âmour* (alluding both to love, *amour*, and soul, *âme*); *Ça* (alluding both to the French translation of the Freudian 'Id' and to the 'S' as linguistic shorthand for the signifier); *poubellication* (suggesting that the serious practice of 'publication' is like placing rubbish in a dustbin, *poubelle*); *j'ouis* (meaning both to enjoy, *jouir*, and to hear, *ouier*); or his frequent play on the curious homophony of *lettre*, *l'être* and *l'autre*. By engaging in such word play Lacan is not merely intending to amuse his readers or listeners (most of Lacan's seminars were delivered as spoken lectures), but also to demonstrate how one signifier can displace or substitute for another in an open-ended chain of signifiers which bespeaks the language of the unconscious. In this way, Lacan managed to communicate his structuralist convictions (I) that "dream-work follows the laws of the signifier", and (II) that the signifiers of dreams are 'overdetermined' (in the sense that one signifier is related to a plurality of different meanings). The Lacanian invitation to play with words, to communicate ex-centrically, is an invitation to respond to the structural play of unconscious desire.

The radicality of Lacan's gesture is neatly expressed in his formula

$$\frac{\text{signifier } S}{\text{signified } s}$$

By capitalising the Signifier and by placing it on the upper side of the bar, Lacan is graphically displaying the priority of the Signifier over the signified. And by affirming that they are separated by a radical cleavage or barrier, he is liberating the Signifier from any fixed, one-to-one reference to the signified. He thereby suggests how the unconscious releases words from their normal chore of representing empirical facts and delights in an endless play of 'sliding' or 'floating' signifiers. This implies, further, that there is no such thing as a pre-linguistic reality which the signifier could be said to represent. The Real is always already structured by the Imaginary and the Symbolic. There can be no human experience that does not bear the traces of a signifying play. We do not *first* exist and *then* enter into language. We exist only in and through language. "It was certainly the Word that was in the beginning", comments Lacan, "and we live in its creation, but it is the action of our spirit that continues this creation by constantly renewing it . . . It is the world of words that creates the world of things . . . Man speaks them, but it is because the symbol has made him man" (*ibid.*).

Because the unconscious order of the signifier is autonomous it is forever lacking its ultimate signified; it expresses itself as an unrequited desire for its *other*. Lacan refers to it accordingly as an errant knave whose errancy is inexhaustible, an endless chain of signifiers where each meaning perpetually displaces or replaces another. He also identifies this signifying process in the Freudian terms of a desire for the symbolic phallus of full presence, plenitude and power. But the phallus is precisely that which is always lacking, absent, other. It is often associated with 'the Name of the Father' whose prohibition of fusion with the mother first sets the signifying chain of desire in motion and forbids it from coming to an end in imaginary identifications – the 'idols' of the ego. The paternal other, as Lacan points out, is the symbolic impossibility of fulfilment. For the phallus is the symbol of the signified that forever slips beneath the signifiers of desire, thus reminding us that we are permanently estranged, at odds with ourselves, haunted by an absence that we can never make present, by an ideal that we can never possess.

This is why for Lacan the true function of psychoanalysis is to encourage the subject to embrace the interminable play of its own unconscious desire rather than to try to bring it to an impossible full stop. We must learn to live with the reality of the unconscious as a dialectic of unpredictable dispersal; we must consent to become, as it were, the privileged playthings of its language. The ultimate purpose of the analyst is, in short, to permit the analysand to break free from the illusory order of the imaginary and to enter, with carefree gaiety and undeceiving abandon, into the open-ended order of the symbolic.

Lacan provides us with a suggestive illustration of how the unconscious signifier functions in his reading of Poe's story 'The purloined letter'. Poe tells of how a compromising secret letter addressed to a Queen is stolen by a Court Minister, unbeknown to the King, but in front of the Queen who is helpless to intervene for fear of alerting the King's attention. The letter is searched for in vain by the police and eventually recovered by a clever detective who, unbeknown to the police, finds it in the most obvious place of all: in full view on the Minister's desk – the one place the police had never thought of looking. The letter, however, is never actually read; so the reader, and indeed the participants in the story, while seeking the floating letter – the unconscious signifier of desire – through an endless chain of signifiers, never succeed in disclosing the signified.

Lacan's point seems to be that it is the floating letter itself which determines the roles and reactions of the various characters in the plot. It is not they, as conscious agents, who have mastery over the language of desire, but this language of desire which governs their sense of identity and purpose – the hidden logic of their intersubjective relations. The fable shows that it is the unconscious letter and its unpredictable diversions which regulates their stage entries and exits in the play of consciousness. "Falling in possession of the letter – admirable ambiguity of language – its meaning possesses them." We are thus reminded of the fact that we are not the authors of meaning. The unconscious usually means something other than what we take it to mean. And whenever the speech of the individual ego presumes to be self-possessed, in control, the unconscious language of desire – which it is the aim of Lacanian analysis and writing to evoke – unleashes a new play of contradictory meanings which shatter this presumption. "The subject is spoken rather than speaking", insists Lacan.

VI: CONCLUSION

There is no doubt that Lacan's structuralist reading of the unconscious represents a radicalisation of Freud. Where the orthodox Freudians often spoke of the language of dream and symbol in terms of 'psychic distortions' which analysis would unravel and make plain, Lacan views such unconscious deviations of meaning as playful gestures of desire which should be celebrated precisely as they are. This is what he means by his unorthodox interpretation of the Freudian maxim: 'where the 'Id' is that is the place to which the 'Ego' must come'. For Lacan metaphor and metonymy are *not* considered as secondary symbolisations which 'represent' some pre-symbolic reality. The unconscious reality *is* rhetorical through and through. It is a system of interrelating signifiers with no fixed reference or signified outside of itself. Lacan's own writings testify to this fact by virtue of their very inconclusiveness. They enjoin the reader to embrace the rhetorical inventiveness of language as a free play of association and allusion. They are intentionally fragmented and incomplete. As Vincent Leitch observes: "Unmistakeably, Lacan plays, like some latter-day gingerbread man, the elusive visionary, refusing with much refinement and rarity to be caught, systematised, stopped, signified. Jacques Lacan is emperor of the exquisite and alluring ellipsis" (*Deconstructive Criticism*, 1983). To prevent his work ever becoming a monument of official learning, a new orthodoxy in its own right, Lacan constantly performed a disappearing act. He played the ambiguous role of prodigal son and 'severe father', the joker in the pack who can never be assigned a predictable place, refusing to respond to our conscious need for a fixed identity of meaning. As he appropriately remarked when dissolving his own school, *l'école freudienne* (first founded in 1964): "*Je pére-sévère*". But whether Lacan's elliptical writings fill us with admiration or indignation, we cannot fail to concede that his conflation of structuralist and psychoanalytic methods represents a provocative contribution to modern Continental thought.

Michel Foucault

Michel Foucault was born in Poitiers, France in 1926 and taught for many years as Professor of the History and Systems of Thought at the Collège de France in Paris. Although his books were by no means simple, conceptually or terminologically, Foucault has become an immensely popular thinker. He brought complex intellectual debates into the public arena. One could say that what Sartre and Camus were to existentialism, the young Foucault was to structuralism. He belonged to that French tradition of outspoken philosophers who passionately believed in the 'committed' nature of thinking. Foucault was always *more* than a scholarly academic – though he was that too. A brilliant media debater and a relentless champion of human rights, whether it concerned the rights of oppressed women, prisoners, homosexuals or the victims of international power politics (e.g. the Vietnamese 'boat people'), Foucault was forever at the forefront of public controversy up to his death in 1984.

I

Foucault's bestselling book, *Les Mots et les Choses* (1966, translated into English as *The Order of Things*, 1973), did more perhaps than any other work – with the possible exception of Lévi-Strauss's *Tristes Tropiques* – to introduce structuralism to the public. Foucault's use of 'structuralist' methods was never what might be described as purist. On several occasions indeed he expressed overt disapproval of the label (in the manner of Althusser, one of his most influential mentors). It is certain that Foucault's contributions to the structuralist debate were more wide-ranging and electric than those of his predecessors. For while the latter had tended to confine their 'structuralist' analysis to one specific discipline of the human sciences – e.g. Saussure to linguistics, Lévi-Strauss to anthropology, Lacan to psychoanalysis and so on – Foucault energetically embraced a 'multidisciplinary' approach. His structural investigations ranged from psychopathology (*Madness and Civilisation: A History of Insanity in the Age of Reason*, 1961) and medicine (*The Birth of the Clinic: An Archaeology of Medical Perception*, 1963), to criminology (*Discipline and Punish: The Birth of the Prison*, 1976) and a final three volume *History of*

Sexuality (only two of which were completed by the time of his death).

One would be entirely incorrect, however, to interpret the diversity of Foucault's works as a symptom of divided intellectual allegiance or of overall lack of purpose. There is a basic, if at times oblique, continuity running through Foucault's researches. It manifests itself particularly in the author's concern to establish an epistemological critique of the strategic practices or structures of knowledge (what in the early works he called *epistemes*) on the basis of a new understanding of the dominant discourses of Western culture. As it applies to his first writings, this approach has been frequently described as a 'structuralist epistemology'. Foucault himself, it is true, preferred the term 'archaeology'. He felt that such a term would be free from traditional metaphysical connotations while at the same time suggesting the necessity of a scientific exploration of the hidden structures of knowledge which ultimately determine the ways in which we experience and perceive our role in society.

In *The Order of Things*, subtitled *An Archaeology of the Human Sciences*, Foucault provides a compelling critique of the post-Renaissance history of 'discourse' as it moves or 'mutates' through a series of epistemic jumps. He demonstrates how one period's 'code of knowledge' (*episteme*) replaces another not in terms of a continuous progression but in terms of discontinuous ruptures. Rejecting the Enlightenment notion of linear progress, epitomised by the philosophy of humanist rationalism, Foucault focuses his critical lens on those pre-rational structures of the 'Classical period' of modern Western civilisation which he defines as the 'positive unconscious' of our cultural knowledge. In this seminal work he appears to endorse the structuralist premiss that traditional concepts like 'meaning', 'intention', 'will', 'reason' or indeed, the 'individualized subject' are but superficial items in the play of underlying systems of signification. Developing this vocabulary of the structuralists, Foucault affirms that the overall system of discourse in any given period must be properly understood as a structured ensemble of correlations which functions independently of the individual counters which it keeps in play. He defines the structural ensemble of the Classical period as a concealed order which predetermines the apparent orders of rational consciousness operating in a variety of new scientific discourses, linguistic (language), biological (life), and economic (labour). The task of his archaeological analysis is to 'decode' these epochal forms of knowledge so as to discover the subjacent structural laws which govern them. In the following passage from his 'Foreword' to the English edition of *The Order of Things*, he makes plain his purpose:

What I would like to do . . . is to reveal a *positive unconscious* of knowledge: a level that eludes the consciousness of the scientist and yet is part of scientific discourse, instead of disputing its validity and seeking to diminish its scientific nature. What was common to the natural history, the economics and the grammar of the Classical period was certainly not present to the consciousness of the scientist . . . but unknown to themselves, the naturalists, economists, and grammarians employed the same rules to define the objects proper to their own study, to form their concepts, to build their theories. It is these rules of formation, which were never formulated in their own right, but are to be found only in widely differing theories, concepts, and objects of study, that I have tried to reveal, by isolating, as their specific locus, a level that I have called, somewhat arbitrarily perhaps, archaeological. Taking as an example the period covered in this book, I have tried to determine the basis or archaeological system common to a whole series of scientific 'representations' or 'products' dispersed throughout the natural history, economics, and philosophy of the Classical period. (*The Order of Things*)

Foucault is fully aware that this 'comparative' or cross-disciplinary method produces results strikingly at variance with those found in single-discipline studies. He thus brushes the traditional scientific approach against the grain. He redraws the frontiers, exposing hitherto unremarked overlaps and bringing together things usually far apart. So that instead, for example, of relating "biological taxonomies to other knowledge of the living being (the theory of germination, or the physiology of animal movement, or the statistics of plants)", Foucault chooses to compare them "with what might have been said at the same time about linguistic signs, the formation of general ideas, the language of action, the hierarchy of needs, and the exchange of goods" (*ibid.*)

Perhaps the most startling feature of Foucault's analysis was the claim that the revered Western notion of 'man' is itself a conditioned 'product' of a specific 'epistemic epoch' (i.e. the modern) which is now beginning to disappear. Far from being the creator of the scientific codes of discourse, as humanism held, 'man' is now revealed as no more than a category created by these codes. We do not produce science, it produces us. And if it is true that science once served to objectively legitimate the construct of the human subject as an autonomous substance or individual consciousness, it is now in the process of dismantling this construct. And so Foucault announces that the famous era of the *death of God*, ushered in by Nietzsche and the existentialists, is now being superceded by a new era whose signal achievement is the *death of Man*.

This epochal 'death of man' dramatically alters our whole understanding of the human sciences. Foucault endeavours to show how what we have been accustomed to consider as individual or 'original' expressions of the human subject are no more than surface 'effects' of an anonymous system of Language or Thought. Works of art, for instance, are not created by individual persons but by the complex structure of interacting cultural codes which prevail in the 'epistemic' epoch during which these works emerged. One cultural epoch differs from another not by virtue of the acts of subjective genius or creative imagination (as romanticism maintained) but by virtue of an epistemological rupture in the system of relations which governs them. Thus while the 'contents' of the empirical relations between human subjects may be said to differ or develop 'diachronically' within any given epoch, the 'formal' system which predetermines these relations remains the *same* and informs each epoch with an internally 'synchronic' and permanent structure. And in so far as there are differences between one synchronic epoch and another, Foucault chooses to describe them in terms of 'leaps', 'ruptures' or 'mutations' (ie. structural *discontinuity*) rather than as a continuous process of causal development.

The primary aim of Foucault's archaeology is to uncover the unconscious laws of language and thought which precondition the cultural transformations within knowledge. Whereas most human sciences concern themselves with particular isolated institutions or ideologies which arise within their period of inquiry (e.g. utilitarianism in the eighteenth century), Foucault's science of the human sciences takes a step back from such immediate identifications and uncovers those infra-structures which made such institutions or ideologies possible in the first place. These latent structures are what Foucault calls *epistemes*. An *episteme* represents a general field of knowledge which functions as the 'historical *a priori*' of the given epoch. It serves as a sort of 'intellectual underground' which all of the scientific minds of that epoch unconsciously tap or presuppose. But one would be wrong to think of the *episteme* of an historical period as merely the sum of its knowledge or the general style of its research. It may be more properly understood as the total configuration of structural relations which regulates the manner in which a multiplicity of scientific discourses emerge, predominate and interact in any period. It is, in short, what ultimately determines what can be said and what cannot be said. Foucault defines the *episteme* accordingly as a hidden 'archive' which comprises 'a general system of the formation and transformation of statements'.

Foucault argues that as we enter the new structural epoch of contemporary history, we come to realise that it is not us, *qua* individual subjects, who invent the *episteme* of our time. The *episteme* pre-exists the human subject and conditions the specific form of its every thought and action. In particular, it decides the fundamental relation which exists between things (*les choses*) and our own understanding – that is, our conceptual representations

– of these things in and through language (*les mots*). This relation between 'things' and 'words' differs from one epoch to the next depending on the *episteme* which informs this relation.

II

Foucault provides the reader with specific examples to illustrate his rather abstract arguments. (Though even here, it must be admitted, Foucault's analysis is largely methodological for his stated aim remains a critical *science of science*, that is, an exploration of the theoretical conditions of possibility of scientific knowledge.) In *The Order of Things*, Foucault excavates, as it were, the principal 'epistemic' sites of Western systems of knowledge from the Renaissance to the present day. The materials he unearths in this archaeological fieldwork are not those 'facts' with which the traditional historian would be concerned (e.g. famous personalities, decisive empirical events or discoveries and so on). What Foucault is interested in discovering are those theoretical archives which tell us how the 'facts' were interpreted in a specific epoch. Or to put it in another way, he is less preoccupied with the 'things' of a particular cultural period than with the 'words' which were used to signify these things, that is, the ways in which these things were perceived, expressed and thereby *known*.

Foucault begins with the Renaissance. By means of a thorough analysis of representative documents of the period, he is able to show that the *episteme* which prevailed here determined that *things were seen as words*. The world was deemed to be a Divine Script authored by God Himself for man to read. Things were thought to 'resemble' each other as signs of the Creator's revelatory text. Man viewed Nature accordingly as a network of spiritual symbols and mystical correspondence with an appointed place for everything and with everything in its appointed place. Dante's *Divine Comedy* offers an early illustration of this kind of universe where words were symbolically ordered amongst themselves in the same manner as things and were read as perfect mirrorings of things. The *episteme* of the Renaissance could thus be summed up as a system of *resemblance*. Here words resembled things and things resembled words.

The next major 'epistemic' period which Foucault analyses is the 'Classical Age' of the seventeenth and eighteenth centuries. Here the structural relation between words and things shifts from an *episteme* of 'resemblance' to an *episteme* of 'representation'. A gap or 'difference' now emerges between words and things. Words come to function as representational ideas whose purpose it is to classify, measure and compute the things of the world. One can no longer assume that words are naturally *like* things; they have to be made like things and things have to be made like words. This is the Classical framework which gave rise to Descartes' idealism in France and Hume's empiricism in Britain. The philosopher or scientist thus begins with a separation of words and things, the former being consigned to the human subject and the latter to the world of objects. In other words, objective things are no longer presumed to be identical with the language or thought of man. It is the business of the human enquirer to try to get to know these things by means of his own subjective representations (whether these are 'innate' as in Descartes or empirically acquired through the subject's sensory experience as in Hume). All this means, of course, that man is no longer able to read the world directly as if things were quasi-mystical symbols orchestrated and guaranteed by an Omnipotent Deity omnipresent in all of his works. God becomes an absent God, a *Deus Absconditus*. And the world in turn becomes an autonomous material universe which man tries to master by means of his conceptual acts of representation. The world of objects (the order of things) only acquires meaning consequently in so far as it is presented by the subject (the order of words or word-ideas). In this manner, the Renaissance model of language as a system of revelatory symbols (intrinsically related to things) is replaced by the Classical model of language as a system of representational signs. Foucault concludes accordingly that the historical *a priori* which epitomises the *episteme* of the Classical Age is manifested in a common attempt by both the human and natural sciences to deploy new forms of classification to make sense of the things of the world as *represented* in the thoughts of the human subject.

Foucault then goes on to analyse how this Classical Age of 'representation' is replaced by the Modern Age of 'self-reference'. This shift is accompanied by another 'epistemic break' which establishes a total severance, rather than a merely partial separation, between words and things. Words and things are no longer simply different; they are now bereft of any correlation whatsoever, be it one of resemblance or representation. In the Modern Age of the nineteenth century, words function neither as symbols which reveal things directly to us, nor as signs which represent things indirectly to us, but simply as a self-referential discourse of a transcendental human subject with itself. Otherwise put, words now reflect the human subject to himself. Foucault defines this modern *episteme* as 'anthropologism': the anthropological formation of man as a self-sufficient autonomous subject requiring no external support for his knowledge – either in God or in nature. (Perhaps the most influential philosophical exponent of this *episteme* is Kant, whose *Critique of Pure Reason* sought to establish the 'transcendental ego' as privileged subject of all scientific knowledge). What occurs here is that man becomes both the subject and the object of his own knowledge. One of the consequences of this position is that the exact or natural sciences are complemented by the transcendental sciences of psychology, sociology and the anthropological study of myth and the history of art – sciences which take the human subject *per se* as their primary object of investigation. In the Modern Age the proper study of man becomes man himself.

Foucault argues, however, that the story of knowledge does not stop here. The modern humanist preoccupation with the knowledge of man is gradually giving way, he maintains, to a new 'post-modern' and basically anti-humanist conviction that the human subject is itself a limited consciousness subject to laws which are not of his own choice or making. At this point we touch once again on the great debate between modern existentialism – with its origins in nineteenth-century German idealism – and post-modern structuralism. Foucault's argument is that man's increasing knowledge of himself does not result in a confirmation of the humanist notion of a transcendentally free and creative subject, but in a dismantling of this notion. In the post-modern epoch we find man becoming aware of unconscious structural laws which ultimately predetermine what we had previously deemed to be the free activities of the human consciousness. Thus we have humanistic psychology being undermined by structural psychoanalysis (Lacan), sociology by structural ethnology (Lévi-Strauss), romantic criticism by semiological linguistics (Saussure): and perhaps most relevant for present considerations, we have existentialism being replaced by Foucault's own archaeology. *The Order of Things* may be read accordingly as a sort of meta-theory of structuralism itself.

Not surprisingly, Sartre was to prove one of Foucault's major adversaries in the whole debate which followed the publication of *The Order of Things*. While Sartre and others were declaring that existentialism was the most authentic philosophy of our age because it was a 'humanism' which affirmed the primacy of freedom and of man, Foucault replied that the very concept of man is an epistemological construct of a specific historical epoch. Foucault explained that his structural archaeology of knowledge deals not with man as an existential reality but with the epistemic field called 'man' which makes possible every kind of knowledge about this field – the human sciences.

In so far as structuralism reveals how the unconscious, both psychic and social, is structured as a system of language, it emerges as the post-modern science *par excellence*. Structuralism dispenses with the study of *Man* in favour of the study of *Language* itself. The post-modern age is therefore the age of structuralism.

Foucault is thus in a position to conclude that the ultimate *episteme* of the post-modern era of structuralism is characterised by the historical *a priori* of the 'demise of man'. As he puts it in *The Order of Things*: "The archaeology of our thought shows with ease that man is an invention of recent date. And perhaps also his approaching end". Words, as the discourse of the so-called 'transcendental subject' of man, are now seen to be no more than the external workings of the system of language. Otherwise stated, words refer neither to things, nor to representations of things, nor indeed to the self-representation of the human subject. They refer quite simply to words themselves. Perhaps the most epoch-making discovery of structuralism is that *language speaks itself*. This appearance of language coincides with the disappearance of man. In the contemporary *episteme* of the structural age, the individual discourse of the human subject (*parole*) is dissolved into the more anonymous codes of language itself (*langue*).

Several modern writers may be said to have anticipated this return of language to itself. Mallarmé, for example, proposed to enclose "all discourse within the fragile density of the word". Joyce and Beckett wrote works about the workings of language – an attitude aptly summed up by Beckett when he declared that Joyce's *Ulysses* was not *about* something but was that something itself. And there exists a host of other contemporary authors and artists who have explored the whole complex relationship between 'signs' and the unconscious world of language which resides beneath or beyond the individual human 'creator'. Foucault views such movements in the arts as well as in the sciences as prefigurations of the death of man – as cultural symptoms of how the humanistic rule of reason is being steadily eroded by the anti-humanistic rule of language. All of this, he contends, is working towards the provision of a science (archaeology) which is making it less and less possible to speak of the 'sciences of man' in the established sense of the term. "A 'human science' exists", writes Foucault, "not wherever man is in question, but wherever there is analysis – within the dimension proper to the unconscious – of norms, rules, and signifying totalities which unveil to consciousness the conditions of its forms and contents. To speak of 'sciences of man' in any other case is simply an abuse of language" (*The Order of Things*).

III

While Foucault's analysis in *The Order of Things* (1966) and *The Archaeology of Knowledge* (1969) focused on the general epistemic structures of historical periods, in other works he turned his attention to more concrete instances of how knowledge functions as a social power.

Foucault did not believe that knowledge was innocent or neutral. Behind the conventional veneer of the knower as a disinterested transcendental spectator, Foucault identified ways in which truth was often monopolised by certain repressive institutions. This resulted in attempts to circumscribe knowledge in such a manner that whatever surpassed its official limits was categorised as a form of 'deviancy'. Thus in *Madness and Civilisation*, for example, Foucault examines the historical presuppositions of the emergence of different categories of the 'insane'. In *The Birth of the Clinic* he applies a similar critique to the strategies concealed behind the clinical categorisations of the 'sick'. In *Discipline and Punish* he investigates the conceptual underpinnings of the institutional confinement of the 'criminal' in enclosed spaces subject to surveillance. And in his final work on the *History of Sexuality*, Foucault analyses the 'confessional' rationale behind the rise of the *scientia sexualis* in the West which produces classifications of (psychiatric and legal) sexual abnormality or 'perversion'. Foucault's respective studies of psychology, medicine, law and sexuality express his resolve to ascertain the covert epistemological codes by means of which society contrives to legitimate certain formal practices of knowledge by outlawing others. The history of these strategic divisions into 'official' and 'deviant' modes of experience, into 'normal' and 'abnormal' practices, is characterised by the later Foucault as a hidden history of *power*.

In this manner, Foucault's critical project combines (1) a methodological concern with the epistemic structures of knowledge with (2) a more concrete investigation of how these structures underpin the various institutionalisations of the knowledge of man (as confessional 'subject' or incarceral 'object') in the interests of domination. This approach enables Foucault to demonstrate how 'deviancy' and 'legitimacy' are relative concepts whose purpose it is to control the contradictions, differences or inconsistencies which proliferate in a society so as to cultivate the illusion of a manageable social totality. The various scientific attempts to standardise our modes of perception by constructing supposedly 'objective' definitions of the criminal, the sick, the insane or the perverse, ultimately signify a 'will-to-knowledge' whose purpose is the maintenance and extension of social control. Scientific disciplines, in short, serve the interests of *discipline*.

Foucault's attack on the oppressive origins and aims of 'reason' may be seen as a central feature of his critical *oeuvre*. It finds its initial outline in *Madness and Civilisation* published in 1961. As this is one of Foucault's most accessible works we shall rehearse its arguments in some detail.

Here Foucault scrutinises a wide variety of documents ranging from the late Middle Ages to the present day with a view to showing how the very concept of 'madness' arose at a certain stage of Western 'rationalist' civilisation. (Hence the subtitle of this work, *A History of Insanity in the Age of Reason*.) He reveals how the genesis of this concept coincided with the realisation by the social establishment that it could no longer rely on such traditional categories as the 'leper' or the 'demonically possessed' to satisfy the need for social outcasts – whose very 'otherness' justified the privileged consensus of the status quo. And so the category of 'madness' was invented largely in response to a specific social need to centralise and conserve power, that is, to exclude from the social fold those who did not conform to the established codes of 'normal behaviour'. In other words, the invention of the term 'madness' served ideological and institutional purposes. Society kept itself pure, gave itself a 'good conscience' as it were, by proclaiming the necessity to 'purge' itself of those undesirable elements of 'difference' which threatened its sense of legitimacy. The madman become the scapegoat in the age of reason. "The absolute privilege of folly", as Foucault ironically remarks, "was to rule over everything that is bad in man" (*Madness and Civilization*).

Even in his early work, Foucault was analysing western history in terms of shifts and ruptures between different prevailing codes of knowledge. In the pre-Renaissance period, still largely conditioned by religious values, the notion of madness played a somewhat ambiguous role as a sort of mediation between the opposed orders of the divine and the demonic, sense and non-sense, truth and falsehood. The role of the 'holy fool' is a good case in point. Towards the end of the Middle Ages, one confronts the curious phenomenon of the 'ship of fools' – a floating public spectacle moving from one European port to another. This phenomenon served society's need to manifest to itself the image of unreason-in-exile in order to consolidate its own sense of reason-in-settlement. By the seventeenth century the 'mad' were beginning to be treated as dangerous beings who needed to be enclosed in prison-like asylums such as the Hôpital Général de Paris, founded in 1656. It is significant for Foucault that many of these 'asylums' were in fact reconverted leprosariums. This institutionalisation of the 'insane' – the new lepers of unreason – in punitive conditions of confinement had the purpose, and indeed the effect, of criminalising those who transgressed the limits of what was considered to be a rationally acceptable code of behaviour. From the seventeenth century onwards, the confinement of the 'insane' was regulated by increasingly scientific rules of knowledge serving the interests of social domination. This practice of confinement, as Edith Kurzweil comments, "marked the beginning of a new age: madness still preserved its ambivalences and appearances but was also tied to the rise of scientism and to the loss of religious values. Now the mad were available for discussion and treatment, for legal regulation and scientific diagnosis, even though it was not until the nineteenth century that they were separated from thieves and criminals, squanderers and beggars, vagabonds and unemployed. Their separation from other deviants became a scientific question occupying doctors, lawyers, and police" ('Foucault: structures of knowledge' in *The Age of Structuralism*, 1980).

The irony here, of course, was that the more insanity became an acknowledged object of scientific knowledge, the more the original scientific distinction between reason and unreason was itself undermined. Thus with the rise of humanistic psychology in the nineteenth century, the thin line separating rational and non-rational behaviour was increasingly blurred, eventually leading to the psychoanalytic discovery in our own century of the 'unconscious' as a suppressed language of desire and transgression. It is true that Freud's theory of the unconscious libido originally served to codify deviant energies into a science of sexuality (*scientia sexualis*) whose secular forms of confessional 'ritualisation' (i.e. the 'talking cure') established a new model of social 'adaptation' and behavioural regulation. But at the same time the discoveries of psychoanalysis threatened to destabilise its own authority as a rational discipline of the positive sciences.

The culmination of the modern era of science witnesses therefore a subtle erosion of the conventional division between the categories of rationality and irrationality. And this is perhaps most manifest at the level of *language*. For while it was language – as a system of codes and significations – which originally provided the means of scientifically classifying our discourses about the insane (what Foucault calls 'discursive regularities'/ *enoncés*), it is also language which is finally shown to possess the *same* unconscious structure as so-called 'madness'. The dialectic of the science of madness parallels that of the science of language. With the rise of modern linguistics and psychoanalysis, notes Foucault, science becomes a structural archaeology of its own epistemological foundations, and thus heralds its own demise as an authoritative order of knowledge. In Foucault's own studies, those medical, psychiatric and legal institutions which had previously turned certain categories of people into 'cases', themselves become 'cases' to be deciphered and exposed.

Foucault also shows how the bourgeois code of 'puritanism' both fashions and suppresses its adversary 'deviancy'. For example, at an economic level, the puritan ethic sets a lucrative price on prohibited pleasure and thereby profits from the repression of sexuality; while at the psychological level, bourgeois puritanism celebrates the cultural spectacle of the bizzare, infantile, eccentric or marginal at the same time as its disciplinarian moralism punitively condemns the social manifestations of these same qualities as 'deviant'. In short, the codes of our modern Western civilisation frequently work in a duplicitous or self-contradictory way, condemning those very 'outsiders' they themselves have created. The deviant of unreason is someone whom the puritan of reason loves to hate yet never ceases to cultivate.

By exposing the strategic complicities between science and power, Foucault subverts the established distinctions between sane and insane, normal and abnormal, conscious and unconscious, healthy and sick etc. He discloses the 'unthought' collusion which exists between these conventional oppositions of 'thought', and thus challenges the hallowed codes of bourgeois civilisation. Foucault goes so far as to suggest that the fundamental concepts of our revered Western humanism are not only unfounded but often fundamentally *inhuman*. At times, indeed, he recommends that we acknowledge and playfully affirm the 'madness' that is in us, rather than banishing it to a 'ship of fools', an asylum or a psychiatrist's couch. Foucault begins *Madness and Civilization* by approvingly citing Dostoyevsky's view that "it is not by confining one's neighbour that one is convinced of one's own sanity". He concludes it by celebrating the works of Nietzsche, Van Gogh, and other artistic madmen, other visionary 'fools', as harbingers of a new apocalyptic age of insanity:

> Henceforth, and through the mediation of madness, it is the world that becomes culpable (for the first time in the Western world) in relation to the work of art, obliged to order itself by its language, compelled by it to a task of recognition, of reparation, to the task of restoring reason *from* that unreason and *to* that unreason. The madness in which the work of art is engulfed is the space of our enterprise, it is the endless path to fulfilment, it is our mixed vocation of apostle and exegete . . . madness is contemporary with the work of art since it inaugurates the time of its truth. The moment when, together, the work of art and madness are born and fulfilled is the beginning of the time when the world finds itself arraigned by that work of art and responsible before it for what it is. Ruse and new triumph of madness: the world that thought to measure and justify madness through psychology must justify itself before madness . . . (*ibid.*)

IV

In conclusion, we shall make some brief remarks on Foucault's innovative

interpretation of history. By identifying 'epistemic breaks' which demarcate historical epochs in terms of self-contained systems of dominant
knowledge, Foucault succeeded in combining the synchronic model of
structuralism with the diachronic model of history. Unlike certain orthodox
structuralists Foucault does not eliminate history. But he does reject
conventional notions of historical time as a single, homogenous continuity.
"The traditional devices for constructing a comprehensive view of
history", he submits, "and for retracing the past as a patient and continuous
development must be systematically dismantled ... History becomes
'effective' to the degree that it introduces discontinuity into our very being"
(*Language, Counter-Memory, Practice*, 1977). The Enlightenment idea of a
linear Progress of Reason is thus debunked in favour of the view that
history is made of a plurality of 'fields of discourse' with no direct causal
link between them. Foucault dispels the notion of history as an evolving
continuum. Employing a sort of 'free association' or 'cross-linking' between the concepts of diverse scientific disciplines such as economics,
medicine, sociology, grammar and biology, Foucault points out how the
historical changes in man's social perceptions reflect 'epistemic ruptures'
at the unconscious level of language.

But while Foucault appears to subscribe to the structuralist premiss that
nothing escapes the rule of language, his later writings give this premiss a
somewhat 'post-structuralist' inflection by replacing the notion of linguistic
'totality' with the notion of linguistic 'plurality' (or, more precisely, of a
plurality of totalities). Thus, where Lévi-Strauss, for example, endorsed a
study of 'society without history', Foucault favours a study of 'history within
societies', that is, *within the discourses of societies*. Only in this way, he
suggests, can we refute the historicist concept of history as a teleological
progression of chronological events and recognise it for what it really is: a
multiplicity of coded discourses, each one of which sets entirely new terms
for the regulation of the division between what can be legitimately thought
and what cannot, between what is reason and what is unreason, and so on.

In complete contrast, therefore, to the customary approach of the historian who searches for beginnings and tries to trace events through some
linear evolution over time, Foucault dispenses with such humanist models
of causality. Indeed the very 'epistemic' break between the 'historical *a
priori*' of *humanism* (which preconditioned the dominant discourses of
modern idealism, empiricism and existentialism) and that of *structuralism*
(which preconditions the new post-modern discourses of Saussure's linguistics, Lévi-Strauss' anthropology, Lacan's psychoanalysis and Foucault's own archaeology) is itself a cogent example of the operation of
discontinuity and rupturing which Foucault identifies with history. By

excavating the gaps, rifts and contradictions which inform the historical order of thought, Foucault retrieves those hidden texts of the unthought, of unreason, whose repressed capacities for radical transgression herald both the 'end of man' and the 'end of history' as we have known them. In such mature works as *Discipline and Punish* and *The History of sexuality*, Foucault moves beyond structuralist and neo-Marxist idioms towards a more Nietzschean approach to history (as 'genealogy' rather than 'archaeology'). Furthermore, by stressing the centrality of a discourse/practice model he suggests that a critique of *modes of information* may – as Habermas argued in another philosophical context – be more appropriate to a social history of advanced capitalist society than the common emphasis on the primacy of *modes of production*.

POSTSCRIPT

Our treatment of Foucault has been necessarily selective. In order to highlight the 'structuralist' aspects of Foucault's *oeuvre* we have concentrated mainly on his early works and particularly *The Order of Things* (whose real subtitle, as Foucault admitted to Hubert Drefus and Paul Rabinow – authors of a comprehensive English commentary on his work – was *The Archaeology of Structuralism*). For reasons of economy we have played down Foucault's own shift away from structuralist methods in his later writings where he replaces the formative 'archaeological' approach with a more 'genealogical' one which foregoes the quest for a universal theory of discourse in favour of concrete readings of the social strategies adopted by the discursive practices of the human sciences. Indeed, Foucault's final works may be construed as, amongst other things, an auto-critique of his former attempts to establish a system of autonomous discourse on the basis of a structuralist vocabulary. In a late essay, 'The subject and power' – published as an 'Afterword' to Drefus and Rabinow's *Michel Foucault: Beyond Structuralism and Hermeneutics* (1982) – Foucault furnishes a useful summary of his overall project which seeks to explain the transition from his early 'linguistic' approach to his later 'historical' one. As a corrective to simplistic interpretations of Foucault as an orthodox structuralist who dispenses altogether with notions of history or the human subject, this essay merits quotation at some length:

> My objective has been to create a history of the different modes by which, in our culture, human beings are made subjects. My work has dealt with three modes of objectification which transform human beings into subjects. The first is the modes of inquiry which try to give themselves the status of sciences; for example, the objectivizing of the speaking subject in *grammaire générale*, philology, and linguistics . . . In the second part of my work, I have studied the objectivizing of

the subject in what I call 'dividing practices'. The subject is either divided inside himself or divided from others . . . Examples are the mad and the sane, the sick and the healthy, the criminals and the 'goods boys'. Finally, I have sought to study – it is my current work – the way a human being turns him- or herself into a subject. For example, I have chosen the domain of sexuality – how men have learned to recognize themselves as subjects of 'sexuality' . . .

It soon appeared to me that, while the human subject is placed in relations of production and of signification, he is equally placed in power relations which are very complex. Now it seemed to me that economic history and theory provided a good instrument for relations of production; that linguistics and semiotics offered instruments for studying relations of signification; but for power relations we had no tools of study. We had recourse only to ways of thinking about power based on legal models, that is: What legitimates power? Or we had recourse to ways of thinking about power based on institutional models, that is: What is the state? It was necessary therefore to expand the dimensions of a definition of power if one wanted to use this definition in studying the objectivizing of the subject. Do we need a theory of power? Since a theory assumes a prior objectivi-cation, it cannot be asserted as a basis for analytical work. But this analytical work cannot proceed without an ongoing conceptualization. And this conceptuali-zation implies critical thought – a constant checking. The first thing to check is what I should call the 'conceptual needs'. I mean that the conceptualization should not be founded on a theory of the object – the conceptualized object is not the single criterion of a good conceptualization. We have to know the historical conditions which motivate our conceptualization. We need a historical awareness of our present circumstance . . .

The relationship between rationalization and excesses of political power is evident. And we should not need to wait for bureaucracy or concentration camps to recognise the existence of such relations. But the problem is: What to do with such an evident fact? . . . It may be wise not to take as a whole the rationalization of society or of culture, but to analyze such a process in several fields, each with reference to a fundamental experience: madness, illness, death, crime, sexuality, and so forth . . . I would like to suggest . . . a way that is more empirical, more directly related to our present situation, and which implies more relations between theory and practice. It consists of taking the forms of resistance against different forms of power as a starting point . . . For example, to find out what our society means by sanity, perhaps we should investigate what is happening in the field of insanity. And what we mean by legality in the field of illegality. And, in order to understand what power relations are about, perhaps we should investi-gate the forms of resistance and attempts made to dissociate these relations . . . opposition to power of men over women, of parents over children, of psychiatry over the mentally ill, of medicine over the population, of administration over the ways people live. ('The subject and power', 1982)

Foucault's sustained critique of Western society's most venerated insti-tutions, traditions and professional establishments has proved immensely popular with the iconoclastic young generations. His ability to reconcile a commitment to scientific rigour of research with a celebration of anti-tota-litarian dissent, sexual pleasure and poetic excess epitomises the new 'anti-establishment' philosophy of the post-modern era. Foucault has been hailed as a defender of the marginal and outlawed, a champion of the ludic liberties of folly and transgression. It is in this context that we can perhaps best understand Foucault's controversial claim: "We renounce the 'will-to-knowledge' and its sacrifice of life . . . We revere a certain practice of *stupidity*" (*Language, Counter-Memory, Practice*).

Louis Althusser

Louis Althusser was born in Algeria in 1918. In 1948, when he was thirty, he became a teacher of philosophy and joined the Communist Party in France. He taught for many years at the Ecole Normale Supérieure in Paris and was hailed in the sixties and seventies as the most innovatory theorist of the Party. What marked Althusser off from most Marxist intellectuals in Western Europe in our century was his insistence that a new reading of Marxism was necessary to retrieve it from the 'humanist' excesses of various existentialist and neo-Hegelian reinterpretations (e.g. Lukács, the Frankfurt School and the later Sartre). Such reinterpretations, Althusser argued, deprived Marx's work of its scientific basis; they rehabilitated several concepts of the early Marx – 'labour' or 'alienation', for example – within a philosophical framework of bourgeois humanism alien to the mature scientific project of Marxism. In order to live up to its true vocation as a *scientific theory of practice*, Marxism needed to be read in terms of Marx himself. All attempts to re-read Marx in terms of non-Marxist philosophies of idealism, empiricism or existentialism were doomed to failure. Such efforts to reduce Marxism as a theory of structural relations to a philosophy of the human subject, are denounced by Althusser as 'ideologies'.

I

Against those who reject Marx out of hand or distort his work with ideological interpretations, Althusser declares his intention to re-empha-sise Marx's monumental discovery of history – 'the discovery that opens for men the way to a *scientific* (materialist and dialectical) understanding of their own history as a history of the class struggle' ('Foreword' to *Lenin and Philosophy and Other Essays*, 1969). In order for Marx to have been able to carry out his scientific work, it was necessary for him to go beyond the ruling ideology of bourgeois positions to which he was still subject in his early writings. It was only when he came to analyse the mechanisms of class society – masked by the prevailing ideology – that Marx was able to produce a scientific knowledge of it, i.e. to conceive a scientific critique of the relations of production in class society. Althusser demonstrates how this coincided with (1) Marx's departure from the erstwhile philosophical consciousness' of his early Hegelian phase and (2) his adoption of the class position of the proletariat. In short, this 'change of position' from a bourgeois to a proletariat point of view, was essential both at the level of *theory* and *praxis*. Althusser writes accordingly:

> Without the proletariat's class struggle, Marx could not have adopted the point of view of class exploitation or carried out his scientific work. In this scientific work . . . he has given back to the Worker's Movement in a theoretical form what he took from it in a political and ideological form . . . The struggle for Marxist science and Marxist philosophy is today, as it was yesterday, a form of political and ideological class struggle. This struggle entails a radical critique of all forms of bourgeois ideology and of all 'bourgeois' interpretations of Marxism. (*ibid.*)

In this way, Althusser endorses what he considers to be the greatest thesis of Marx and Lenin – *that philosophy is fundamentally political*. But for philosophy to become political means that politics must become philosophical. And this requires that 'class instinct', which is subjective and spontaneous, be translated into a 'class position' which is objective and rational – and therefore *scientific*. Althusser states that this crucial transition involves a process of *education* "determined by proletarian class struggle conducted on the basis of the principles of Marxist-Leninist *theory*" ('Philosophy as a revolutionary weapon' in *Lenin and Philosophy*, 1969). The resulting fusion of Marxist theory and the Workers' Movement thus represents for Althusser the most important event in the whole of human history, whose first effects are witnessed in the socialist revolutions.

Althusser compares Marx's discovery of the new science of historical materialism with two previous scientific discoveries of new 'continents': Thales' discovery of the continent of mathematics and Galileo's discovery of the continent of physics. The third continent is that of history, which Marx's work opens to scientific knowledge for the first time. Moreover, Althusser claims that decisive transformations in philosophy always depend on such great scientific breakthroughs. So that just as Platonic metaphysics was founded upon Thales' science of mathematics and Descartes' idealism upon Galileo's science of physics, so too the Marxist philosophy of dialectical materialism is founded upon Marx's science of history. This explains why philosophy has lagged behind science in Marxist theory making it susceptible to all kinds of humanist misinterpretations. Althusser sees his own work as an attempt to bring them back into line by 'returning to Marx'. He holds that philosophers after Marx – with a few notable exceptions such as Engels and Lenin – continued to dabble in bourgeois pseudo-sciences like political economy, sociology, anthropology and so on. This for Althusser is a form of 'ideological anachronism' comparable to the survival of Aristotelian physics after Galileo. The most pressing task for the

Communist Movement in *theory* (which Althusser advances) is to conquer for the real science of historical materialism the human and social sciences which have occupied as imposters the continent of history to which Marx has given us the keys. Althusser identifies this task more precisely as a "struggle against the bourgeois and petty-bourgeois world outlook which always threatens Marxist theory . . . The *general* form of this world outlook: *Economism* (today 'technocracy') and its 'spiritual complement' *Ethical Idealism* (today 'Humanism') . . . The current *philosophical* form of this world outlook [is] *neo-positivism* and its 'spiritual complement' existentialist-phenomenological subjectivism" ('Philosophy as a revolutionary weapon').

The ultimate stake in the struggle *against* bourgeois ideologies – religious, ethical, legal, political, aesthetic – is the struggle *for* scientific knowledge. Althusser conceives *philosophy* accordingly as a battle conducted on the frontiers between the *ideological* and the *scientific*. Philosophy, as he puts it, 'represents the people's class struggle in theory' (*ibid.*). It is here that the idealist philosophies which exploit science engage with the materialist philosophies which serve science. Hitherto, idealism has always won this philosophical combat which reflects the class struggle between world outlooks. But Marx has made possible the reversal of the outcome. Now for the first time, materialism can dominate idealism, not only in theory (that is, in Althusser's philosophy) but also, if the political conditions are realised, in revolution. Althusser urges that if we are to 'read' Marx's *Capital* properly we must directly experience the two *realities* which determine the science of historical materialism: (i) the reality of theoretical practice in its concrete life; and (ii) the reality of the practice of revolutionary class struggle in its concrete life (in contact with the masses). Historical materialism requires, in other words, that we both *know* history and *change* it. Against bourgeois humanism which holds that it is 'man' who makes history, Althusser retorts that scientific Marxism knows that it is the 'masses' who make history.

II

Althusser maintains that Marxism is far more therefore than an anthropology of human behaviour or a pragmatic manual of political strategy. Above all, it is a *science of structural relations*. It is a method of revolution precisely because it is a 'revolution in method'.

Das Kapital, Althusser contends, is the key work for a true understanding of Marxism and not the early *Economic and Philosophical Manuscripts* as the 'humanist' Marxists of Critical Theory often argue. For it is in *Das Kapital* that the mature Marx proposes a radically new 'logic' of structural relations which enables us to treat of historical and social *praxis* in a rigorously scientific way. A proper task for philosophers after Marx is, Althusser submits, to return to this central work and to read it in such a way that this 'logic' may be made more explicit and more effective. In this respect, Althusser's work is a sort of *rappel aux sources*.

If it is true that Althusser has been frequently treated as an exponent of 'structuralism' and features in many anthologies on the subject, it must be pointed out that this label was rejected by Althusser himself. This rejection is most explicit in his contentious foreword to the Italian edition of *Reading Capital* (reproduced in the English edition) where he refers disparagingly to the 'idéologistes structuralistes'. Althusser's own repudiation of the term was no doubt in part due to his reluctance to be equated with the fashionable movement of French Structuralism (though he was influenced by Lacan and exerted a considerable influence on Foucault). Marx, not Saussure, is Althusser's theoretical master. Nonetheless he did acknowledge that Marx was the first proponent of a structural method of scientific analysis which give priority to the totality of the system over the individual historical subjects which operate as parts within the whole. In so far as Althusser develops this methodological discovery of Marx in a manner especially appropriate to the post-humanist climate of much modern thought, his work has, not surprisingly, been associated with the structuralist movement. Mindful of the particularity of Althusser's position, the following analysis will attempt to outline some of the main aspects of his controversial reading of Marxism as a science of structural relations.

In two major works, *For Marx* (1965) and *Reading Capital* (1968 co-authored with Balibar), Althusser expounds his famous 'symptomatic' interpretation of the Marxian corpus. This interpretation resembles in several significant respects the models of both linguistic and psychoanalytic structuralism. Althusser argues here that the philosophical and economic texts of Marx should be read not solely in terms of their surface or 'visible' meanings, but by attending to a 'different invisible discourse' which represents a sort of textual unconscious. Adopting a method analogous to Saussure's analysis of *langue* and Lacan's theory of 'symptoms' (as a chain of unconscious signifying relations reflected in the contradictions of conscious speech), Althusser affirms the possibility of restoring to the totality of Marx's work its true scientific basis by reading its apparent contradictions (e.g. the discrepancies between the early 'humanist' thinker and the later 'political economist') in a structural or, as he puts it, 'symptomatic' manner.

Thus Althusser sets out to recover the *real* thought of Marx – as in another context Lacan had done with Freud. Althusser concedes that Marx did at times employ Hegelian and idealist language. But this he insists was a superficial aberration necessitated by the limited conceptual apparatus available in his day, an apparatus which was not fully adequate to the 'scientific' core of his thinking. Only by means of a deep structural reading capable of identifying the idealist inflections in Marx as 'symptoms' of an underlying unconscious logic of relations – which is the object of his analysis – would it be possible to accord to Marxism the revolutionary scientific status it deserves. Such a 'symptomatic' reading permits us to distinguish between (1) the *ideological phase of Marxism as a humanist philosophy* still informed by such idealist categories as 'subject, 'essence', 'history' etc. and (2) its properly *scientific phase as a rigorous theory* (a science of science) which dispenses with all such categories. While the former phase focused on human relations between *persons*, the latter penetrates deeper to the formal relations between the *terms of production*. Indeed Althusser goes so far as to claim that Marxism is scientific theory in its highest form since it conceptually constitutes its own object and deals with the origin and end of forms of knowing as a 'practice of production'.

In this respect, Althusser inverts the traditional philosophical view that knowledge precedes production. By equating scientific theory with the forces of production – an equation which he believes to be one of the most pioneering insights of Marxism – Althusser is led to the conclusion that the real subjects are not what they *appear* to be (i.e. human individuals) but the hidden relations of production which ultimately determine what function individuals fulfil in the system of production. His rigorously 'scientific' interpretation of Marx thus reveals that the latter located the motive source of history not in the existential consciousness of men but in the structural order of a 'social totality' which predetermines this consciousness. Vincent Descombes provides a succinct account of this opposition between existential and structural Marxism in *Modern French Philosophy*:

Post-war 'existential Marxism' was presented as a philosophy of history. It provided a connection between the course of events (from human origins through to the end of history) and the subjective experience of individuals. It sought to endow Marxism with a phenomenological foundation ('being' as the 'presentation of a meaning to a consciousness'). The truth of Marxist theories of class struggle and the necessity of revolution lay in the experience of the individual, consciously existing as exploited or exploiter and freely choosing to invest his life with the meaning of struggle for or against a society of universal recognition between consciousnesses. Now all this had the air of a myth. The lived meaning, as Lévi-Strauss explains, is never the correct one. Althusser's definition of *ideology* (in the pejorative sense of 'false representation') invokes this very discrepancy between experience and knowledge. Ideology, he says, is the expression of the lived relations of men to their conditions of existence, given that this expression of a (real) relationship is never synonymous with knowledge of it, and always includes an element of the imaginary. The truth of Marxism can no longer be guaranteed by the testimony of consciousness. Another basis has therefore to be found. So we arrive at what might be called the formula of the Althusserian intervention: it is not in a philosophy of freedom, or *praxis*, that the foundation of Marxism must be sought, but rather in an *epistemology* whose central thesis would be the opposition of consciousness and concept (and as a result the impossibility of all phenomenology). (*Modern French Philosophy*, 1980)

Such an argument had immediate implications for the contemporary debate on determinism. It appeared that Althusser was eliminating the notion of man as the privileged subject of history. And this raised the vexed question of whether one could still talk of human freedom in any meaningful way. Predictably, many suspected that Althusser's position was intimately aligned with the structuralist priority of the system over the subject, of *langue* over *parole*. And this suspicion was strengthened when Althusser vigorously opposed the philosophical stance taken by the French Marxist, Rober Garaudy, whose humanist reading of Marx sought to make common cause with a broad alliance of left-wing Christians, socialists and existentialists. Where Garaudy and his intellectual allies emphasised the importance for Marxism of notions like human will, choice, creativity and responsibility, Althusser tended to dismiss such emphasis as signalling a return to bourgeois liberalism.

The critique of ideology plays a central role in the Althusserian project. For Althusser the particular events of our everyday life and its struggles are invariably experienced in 'ideological' terms; whereas 'knowledge' about the ultimate causes of these struggles can only be identified at the 'scientific' level of a theoretical practice. All non-scientific representations of the social process in terms of free individual subjects are necessarily ideological constructions. Such representations do no more than reinforce the illusion of a 'natural world' perceived on the surface, and as such reflect the dominant ideology. The particular ideology of modern times, the bourgeois ideology, constructs the fiction of free, autonomous, non-contradictory individuals who experience society as something which exists over and above them. And a major consequence of this ideology is that the underlying structural contradictions of the social formation are concealed by the construction of myths – the most notable being the bourgeois myth of some natural 'human condition'.

Althusser points out that the notion of human *subjectivity* as a natural condition of freedom, is in reality no more than an ideological strategy of *subjection* to the powers that be. Ideology, in other words, summons human individuals to respond freely to the 'false representations' of social exist-ence which ideology has already imposed on them. It functions as a subtle form of double-think which at once affirms and denies the phenomenon of individual free will. For Althusser there is 'no ideology except by and for subjects'; and the primary purpose of ideology is to represent each individ-ual as a *subject of* autonomous freedom in order that he may accept a social position *subject to* the prevailing social formation. Exploiting the ambiguity in the term 'subject' – meaning both freedom *and* constraint – Althusser explains how ideology works to isolate human beings from one another in such a way that society itself assumes the form of an unchallenged and unchangeable power. He thus exposes ideology as a non-systematic and often conflicting use of concepts devoid of any coherent totality. He writes:

> The whole mystery of this (ideological) effect lies . . . in the ambiguity of the term *subject*. In the ordinary use of the term, subject in fact means: (1) a free subjecti-vity, a centre of initiative, author of and responsible for its actions; (2) a subjected being, who submits to a higher authority, and therefore is stripped of all freedom except that of accepting freely his submission . . . the individual *is interpellated as a (free) subject in order that he shall submit freely to the commandments of the Subject, i.e. in order that he shall (freely) accept his subjection*, i.e. in order that he shall make the gestures and actions of his subjection 'all by himself'. *There are no subjects except by and for their subjection*. That is why they 'work all by themselves'. ('Ideology and ideological state apparatuses' in *Lenin and Philosophy*)

The implications of Althusser's concept of 'science' are complex and far-reaching. Since Althusser accepts the structuralist premiss that every reading of a text determines the meaning of that text, it follows that the "pre-condition of a reading of Marx is Marxist theory" (*For Marx*). And since, furthermore, 'Marxist theory' comprises the conceptual totality of Marxist texts, a scientific 'reading' of the texts requires us to 'decode' their internal transitions, transformations and contradictions as 'diachronic' parts which are structurally interrelated within a 'synchronic' whole. Only in this way, Althusser suggests, is 'scientific socialism' possible.

Althusser's structural analysis discloses the existence of an 'epistemolo-gical break' in the 'objective text' of Marx's writings. He locates this break between the early works of the 1840s and later works such as the *Grundrisse* (1957) and the *Kapital* (Vol. I, 1867). On the basis of this disclosure, Althusser maintains that the early 'historical' reading of concepts such as 'alienation', 'labour' and 'negativity' in terms of preceding philosophical traditions (e.g. as in certain passages of the 1844 *Paris Manuscripts*), must be replaced by a mature 'structural' reading of such concepts within the synchronic system of Scientific Marxism. More exactly, it is only in the light of the later scientific works that Marx's early writings – which are ideological productions and so excluded from Marxist theory proper – can be analyzed from a truly Marxist perspective.

The principal target of Althusser's criticism here is Hegel. Openly hostile to the numerous modern attempts to resituate Marx in some kind of continuous relation to Hegel – witnessed for example in Lukács, Sartre and Marcuse – Althusser pledges to read Marx in terms of Marx alone. "We need more light on Marx", Althusser observes, so that "the phantom of Hegel can return into the night" (*For Marx*). Marxism is thus revealed as a self-sufficient system which can neither be derived from nor translated into any other theory. With Marx, there is no before or after. His work can only be properly understood on its own terms.

III

We are now perhaps in a better position to assess what has often been described as the 'structuralist' character of Althusser's analysis. Just as the workings of language can only be structurally understood within the system of language (Saussure) and the workings of the unconscious within the system of the unconscious (Lacan), so too Marx can only be properly understood within the structural system of Marxism itself (Althusser). All of the 'mixed' concepts of Marx's early work – which suggest borrowings from bourgeois philosophy – must be comprehended retrospectively as the *prehistory* of scientific Marxism. This prehistory embraces the 'adolescent phases' of Marx's rationalist humanism (the heritage of Kant and Fichte), materialist humanism (the heritage of Feuerbach) and dialectical humanism (the heritage of Hegel). But it would be entirely wrong to suppose that Marx can thus be 'read' through Hegel and the other intellectual predecessors of Marxism. If anything, these humanist philosophers must be 're-read' through Marx. It is at this point that Althusser affirms the existence of an unbridgeable dichotomy or 'rupture' between *ideology* (referring to all pre-Marxist, i.e. pre-scientific, philosophies and all the ideas and representations which comprise the lived relation of people to the world) and *science* (which overcomes the errors and illusions of ideology by transforming ideological material into rigorous and systematic theory by various structural procedures).

Althusser develops his 'structural' analysis in order to produce/construct Marxist concepts which may only be implicit in Marx's writings but which represent the underlying structural relations which comprise the scientific theory of Marxism. In this way, Althusser's reading proposes an order of concepts not previously available.

Althusser did not of course see himself as translating Marxism into structuralism – as if the latter were some post-Marxist method which could make new and better sense of Marx. This, quite evidently, would be in contradiction with his overriding premiss that Marxism is a self-sufficient conceptual totality. For Althusser Marxism is a 'scientific theory of theoretical practice' which precedes the contemporary movement of structuralism. Marx was the first to insist that contradictions between the forces and modes of production are not 'reflections' of some absolute Spirit, but structural relations within a structural system. Similarly, for Marx, the class struggles of history cannot be interpreted in terms of conflicting consciousness, still less in terms of isolated empirical contents, but only as an interplay of formal laws which govern both the reality of consciousness and of history.

It is clear that Althusser's approach has much in common at times with Saussure, Lévi-Strauss, Lacan and other self-acknowledged structuralists. But there are fundamental differences of emphasis. Whereas Saussure had situated the basis of structural relations at the level of phonemic oppositions, Lévi-Strauss at the level of mythemic polarities, and Lacan at the psychic level of unconscious signifiers, Althusser spoke of different 'fields' or partial 'instances' which constitute structural oppositions within the social formation of Marxism itself. These different 'fields' – the political, the theoretical, the economic etc. – are shown to operate as autonomous but interrelated instances determined by a single 'dominating structure'.

This dominating structure differs from one historical epoch to the next: at one stage it may be predominantly religious, at another political, at another economic and so on. But while the 'instances' thus undergo diachronic alterations, the system of structural relations remains a synchronic totality. In this way, Althusser was able to reject the 'economistic' error which construed the economic structure as 'causing' the political structure and the latter as 'causing' the ideological structures of religion and philosophy etc. By according a certain autonomy to both the political superstructures and the economic infrastructures in the total system of structural relations, Althusser was capable of explaining, for example, how even certain Marxist societies (e.g. the USSR under Stalin) were guilty of ideological perversions, *without* having to indict the economic infrastructure of socialism. In the following passage in *For Marx*, Althusser suggests how a structural analysis of Marxism enables us to understand its internal historical phases as relatively autonomous parts within the synchronic whole:

We can argue from the specific structure of the Marxist whole that it is no longer possible to think the process of development of the different levels of the whole in *the same historical time*. Each of these different 'levels' does not have the same type of historical existence ... The fact that each of these times and each of these histories is *relatively autonomous* does not make them so many domains which are *independent* of the whole: the specificity of each of these times and each of these histories – in other words, their relative autonomy and independence – is based on a certain type of *dependence* with respect to the whole. (*ibid.*)

IV

Althusser thus rejects the crude excesses of 'economism' which reduces history to a series of mechanical causes. He ironically rebukes the clichéd idea of 'superstructures' scattering before 'His Majesty the Economy as he strides along the royal road to the Dialectic'. But he does not deny for all that that the economic instance of the social totality is the 'last instance', even if it never actually manifests itself as such (that is, never completely dominates the other superstructural instances). The economic instance "is determinant in the last instance", he writes, "(but) the lonely hour of the 'last instance' never comes".

In other words, the relative autonomy and even invisibility of the economy in relation to the other instances does not preclude its role of ultimate determination within the 'unity of the totality'. For while the 'structure-in-dominance' may vary historically between the ideological, political or economic instances, it is always the economic instance which in the last analysis is seen to determine which instance (itself or another) is to be dominant and which subordinate at a particular stage in history. As Alex Callinicos explains in his commentary on Althusser, the specific superstructural instances of the totality, though remaining relatively autonomous, "possess a certain order, are organised into a certain hierarchy, according to the determination of the economy, which displaces the role of dominant instance onto a particular instance and allocates to the other instances their specific role ... The complex character of the complex unity is one in which the superstructures, the political and the ideological, are treated as consisting of specific distinct instances of the whole, articulated upon each other and upon the economy, but in which they are ordered by the economy in a specific relation of domination and subordination" (*Althusser's Marxism*, 1976).

Althusser is insistent that the determining structure of the economy operates neither in the positivist manner of linear cause and effect, nor in the idealist manner of appearances 'reflecting' some transcendental spiritual essence. The economy must be understood in the dialectical terms of a unique, if often unobservable, 'structural causality' wherein the specific infrastructural instance serves as the precondition of the superstructural instances and vice versa. This causality of structure is one of reciprocal relation where part and whole are mutually necessary for each other's existence. Or as Althusser puts it in typically cryptic fashion: "The *difference* of the essential contradictions and their structure in dominance, is the very existence of the whole" (*For Marx*). This implies that the structural cause of the whole upon the parts is a structural combination of partial effects and cannot exist outside of or apart from these effects. The whole is the interplay of its parts. The one cannot function without the other.

To rephrase this in the terminology of linguistic structuralism, one could say that the superstructural instances of politics and ideology do not relate to the infrastructural instance of the economy as signifiers to signified but as signifiers to another signifier. Rather like Lacan's 'floating signifier' of the unconscious, the 'economic structure' unfolds in the Althusserian system as an endless, dialectical chain of signifiers, which never comes to a stop, which is never exhausted by reference to any single empirical signified. The structural causality which historical materialism advances, according to Althusser's reading, "makes the ruling cause an absent one, for it effaces, eclipses and 'surpasses' the mechanist category of cause, conceived as *the* billiard-ball in person, that one can get hold of, the cause identified as *the substance*, *the* subject etc" (*Ibid.*). In the Althusserian dialectic, the notion of 'cause' appears not as a person present on the stage of history but as a structural link which relates one signifier to another.

It is significant that Althusser invokes here the Lacanian/Freudian notion of 'overdetermination' to describe how one particular instance of contradiction can become charged with the unconscious interplay of relations between other instances of contradiction. The economic signifier which governs the subordination of one instance to another cannot be understood as some sort of transcendental essence existing outside of the system of signifiers. And if it is indeed 'absent', in the sense of being invisible to normal 'ideological' consciousness, this is only because it is hidden *within* the system as the 'overdetermined' structural interrelationship of parts and whole: "The absence of the cause in the structure's 'metonymic causality' on its effects is not the fault of the exteriority of the structure with respect to the economic phenomena; on the contrary, it is the very form of the interiority of the structure, in its effects". (*Reading Capital*).

But if the structural cause does not appear as a person on the stage of history, it does produce historical effects. Indeed were Althusser to deny this he could not be considered a Marxist in any sense of the term. It is by linking the concept of 'overdetermination' with the concept of 'symptomology' (also of Freudian/Lacanian derivation), that Althusser explains this complex rapport between structural cause and historical effect. His account of Marxist revolution runs something as follows. When different

kinds of contradiction form a certain structural 'conjuncture', rev·lu-
tionary mutations can occur. This happened in Russia, for exa ple, in
1917 when the convergence of a number of 'symptomatic' contr. .lictions
(e.g. imperial politics, agrarian feudalism, urban industrialisation and a
conservative Tsarist ideology) made it possible for a socialist revolution to
displace the preceding order. Revolution does not result solely from an
economic crisis or collapse – if so every society would have had its revolution – but from a certain interplay of contradictions at a variety of levels.
Unlike the Hegelian notion of contradiction as a single identity which splits
itself into two contradictory parts before reconciling them again in a new
identity, Althusser construes contradiction as a complex of several contradictions, any one of which may function as a 'dominant instance' which
nonetheless reflects the complexity of the whole. For Althusser, any contradiction may be said to be 'overdetermined' in the sense that it internally
reproduces the relations pertaining within the social formation as a whole.
Michael Kelly provides a useful commentary on this difficult argument in
his treatment of Althusser in *Modern French Marxism*:

> The basic contradiction between forces and relations of production, embodied in
> the struggle of antagonistic classes, is not in itself sufficient to provoke revolution
> . . . What is necessary is that it should 'fuse' [*fusionner*] with other contradictions
> in a unity which provokes radical change. This unity of fused contradictions, he
> suggests, reveals its own nature, which is that contradiction is inseparable from
> its conditions of existence and from the moments, or instances, it governs.
> Determining and determined by the various levels and moments of the social
> formation, contradiction is therefore 'overdetermined' . . . He contrasts [Hegel's
> notion of dialectic] with Marx's dialectic which recognizes that the basic contra-
> diction between Capital and labour is always specified by the concrete historical
> forms and circumstances in which it occurs, including political, ideological and
> religious superstructures, and national and international historical developments
> (*Modern French Marxism*, 1982).

V

One of the most radical consequences of Althusser's analysis is the structural equation of science and practice. Marxism is thus revealed to be, above
all else, a science of historical practices. Althusser, of course, saw this as no
more than an explicitation of Marx's resolve to overcome the traditional
division between theory and praxis. But not all Marxists agreed. Indeed
Geraudy denounced the Althusserian solution as a reduction of the Marxist project of concrete liberation to an abstract system of structural
determinism in which the free human agent is eliminated. Others argued
that Althusser's structuralism was nothing short of a betrayal of Marxism in
so far as it dissolved the actual *content* of practice (that is, the revolutionary

struggle of the working class as something concretely experienced by living human subjects) into a scientific *form* of practice. The ultimate consequence of this move, Althusser's critics suggested, was a scientific Marxism which held the primary aim of 'practice' to be the production of objective knowledge.

Althusser responded by accusing his opponents of treating Marxism as no more than an 'ideological' product of consciousness. He berated them for divorcing theory from the *real* reality of history – which is *not* an existential stagedrama of human subjects but a system of structural relations. Socialism, he pursued, can only attain to its true 'objective' status if it expresses itself as a scientific system whose *theoretical* practice is at one and the same time a *material* practice. It is the identification of these two aspects of practice in Marxism which results in the category of the 'concrete-in-thought' (Marx's *'Gedankenkonkretum'* from the 1857 'Introduction' usually printed with the *Grundrisse*). This is why Althusser so emphatically affirms that the science of socialism represents an 'epistemological break' with the ideological 'pre-history' of all bourgeois philosophies. For these philosophies viewed the very notion of science as a superstructural mode of thought removed from the material world of historical practice. By contrast, Marxism constitutes a science that does not simply reflect or represent material reality at some secondary level. The science of Marxism *is* material reality. It is not *about* anything other than itself. Or to put it in another way, it is not some abstract theorising about the appropriation of the real; it is this very mode of appropriation. And this is why, by its very nature, Marxism could never be an 'ideology'. For an 'ideology' is a false representation, that is, the representation of something true (the real) in terms of something false (the imaginary). But Marxism, as a theory which is also practice, as a science which is also reality, cannot be a false representation since it must always represent itself in terms of itself, since it *is* itself. Once Marxism unites theoretical with real practice in this way, after the break from bourgeois ideology (which was based on the separation of theory and reality), "it has no need for verification from *external* practices to declare the knowledges it produces to be true" (*Reading Capital*).

It is Althusser's firm conviction then that Marx transcended the traditional dichotomy between the historical development of reality and its structural development in thought. Marxism, he claims, is that science of theoretical practice which itself functions as a mode of *production* in so far as it transforms ideological representations into knowledge. More precisely, theory may be construed as a practical production in that it transforms the *raw materials* of ideology (e.g. political economy) into a new *product*: the structural science of socialism.

Marxism is, for Althusser, a science which expresses 'the development of things in general'. As such, theory also differs significantly from such non-scientific practices as art or literature. In 'A letter on Art in reply to André Daspre', Althusser makes it clear that he does not rank 'real art' among the ideologies, although it does have a specific relationship to ideology. Taking the examples of Balzac and Solzhenitsyn, he affirms that while neither give us any *knowledge* of the world they describe, they do enable us to 'see', 'perceive' or 'feel' the reality of the ideology of that world. Since ideology slides into all human activity and experience, great works of literature can make us 'see' ideology in the experience of individuals as it is *spontaneously lived*; but they cannot make it *scientifically known*. Ideology, as the lived experience of individuals, is the common concern of both art and science. But it is comprehended in each case in a radically distinct manner. 'The real difference between art and science', writes Althusser, 'lies in the *specific form* in which they give us the same object in quite different ways: art in the form of "seeing" and "perceiving" or "feeling", science in the form of *knowledge* (in the strict sense, by concepts) . . . if Solzhenitsyn does "make us see" the "lived experience" of the "cult of personality" and its effects, in no way does he give us *knowledge* of them: this knowledge is the conceptual knowledge of the complex mechanisms which eventually produce the "lived experience" that Solzhenitsyn's novels discuss' ('A letter on Art' in *Lenin and Philosophy and Other Essays*). Althusser concludes accordingly:

> . . . in order to answer most of the questions posed for us by the existence and specific nature of art, we are forced to produce an adequate (scientific) *knowledge* of the processes which produce the "aesthetic effect" of a work of art . . . like all knowledge the knowledge of art presupposes a preliminary *rupture* with the language of *ideological spontaneity* and the constitution of a body of scientific concepts to replace it . . . if it is a matter of *knowing* art, it is absolutely essential to begin·with "*rigorous reflection on the basic concepts of Marxism*": there is no other way . . . not in order ot pass art silently by or to sacrifice it to science : it is quite simply in order to *know* it, and to give it its due. (*ibid.*)

Thought is revealed as the highest form of the organisation of matter (in sharp contrast with Hegel and other 'ideological' thinkers for whom matter was but an externalisation or 'alienation' of thought). Properly understood, Marxism is not, Althusser submits, a question of reducing either thought to matter (mechanical materialism) or matter to thought (speculative idealism). It is a question of recognising that true theory is itself a social practice, a practical activity which organises our 'lived experience' *as* thought.

The difficulty here, however, is that Althusser sometimes appears to deny that theory – as the practical activity of knowing – can have any starting point *outside* of thought. And so some critics objected that Althusser was in fact transmuting Marxism into a new kind of speculative rationalism. Althusser dismisses such suggestions on the grounds that they completely ignore the radical *discontinuity* between the ideological and scientific approaches to theory, which precludes the possibility of reading Marxism in traditional rationalist terms. Hegelianism and other forms of bourgeois rationalism must be seen as ideological instances contained within the 'pre-history' of Marxism itself. Abolishing, as we saw, the idea of an organic transition between Hegel and Marx – an idea which had informed most humanist Marxist theories from Lukács and the Frankfurt school to the existentialist Marxism of the fifties (e.g. Sartre and Merleau-Ponty) – Althusser injected new theoretical blood into Marxist studies on the Continent and exerted a profound and many believe liberating influence on thinking within the French Communist Party and, for a brief dramatic period, on the emerging groups of Maoist students.

CONCLUSION

Althusser's structural reading of Marx's work necessitated a radical rethink of the basic aims and categories of dialectical materialism. Many commentators have adverted to this 'structuralist' character of Althusser's approach (even if they have not always explored it). A good case in point is Alex Callinicos who provides the following summary outline of the relationship between Althusser and structuralism:

> There are certain parallels between the preoccupations of Althusser and those of figures like the anthropologist Lévi-Strauss, the psychoanalyst Lacan, or the epistemologist Foucault. They appear to share a common preoccupation with the unconscious structures presupposed by the activities of human subjects, with the complex and opaque forms taken up by human discourse, with alternatives to a humanism that treats the conscious human subject as sovereign. The cross-fertilisation of ideas (the influence, say, of Lacan on Althusser, or of Althusser on Foucault) and their common debt to Freud are other arguments for a common treatment. (*Althusser's Marxism*)

Our concentration on those aspects of Althusser's thinking which relate, directly or otherwise, to the structuralist movement, has meant that we have had to forego discussion of other important aspects – in particular, the historical and political consequences of his work; the major reworking of his position after 1968; his marked preference for Spinoza over Hegel. But we do hope, within the set limits of our study, to have touched on some of the key concepts in Althusser's theory of the social formation as an interplay of structural relations.

In conclusion, we offer a summary of the principal features which Althusser's analysis shares, at least in part, with structuralism. Firstly, it displays a definite preference for a 'science' of knowledge over a 'phenomenology' of lived experience. Secondly, it provides a 'synchronic' explanation of the dialectic within a complex totality in opposition to a 'diachronic' explanation in terms of a generative progress from alienated past to critical present to utopian future. Thirdly, it replaces the 'historicist' notion of cause and effect with a 'structural' model of causality as a dialectical isomorphism between infrastructure and superstructure – a model which in fact purports to do away with the dichotomy altogether. And lastly, Althusser proposes a 'systematic' reading of Marxism as an interplay of determining and determined relations, which dismisses the 'humanist' concept of the free individual subject as an ideological mystification.

APPENDIX: ALTHUSSER AND LACAN

It may be useful to take a brief look at Althusser's famous essay on 'Freud and Lacan', for it is here that he comes closest to a positive assessment of the contribution which a structuralist analysis of the unconscious can make to a Marxist critique of ideology.

In this study, Althusser urges Marxists to recognise the 'scientificity' of psychoanalysis – which had been 'officially' condemned by the Communist Party in the fifties as a 'reactionary ideology' – and the importance of Lacan's interpretation of it. In particular, Althusser commends the possibilities of a structural analysis of the 'familial ideology' (of paternity–maternity–conjugality–infancy and their interaction) which Lacan discloses as a central instance of the unconscious. Needless to say, Althusser argues that such an analysis implies the conclusion – which Lacan himself could not express given the limits of his theoretical formation – that no theory of psychoanalysis is complete unless it is founded upon the science of historical materialism which alone can fully explain the social formulation of familial ideology.

Althusser approves Lacan's endeavour to combat the 'revisionism' which assisted the ideological exploitation of psychoanalysis in the West as a 'mystification of consciousness'. Just as Marxist revisionism coincided with the fall of historical materialism into the bourgeois interpretations of 'economism, technocratism and humanism', so Freudian revisionism coincided with the fall of psychoanalysis into 'biologism, psychologism and sociologism'. Althusser thus draws a parallel between his own attempt to restore Marxism to a scientific status and Lacan's attempt to effect a scientific retrieval of Freud from mechanistic misreadings. He interprets Lacan's 'return to Freud' as (I) an *ideological critique* of the reactionary exploitation of psychoanalysis as a crude mystification, and (2) an *epistemological elucidation* which enables us to identify in the pre-scientific concepts which Freud himself had to use (e.g. concepts imported from the biology, thermodynamic physics and political economy of his day), the true scientific relation between these concepts and their thought content: the instance of the unconscious. According to Althusser, both Marx and Freud represent 'births of sciences and criticism' which threatened the ideological defences of Western society and were thus 'revised' so as to take the harm out of them.

By rescuing the science of psychoanalysis from bourgeois revisionism, Lacan put the real harm back into Freud just as Althusser put the harm back into Marx. Lacan sought to give the practice of analysis a theory and thus prevent it serving as a mere shamanistic technique: 'the social magic of modern times'. The importance of Lacan was to recognise that Freud had opened up the possibility of a new science with a new object – the unconscious. So doing, he demonstrated that psychoanalysis has a specific *theory* which allows for the knowledge and transformation of its object (the unconscious) in a specific practice. But it is precisely this identification of psychoanalysis with a scientific theory of the unconscious as a system of structural relations (analogous to the system disclosed by Saussure's linguistics) that contemporary bourgeois analysis – especially in America – rejects by annexing Freud to its own ideological pseudo-sciences or myths: e.g. to behaviourist psychiatry (Dalbiez), existential psychology (Sartre, Merleau-Ponty, Binswanger) or to anthropological sociology (Margaret Mead). "Thus subordinated to psychology or sociology", observes Althusser," psychoanalysis is usually reduced to a technique of 'emotional' or 'affective' re-adaptation, or to a re-education of the 'relational function', neither of which has anything to do with its real object – but which unfortunately respond to a major demand, and what is more, to a demand that is highly tendentious in the contemporary world. Through this bias, psycho-analysis has become an article of mass consumption in modern culture, i.e. in modern ideology" ('Freud and Lacan' in *Lenin and Philosophy*).

It is significant that Althusser defends the 'artifice' and strange 'hermeticism' of Lacan's style as a necessary strategy for presenting the theory of the unconscious to doctors and analysts with a 'dumbshow equivalent to the language of the unconscious' (i.e. as *witz*, pun and metaphor). Lacan's disclosure of the 'familial ideology' at work in the Oedipal phase, where a 'small animal conceived by a man and a woman is transformed into a small human child', is no business for the biologist, Althusser argues, nor indeed for the neurologist, anthropologist or sociologist. Psychoanalysis – like Marxism – has a right to a specificity of concepts in line with its own specific object (the unconscious and its effects).

It is equally significant that Althusser concedes that Lacan's revolutionary theorising of psychoanalysis along scientific lines would have been impossible without the emergence of the new science of structural linguistics. For it was Saussure's discovery which enabled Lacan to adequately articulate Freud's discovery that the 'unconscious is structured like *language*'. As this aspect of Althusser's commentary on Lacan is one of the most explicit acknowledgements of the contribution made by the structuralist method (which he elsewhere dismisses as an 'ideology') to the formation of scientific theory, we shall cite it at some length:

> It is in the nature of the history of the sciences that one science may often not become a science except by recourse to a detour through other sciences, not only sciences that existed at its baptism but also some new late-comer among sciences that needed time before it could be born. The temporary opacity of the shadow cast on Freudian theory by the model of . . . thermodynamic physics has been dispersed today by the light that structural linguistics throws on its object, making possible an intelligible approach to that object. Freud himself said that everything depended on language. Lacan makes this more precise: 'the discourse of the unconscious is structured like a language'. In his first great work *The Interpretation of Dreams*, Freud studies the 'mechanisms' and 'laws' of dreams, reducing their variants to two: *displacement* and *condensation*. Lacan recognized these as two essential figures of speech, called in linguistics metonymy and metaphor. Hence slips, failures, jokes and symptoms, like the elements of dreams themselves, became *signifiers*, inscribed in the chain of an unconscious discourse . . . Hence we are introduced to the paradox, formally familiar to linguistics, of a double yet single discourse, unconscious yet verbal, having for its double field only a single field, with no beyond except in itself: the field of the 'signifying chain'. Hence the most important acquisitions of de Saussure and of the linguistics that descends from him began to play a justified part in the understanding of the process of the unconscious as well as that of the verbal discourse of the subject and of their inter-relationship, i.e. of their identical relation and non-relation, in other words, of their reduplication and dislocation. Thereby philosophico-idealist interpretations of the unconscious as a second consciousness, of the unconscious as bad faith (Sartre), of the unconscious as the cankerous survival of a non-current structure or non-sense (Merleau-Ponty), all the interpretations of the unconscious as a biologico-archetypical 'id' (Jung) became what they were: not the beginnings of a theory but null 'theories', ideological misunderstandings". (*ibid.*).

The parallel between Lacan's use of structural models to salvage Freud from ideological misinterpretations and Althusser's own procedure with regard to Marx is suggestive. Quite clearly Althusser is here enlisting Lacan's structuralist model as an ally in the struggle against the common enemy of ideology. Of especial interest to Althusser is the manner in which Lacan revealed the mechanisms whereby the formal structures of language play a primary role in the 'forced *humanization* of the small human animal into a *man* or a *woman*', that is, the production of a gendered human subject. Lacan had shown how the transition from biological existence to human existence is achieved within the symbolic order of language (the Law of Order and of Culture). This transition, he argued, is highlighted in the move from (1) the pre-Oedipal relationship between child and mother which is lived as an 'imaginary fascination of the ego, being itself *that* other, *every* other, all *the others* of primary narcissistic identification, never able to take up the objectifying distance of the third *vis-à-vis* either the other or itself; to (2) the Oedipal relationship when the third (the father) intrudes into the imaginary fascination of mother and child and introduces the child to the *Symbolic Order* of objectifying language which enables the child to become *human* by allowing it to say: I, you, he, she or it (i.e. to situate itself as a human child in a world of adult thirds).

By disclosing the structural codes which govern this transition from the Imaginary to the Symbolic Order of language Lacan permits us to have a *conceptual* hold of the discourse of the unconscious. 'The whole dialectic of the transition', remarks Althusser, 'is stamped by the seal of Human Order, of the Symbolic, for which linguistics provides us with the *formal* laws, i.e. the *formal concept*' (*ibid.*) Furthermore, just as Althusser called for a theoretical science of Marxist concepts to coincide with concrete historical practice (the revolution), so too Lacan provides Freudian concepts with a scientificity which contains the measure – or law of structure – of their concrete application in analytic practice (the cure). In this way, Lacan's use of structural linguistics opens up the possibility of a scientific grasp of the power structures operative in the 'familial ideology' of paternity, maternity, childhood etc. This recognition of psychoanalysis as a critique of ideology raises a number of crucial questions for Althusser:

For example, how can we rigorously formulate the relation between the *formal* structure of language, the absolute precondition for the existence and intelligibility of the unconscious, on the one hand, the concrete kinship structures on the other, and finally the concrete ideological formations in which the specific functions implied by the kinship structures (paternity, maternity, childhood) are lived? . . . What relations are there between analytic theory and (1) the historical preconditions of its appearance, and (2) the social preconditions of its application? . . . The test (implied by these questions) is rooted in the test Freud, in his own field, applied to a particular legal, ethical and philosophical, i.e. definitively ideological, image of 'man', of the human 'subject'. Not in vain did Freud sometimes compare the critical reception of his discovery with the upheavals of the Copernican Revolution. Since Copernicus, we have known that the earth is not the 'centre' of the universe. Since Marx, we have known that the human subject, the economic, political or philosophical ego is not the 'centre' of history – and even, in opposition to the Philosophers of the Englightenment and to Hegel, that history has no 'centre' but possesses a structure which has no necessary 'centre' except in ideological misrecognition. In turn, Freud has discovered for us that the real subject, the individual in his essence, has not the form of an ego, centred on ... 'consciousness' or on 'existence', that the human subject is de-centred, constituted by a structure which has no 'centre' either, except in the imaginary misrecognition of the 'ego', i.e. in the ideological formations in which it 'recognizes' itself. ('Freud and Lacan').

By leading us to a more scientific understanding of Freud's discovery of the 'structure of misrecognition', Lacan has in Althusser's view provided Marxists with new insights into the workings of ideology. Indeed, in 'Ideology and ideological state apparatuses' (also published in *Lenin and Philosophy*), Althusser invokes Lacan's structural model of the linguistic unconscious when he states that '*ideology is eternal*, exactly like the unconscious'. In other words, ideology is a denial of history in so far as it operates as an empty dream or 'imaginary assemblage'. But it is at this point that Lacan's structural science of psychoanalysis needs to be complemented by Althusser's structural science of historical materialism. As Althusser observes in a note to his 'Freud and Lacan' essay:

> The law of Culture, which is first introduced as language and whose first form is language, is not exhausted by language; its content is the real kinship structures and the determinate ideological formations in which the persons inscribed in these structures live their functions. It is not enough to know that the Western family is patriarchal and exogamic (kinship structures) – we must also work out the ideological formations that govern paternity, maternity, conjugality and childhood ... A mass of research remains to be done on these ideological formations. This is the task for *historical materialism*. (*ibid.*)

Roland Barthes

Roland Barthes is probably best known in the English-speaking world as the Frenchman who applied structuralism to literary criticism. It is true that Barthes provided masterly 'structuralist' readings of literature, ranging from such classical authors as Racine, Michelet and Balzac to modern experimental writers like Robbe-Grillet and Sarraute, inaugurators of the *nouveau roman*. But Barthes is more than a 'literary critic'. One would do better to think of him as a 'cultural critic' with radical philosophical intentions. Barthes' intellectual career is versatile and multi-faceted; yet it bears witness to a common purpose: the application of the science of signs – *semiology* – to such diverse cultural discourses as sociology, art, politics, anthropology and the popular media. This original blending of a multiplicity of contents with a unity of method is aptly reflected in the title of Barthes' chair at the *Ecole Pratique des Hautes Etudes* in Paris, where he taught for many years – Director of the Sociology of Signs, Symbols and Collective Representations.

I

Barthes, it might be said, did for the French intellectual generation of the sixties and seventies, what Sartre and Merleau-Ponty had done for the generation of the forties and fifties – that is, introduce a new methodology which corresponded to the particular cultural climate of the time. Where Sartre and the existentialists had employed a phenomenology of free consciousness in response to the post-war experience of spiritual crisis, Barthes chose the Saussurian model of structural linguistics as a more appropriate method for a critical understanding of the modern era of advanced technology and mass-media advertising. In one of the most basic formulations of his structuralist philosophy, *Elements of Semiology* (1964), Barthes states his initial position as follows:

> In his *Course in General Linguistics*, first published in 1916, Saussure postulated the existence of a general science of signs, or Semiology, of which linguistics would form only one part. Semiology therefore aims to take in any system of signs, whatever their substance and limits; images, gestures, musical sounds, objects, and the complex associations of all these, which form the content of ritual, convention or public entertainment: these constitute, if not *languages*, at

least systems of signification. There is no doubt that the development of mass communications confers particular relevance today upon the vast field of signifying media, just when the success of disciplines such as linguistics, information theory, formal logic and structural anthropology provide semantic analysis with new instruments. There is at present a kind of demand for semiology, stemming not from the fads of a few scholars, but from the very history of the modern world. (*Introduction* to *Elements of Semiology*)

Barthes acknowledges from the outset the tentative nature of semiology. He describes it as a science which explores 'the field of intellectual imagination in our time'. This field refers primarily to the systems of structural classification, opened up by Saussure, Lévi-Strauss and Lacan. Such systems, Barthes maintains, constitute a kind of 'meta-language' which reflects the new discoveries of the contemporary social sciences.

It is arguably in this extension of the structuralist model into the realm of social science, with all its radical consequences, that Barthes' most original contribution lies. With Barthes semiology comes to function as a sociology of signs capable of analysing such divergent 'signifying systems' as a Charlie Chaplin film, a soap powder ad, a women's fashion magazine, a modern avant-garde novel or a mystical text by Saint Ignatius Loyola. This broad application of the structuralist model is what Barthes calls *translinguistics*. It presupposes that every sign – be it an image, gesture or political slogan – operates not in isolation but within a system of signifying relations. No sign has meaning independently of its interplay with other signs. Or as Barthes puts it, "there is no meaning which is not designated, and the world of signifieds is none other than that of language" (*Elements of Semiology*).

By developing semiology as a 'translinguistic' critique of our prevailing cultural discourses – or what he calls 'the great signifying unities of discourse' – Barthes advances a mode of research capable of embracing the materials of such diverse disciplines as anthropology, psychoanalysis, stylistics, and of course, sociology. The basis for such an interdisciplinary approach is the supposition (1) that every object in our world is a sign, (2) that every sign is linguistic or trans-linguistic to the extent that its signification always involves its structural relation to other signs and (3) that this relation is determined by the hidden codes of a language system. In this respect, Barthes confirms Jakobson's famous maxim: 'there are no things, only relations between things'.

For Barthes, the structuralist method is more than just a technique of analysis. It presupposes a new philosophical understanding of the world and of society. Barthes' structural investigation of a work of art or literature, for example, is fundamentally opposed to both an idealist philosophy which treats the artwork as a mere intention of consciousness and an empiricist philosophy which reduces it to an isolated datum of experience. Barthes insists that the text – be it literary or otherwise – must be seen as a complex interplay of structural relations, governed by a social or collective system of signification. Barthes thus replaces the interpretative model of humanist psychology with that of a structuralist sociology. When it comes to understanding the meaning of a text, the author's personal identity (whether he be French, Catholic, Communist etc.) is irrelevant. And the reader's biography is, in most cases, equally beside the point. The ultimate significance of a work lies in the transformation and substitution of signs internal to the systems of signification which the work exemplifies. It is not the author therefore who produces the text; it is the text which produces the author. The private intentions of the sender or receiver of textual messages is not what matters but the overall system which governs the structural codification of such messages. Or to put it in another way, texts do not signify by representing ideas or things which exist outside of language; they signify by virtue of their relation to a system of social signification which precedes and predetermines them. By radically *depsychologizing* our understanding of the text, Barthes turns our attention to those collective unconscious codes which ultimately structure the production of meaning.

But Barthes is clearly more of a textual practitioner than a grand theorist and as such feels at liberty to shift his position repeatedly throughout his career.

II

It may be useful at this point to cite some concrete examples of Barthes' method. Already in his first work of literary criticism, *Writing Degree Zero* (1953), Barthes anticipates his later structuralist position by declaring that literature must be understood as a function of *writing (écriture)*, rather than as an expression of *style* (i.e. an expression of the individual character of the author). While Barthes is prepared to acknowledge in this work that one of the purposes of literature may well be a socio-political commitment – as Sartre had so powerfully argued in *What is Literature?* (1947) – he insists that literature's primary role is a *formal* one. Though clearly in sympathy with Marxism, Barthes repudiates the crude reductionism of 'Socialist Realism' (the official aesthetic of the Soviet Communist Party) for claiming that literature can only be properly evaluated in terms of its representational *content*. Socialist Realism had tended to dismiss much modernist and post-modernist writing – and particularly that of Joyce, Beckett, Borges and the *nouveau roman* – as a symptom of decadent bourgeois nihilism. Barthes, by contrast, sees such avant-garde writing as revolutionary in form. By exposing the alienation and disintegration of bourgeois consciousness, it signals the 'deanthropomorphising' of romantic humanism and the promotion of new 'colourless, zero-degree writing' which expresses itself in a 'multiplication of modes of writing'. This multiplication of experimental forms, abolishes the traditional view of literature as some monolithic and sacramental exercise. Here at last, claims Barthes, "literature is openly reduced to the problematics of language" (*Writing Degree Zero*). This return of language to itself has radical rather than reactionary consequences. Modernist writing explodes all conventional attitudes to consciousness and creativity by reminding us that 'there is no thought without language'; and that the endless proliferation of experimental forms of writing "brings a new literature into being in so far as the latter invents its language only in order to be a project: literature becomes the utopia of language" (*Writing Degree Zero*).

Some of the most vivid examples of Barthes' overtly 'structuralist' critique are to be found in three collections of essays *Mythologies* (1957), *Critical Essays* (1964) and *Image–Music–Text* (1977). Here we find Barthes brilliantly employing the techniques of structural decoding in order to 'read' contemporary culture as an interlocking play of signifying systems which determine the dominant myths and metaphors of the social order. Barthes' analysis in these works clearly owes much to Lévi-Strauss' understanding of myths as collective strategies for resolving the contractions of everyday social existence. Barthes identifies such strategies with bourgeois ideology.

In *Mythologies*, Barthes combines the structuralist approach to myth with the Marxist critique of the fetishisation of consumer commodities under capitalism. This confluence of methods produces an eclectic and at times idiosyncratic investigation of the 'myths' of mass culture in the modern industrial era. In the preface to the 1970 edition of *Mythologies*, Barthes declares his intention to analyse semiologically the mechanics of the language of mass culture. By treating collective representations as sign systems, he hopes "to go further than the pious show of unmasking them and account *in detail* for the mystification which transforms petit-bourgeois culture into universal nature" (*Mythologies*). Barthes explicitly avows his commitment to a critique of ideology which identifies its enemy as the 'bourgeois norm'. There is no semiology, as he notes at one point, which cannot in the final analysis function as 'semioclasm'.

The 'bourgeois norm' is based on the strategic substitution of *nature* for *history* (with nature being understood as that which is eternal and unchanging). Barthes points to obvious examples of this in the media myths which represent reality as if it were somehow devoid of history – as if it were some immaculately conceived child of nature. The twenty-eight essays contained in *Mythologies*, treating of such diverse media phenomena as films, newspaper articles, fashion ads or cuisine fads, all share a common purpose: "to track down, in the decorative display of *what-goes-without-saying*, the ideological abuse which . . . is hidden there".

These exercises in 'semioclastic' critique presuppose the basic structuralist principle that all popular myths – even those dealing with such ostensibly non-linguistic phenomena as a wrestling match or plastics exhibition – ultimately function as a *language*. It is, moreover, this extended 'trans-linguistic' model which enables Barthes to combine the resources of scientific method and literary irony as the most appropriate means of detecting the hidden workings of our contemporary myths. "I cannot countenance the traditional belief", writes Barthes, "which postulates a natural dichotomy between the objectivity of the scientist and the subjectivity of the writer, as if the former were endowed with a 'freedom' and the latter with a 'vocation' equally suitable for spiriting away or sublimating the actual limitations of their situation. What I claim is to live to the full the contradiction of my time, which may well make sarcasm the condition of truth" (1957 Preface to *Mythologies*).

Barthes analyses myth as a 'message' which functions within a signifying system. The most important aspect of myth, he contends, is not so much the visible reference or object of the message but the invisible way in which the message is conveyed. Barthes subscribes here to the central structuralist premiss that it is the *form* rather than the *substance* of a sign that is ultimately constitutive of its meaning. But Barthes goes further than Saussure in affirming that myth is not just subject to *formal* considerations but also *historical* ones; he declares the sociological and ideological conditions of its usage to be of paramount significance. Myths, for Barthes, are not eternal archetypes of some cosmic unconscious; nor are they miraculous inspirations of consciousness; nor do they evolve organically from the 'nature' of things. Myths are structural conversions of social reality into language which serve a specific social purpose.

Barthes thus arrives at his innovative definition of 'mythology' as a subsection of semiology devoted to certain kinds of ideological discourse governing the popular consciousness of a society. 'Mythologies' are 'ideas-in-form' which have been invested with ideological meaning by mass media publicity, the national press or radio and other 'rites of communication' informing social appearances. Barthes detects 'mythologies' everywhere. In fact, he argues that it is nearly impossible to come across 'non-signifying fields' in our modern world (that is, events or things that have not been *formalised* in terms of some ideological connotation). Even our perception of something as ostensibly natural as the 'seaside', observes Barthes, is shot through with surrounding semiological messages, e.g. signboards, clothes, advertising slogans, suntan and so on.

Myth works in terms of double meanings. It takes as its starting point an already existing sign (be it a written sentence, a photograph, a newsreport or whatever) which it then recharges with some borrowed ideological signification. In this respect, the myth is a kind of covert language which has reworked an already existing language. In the final chapter of *Mythologies*, entitled 'Myth today', Barthes offers his famous analysis of the *Paris Match* magazine cover showing a negro in French uniform, with eyes uplifted, saluting the national flag. As this example is particularly instructive, we shall examine it here in some detail.

III

There are two orders of signification operating in our perception of the *Paris Match* cover. The first-order signification reads as follows: *a black soldier is giving the French salute.* But behind this surface meaning, there lurks a second order of signification: *France is a great colonial empire and all her sons, regardless of colour, faithfully serve under her flag.* The semiological system of 'myth' thus comes into operation when the first-order sign (negro-saluting-flag) starts to function as a second-order 'signifier' whose 'signified' is the ideological message that French patriotism is compatible with military colonialism.

Barthes points out that in this transition, the original linguistic sign of negro-saluting-flat is effectively emptied of its own particular meaning – for example, the personal characteristics of the negro – in order that it may serve as a purely *formal* signifier for the new mythic signified: the concept of colonial imperialism. But Barthes notes that this transition must also be a reversible process. Otherwise the myth might prove *too* obvious and thereby expose its own ideological purpose of propaganda and persuasion. Barthes writes:

> the (first-order) meaning loses its value, but keeps its life, from which the (second-order) form of the myth will draw its nourishment. The meaning will be for the form like an instantaneous reserve of history, a tamed richness, which it is possible to call and dismiss in a sort of rapid alternation: the form must constantly be able to be rooted again in the meaning and to get there what nature it needs for its nutriment; above all, it must be able to hide there. It is this constant game of hide-and-seek between the meaning and the form which defines myth . . . the negro who salutes is not the symbol of the French Empire: he has too much

presence, he appears as a rich, fully experienced, spontaneous, innocent, *indisputable* image. But at the same time this presence is tamed, put at a distance, made almost transparent; it recedes a little, it becomes the accomplice of a concept which comes to it fully armed, French imperiality. (*Mythologies*)

Myths emerge, accordingly, when the original meaning of signs is *appropriated* in order to correspond to a strategic ideological function. But this suggests that the same ideological function – the promotion of French imperialism – could have been served by a variety of different signifiers – e.g. by not only the *Paris Match* cover of a negro saluting a flag but by an excerpt from the film of the French Foreign Legion, *Beau Geste*, or from a right-wing history text or from a government radio broadcast and so on. There is no permanent one-to-one corespondence between signifier and signified. Barthes is echoing here Saussure's discovery of the 'non-natural' relation between signifier and signified.

Myths fulfill their ideological role as 'hidden persuaders', in short, by alienating or emptying the original meaning of a sign in order to create a new artificial meaning. This requires a structural interplay of ambiguous alternation between the so-called 'natural' meaning of the sign and its 'imposed' ideological meaning. Thus we find the original image of the negro saluting the flag being used to 'present' the ideological message of French imperialism at the same time as this message 'outdistances' the image. This dialectical interplay between the two orders of signification in myth is compared by Barthes to looking at scenery through a car window:

At one moment I grasp the presence of the glass and the distance of the landscape; at another, on the contrary, the transparence of the glass and the depth of the landscape; but the result of this alternation is constant: the glass is at once present and empty to me, and the landscape unreal and full. The same thing occurs in the mythical signifier: its form is empty but present, its meaning absent but full. (*ibid.*)

During the course of the analysis, Barthes departs from the strictly neutral stance of the scientist and implies that a semiological critique of myth carries a political duty to expose its ideological subterfuges. In other words, the semiological reading of mythologies must be not only *structural* but *historical* (in the Marxist sense). It is not sufficient to merely decode and decipher the duplicitous messages of myth; one must also demystify them. Invoking both the Freudian analysis of dreams and the Marxist critique of the fetishisation of commodities, Barthes asserts that it is necessary to debunk myth as a magical timeless appearance by reminding the reader of the precise historical context of its production (why was the *Paris Match* cover made at this particular juncture of French colonial history?) and of its consumption (what kind of audience – French middle class or working class – is it aimed at?) By thus relocating myths in their historical context, the critical semiologist reveals that what seems 'natural' is in reality 'contrived', that what postures as a univeral fact is no more than a particular ideological fabrication.

Barthes' primary aim in *Mythologies* is to demonstrate that myth is not an empirical but a semiological phenomenon. And while Barthes acknowledges that myths have always existed since time immemorial, he insists that a 'semioclastic' reading of *contemporary* myths is particularly important. This is so because the modern Western society of advanced capitalism functions as an ideological system which produces myths in order to conceal its own ideological motivations. Indeed, as Barthes notes, the modern bourgeoisie no longer even calls itself 'bourgeois'; for that would be to acknowledge that there exists outside of it a class of people and interests which might subvert it: the proletariat. The bourgeoisie deploys secular mythologies, rituals and ceremonials, in order to represent itself as a universal social totality, as the one and only incarnation of 'human nature' itself, as *Eternal Man*. "The whole of France", observes Barthes, "is steeped in this anonymous ideology" (*Mythologies*). In this way bourgeois ideology translates the reality of the world into an image of the world; it contrives to reduce history to nature. Thus while the actual status of the bourgeoisie remains historically situated in a particular time, it projects an image of man as eternal and unalterable. Bourgeois myths drain things of their memory, of their social genesis. They present the world as blissfully clear and uncomplicated, without contradiction or depth. And in the process, human actions are depoliticised and transformed into unquestionable matters of fact. The result is that one no longer needs to choose one's world, merely to conform to it. Revolutionary discourse, Barthes maintains, is therefore the antithesis of mythical discourse. Whereas the bourgeoisie hides the fact that it is bourgeois by means of myth, "revolution announces itself openly as revolution and thereby abolishes myth" (*ibid.*).

We are now perhaps in a better position to appreciate what Barthes meant exactly when he suggested that the most fitting attitude for the critical semiologist is 'sarcasm'. To dismantle the alienating myths of our prevailing social language, the reader must consciously alienate himself from this language. To negate the negation (as Hegel or Marx would put it), one must take up a position on the margins of language, adopt a sort of 'unnatural' subversiveness in order to strip away the 'natural' veneer of bourgeois discourse. This is why the stance of the semioclast is necessarily a negative one. What will replace the negation of the bourgeois order of mythology is not a matter for consideration now. The critic of myth must resist the role of prophecy. He can lead us through the desert but not out of it. "He cannot see the promised land", writes Barthes, "tomorrow's positivity is entirely hidden by today's negativity. All the values of his undertaking appear to him as acts of destruction" (*ibid.*). In this rather apocalyptic conclusion to *Mythologies*, Barthes seems to be moving beyond the limits of a 'structuralist' position towards a 'post-structuralist' one. He would appear, that is, to be advancing a more radical 'deconstructionist' strategy which treats the structural totality of language as inherently repressive and refractory to those anarchic qualities of excess and eccentricity which defy the centralising codes of the established language.

IV

In subsequent works, Barthes spells out some of the implications of this critical strategy of 'sarcasm'. In his preface to *Sade/Fourier/Loyola* (1971), he goes so far as to suggest that there is no innocent site of language outside of bourgeois ideology, no discourse that has remained unadulterated by its distortions. The only possible rejoinder to the prevailing bourgeois language is not 'confrontation' – for that would be to tackle it on its own terms – but 'theft'. Thus we find Barthes counselling his readers to "fragment the old texts of culture, science, literature and change its features according to formulae of disguise, as one disguises stolen goods" (*Sade, Fourier, Loyola*). Barthes equates this attitude of subversive stealth with a 'terrorist' raid on language whose very 'violence enables it to *exceed* the laws that a society, an ideology, a philosophy establish for themselves in order to agree among themselves in a fine surge of historical intelligibility. This excess is called: writing" (*ibid.*)

Writing is for Barthes a textual trojan horse in the city of language. It attacks from within. Writing sponsors an endless multiplicity of different meanings which the totalising system of so-called 'naturalised' language seeks desperately to eradicate. It decentres the established practice of language which ties each signifier to one signified, and thereby unleases an exuberant polyphony of playful readings. By disclosing the arbitrariness of meaning (as the relation between signifier and signified), writing reminds the reader that meaning can be *otherwise*. Each reading of the text thus becomes a renewed writing of it. And this, claims Barthes, involves a radical shift of emphasis from the author (as supposed centre or origin of the text's 'true' meaning) to reader (who emancipates the text into an infinite plurality of meanings). In a celebrated essay in *Image–Music–Text*, (1977), entitled 'The death of the author', Barthes explains this revolutionary reversal of roles as follows:

Writing is the destruction of every point of origin . . . In the multiplicity of writing, everything is to be *disentangled*, nothing *deciphered*; the structure can be followed, 'run' (like the thread in a stocking) at every point and at every level; but there is nothing beneath: the space of writing is to be ranged over, not pierced; writing ceaselessly posits meaning ceaselessly to evaporate it, carrying out a systematic exemption of meaning. In precisely this way, [writing] by refusing to assign a 'secret', an ultimate meaning, to the text (and to the world of the text), liberates what may be called an anti-theoretical activity, an activity that is truly revolutionary since to refuse to fix meaning is, in the end, to refuse God and his hypostases – reason, science, law . . . The true place of writing is reading . . . The birth of the reader must be at the cost of the death of the author. (*ibid.*)

Thus Barthes desacralises the traditional relation of author to text as father to child, as quasi-divine Creator to creature, as fixed subject existing before and after the book which is its predicate. Writing, Barthes insists, only exists in the here and now of each enunciation, of each reading.

Now we begin to detect more clearly the consequences of Barthes' transition from a 'structuralist' to a 'post-structuralist' perspective. For the later Barthes a genuinely revolutionary discourse may no longer be conceived as a deciphering or unmasking of hidden coded messages – since this implies a certain hierarchy of meanings, that some meanings are deeper or more fundamental than others. Revolutionary discourse is now defined as a libertine excess of multiple signification which frees the *signifier* from any fixed *signified* (or fixed order of signifieds); it exults in the comic play of multi-dimensional asssociations. One is therefore no longer justified in trying to uncover the hidden ideological motivation behind a given myth or text. Every text, be it mythic or otherwise, is now treated as an intertextual play of signifiers without any identifiable reference or purpose – "a tissue of quotations drawn from innumerable centres of culture" (*ibid.*) And just as every reader becomes a writer, so too every writer becomes a reader in that he becomes aware that his role as 'scriptor' is not to 'express' his inner feelings or intentions but to serve as a textual rereading or rewriting which knows no beginning or end.

The revolutionary overthrow of the bourgeois notion of a 'natural' language (i.e. that texts somehow imitate or represent the things of nature) requires an aesthetic of irreverent pleasure (*jouissance*) and 'profound ridiculousness'. Only by means of such an aesthetic can we begin to appreciate that the very idea of 'nature' is no more and no less than a cultural product of language, a particular kind of text which has become reified because it has forgotten that it is a text. "Life never does more than imitate the book", writes Barthes, echoing the deconstructionist idioms of Derrida, "and the book itself is only a tissue of signs, an imitation that is lost, indefinitely deferred" (*ibid.*).

V

It is this post-structuralist stance of textual anarchism which dominates Barthes' mature writings from *The Empire of Signs* and *S/Z* (both published in 1970) to *Barthes by Barthes* (1975) and *A Lover's Discourse* (1977). But perhaps Barthes's most definitive statement of his later position – in so far as one can attribute 'definitive' statements to a writer who repudiates the very notion of a continuous authorial identity – is to be found in his inauguration lecture at the Collège de France in 1977. Here Barthes explicitly makes common cause with Derrida's programme of deconstruction and Foucault's critique of power, in his refusal of all repressive dogmatisms of language. He declares his aim to disengage discourse from the overriding 'will-to-possess' (*libido dominandi*) which the system of language manifests. Barthes defines as a language of power any authoritarian discourse which "engenders blame, hence guilt, in its recipient" (*Collège de France Inauguration Lecture*). Indeed he goes so far as to accuse the prescriptive system of language of being 'fascist' in itself. If freedom is to be understood not only as the capacity to liberate oneself from power but also as a capacity to avoid imposing power on others, then 'freedom can only exist outside of language' (*ibid*). But this, according to Barthes' fundamental view that there is no 'outside' to language, is impossible. And so the best one can do is to take recourse to intra-literary devices for 'cheating' speech. "This salutary trickery", he writes, "this evasion, this grand imposture which allows us to understand speech (*langue*) *outside the bounds of power*, in the splendour of the permanent revolution of language, I for one call literature" (*ibid.*).

Of course, Barthes understands by literature not some august body of officially approved works, but the broad practice of 'writing' as an open interplay of signifiers. It is thus *within* the textual writing and rewriting of speech that speech itself may be fought, led astray "by that play of words of which it is the theatre" (*ibid.*). This radical potential of literature is found in the textual labour of an endless 'displacement' of meanings which the work brings to bear on language, and *not* in some overt or covert political content.

Bringing together a wide diversity of different kinds of knowledge – drawn from the natural sciences, history, sociology, technology, anthropology etc. – the literary text serves in fact to *displace* them, to defetishise them by exploding their respective pretensions to an autonomous, clearly defined, fixed discourse. Literature, for Barthes, has the advantage of being able to work away in the 'interstices of science', undermining its self-inflated conformism and opening up a new space, a no-place (*u-topos*), where knowledge can be emancipated into a play of plural meanings that can never be completed or finalised. In this wise, literature makes knowledge 'festive'. "It *stages* language", as Barthes puts it, "instead of simply using it ... Through writing, knowledge ceaselessly reflects on knowledge, in terms of a discourse which is no longer epistemological, but dramatic" (*ibid.*). Literature is, consequently, the privileged medium of revolt, he goes on, because it enables us to experience words not as simple instruments (as the scientific attitude dictates) but as 'explosions, vibrations, devices, flavours'. And in so doing it reveals knowledge to be at its best when it acknowledges itself as an infinitely playful performance of signification to be hedonistically savoured in all its pluri-dimensional richness. Literature, in short, reconverts knowledge into desire.

In the same inauguration lecture, written only three years before his death in 1980, Barthes makes a particular act of faith in the modernist project of writing, first announced by Mallarmé and espoused by many other 'experimental' authors of our time. He hails this project as an attempt to establish a utopia of language, where there could be as many languages as there are desires and as many desires as there are readers. This pluralising manoeuvre of literature – which seeks out 'unclassified, atopic sites' in opposition to the *topos* of dogmatic discourse – also carries an implicit demand for a social utopia; for as Barthes ruefully observes, "no society is yet ready to admit the plurality of desire" (*ibid.*). In the absence of such a society, the best one can do is to endorse the literary subversion of all hierarchical systems of language which institutionalise one form of discourse by repressing all non-conformist alternatives. Only when this negative work of subversion – or 'sarcasm' – has been achieved, might it be possible for language to realize that utopian condition where each subject may know without remorse or repression, the bliss of speaking "according to his perversions, not according to the Law" (*ibid.*). Barthes' final position raises the vexed question as to whether his strategy of textual 'deconstruction' is a Marxism by other means (and therefore compatible with his early position in *Mythologies* for example) *or* a critique of all scientific and political discourses (including Marx and Althusser etc.).

The later Barthes thus finds himself in a position to redefine semiology as the 'deconstruction of linguistics' (understood as the system of language worked on by power). But while avowing the multiple detours and digressions which his intellectual career has taken, Barthes suggests that his initial semiological project to combine the 'social criticism' of Brecht and Sartre with Saussure's structuralist 'science of signs', still commands his loyalty. He still sees semiology as providing the best means for analysing "how a

society produces stereotypes, ie. triumphs of artifice, which it then con-
sumes as innate meanings, ie. triumphs of nature" (*ibid.*).

Barthes' final 'post-structuralist' phase should be viewed therefore not
as a departure from his early work but as a radical rewriting of it. Although
the moral seriousness of the early texts has been replaced by a tone of
amoral playfulness, the basic purpose remains the same: the liberation of
language from the abuses of power and domination. In his conclusion to
the Inauguration Lecture, we find Barthes championing semiology as that
labour of *non-power* which "collects the *impurity* of language, the *waste* of
linguistics, the immediate corruption of the message: nothing less than the
desires, fears, appearances, intimidations, advances, blandishments,
protests, excesses and aggressions, the various kinds of music out of which
active language is made" (*ibid.*). Henceforth, semiology no longer claims to
function as some kind of superior scientific metalanguage uncontaminated
by the languages of power. In the final analysis, semiology has no choice but
to work within the totalitarian edifice of language, launching seditious
sorties to loosen the bricks and morter of its authoritarian stature, breaking
gaps in its wall of defence so that unlegitimised pleasures – the excesses of
jouissance – may have their say. "It is a moment at once decadent and
prophetic, a moment of gentle apocalypse, a historical moment of the
greatest possible pleasure", concludes Barthes with customary gusto, ". . .
and I am increasingly convinced, both in writing and teaching, that the
fundamental operation of this loosening method is, if one writes, fragmen-
tation, and if one teaches, digression, or to put it in a preciously ambiguous
word, *excursion.*" The ultimate goal of all such semiological excursions is,
he adds, "*Sapientia*: no power, a little knowledge, a little wisdom, and as
much flavour as possible" (*ibid.*).

SELECT
BIBLIOGRAPHY

WORKS BY AND ON HUSSERL IN ENGLISH

Primary sources

Logical Investigations, Humanities Press, 1970
Ideas: General Introduction to Pure Phenomenology, Collier Books, 1962
The Idea of Phenomenology, Nijhof, The Hague, 1973
The Phenomenology of Internal Time Consciousness, Nijhoff, The Hague, 1964
Phenomenology in *The Encyclopaedia Britannica*, Vol. 17, 1929
Formal and Trascendental Logic, Nijhoff, The Hague, 1969
Cartesian Meditations, Nijhoff, The Hague, 1960
Experience and Judgement, Northwestern University Press, 1973
Phenomenology and the Crisis of Philosophy (*Philosophy as a Rigorous Science* and
    Philosophy and the Crisis of European Man), Harper and Row, 1965
The Crisis of European Sciences and Transcendental Phenomenology, Northwestern
    University Press, 1970 (this work includes 'The origin of gemoetry' as an
    appendix).

Secondary sources

D. Carr, *Phenomenology and the Problem of History*, Northwestern University Press,
    1974
F. Elliston and P. McCormick, eds. *Husserl, Expositions and Appraisals*, University of
    Notre Dame Press, 1977
R. O. Elverton, ed. *The Phenomenology of Husserl: Selected Critical Readings*,
    Quadrangle Books, 1970
M. Farber, *The Foundation of Phenomenology*, Harvard University Press, 1943
R. Grossman, *Phenomenology and Existentialism: An Introduction*, Routledge and
    Kegan Paul, 1984
A. Gurwitsch, *Studies in Phenomenology and Psychology*, Northwestern University
    Press, 1966
J. Kockelmans, ed. *Phenomenology: The Philosophy of Edmund Husserl and its Inter-
    pretations*, Anchor Books, 1967
L. Kolakowski, *Husserl and the Search for Certitude*, Yale University Press, 1975
Q. Lauer, 'Introduction' to Husserl's *Phenomenology and the Crisis of Philosophy*,
    Harper and Row, 1965
    The Triumph of Subjectivity, Fordham University Press, 1958; reprinted as *Phe-
    nomenology: Its Genesis and Prospect*, Harper and Row, 1965
W. Luijpen, *Phenomenology and Humanism*, Duquesne University Press, 1966
P. Ricoeur, *Husserl: An Analysis of his Philosophy*, Northwestern University Press,
    1967
    Hermeneutics and the Human Sciences, Cambridge University Press, 1981

R. Sokolowski, *Husserlian Meditations*, Northwestern University Press, 1974
H. Spiegelberg, *The Phenomenological Movement: A Historical Introduction*, Nijhoff, The Hague, 1960
D. Welton, *The Origins of Meaning: A Critical Study of the Thresholds of Husserlian Phenomenology*, Nijhoff, The Hague, 1983
R. Zaner and D. Ihde, *Phenomenology and Existentialism*, Capricorn Books, 1973

WORKS BY AND ON HEIDEGGER IN ENGLISH

Primary sources

Being and Time, Blackwell, 1962
Kant and the Problem of Metaphysics, Indiana University Press, 1962
Introduction to Metaphysics, Yale University Press, 1959
What is Called Thinking?, Harper and Row, 1967
Discourse on Thinking, Harper and Row, 1970
Identity and Difference, Harper and Row, 1960
What is a Thing?, Gateway Books, 1967
Poetry, Language, Thought, Harper and Row, 1971
On the Way to Language, Harper and Row, 1971
On Time and Being, Harper and Row, 1972
Early Greek Thinking, Harper and Row, 1975
The End of Philosophy, Harper and Row, 1973
The Piety of Thinking, Indiana University Press, 1976
The Question Concerning Technology, Harper and Row, 1977
Basic Writings, Harper and Row, 1977
What is Philosophy?, Twayne Publishers, 1958
Nietzsche (4 Vols), Harper and Row, 1979–
The Essence of Reason, Northwestern University Press, 1969
Hegel's Concept of Experience, Harper and Row, 1970
What is Metaphysics? in *Existence and Being*, Vision Press, 1949
Hölderlin and the Essence of Poetry in *Existence and Being*, Vision Press, 1949

Secondary sources

H. J. Blackham, *Six Existentialist Thinkers*, Routledge and Kegan Paul, 1953
J. O. Caputo, *The Mystical Element in Heidegger's Thought*, Ohio University Press, 1978
M. Gelven, *A Commentary on Heidegger's 'Being and Time'*, Harper and Row, 1970
L. Goldmann, *Lukács and Heidegger*, Routledge and Kegan Paul, 1977
M. Greene, *Martin Heidegger*, London, 1957
D. Halliburton, *Poetic Thinking, An Approach to Heidegger*, University of Chicago Press, 1981
M. King, *Heidegger's Philosophy*, New York, 1964
J. Kockelmans, *Martin Heidegger: A First Introduction to his Philosophy*, Duquesne University Press, 1965
T. Langan, *The Meaning of Heidegger*, London, 1959
J. L. Mehta, *The Philosophy of Martin Heidegger*, Harper and Row, 1971
M. Murray, ed. *Heidegger and Modern Philosophy*, Yale University Press, 1978

J. Perotti, *Heidegger on the Divine,* Ohio University Press, 1974

J. Robinson and J. Cobb, *The Later Heidegger and Theology,* Greenwood Press, 1963

W. Richardson, *Heidegger: Through Phenomenology to Thought,* Nijhoff, The Hague, 1963

J. Sherover, *Heidegger, Kant and Time,* Indiana University Press, 1971

T. Sheehan, ed. *Heidegger, The Man and the Thinker,* Precedent Press, 1981

G. Steiner, *Heidegger,* Fontana, 1978

L. M. Vail, *Heidegger and Ontological Difference,* Penn State University, 1972

WORKS BY AND ON SARTRE IN ENGLISH

Primary sources

Imagination: A Psychological Critique, University of Michigan Press, 1962

The Psychology of Imagination, Philosophical Library, 1948

Sketch for a Theory of the Emotions, Methuen, 1962

Being and Nothingness, Philosophical Library, 1956

What is Literature?, Methuen, 1950; *Existentialism and Literature,* Citadel Press, 1972

Existentialism and Humanism, Methuen, 1948

The Portrait of an Anti-Semite, Secker and Warburg, 1948

Politics and Literature, Calder and Boyers, 1973

Saint Genet, Actor and Martyr, Braziller, 1963

Critique of Dialectical Reason, NLB, 1976

The Philosophy of J.–P. Sartre (a selection from his works edited by R. Denoon Cumming, Random House, 1965).

Baudelaire, Hamilton, 1964

Essays in Aesthetics, Washington Square Press, 1966

Situations, Hamilton, 1965

Literary Essays, Philosophical Library, 1957

Words, Hamilton, 1964

Search for a Method, Vintage Books, 1968

Between Existentialism and Marxism, NLB, 1974

Life/Situations, Pantheon Books, 1977

'Merleau-Ponty (1)' in *Journal of the British Society of Phenomenology,* Vol. 15, No. 2, 1984

Flaubert: The Idiot of the Family, Chicago University Press, 1981.

The Childhood of a Leader in *Intimacy,* Panther, 1960

Secondary sources

E. Allen, *Existentialism from Within,* MacMillan, 1952

D. Archard, *Marxism and Existentialism,* Blackstaff Press, 1980

H. J. Blackham, *Six Existentialist Thinkers,* Harper and Row, 1957

J. Collins, *The Existentialists,* Regnery/Chicago, 1952

M. Cranston, *Sartre,* Oliver and Boyd, 1962

W. Desan, *The Tragic Finale: An Essay on the Philosophy of J.–P. Sartre,* Harper and Row, 1960

The Marxism of J.–P. Sartre, Doubleday, 1965

M. Greene, *J.-P. Sartre: The Existentialist Ethic*, Michigan University Press, 1960
R. Grossman, *Phenomenology and Existentialism: An Introduction*, Routledge and Kegan Paul, 1984
E. Casey, *Imagining: A Phenomenological Study*, Indiana University Press, 1977
E. Kaelin, *An Existentialist Aesthetic, The Theories of Sartre and Merleau-Ponty*, University of Winconsin Press, 1962
W. Kaufman, ed. *Existentialism: From Dostoyevsky to Sartre*, Meridian Books, 1956
R. Lafarge, *J.-P. Sartre: His Philosophy*, Gill and Macmillan, 1970
A. Manser, *Sartre: A Philosophical Study*, Athlone Press, 1966
I. Murdoch, *Sartre: Romantic Rationalist*, Fontana, 1967
M. Warnock, *The Philosophy of Sartre*, Hutchinson, 1965

WORKS BY AND ON MERLEAU-PONTY IN ENGLISH

Primary sources

The Structure of Behaviour, Beacon Press, 1963
Phenomenology of Perception, Humanities Press, 1962
The Primacy of Perception, Washington University Press, 1964
Signs, Northwestern University Press, 1964
Sense and Non-Sense, Northwestern University Press, 1964
Adventures of the Dialectic, Northwestern University Press, 1973
The Prose of the World, Heinemann, 1974
Humanism and Terror, Beacon Press, 1969
The Visible and the Invisible, Northwestern University Press, 1968
Eye and Mind in *Phenomenology, Language and Sociology: Selected Essays of Merleau-Ponty*, ed. John O'Neill, Heinemann, 1974
Themes from the Lectures at the Collège de France 1952–1960, Northwestern University Press, 1970
In Praise of Philosophy, Northwestern University Press, 1963

Secondary sources

D. Archard, *Marxism and Existentialism*, Blackstaff Press, 1980
R. Aron, *Marxism and the Existentialists*, Harper and Row, 1969
M. R. Barral, *The Role of the Body-Subject in Merleau-Ponty*, Duquesne University Press, 1965
J. Bannan, *The Philosophy of Merleau-Ponty*, Harcourt, Brace and World, 1967
V. Descombes, *Modern French Philosophy*, Cambridge University Press, 1980
A. Fischer, ed. *The Essential Writings of Merleau-Ponty*, Harcourt, Brace and World, 1969
G. Garth, *The Horizons of the Flesh: Critical Perspectives on the Thought of Merleau-Ponty*, Southern Illinois University Press, 1973
R. Grossman, *Phenomenology and Existentialism: An Introduction*, Routledge and Kegan Paul, 1984
E. Kaelin, *An Existentialist Aesthetic, The Theories of Sartre and Merleau-Ponty*, University of Winsconsin Press, 1962
J. Kocklemans, *Phenomenology*, Doubleday/Anchor, 1967
R. Kwant, *The Phenomenological Philosophy of Merleau-Ponty*, Duquesne University

Press, 1963

From Phenomenology to Metaphysics, the Later Work of Merleau-Ponty, Duquesne University Press, 1966

T. Langan, *Merleau-Ponty's Critique of Reason*, Yale University Press, 1966

A. Robil, *Merleau-Ponty: Existentialist of the Social World*, Columbia University Press, 1967

J.–P. Sartre, 'Merleau-Ponty I', in *Journal of the British Society of Phenomenology*, Vol. 15, No. 2, 1984

G. Schrader, *Existential Philosophers: Kierkegaard to Merleau-Ponty*, McGraw-Hill Press, 1967

H. Spiegelberg, *The Phenomenological Movement*, Nijhoff, The Hague, 1960

R. Zaner, *The Problem of Embodiment*, Nijhoff, The Hague, 1964

R. Zaner and D. Ihde, *Phenomenology and Existentialism*, Capricorn Books, 1973

WORKS BY AND ON RICOEUR IN ENGLISH

Primary sources

Freedom and Nature: The Voluntary and the Involuntary, Northwestern University Press, 1966

Husserl: An Analysis of his Phenomenology, Northwestern University Press, 1967

History and Truth, Northwestern University Press, 1965

Fallible Man, Regnery/Chicago, 1965

The Symbolism of Evil, Harper and Row, 1967

Freud and Philosophy: An Essay on Interpretation, Yale University Press, 1970

The Conflict of Interpretations: Essays in Hermeneutics, Northwestern University Press, 1974

The Rule of Metaphor: Multi-disciplinary Studies of the Creation of Meaning in Language, Routledge and Kegan Paul, 1978

Political and Social Essays, ed. D. Stewart and J. Bien, Ohio University Press, 1974

Interpretation Theory: Discourse and the Surplus of Meaning, Texas Christian University Press, 1976

Hermeneutics and the Human Sciences, ed. J. B. Thompson, Cambridge University Press, 1981

The Philosophy of Paul Ricoeur: An Anthology of his Work, ed. C. Reagan and D. Stewart, Beacon Press, 1978

Time and Narrative, vol. I, University of Chicago Press, 1984

Secondary sources

J. Bleicher, *Contemporary Hermeneutics*, Routledge and Kegan Paul, 1980

D. Ihde, *Hermeneutic Phenomenology: The Philosophy of Paul Ricoeur*, Northwestern University Press, 1971

R. Kearney, *Dialogues with Contemporary Continental Thinkers*, Manchester University Press, 1984

D. Stewart, 'Paul Ricoeur and the phenomenological movement' in *Philosophy Today*, Winter, 1968

J. B. Thompson, 'Introduction' to Ricoeur's *Hermeneutics and The Human Sciences*, Cambridge University Press, 1981

Critical Hermeneutics: A Study in the Thought of Paul Ricoeur and Jürgen Habermas, Cambridge University Press, 1981

T. M. Van Leewan, *The Surplus of Meaning: Ontology and Eschatology in the Philosophy of Paul Ricoeur*, Amsterdam Studies in Theology, Rodopi, 1981

R. Zaner and D. Ihde, *Phenomenology and Existentialism*, Capricorn Books, 1973

C. Regan (ed.), *Studies in the Philosophy of Paul Ricoeur*, Ohio University Press, 1979

WORKS BY AND ON DERRIDA IN ENGLISH

Primary sources

Edmund Husserl's 'Origin of Geometry': An Introduction, Nicholas Hays, 1978

Writing and Difference, University of Chicago Press, 1978

Speech and Phenomena and other Essays in Husserl's Theory of Signs, Northwestern University Press, 1973

Of Grammatology, Johns Hopkins University Press, 1977

Positions, University of Chicago Press, 1977

Spurs: Nietzsche's Styles, University of Chicago press, 1979

Margins of Philosophy, University of Chicago Press, 1983

Dissemination, Athlone Press, 1981

The Postcard: From Socrates to Freud and Beyond, University of Chicago Press (forthcoming).

The Archaeology of the Frivolous, Duquesne University Press, 1981

'Deconstruction and the Other': Dialogue with Richard Kearney in *Dialogues with Contemporary Continental Thinkers*, Manchester University Press, 1984

Secondary sources

J. Culler, *On Deconstruction: Theory and Criticism after Structuralism*, Cornell University Press, 1982

The Pursuit of Signs: Semiotics, Literature, Deconstruction, Cornell University Press, 1981

'Derrida' in *Structuralism and Since: From Lévi-Strauss to Derrida* (ed. J. Sturrock), Oxford University Press, 1979

V. Descombes, *Modern French Philosophy*, Cambridge University Press, 1980

T. Eagleton, *Walter Benjamin: Towards a Revolutionary Criticism*, NLB, 1981

J. V. Harari, ed. and introduction, *Textual Strategies: Perspectives in Post-Structuralist Criticsm*, Cornell University Press, 1979

B. Johnson, 'Introduction' to Derrida's *Dissemination (op.cit.)*

B. Johnson, *The Critical Difference*, Johns Hopkins U.P. 1980

V. B. Leitch, *Deconstructive Criticism: An Advanced Introduction*, Hutchinson Press, 1983

R. Murray and E. Donato, eds. *The Structuralist Controversy*, Johns Hopkins University Press, 1970

R. Magliola, *Derrida On the Mend*, Purdue University Press, 1984

A. Montefiori, ed. *Philosophy in France Today*, Cambridge University Press, 1983

C. Norris, *The Deconstructive Turn*, Methuen, 1983

Deconstruction: Theory and Practice, Methuen, 1982

M. Ryan, *Marxism and Deconstruction*, Johns Hopkins U.P. 1982

G. Spivak, 'Introduction' to Derrida's *Of Grammatology (op.cit.)*

R. Young, ed. *Untying the Text: A Post-Structuralist Reader*, Routledge and Kegan Paul, 1981

R. Rorty, 'Signposts along the way that Reason went' in *The London Review of Books*, 1984

D. C. Wood and R. Bernasconi, eds. *Derrida and Difference*, Parousia Press, University of Warwick, 1985

WORKS BY AND ON LUKÁCS IN ENGLISH

Primary sources

History and Class Consciousness, Merlin Press, 1971

Studies in European Realism, Hillway, 1950

The Historical Novel, Merlin Press, 1962

Theory of the Novel: A Historico–Philosophical Essay on the Forms of Great Literature, M.I.T. Press, 1971

The Meaning of Contemporary Realism, Merlin Press, 1962 (includes 'The Ideology of modernism')

Goethe and His Age, Merlin press, 1968

Marxism and Human Liberation: Essays on History, Culture and Revolution, Delta Books, 1973 (includes 'The Twin Crises' and 'The Ideology of modernism')

Essays on Thomas Mann, Grosset and Dunlop, 1965

Solzhenitsyn, Merlin Press, 1970

Lenin: A Study on the Unity of His Thought, New Left Books, 1970

Writer and Critic and Other Essays, Merlin Press, 1970

Ontology, Merlin Press, Vol. I, 1978–

The Destruction of Reason, Merlin Press, 1979

Secondary sources

H. Arvon, 'Bertolt Brecht and Georg Lukács' in *Marxist Esthetics*, Cornell University Press, 1973

L. Goldman, *Lukács and Heidegger: Towards a New Philosophy*, Routledge and Kegan Paul, 1977

F. Jameson, 'The Case for Georg Lukács' in *Marxism and Form*, Princeton University Press, 1971

G. Lichtheim, *Lukács*, Fontana, 1970

M. Löwy, *Georg Lukács – From Romanticism to Bolshevism*, London, 1979

G. Parkinson, ed. *Georg Lukács: The Man, His Work and His Ideas*, Random House, 1970

M. Solomon, 'Georg Lukács' in *Marxism and Art*, Harvester Press, 1979

J. Todd, 'Aesthetic experience and contemporary capitalism: notes on Georg Lukács and Walter Benjamin' in *The Crane Bag Journal*, Vol. 7, No. 1, 1983

V. Zitta, *Georg Lukács Marxism: Alienation, Dialectics, Revolution*, Nijhoff, 1965

WORKS BY AND ON BENJAMIN IN ENGLISH

Primary sources

Illuminations, with an introduction by Hannah Arendt, Fontana, 1973
One Way Street, NLB, 1979 (includes 'Critique of violence', 'On language as such and on the language of men', 'The destructive character')
The Origin of German Tragic Drama, NLB, 1977
Understanding Brecht, NLB, 1973
Charles Baudelaire: A Lyric Poet in the Era of High Capitalism, NLB, 1973

Secondary sources

A. Arato and E. Gebhardt, *The Essential Frankfurt School Reader*, Urizen Books, 1978
H. Arendt, 'Introduction: Walter Benjamin 1892–1940' in *Illuminations (op. cit.)*
T. Eagleton, *Walter Benjamin: or Towards a Revolutionary Criticism*, NLB, 1981
F. Jameson, 'Walter Benjamin; or nostalgia' in *Marxism and Form*, Princeton University Press, 1971
M. Solomon, 'Walter Benjamin' in *Marxism and Art*, Harvester Press, 1979
J. Todd, 'Aesthetic experience and contemporary capitalism: notes on Georg Lukács and Walter Benjamin'
in *The Crane Bag Journal*, Vol. 7, No. 1, 1983
J. Roberts, *Walter Benjamin*, Macmillan, 1982
M. Jay, *The Dialectical Imagination: A History of the Frankfurt School*, Heinemann Books, 1973
R. Wolin, *Walter Benjamin: An Aesthetic of Redemption*, Columbia University Press, 1982

WORKS BY AND ON GRAMSCI IN ENGLISH

Primary sources

Selections from the Prison Notebooks, Lawrence and Wishart, 1971
Political Writings, 1910–1920, Lawrence and Wishart, 1977
Political Writings, 1921–1926, Lawrence and Wishart, 1978

Secondary sources:

C. Boggs, *Gramsci's Marxism*, Pluto Press, 1976
C. Buci, *Glucksmann, Gramsci and the State*, Lawrence and Wishart, 1980
J. Camett, *Antonio Gramsci and the Origins of Italian Communism*, Stanford University Press, 1967
M. Clark, *Antonio Gramsci and the Revolution that Failed*, Yale University Press, 1977
A. Davidson, *Antonio Gramsci: Towards an Intellectual Biography*, Merlin Press, 1977
J. Davis, ed. *Gramsci and Italy's Passive Revolution*, Croom Helm, 1979
G. Fiori, *Antonio Gramsci*, NLB, 1977
E. Hobsbawm, 'Gramsci and Marxist political theory' in *Approaches to Gramsci*, ed. A. Showstack Sassoon, Writers and Readers Publishing Coop., 1982
J. Joll, *Gramsci*, Fontana, 1977

E. Laclau, *Politics and Ideology in Marxist Theory*, NLB, 1979
C. Mouffe, ed. *Gramsci and Marxist Theory*, Routledge and Kegan Paul, 1979
A. S. Sassoon, ed. *Approaches to Gramsci*, Writers and Readers Coop., 1982
R. Simon, *Gramsci's Political Thought: An Introduction*, Lawrence and Wishart, 1982
M. Solomon, 'Gramsci' in *Marxism and Art*, Harvester Press, 1979
P. Togliatti, *Gramsci and Other Essays*, Lawrence and Wishart, 1979
G. Vacca, 'Intellectuals and the Marxist theory of the state' in *Approaches to Gramsci*, ed. A. S. Sassoon, *op.cit.*

WORKS BY AND ON BLOCH IN ENGLISH

Primary sources

A Philosophy of the Future, Herder and Herder, 1970
On Karl Marx, Herder and Herder, 1971
Atheism in Christianity, Herder and Herder, 1972
Man on His Own, Herder and Herder, 1978
Aesthetics and Politics, NLB, 1979
'Man as possibility' in *Cross Currents*, XVIII, 1968

Secondary sources

P. M. Green, 'Ernst Bloch's revision of atheism' in *Journal of Religion*, Vol. 49, No. 2, 1969
D. Cross, 'Ernst Bloch: the dialectics of hope' in *The Unknown Dimension: European Marxism since Lenin*, ed. by Howard and Klare, Basic Books, 1972
J. Habermas, 'Ernst Bloch: A Marxist Schelling' in *Philosophical–Political Profiles*, Heinemann, 1983
W. Hudson, *The Marxist Philosophy of Ernst Bloch*, Macmillan, 1982
D. Howard, 'Marxism and concrete philosophy: Ernst Bloch' in *The Marxian Heritage*, Macmillan, 1977
F. Jameson, 'Ernst Bloch and the Future' in *Marxism and Form*, Princeton University Press, 1971
M. Solomon, 'Ernst Bloch' in *Marxism and Art*, Harvester Press, 1979
R. Taylor, ed. *Aesthetics and Politics* (Debates between Bloch, Lukács, Brecht, Benjamin and Adorno, with an afterword by F. Jameson, NLB, 1977)

WORKS BY AND ON MARCUSE IN ENGLISH

Primary sources

Reason and Revolution: Hegel and the Rise of Social Theory, Oxford University Press, 1941
Eros and Civilization: A Philosophical Inquiry into Freud, Beacon Press, 1955
Soviet Marxism: A Critical Analysis, Columbia University Press, 1958
One-Dimensional Man: Studies in the Ideology of Advanced Industrial Society, Beacon Press, 1964
An Essay on Liberation, Beacon Press, 1969

Negations: Essays in Critical Theory, Beacon Press, 1968
Revolution or Reform: A Confrontation (with Karl Popper), ed. A. Ferguson, Chicago, 1976
Five Lectures, Beacon Press, 1970
Counter-Revolution and Revolt, Beacon Press, 1972
Studies in Critical Philosophy, Beacon Press, 1973
The Aesthetic Dimension: Toward a Critique of Marxist Aesthetics, Beacon Press, 1978

Secondary sources

A. Arato and E. Gebhart, *The Essential Frankfurt School Reader*, Urizen Books, 1978
D. Breines, *Critical Interruptions: New Left Perspectives on Herbert Marcuse*, Herder and Herder, 1972
J. Fry, *Marcuse: Dilemma and Liberation*, Harvester, 1978
V. Geoghegan, *Reason and Eros: The Social Theory of Herbert Marcuse*, Pluto Press, 1981
D. Held, *Introduction to Critical Theory*, Hutchinson, 1980
D. Howard, *The Marxian Legacy*, Macmillan, 1977
F. Jameson, 'Marcuse and Schiller' in *Marxism and Form*, Princeton University Press, 1971
M. Jay, *The Dialectical Imagination*, Heinemann, 1974
B. Katz, *Herbert Marcuse and the Art of Liberation*, NLB, 1982
R. Kearney, 'The philosophy of art and politics: dialogue with Herbert Marcuse' in *Dialogues with Contemporary Continental Thinkers*, Manchester University Press, 1984
D. Kellner, *Herbert Marcuse and the Crisis of Marxism*, Macmillan, 1984
P. Lind, *Marcuse and Freedom*, Croom Helm, 1985
A. MacIntyre, *Marcuse*, Fontana, 1970
R. Marks, *The Meaning of Marcuse*, Ballantyre, 1972
F. Olafson, 'Heidegger's politics: Interview' in *Graduate Faculty Philosophy Journal*, 6, 1, New York, 1977
M. Schoolman, *The Imaginary Witness: The Critical Theory of Herbert Marcuse*, Macmillan, 1980
P. Slater, *The Origin and Significance of the Frankfurt School*, Routledge and Kegan Paul, 1977
M. Solomon, *Marxism and Art*, Harvester, 1979
H. Wolff and B. Moore, eds. *The Critical Spirit: Essays in Honour of Herbert Marcuse*, Beacon Press, 1967

WORKS BY AND ON HABERMAS IN ENGLISH

Primary sources

Knowledge and Human Interests, Beacon Press, 1972
Theory and Practice, Beacon Press, 1973
Legitimation Crisis, Beacon Press, 1973
Towards a Rational Society (including 'Technology and science as "ideology"') Beacon Press, 1970
Communication and the Evolution of Society, Beacon Press, 1979

Philosophical–Political Profiles, Heinemann, 1983
The Theory of Communicative Action, Vol. I, Heinemann, 1985

Secondary sources

T. Adorno and M. Horkheimer, *Dialectic of Enlightenment*, Herder and Herder, 1972
J. Bleicher, *Contemporary Hermeneutics*, Routledge and Kegan Paul, 1980
H. G. Gadamer, *Truth and Method*, Sheed and Ward, 1975
D. Howard, *The Marxian Heritage*, Macmillan, 1977
M. Jay, *The Dialectical Imagination: A History of the Frankfurt School*, Heinemann Books, 1973
D. Lane, 'Habermas and Praxis' in *Foundations for a Social Theology*, Gill and Macmillan, 1984
T. McCarthy, *The Critical Theory of Jürgen Habermas*, MIT Press, 1978
P. Ricoeur, 'Hermeneutics and the critique of ideology' in *Hermeneutics and the Human Sciences*, Cambridge University Press, 1981
J. Thompson, *Critical Hermeneutics: A Study in the Thought of P. Ricoeur and J. Habermas*, Cambridge University Press, 1981
J. Thompson and D. Held, *Habermas: Critical Debates*, Macmillan, 1982

WORKS BY AND ON SAUSSURE IN ENGLISH

Primary sources

F. de Saussure, *Course in General Linguistics*, The Philosophical Library, 1959

Secondary sources

D. Archard, 'The unconscious and language' in *Consciousness and the Unconscious*, Hutchinson, 1984
P. Caws, 'What is structuralism?' in *Partisan Review*, 1968
J. Culler, *Saussure*, 1976
    Structuralist Poetics, Cornell University Press, 1975
R. and F. de George, *The Structuralists*, Doubleday/Anchor, 1972
J. Ehrmann, ed. *Structuralism*, Doubleday, 1970
T. Hawkes, *Structuralism and Semiotics*, University of California Press, 1977
F. Jameson, *The Prison House of Language*, Princeton University Press, 1972
M. Lane, *Introduction to Structuralism*, Basic Books, 1970
Structuralism, A Reader, Cape, 1970
P. Petit, *The Concept of Structuralism*, Gill and Macmillan, 1976
B. McNicholl, 'Structuralism' in *Irish Theological Quarterly*, 1968
J. Sturrock, ed. *Structuralism and Since*, Oxford University Press, 1979
D. Robey, ed. *Structuralism: An Introduction*, Clarendon Press, 1973
A. Wilden, *System and Structure*, Tavistock, 1977

WORKS BY AND ON LÉVI-STRAUSS IN ENGLISH

Primary sources

Race and History, UNESCO, 1958
Structural Anthropology, Basic Books, 1963
The Raw and the Cooked, Harper and Row, 1969
From Honey to Ashes, Cape, 1970
The Scope of Anthropology (Inauguration Lecture to the Collège de France, 1960),
　Cape, 1967
The Savage Mind, University of Chicago Press, 1966
Totemism, Beacon Press, 1963
Tristes Tropiques, Anthenaeum, 1964
The Origin of Table Manners, Cape, 1973
The Naked Man, Cape, 1981
Myth and Meaning, Routledge and Kegan Paul, 1978
The Elementary Structures of Kinship, Eyre and Spottiswoode, 1969

Secondary sources

C. R. Badcock, *Structuralism and Sociological Theory*, Hutchinson, 1975
J. Boon, *From Symbolism to Structuralism*, Harper and Row, 1972
R. Boudon, *The Uses of Structuralism*, Heinemann, 1971
G. Charbonnier, *Conversations with Claude Lévi-Strauss*, London, 1969
J. Ehrmann, ed. *Structuralism*, Doubleday Anchor, 1966
R. and F. de George, *The Structuralists*, Anchor, 1972
E. and T. Hayes, *Claude Lévi-Strauss: The Anthropologist as Hero*, MIT Press, 1970
T. Hawkes, *Structuralism and Semiotics*, University of California Press, 1977
E. Kurzweil, 'Claude Lévi-Strauss: the father of structuralism' in *The Age of
　Structuralism*, Columbia University Press, 1980
M. Lane, *Introduction to Structuralism*, Basic Books, 1970
Structuralism, A Reader, Cape, 1970
O. Paz, *Claude Lévi-Strauss, An Introduction*, Cornell University Press, 1970
E. Leach, *Lévi-Strauss*, Fontana, 1970
　ed. *The Structuralist Study of Myth and Totemism*, Tavistock, 1967
D. Sperber, 'Claude Lévi-Strauss' in *Structuralism and Since*, ed. J. Sturrock,
　Oxford University Press, 1979

WORKS BY AND ON LACAN IN ENGLISH

Primary sources

Écrits: A Selection, Tavistock, 1977
The Four Fundamental Concepts of Psychoanalysis, Penguin, 1977
The Language of the Self: The Function of Language in Psychoanalysis (with
　Introduction and Essay by A. Wilden), Johns Hopkins University Press, 1968
Feminine Sexuality: Jacques Lacan and the 'École Freudienne' (selections from Lacan
　with an introduction by J. Mitchell and J. Rose), Macmillan, 1982

Secondary sources

D. Archard, *Consciousness and the Unconscious*, Hutchinson, 1984

J. Bird, 'Jacques Lacan – the French Freud?' in *Radical Philosophy*, No. 30, 1982

M. Bowie, 'Jacques Lacan' in *Structuralism and Since*, ed. J. Sturrock, Oxford University Press, 1979

R. and F. De George, *The Structuralists*, Anchor, 1972

J. Ehrmann, ed. *Structuralism*, Doubleday Anchor, 1970

E. Kurzweil, 'Structuralist psychoanalysis' in *The Age of Structuralism*, Columbia University Press, 1980

J. Laplanche and J. Pontalis, *The Language of Psychoanalysis*, London, 1973

V. Leitch, *Deconstructive Criticism*, Hutchinson, 1983

R. Macksey and E. Donato, ed. *The Structuralist Controversy: The Languages of Criticism and the Sciences of Man*, Johns Hopkins University Press, 1970

J. Muller and W. Richardson, *Lacan and Language: A Reader's Guide to Ecrits*, International University Press, 1982

E. Ragland-Sullivan, *Jacques Lacan and the Philosophy of Psychoanalysis*, Croom Helm 1985

S. Schneiderman, ed. *Returning to Freud: Clinical Psychoanalysis in the School of Lacan*, Yale University Press, 1980

R. Skelton, 'Reason and rationality in Lacan' in *Irish Philosophical Journal*, II, 1, 1985

J. Smith and W. Kerrigan, ed. *Interpreting Lacan*, New Haven, 1983

WORKS BY AND ON FOUCAULT IN ENGLISH

Primary sources

Madness and Civilization: A History of Insanity in the Age of Reason, Random House, 1965

The Order of Things: An Archaeology of the Human Sciences, Pantheon, 1970/Tavistock, 1972

The Archaeology of Knowledge, Pantheon, 1972

I, Pierre Rivière . . . Pantheon, 1975

Discipline and Punish: The Birth of the Prison, Random House, 1979

The History of Sexuality, Volume I: An Introduction, Random House, 1980

Language, Counter-Memory, Practice, Blackwell, 1977

Power/Knowledge: Selected Interviews and Other Writings 1972–1977, ed. C. Gordon, Pantheon, 1980

The Birth of the Clinic: An Archeology of Medical Perception, Randon House, 1975

'The Subject of Power'/Afterword to *Michel Foucault: Beyond Structuralism and Hermeneutics*, ed. H. Dreyfus and P. Rabinow, Harvester Press, 1982

Secondary sources

V. Descombes, *Modern French Philosophy*, Cambridge University Press, 1980

H. Dreyfus and P. Rabinow, *Michel Foucault: Beyond Structuralism and Hermeneutics* (With an afterword by Michel Foucault: 'The subject and power'), Harvester, 1982

E. Kurzweil, 'Michel Foucault: structuralism and the structures of knowledge' in *The Age of Structuralism*, Columbia University Press, 1980
V. Leitch, *Deconstructive Criticism*, Columbia University Press/Hutchinson, 1983
A. Sheridan, *Michel Foucault: The Will to Truth*, Tavistock, 1980
B. Smart, *Foucault, Marxism and Critique*, Routledge and Kegan Paul, 1983
H. White, 'Michel Foucault' in *Structuralism and Since*, ed. J. Sturrock, Oxford University Press, 1979

WORKS BY AND ON ALTHUSSER IN ENGLISH

Primary sources

For Marx, Pantheon, 1972
Reading Capital (co-authored with E. Balibar) NLB, 1970
Lenin and Philosophy and other Essays, NLB, 1971
Politics and History, NLB, 1972
Essays in Self-Criticism, NLB, 1976

Secondary sources

A. Callinicos, *Althusser's Marxism*, Pluto Press, 1976
S. Clark (*et.al.*), *One-Dimensional Marx: Althusser and the Politics of Culture* (Alison and Busby, 1980).
V. Descombes, *Modern French Philosophy*, Cambridge University Press, 1980
W. Dowling, *Jameson, Althusser, Marx*, Methuen, 1984
R. Fowler, ed. *Style and Structure in Literature*, Cornell University Press, 1975
D. Howard and K. Klare, eds. *The Unknown Dimension*, Basic Books, 1972
M. Glucksmann, *Strucuturalist Analysis in Contemporary Social Thought*, Routledge and Kegan Paul, 1974
E. Kurzweil, 'Althusser: Marxism and Structuralism' in *The Age of Structuralism*, Columbia University Press, 1980
M. Kelly, *Modern French Marxism*, Blackwell, 1982
G. Lichtheim, *Marxism in Modern France*, Columbia University Press, 1966
 'A new twist in the dialectic' in *From Marx to Hegel and Other Essays*, Herder and Herder, 1971
M. Pecheux, *Language, Semantics, Ideology*, St. Martin's Press, 1982
H. Veltmeyer, 'Towards an assessment of the structuralist interrogation of Marx: Claude Lévi-Strauss and Louis Althusser' in *Science and Society*, Winter, 1975

WORKS ON AND BY BARTHES IN ENGLISH

Primary sources

Writing Degree Zero, Cape, 1967
On Racine, Hill and Wang, 1964
Critical Essays, Northwestern University Press, 1972
S/Z, Hill and Wang, 1974
The Pleasure of the Text, Hill and Wang, 1975

Mythologies, Cape, 1972
Image-Music/Text, Fontana, 1977
Elements of Semiology, Hill and Wang, 1968
Sade, Fourrier, Loyola, Hill and Wang, 1976
Barthes by Barthes, Hill and Wang, 1977
A Lover's Discourse, Hill and Wang, 1978
New Critical Essays, Hill and Wang, 1980
'Inaugural Lecture at the Collège de France', 1977, in *Oxford Literary Review*, Vol.
   4. No. 1, 1979
Fashion Systems, Cape, 1985
Camera Lucida, Fontana, 1984

Secondary sources

R. Fowler, ed. *Style and Structure in Literature*, Cornell University Press, 1975
T. Hawkes, *Structuralism and Semiotics*, University of California Press, 1977
E. Kurzweil, 'Roland Barthes: literature, structuralism and erotics' in *The Age of Structuralism*, Columbia University Press, 1980
V. Leitch, *Deconstructive Criticism*, Hutchinson, 1983
P. Petit, *The Concept of Structuralism*, Gill and Macmillan, 1976
L. le Sage, *The French New Criticism*, Pennsylvania State University Press, 1976
R. Scholes, *Structuralism in Literature*, Yale University Press, 1974
S. Sontag, ed. *A Barthes Reader*, Hill and Wang, 1983 (also includes Barthes's Collège de France Inaugural Lecture)
J. Sturrock, 'Roland Barthes' in *Structuralism and Since*, ed. Sturrock, Oxford University Press, 1979